THEOLOGY
OF THE PSALMS

HANS–JOACHIM
KRAUS

THEOLOGY
OF THE PSALMS

Translated by
Keith Crim

AUGSBURG PUBLISHING HOUSE
MINNEAPOLIS

THEOLOGY OF THE PSALMS

First published 1979 by Neukirchener Verlag, Neukirchen-Vluyn, under the title *Theologie der Psalmen* in the Biblischer Kommentar Series.

First Published in English 1986 by Augsburg Publishing House in the U.S.A. and in Great Britain by SPCK, Holy Trinity Church, Marylebone Road, London NW1 4DU.

Library of Congress Cataloging-in-Publication Data

Kraus, Hans-Joachim.
   THEOLOGY OF THE PSALMS.

   Translation of: Theologie der Psalmen.
   Bibliography: p.
   Includes indexes.
   1. Bible. O.T. Psalms—Theology. I. Crim, Keith.
II. Title.
BS1430.5.K7313   1986   223′.206   86-17267
ISBN 0-8066-2225-3

Manufactured in the U.S.A.   APH 10-6292

1   2   3   4   5   6   7   8   9   0   1   2   3   4   5   6   7   8   9

Contents

Contents

Translator's Preface

My basic principle in preparing this translation has been to express the meaning of the original text in clear and idiomatic English. Technical terminology of biblical scholarship has been translated by the equivalent scholarly terms in English, rather than using a literal translation of the German.

The author, in the German edition, gave in full the sources of citations and quotations in the text itself, rather than in notes. Since this would result in a certain overburdening of the English translation, they are identified in this translation by only the name of the author, the date of publication of the work, and, where appropriate, by the page or pages to which reference is made. Fuller bibliographical data may be found at the end of the volume, where the works cited are listed by date under the name of the author in alphabetical order.

While the publisher has agreed to retain the Hebrew, Greek, and Latin words found in the German edition, these have also been transliterated or translated, as seemed appropriate, in the text, in order to make this work accessible to a larger circle of readers.

Almost all quotations from the Old Testament, the Deuterocanonical books, and the New Testament have been taken from the Revised Standard Version of the Bible, copyright 1946, 1952, and 1971 by the Division of Christian Education of the National Council of Churches. There are occasional quotations from the King James Version and the Jerusalem Bible, where they reflect the author's intentions more clearly than does the RSV. The spelling of all names of persons and places follows the usage of the RSV.

The abbreviation "*Comm.*" in this volume refers to the fifth edition of Kraus's two-volume commentary on the Psalms, published by Neukirchener Verlag in 1978. An English translation of this commentary is now in progress and will be published by Augsburg Publishing House.

Throughout the preparation of this translation for publication the editors of Augsburg Publishing House have been faithful colleagues. Their professional competence and scholarly insights have been of inestimable help, and serve as examples of the fellowship of those who love the Word of the Lord and seek to make that Word known.

KEITH CRIM

9

Introduction

"Israel in the presence of Yahweh (Israel's answer)"—this is how Gerhard von Rad characterized the Psalms within the larger portrayal of biblical theology in his *Theology of the Old Testament*, vol. 1. We must first clarify the assumptions behind this basic position of von Rad's in terms of his whole approach. Note that "Israel's response" as it is expressed in the Psalms is, according to von Rad, viewed in the larger context of Israel's historical traditions. Before dealing with the theology of the Psalms, von Rad made specific reference to the two fundamental complexes of traditions in the Old Testament. "Jahweh twice intervened in Israel's history in a special way, to lay a basis of salvation for his people" (1962, p. 355). "Round the first datum—Israel became the people of Jahweh and received the promised land—lies the Hexateuch with its wealth of traditions, to unfold this work of Jahweh adequately and to interpret it. The other, the choice of David and his throne, became the point of crystallization and the axis for the historical works of the Deuteronomist and the Chronicler" (von Rad, 1962, p. 355). In addition to these basic events to which the blocks of traditional material bear witness, Yahweh revealed himself in the history of his people as Lord. The prophets proclaimed his intervention in history and the new beginnings he made with his people. But not even they could refer to any other bases of saving activity than the revelation at Sinai and the choice of David and his dynasty.

In the light of these two basic events and the traditions around them, von Rad views the situation in the Psalms in the following way. "When these saving acts had happened to her, Israel did not keep silent: not only did she repeatedly take up her pen to recall these acts of Jahweh to her mind in historical documents, but she also addressed Jahweh in a wholly personal way. She offered praise to him, and asked him questions, and complained to him about all her sufferings, for Jahweh had not chosen his people as a mere dumb object of his will in history, but for converse with him. The answer of Israel's, which we gather for the most part from the Psalter, is theologically a subject in itself" (1962, p. 355).

Even though it is appropriate and desirable to deal with a theology of the Psalms, which really is "in itself an object of theological inquiry," under the general theme "Israel in the presence of Yahweh," it is also necessary to be specific about the nature of "Israel's response" as part of a dialog. This must be done, be-

11

cause the "dialogical principle" (Martin Buber) implies certain categories that could lead to a misunderstanding of the distinctive nature of the Psalms. It is clear that in the Psalms Israel spoke to Yahweh in prayer and praise. This could be called an answer inasmuch as it is a reaction to what Yahweh has previously said and done. Problems arise, however, if by bringing in the aspect of dialog we create the impression—which von Rad did not intend—that the two partners are equal to each other and stand on the same level, and that a "dialogical principle" could plumb the mystery of this correspondence. It must be stressed clearly and unequivocally that Israel's praise and prayer rise out of the depths (Psalm 130), even in the hymns and invocations offered on the prominent heights of the sanctuary and from the peaks of religious life. This is always a distance that cannot be ignored. Whenever Israel stood in God's presence or an individual was seeking God they were separated from him by a chasm (compare the Prayers of the People [see *Comm.*,* Intro. §6.2.β] and Ps. 8:5). It is with great astonishment that they experience and praise the חסד ("steadfast love") of God's presence in the sanctuary, the election of Israel (Ps. 33:12), and the exaltation of the אדם ("human") (Ps. 8:6). All this must be kept in mind and carefully considered when the theme "Israel in the presence of Yahweh" is formulated.

If in von Rad's perspective the theology of the Psalms is "in itself an object" of inquiry, it is necessary to define clearly the distinctive features of this object. The Psalter is a collection of the songs, prayers, and wisdom teachings of the Old Testament people of God, which for the most part were sung or spoken in the sanctuary in Jerusalem. We must direct our attention to the cultic center of Israel's life. There we discover the center of the life of the Old Testament people of God. In particular, the songs of Zion (*Comm.*, Intro. §6.4) proclaim the significance of this cultic center. The place itself and the festivals celebrated there give concrete form to the time and space of the worship under which Israel lived and suffered in the presence of God, praising, pleading, giving thanks, and lamenting. When we consider the origin of the Psalms and the history of their transmission (*Comm.*, Intro. §8) the interrelationship of immediate concerns and the language of praise and prayer handed on through the generations becomes a special object of theological interest and reflection. The unimaginable complexity of the manner in which Israel's faith, confession, praise, and prayer were brought together in the Psalms becomes the object of never-ending questions, research, and reflection—especially since all these pieces of evidence from God's people point beyond themselves to the mystery and wonder of the revelation and concealment, the presence and the distance of the God of Israel. The Psalter "might well be called a little Bible. In it is comprehended most beautifully and briefly everything that is in the entire Bible. . . . Anyone who could not read the whole Bible would here have anyway almost an entire summary of it, comprised in one little book" (Martin Luther, 1960 [1528], p. 254). In a similar way the theology of the Psalms could be called "a biblical theology in miniature," but this would not mean that even for an instant we could ignore a theology of the Old Testament and beyond that a biblical theology (cf. H. J. Kraus, 1970). This would also include a consideration of the use made of the Psalter in the New Testament, which will be the object of a thorough investigation in this work.

Comm. in this volume refers to the fifth edition of Kraus's two-volume commentary on the Psalms, published by Neukirchener in 1978; an English translation of this commentary is forthcoming from Augsburg Publishing House.

Once more we should note what Luther said in his "Preface to the Psalms": "Here we find not only what one or two saints have done, but what he has done who is the very head of all saints. We also find what all the saints still do. . . . The Psalter ought to be a precious and beloved book, if for no other reason than this: it promises Christ's death and resurrection so clearly—and pictures his kingdom and the condition and nature of all Christendom—that it might well be called a little Bible" (1960, p. 254). In these statements it is significant that Luther does not speak of a mere prefiguring of Christ in the relationship of the Old and New Testaments, but that the prayer of Christ the Head carries the prayer of the church yesterday and today; thus indeed Christ has become the one who was really praying in the Psalms.

But how are we to define more closely the object with which a theology of the Psalms is concerned? The basic statements of von Rad are significant here as well. To be sure, they were made in reference to the theology of the Old Testament as a whole, but they can also be applied to the theology of the Psalms. "The subject-matter which concerns the theologian is, of course, not the spiritual and religious world of Israel and the conditions of her soul in general, nor is it her world of faith, all of which can only be reconstructed by means of conclusions drawn from the documents: instead, it is simply Israel's own explicit assertions about Jahweh. . .and there is no doubt that in many cases [the theologian] must go back to school again and learn to interrogate each document, much more closely than has been done hitherto, as to its specific kerygmatic intention" (von Rad, 1962, pp. 105-106). This position is a direct rejection of research into the history of Israelite piety; it is also—and this is particularly in question in Psalms research—a rejection of research primarily in terms of the psychology of religion. It is not the pious human being and his religion that are the objects of a theology of the Psalms, but the testimony by which those who sing, pray, and speak point beyond themselves, the "kerygmatic intention" of their praise and confession, their prayers and teachings. Psalm 115:1 says, "Not to us, O Lord, not to us, but to thy name give glory!" Those who sing and pray are not proclaiming their spiritual experience, their personal or private destiny. Everything that they experience, suffer, and undergo becomes praise of Yahweh and proclamation of his name when they speak of their experience and suffering (Ps. 22:22). In the Psalter prayer and praise stand under the negative statement, "Not to us, not to us!" To praise means to give Yahweh the כבוד ("glory") (Ps. 29:1). To pray is to commit to Yahweh all one's capacity and suffering, in body and soul. The test of the objectivity of our theological work and of its faithfulness to its subject matter is whether it really follows the witness of the text, the intention expressed in the language of praise and prayer. This, however, is not to say that we should abandon the realm of the "subjective" for that of the "objective." By analogy we may apply to the Psalms what Karl Barth says about the object and content of the Christian message in his *Church Dogmatics*. "The object and theme of theology and the content. . .is neither a subjective nor an objective element in isolation. This is to say, it is neither an isolated human nor an isolated God, but God and man in their divinely established and effective encounter, the dealings of God with the Christian and of the Christian with God" (*CD* 4/3: 498). If we take this trenchant observation as our starting point, it has inescapable consequences for theological inquiry, so that in dealing with the songs of praise, the prayers, and the instructions of the Psalms we cannot maintain a distance, and cannot eliminate the existential relationship to this event. Especially in relation to the Psalms it is inescapably clear that in their correspondence to their subject matter, praise and prayer are the basic forms of theology. Theology is "a task that not only begins with prayer and is accompanied by it, but one that is to be carried out appropriately and characteristically in the act of prayer" (K. Barth, 1962, pp. 180f.). Only in our encounter with the Psalms are we brought to the basic recognition that anything said of God in the third person is inauthentic; explicitly or implicitly, God can be thought of and spoken of truly and authentically only in the second person of direct address. The wisdom of the Psalms teaches that God sees humans before they begin to think of him or to speak or write about him.

> O Lord, thou has searched me and known me!
> Thou knowest when I sit down and when I rise up;
>   thou discernest my thoughts from afar (Ps. 139:1–2).

The Psalms protect us against the "primordial threat to man"—religion: " 'Religion' comes between God and man and in the end takes the place of that which is irreplaceable" (K. Kerenyi, 1955, p. 20). This phenomenon that Kerenyi has identified must be defined more clearly and precisely. In religion man has taken possession of the divine and set it to work. In religion Israel would no longer be standing before Yahweh, but in a sphere of cultic and ritual mechanisms for making adaptations and producing results, in a world of autonomous experiences. This is not the place to introduce a controversy over the concept of religion and its definition. I want only to point out the "primordial threat to man" which is constantly encountered in the Psalms. Consequently, the theology of the Psalms involves a constant effort to remain true to its subject matter—God and Israel, God and the person in Israel, in their encounter and fellowship, established by God and brought to realization by God. It involves God's dealings with the person and the person's dealings with God.

If this then is the nature of the subject matter of a theology of the Psalms, what methodology is to be used? Gunkel answered this question by insisting that the only appropriate approach was to pay consistent and direct attention to the "categories" found in the Psalter. In the meantime, however, a more complicated situation has developed as the result of research in the history of the transmission of traditions and also in reference to the studies of the language of prayer in the Psalms. The issues are dealt with in the Introduction to the commentary but they may be mentioned here. First, there are a number of areas of overlap. Specific concepts, themes, and traditions of the Old Testament find expression in different categories, and cannot be explained differently in each instance. Conventional formulations of prayer language run through all categories. They cannot be differentiated from each other by topic. Even so, "category research" has a contribution to make to the structure of a theology of the Psalms. This calls for a flexible procedure that coordinates the data and moves between two extremes: an order of loci (topics) which does violence to the subject matter, and an approach which is tied to literary forms alone. We must first ask, "Who is the God whom the Psalms address and of whom they speak? How is he called? Where and how does he make himself known? What pronouncements does he make? (chap. 1, "The God of Israel"). Next, Israel is to be discussed, the people of God who stand in the presence of Yahweh, their calling, their history and destiny, as these find expression in the Psalms. And Israel is also a community assembled for worship, with its rituals, its representatives, and its institutions (chap. 2, "The People of God"). The next chapter will deal in more detail with cultic sites and cultic festivals, including a more direct consideration of such groups of Psalms as the songs of Zion, the festival psalms, and the liturgies (chap. 3, "The Sanctuary and Its Worship"). Next, the royal psalms are to be treated, along with other statements about the "anointed of Yahweh" (Chap. 4, "the King"). The "enemies" are spoken of especially, but not exclusively, in the prayers of the individual and in the prayers of the community. This leads to a careful investigation of this theme (chap. 5, "The Enemy Powers"). Von Rad says of the Psalms, "Here then if anywhere can we hope that the basic features of a theological doctrine of man will become clear—that is, that we may see *the* picture of man set over against the living God, and not merely a variant of the many pictures which man has made of himself" (von Rad, 1962, p. 356). If such an anthropology of the Psalms is to be produced, then the starting place is the prayers of the individual (chap. 6, "The Individual in the Presence of God"). Finally, as has been indicated, the manner in which the Psalms were used in the New Testament is to be investigated and presented (chap. 7, "The Psalms in the New Testament").

The Psalms are artistic poems, whose form cannot be ignored in order to abstract a few bundles of teachings for a theology of the Psalms. In the Old Testament, however, art does not consist of a "dialectical contradiction," as Kierkegaard put it, in the light of the "truth of the eternal" in that poetry. On the contrary, the artistic capacity expressed in the Psalms is indicated in the intensity and concentration of style, the appropriateness of the measures employed, the clarity and beauty, the heights and depths of that which is spoken and sung in the presence of Yahweh. Beauty is only "one specific way of expressing truth" (Hegel, 1937, pp. 135f.). Even where the poetry of the Psalter finds expression only in the use of forms according to traditional rules, where, for example, the acrostic principle is employed, the parallelism of members and the use of meter are able to give expression to the pleasing quality of the rich variety of repetition and the appropriateness of the content being presented. It would be wholly inappropriate to evaluate the content of the Psalms by modern formalist standards, as Gunkel did.

The influence of wisdom teachings on the poetry of the Psalms should be considered here once again. In *Comm.*, Intro. §8, 1, the influence which the reflective thought and the didactic purpose of wisdom literature had on the Psalms, especially on the prayer of the individual and on the hymn of thanks (*todah*), is explained as due to the close relationship between the priestly and wisdom schools in Jerusalem. The כהנים ("priests") as "temple scribes" and the ספרים ("scribes") as "government scribes" lived in close proximity to each other. This in itself explains the fact that the wisdom based on life and experience, the transmission of which was the responsibility of the ספרים ("scribes"), gradually found its way into the language of prayer used by the priests and the temple singers. Theologically this process is of twofold significance. For one thing, the חכמה ("wisdom") tradition of life and experience provided the possibility for that which was lived and suffered, as expressed in the conventional language of prayer and also in the vivid accounts of those rescued from danger, to be elevated to the level of valid knowledge and teachings. The events of suffering and deliverance could be clarified and sublimated in the categories of thought and speech used by חכמה ("wisdom"). Second, the reflective thought, experiential knowledge, and teaching of wisdom literature show unmistakable signs of the beginnings of the formation of theology in the Psalms. The clearly didactic features of wisdom

15

statements in the Psalms thus provide a significant starting point for a theology of the Psalms.

In reflecting on what has been said thus far, one could be excused for thinking that we have in the Psalter the closed world of the Israelite cultic community and the activities carried out in Israel's worship. One might even wonder whether the Psalms are distinctively different from the rest of the Old Testament (except the wisdom literature) in that they present the static world of sacred places and times of worship, while the other books deal with the active dynamic world of the events of history, with its promise of future salvation for all the nations of the world. But such distinctions are not valid. In innumerable significant passages in the Psalter we can note the openness of the songs of praise, the prayers, and the didactic psalms to the world of the nations. In the *todah*, the individual praying wants the kings of the nations to join him in offering thanks (Ps. 138:4). In the presence of the nations he praises the God of Israel (Ps. 57:9; 108:3). The "teleology" of the Psalms is expressed in these words:

> . . .That thy way may be known upon earth,
> thy saving power among all nations (Ps. 67:2).

> Let them know that thou alone,
>   whose name is the Lord,
>   art the Most High over all the earth (Ps. 83:18).

The Psalms raise the banner of universal proclamation and communication. In the old Zion traditions Jerusalem is the "joy of all the earth," the center of creation, the place where all kings and nations gather to worship and adore (Psalms 46; 48; 63:29; 72:10–11; etc.). This has its complement in another theme: Yahweh comes to the nations.

> . . .He comes to judge the earth.
> He will judge the world with righteousness,
>   and the peoples with equity (98:9).

> The Lord has made known his victory,
>   he has revealed his vindication
>   in the sight of the nations (98:2).

Just as these texts warn us against regarding the cult, the distinctive characteristic of the Psalms, as something far removed from history or even antagonistic to it, so too the idea must be rejected that what occurs in the Psalms is of sacral, purely "spiritual" interest, and free from any political significance. It is sufficient to point to the prayers of the people, to the prayers of those who are falsely accused and persecuted, to the themes of "kingship," "enemies," "righteousness," and "innocence." Above all, the influence that the Psalms have had throughout history shows that the poor, the enslaved, the persecuted have been able to express themselves in the language of prayer of the Psalter. Even in the songs of praise, the Psalms are not the hymns and prayers of a church triumphant that exists in liturgical security; they are the language of the עֲנָוִים, the "poor," the people that was chosen and bidden to travel a new and better way among the nations.

1. The God of Israel

A. Yahweh Sebaoth

If Ps. 24:7-10 involves part of the ritual of a solemn entrance ceremony that was observed on Zion (cf. *Comm.* on this passage) then we are justified in regarding יהוה צבאות (*Yahweh Sebaoth*) as the solemn, cultically legitimate name of the God who was present in the sanctuary of Jerusalem and honored there. This divine name, especially the name יהוה (*Yahweh*), points back to the traditions of ancient Israel. In the Psalter the name יהוה occurs about 650 times (according to Lisowsky, 1958, who used Kittel's *Biblia Hebraica* as the basis; according to Jenni, THAT 1:704, it occurs 695 times). It should be kept in mind that in the Elohistic Psalter (see *Comm.*, Intro. §3) instead of the original name יהוה (*Yahweh*) the divine name אלהים (*Elohim*) is found. In the Psalter the shortened form יה or הי is found 43 times (50 times in the entire Old Testament, according to Jenni). For Israel יהוה (*Yahweh*) was purely a name, without any components of meaning that were to be explained etymologically or symbolically. The well-known "definition" of the name Yahweh in Exod. 3:14 presents a theological etymology, but not a philological one, and has no apparent relevance for the Psalms. No less irrelevant are all the attempts to arrive at some "original meaning" of the tetragrammaton by means of philological etymology. Such attempts begin with the question, is the word יהוה (*Yahweh*) a nominal or a verbal form? If, as is usually assumed, a verbal form is involved, we would be led to think of form in the imperfect. But what root is involved? For the various hypotheses, see von Rad (1962) and L. Kohler (1957). But does not the short form יה or הי, which occurs 43 times in the Psalter, represent the more ancient name of Israel's God? G. R. Driver advanced this view (1928). His starting point was the shout of praise הללו יה ("hallelujah"), and he thought he could explain the short form יה as a shout of ecstatic excitement which has an air of originality about it, and which then later, in connection with the events of the exodus from Egypt, was expanded to the longer form יהוה (*Yahweh*). But there is no basis for this explanation. It is much more likely to assume that the shorter form came into use later in shouts during worship and in songs of praise.

The problems in the area of history of religion which are connected with the possibility of discovering the origin of the name *Yahweh* in the ancient world surrounding Israel remain obscure and unresolved. Since the discovery of non-Israelite theophoric names (Yaubidi at Hamath and Azriyau at Sam'al) the question has become pressing, and we must reexamine the hypothesis that the short form may really represent the "original name." Still, nothing more than vague combinations have been suggested. This is also true of the more recent research which has been stimulated by the occurrence of *yw* as the name of a Ugaritic deity (see R. Mayer [1958]; R. Gray [1953]; S. Herrmann [1966]; J. Kinyongo [1970]; E. Jenni [THAT 1:704]; F. M. Cross [1973]).

In the Psalter Yahweh is called אלהי ישראל ("God of Israel"), a usage that must be examined further (Ps. 41:13; 59:5; 68:8; 106:48). He is the "God of Abraham" (Ps. 47:9) and the "God of Jacob" (Ps. 20:1; 24:6; 46:7, 11; 75:9; 76:6; 81:1, 4; 84:8; 94:7). The formula of self-identification, "I am Yahweh, your God" is found in Ps. 50:7; 81:10. On this formula see W. Zimmerli (1978). Thus in the Psalter the ancient Israelite traditions are present through the divine name יהוה (*Yahweh*).

Attempts to explain the name and the solemn divine epithet יהוה צבאות (*Yahweh Sebaoth*) in terms of the history of religion encounter many difficulties. On the problems involved see B. N. Wambacq (1947); O. Eissfeldt (1950); J. P. Ross (1967). While what is probably the original form, יהוה צבאות (*Yahweh Sebaoth*), is found in Ps. 24:10; 46:7, 11; 48:8; 69:6; 84:1, 3, 12, the grammatically easier expression יהוה אלהי צבאות ("Yahweh, God of Sebaoth") is found in Ps. 59:5; 80:4, 7, 14, 19; 84:8; 89:8. Important clues are given in Psalm 80 for the search for the origin of the epithet in terms of tradition history and the cult. In this Psalm יהוה צבאות (*Yahweh Sebaoth*) is designated as ישב הכרובים ("enthroned upon the cherubim") (80:1). The cherubim are mentioned as early as 1 Sam. 4:4 and 2 Sam. 6:2 as components of the sanctuary of the ark of the covenant (cf. 1 Kings 6:23-28). In the Samuel passages and also in 2 Kings 19:15 and Isa. 37:16 the expression ישב הכרובים ("enthroned upon the cherubim") is used. Consequently, we are justified, as has so often been pointed out in the writings on the subject, in assigning the more extensive formula יהוה צבאות ישב הכרובים ("Yahweh of Sebaoth, enthroned upon the cherubim") to the Shiloh sanctuary, where the ark was kept. When the ark was moved to Jerusalem (2 Samuel 6) the archaic name for God went with it to the Zion sanctuary. Since it was in Shiloh that the first Israelite temple was erected, it is logical to assume that the requirements of sacral architecture and the cultic traditions concerning a temple led to the construction of a throne supported by cherubim as an adjunct to the shrine of the ark of the covenant. There can be no doubt that Syrian and Canaanite sacral traditions influenced this new development of a temple structure and a temple cult in Israel.

The question arises of the possible connection between the term ישב הכרובים ("enthroned upon the cherubim"), which is associated with the name *Yahweh Sebaoth*, and the formula וירכב על־כרוב ("he rode on a cherub"), which indicates a Tyrian-Canaanite tradition (cf. Ps. 18:10). Ugaritic texts portray Baal as a "rider of the clouds" (cf. H. Gese, 1969, pp. 122f.) Were the cherubim of the temple the sacral representation of the heavenly realm? Did the cherub throne symbolize the heavenly throne of the god of war? Were these concepts of the Syrian-Canaanite cult transferred to Yahweh at the temple at Shiloh? We can do no more than raise the questions. Nevertheless, there is considerable evidence that the formula ישב הכרוים ("enthroned upon the cherubim") has a direct connection to the designation of Yahweh as "king," so that these concepts must have been received with their background in the history of religion in mind. On this problem see M. Metzger, 1970, pp. 139–158.

But it would be one-sided and shortsighted to try to explain all the traditions connected with the divine name Yahweh Sebaoth in terms of foreign influences on the temple cult at Shiloh and thus in terms of the context of the religion of Syria and Canaan. The ancient Israelite traditions present the ark as a nomadic sanctuary and as the palladium of the holy war. The continuing influence of these traditions should not be underestimated. In discussing the Psalter a degree of caution must be exercised since the ark of Yahweh (ארון) is mentioned only in Ps. 132:8. If, however, we assume that the ceremonial entrance procession in Ps. 24:7-10 presupposes the transfer of the ark (and of the cherubim throne?), then the acclamation of the Lord, "strong and mighty,...mighty in battle (גבור מלחמה) '' (Ps. 24:8), may refer to the connection of the ark with the traditions of the holy war (cf. 1 Sam. 4:3-11).

The meaning of the unusual construct form יהוה צבאות (*Yahweh Sebaoth*) must be explored. Who or what are the צבאות (*Sebaoth*)? What "hosts" or "armies" are meant? To begin by looking at the traditions of the holy war, it is noteworthy that in 1 Sam. 17:45 צבאות (*Sebaoth*) is explained by reference to the hosts of the armies of Israel. Reference could also be made to the construction מלכי צבאות ("kings of *Sebaoth*") in Ps. 68:12, but here we face the problem that in what is probably the original form, יהוה צבאות (*Yahweh Sebaoth*), a proper noun is connected with צבאות (*Sebaoth*). This formula was probably somewhat awkward for the ancient native speaker of Hebrew and required explanation. It was made smoother by the insertion of the construct noun אלהי ("God"). Old Testament research has pursued the question and sought to answer it in other ways. Who are the "hosts"? Are they the army of heavenly beings (Ps. 103:21; 148:2)? Or the army of the stars (Isa. 40:26; 45:12; 34:4; Jer. 33:22)? Or does the expression include all of creation in heaven and earth? The fact that in these passages the singular (צבא, "host") is used speaks against this interpretation. And in any case the unusual construct form remains unexplained. O. Eissfeldt (1950) sought explanations in a different direction. He regarded צבאות (*Sebaoth*) as an "intensive abstract plural." צבאות would then mean "power," and the syntactic relationship would be explained as that of attribution. But this explanation also raises problems, because it robs the expression צבאות of concreteness and specific content. Von Rad (1962, p. 19) rightly asked whether such "an element of cultic epiklesis as old as this is in all circumstances capable of rational explanation." Even so, caution and reserve in the matter do not necessarily require us to renounce all further questions.

In attempting to explain צבאות (*Sebaoth*), it is necessary to take account of the multiplicity of the traditions and their presuppositions and consider the resulting ambiguity of all attempts to explain and understand the expression. Starting at this point, two explanations might be explored: (1) Yahweh as the embodiment of military forces, as the God who alone goes forth and fights for these hosts (von Rad, 1969); and (2) Yahweh as the personification of all the mysterious, mythological powers of the nature religion of Syria and Canaan (Maag, 1950). In the latter explanation the term צבאות (*Sebaoth*) approaches the meaning of אלהים ("gods"). But it must be admitted that the attempt to speak of a concept that "embodies" or "personifies" is far removed from archaic ways of thinking and of understanding relationships. What it means is that the divine reality designated by יהוה (*Yahweh*) could include and connote the צבאות (*Sebaoth*) in the sense that in Yahweh's actions and in his exclusivity those features which were found in the

19

צבאות (*Sebaoth*) are expressed in one being. Yahweh himself was and did that which was represented by the צבאות (*Sebaoth*) in the two senses mentioned above. This is one possible way of attempting to identify the archaic element of cultic terminology in the divine name.

In the Psalms the "name of Yahweh" expresses all the mystery and wonder of revelation, the object of all prayer, praise and reflection. For the expression שם יהוה ("name of Yahweh") in the Psalms see Ps. 7:17; 20:7; 103:1; 113:1-3; 116:4, 13, 17; 118:10-12; 122:4; 124:8; 129:8; 135:1; 148:5, 13. "In Judah God is known, his name is great in Israel" (Ps. 76:1). The earliest evidence of the communication of the name and thus of this basic concept is found in the formula derived from the revelation at Sinai, אנכי יהוה ("I am Yahweh," cf. Ps. 50:7; 81:10). The name has been entrusted to Israel. Israel "knows" this name (Ps. 9:10), "fears" it (Ps. 86:11; 102:15), "loves" it (Ps. 5:11; 69:6; 119:132), and "trusts" in it (Ps. 33:21). Yahweh's שם ("name") is "called on" (Ps. 75:1; 79:6; 80:18; 99:6; 105:1; 116:4, 13, 17; etc.). People "sing" (זמר) this name, and it is "praised" (הלל, ידה, ברך); people exult over it, rejoice in it, break into shouts of joy over it. No one can make use of this name or control it; it is "holy and terrible." It is "majestic" (Ps. 8:1, 9), characterized by כבוד ("glory," Ps. 66:2). A frequent Old Testament expression says that when a person dies or a nation is destroyed, his or her name or its name is "remembered no more" (cf. Ps. 83:4; 109:13). The name means life, identity, presence. It is said of Yahweh's name that it "endures forever" (שמך לעולם), and that his "renown" (זכרך) lasts "through all ages" (Ps. 135:13). This name is to be "celebrated in all generations" (Ps. 45:17). God's name provides protection (Ps. 118:10, 11, 12). The God of Israel "saves" by his name (Ps. 54:1). Since Yahweh is the creator, the majesty of his name is seen throughout all the earth (Ps. 8:1). Tabor and Hermon "joyously praise" his name (Ps. 89:12). And Israel knows that its "help is in the name of the Lord, who made heaven and earth" (Ps. 124:8). As does his name, so too his "praise reaches to the ends of the earth" (Ps. 48:10). All the nations will come and glorify his name (Ps. 86:9), give it that כבוד ("glory") which the heavenly beings bring to Yahweh (Ps. 29:1-2). Thus Israel can call out, "Not to us, O Lord, not to us, but to thy name give glory" (Ps. 115:1).

In addition to this, many religions in the ancient Middle East held a basic concept that the deity had to make his name known among humans. It says in the Old Testament that Yahweh would "cause his name to be remembered" so that he could be worshiped (Exod. 20:24). It was impossible to conceive of worship without knowledge of the name of God, or for there to be communication between God and humans that did not involve a name that could be called on. When Yahweh revealed himself, he communicated his name to his people. The other nations do not know this name (Ps. 79:6). In his name, Yahweh is present in such a manner that every appeal, praise, or question reaches God himself, the *Deus praesens*. As Yahweh himself is holy, so too is his name (Ps. 111:9). This name cannot and must not be used in magic or for any purposes that are not in accord with his will, for such misuse would profane his name. This name is a spring of salvation, deliverance, help, and protection. Indeed the name *Yahweh* is assurance for Israel and every person in the nation of God's people. It expresses the accessibility of Yahweh, his presence, and his faithfulness to his promises. Therefore, in the Psalms the plea is often voiced that the God of Israel intervene, rescue, help, deliver, protect "for his name's sake" (למען שמך). The phrase למען שמך means: because truly your name gives assurance that you will keep your promises and be present to save us (Ps. 23:3; 25:11; 31:3; 106:8; 109:21; 148:5, 13). In Ps. 79:9, as a synonym to לְמַעַן שְׁמֶךָ, the expression עַל־דְּבַר כְּבוֹד־שְׁמֶךָ ("for the glory of thy name") used. The concern here is for the honor, the majesty of the name of Yahweh as a demonstration of help and deliverance. In biblical language the "name" has a dimension and a dynamic that are foreign to our speech and our way of thinking. But this is by no means any reason for claiming that the Old Testament statements about the "name" of God lie in the realm of magical concepts. This is strictly ruled out by the prohibition in the Decalog (Exod. 20:7) of any profaning of the name. Wherever the Old Testament speaks of the "name of Yahweh" there is a depth of mystery in the coinciding of gift and freedom. The "name of Yahweh" is a gift, entrusted to Israel, and in it Yahweh is present. At the same time this name as the reflection of the holiness of Yahweh is itself a force that proclaims God's freedom and that can withdraw and bar access to itself. But the Psalms stress more than anything else that the שֵׁם ("name") is a saving gift, knowing well that this name is "holy and terrible" (Ps. 111:9). The problem of identity and nonidentity that arise in connection with the "name" has depths that cannot be plumbed. Identity means that Yahweh is not only "called" by his name, but that he is the one whom he reveals himself to be and as whom he is addressed. The name is not some designation that is added on, but the self-manifestation and the self-expression of God among his people. The name is what he himself is. "Nomen Dei est Deus ipse" (Calov, 1676, p. 231). And yet the name is Yahweh's external self-manifestation. For the sake of the self-manifestation in Israel the name is enveloped by the secret of nonidentity; it is God's "double." He is the Other, who condescends to manifest himself. The principles of Deuteronomic and Deuteronomistic name-theology extend to the Psalms. In the sanctuary it is not "Yahweh himself" who dwells, but the שֵׁם ("name") as his representative (Ps. 74:7). And yet in the Psalms the presence and gift of the שֵׁם ("name") are constantly the presupposition of all prayer and song, all confidence and hope, all cries and petitions. And this name is the name יהוה (*Yahweh*). Any and all acquaintance with this name is based on the fact that the God of Israel has made himself known. Moreover, every concept of God is based on the fact that he has manifested himself. Those who pray and sing in the Psalms, however, base what they do on the fact that the name is not empty, but that in this name everything is contained—justice and salvation, deliverance and life, knowledge and wisdom.

"There is a reason why the name of God is used to stand for God himself. Because we cannot comprehend the essence of God, insofar as his grace and power are made manifest to us, it is appropriate for us to place our hope in him. Thus by calling on his name, faith is born" (Calvin, CR 59: 208, on Ps. 20:1). "We can know indeed that it really is his name, the name of God, and not the name of a creature, which is here made known to us: the eternal, the holy, the glorious name; the name which is above every name. We can know indeed that in this name we are dealing with God Himself. But we must not be surprised if the name is such that we cannot either hear or express it without remembering that it is a question of Him whom we can only name in consequence of the fact that He has named Himself and as we see and hear this His self-naming. We must not be surprised if this name of His—which we accept, which we praise and laud Him and call upon Him, in which we can know Him, in which He unveils Himself to us—does at the same time accomplish His veiling, so that, looking forward, we are continually referred to Himself, to His own self-unveiling. If it were otherwise, it would not be the name of God" (K. Barth, *CD* 2/1:59–60).

21

The God of Israel

The name distinguishes the God of Israel from all other gods and powers. This opens for us an aspect of the Old Testament that finds particular expression in the Psalms. "The central position of the name included the fact that revelation has always been special revelation, and is and will remain so. God has a name; he is not the nameless one. God is not the All; he becomes known as a reality which is in the world but which is distinguished from the world. God does not come to us as a general reality that is to be found everywhere. Rather, he comes as the most specific reality that can always be sought for and found in a specific place. This does not mean that he is not the most general and the almighty and the one who is everywhere present, but it means that the path to knowledge of him cannot begin with generalities" (Miskotte, 1976, p. 38). Miskotte expresses in theological language the exact perception of that which happens in the Old Testament in the struggle between God and the spirits of nature and heaven, that which is always and everywhere involved in every Old Testament statement in which the name of Yahweh occurs. If the name, Yahweh's self-revelation, is concentrated in a proper name, then this constitutes a warning against any talk of "monotheism" on a theoretical basis. Paul Yorck von Wartenburg wrote to W. Dilthey, "I believe it is desirable to abandon all the categories of pantheism, monotheism, theism, panentheism. In themselves they have no religious value at all; they are only formalities and quantitative designations. They reflect a concept of the world, not a concept of God and constitute only the outline of an intellectual attitude, and thus are only a formal projection. The religious element, however, as well as historical knowledge, depends on the themes of these formal designations" (quoted in Buber, *Werke*, vol. 2 [1964], p. 14). The last sentence of the quotation could be stated more precisely as follows: Theological and historical knowledge depend alone on the name and the fullness of its presentation—the name, not something numinous that has been experienced and explored phenomenologically. A theology of the name, based on the Old Testament and thus also on the Psalms, cannot ignore for a moment what is said of the name of Israel's God in the New Testament and directed toward the future. It is Jesus Christ who has revealed the name of Go d in the eschaton: ἐφανέρωσά σου τὸ ὄνομα ("I have manifested thy name"; John 17:6). Christ Jesus himself has been given the name that is "above every name," the name ΚΥΡΙΟΣ—יהוה (*Kyrios—Yahweh*) (Phil. 2:9). Whatever biblical theology says about the name of God must be related to this eschatological happening (cf. Albertz, 1947, pp. 19–23).

In the Psalter Yahweh is called הלהים (*Elohim*) or אלוה (*Eloah*) 365 times, and is called אל (*El*) 75 times (this term will be discussed in the next section). אלהים (*Elohim*) can be translated as "God," "a god," "the God," "gods," or "the gods." But as a designation of Yahweh the name אלהים (*Elohim*) with its distinctive plural form means "God" in the absolute sense, "the summation of all that is divine," "the only one who exists" (cf. Köhler, 1957, pp. 36ff.). Thus אלהים is the summation of all power and all powers. It contains an element of doxology, of confessing that "Yahweh is Elohim," of polemic, of giving an identifying name. As אלהים (*Elohim*) has become in the Old Testament (and thus also in the Psalms) a strict synonym for Yahweh, the word does not simply denote the highest, holiest, and mightiest in a vague and general manner; rather, אלהים (*Elohim*) is a name, an epithet that represents direct address to Yahweh. In particular the substitution of אלהים (*Elohim*) for יהוה (*Yahweh*) in the Elohistic Psalter (cf. *Comm.*, Intro. §3) makes it clear that אלהים (*Elohim*) has taken the place of the name of God, and thus has the nature of a name. אלהים encodes the fullness that lies hidden in the שׁם יהוה ("name of Yahweh") and explains the riddle of the analogous term צבאות (*Sebaoth*).

The fullness of divine power indicated by the name אלהים (*Elohim*) is made accessible to Israel in the self-disclosure of the name יהוה (*Yahweh*). "Yahweh our God" is the formula by which Israel confessed its faith. That Yahweh is the God of Israel is a fact of prime importance, in comparison with which the question of the existence or the nature of this God is secondary. His being present for Israel expresses the fullness of what it means that Yahweh is אלהים (*Elohim*). Even the fact that Yahweh is the only God, a fact proclaimed again and again in the Psalms, is recognized in the confession, "It is he that made us, and we are his; we are his people, and the sheep of his pasture" (Ps. 100:2). Abstract concepts would lack reality. Yahweh cannot be conceived of apart from the reality of his attentiveness to Israel. He is Israel's God, and as such he is Lord of the nations (Psalms 96; 98). He is the God of Israel, and in this relationship he is the only God, the jealous God who calls Israel to account and brings Israel to judgment (Ps. 50;81). He is אלהים (*Elohim*) who fights in the midst of and for his people against the gods and powers that want to control Israel (cf. §5,1). But whenever Israel turns to Yahweh in praise and prayer, the people proclaim, "For with thee is the fountain of life; in thy light do we see light" (Ps. 36:9). Thus אלהים (*Elohim*) is none other than יהוה (*Yahweh*) in the fullness of his divine power, in his uniqueness; he alone is God and there can be no other.

Yahweh Sebaoth is the living God. "The Lord lives" (Ps. 18:46). He is "the fountain of life" (Ps. 36:9). The longing soul yearns for him, for the "living God" (Ps. 84:2). In terms of the history of religion, the cry חי־יהוה ("live, O Yahweh") is to be seen against the background of the Baal cult. When the dry summer is ended and the fertility deity Baal wakes out of the sleep of death, then the cultic shout rings out חי אלאין בעל ("live, exalted Baal"). But Yahweh is no dying and rising god. When it is said that he "lives" the statement stands against the background of his reality as the one who never tires, who every morning brings forth new salvation and deliverance (cf. Kraus, 1972d, pp. 1-36). "He who keeps Israel will neither slumber nor sleep" (Ps. 121:4). He is *semper actuosus* ("always active"; Luther). Any comparison with Canaanite religion can be only a reference to linguistic analogies. And at the same time the far-reaching fundamental differences must be stressed. In this respect Widengren (1955, p. 69) is wrong (cf. the comments on Psalm 18 in the *Comm.*). Every statement in the Psalms about Yahweh's "sleeping" or "waking" is to be understood in terms of the specific context. When it is said that Yahweh sleeps, it is a metaphor that expresses the hiddenness of Israel's God (Ps. 44:23; 78:65). The cry "Awake!" is synonymous with the petition "save me," "help me," "lift thyself up" (Ps. 7:6; 44:23; 59:4-5, etc.). Yahweh is the living God. He speaks. He acts. He helps. He comes, and "does not keep silence" (Ps. 50:3). He is near to those who call upon him (Ps. 145:18), and to the brokenhearted (Ps. 34:18; 85:9; cf. Amirtham, 1968, pp. 31-55). Yahweh is the living God. He sees (Ps. 10:14; 11:4; 14:2; 33:13-14; 35:22; 94:9; 102:19; 113:6; 138:6; 139:3, 16, 24). He hears and answers (Ps. 4:3; 6:8-9; 69:33; 78:21; 94:9; etc.). He saves, helps, rescues, delivers from trouble and the pangs of death: ישׁע *hiph.*, מלט *piel*, נצל *piel, hiph.*

Köhler (1957, pp. 24-25) was right when, in reference to the many anthropomorphisms, he said, "Their intention is not in the least to reduce God to a rank similar to that of man. To describe God in terms of human characteristics is not to humanize Him. That has never happened except in unreasonable polemic. Rather the purpose of anthropomorphisms is to make God accessible to man. They hold open the door for encounter and controversy between God's will and man's will. They represent God as person. They avoid the error of presenting God as a careless and soulless abstract Idea or a fixed Principle standing over against man like a strong silent battlement. God is personal. He has a will, He exists in controversy ready to communicate Himself, offended at men's sins yet with a ready ear for their supplication and compassion for their confessions of guilt: in a word, God is a living God.'' God is event, action, deed, life in his own incomparable personhood. It is in accordance with his essential nature to make himself known, to express his life in word and deed, to move and to work (Ps. 9:19; 21:13; 57:6; 68:1; 94:2; 99:4; etc.). Therefore ''all flesh'' turns to him. Therefore he is praised and glorified both in the heavenly world and on earth.

B. Appellations of Yahweh

The fact that Yahweh is the Other in distinction from gods and every deity can be established first by inquiring in terms of the history of religion into the appellations of Yahweh. His most specific self-designation is the ''God of Israel'' (Ps. 41:13; 59:5; 68:8; 106:48). He is the ''God of Jacob'' (Ps. 20:1; 24:6; 46:7, 11; 75:9; 76:6; 81:1, 4; 84:8) and the ''God of Abraham'' (Ps. 47:9). He entered unalterably into this relationship through his self-revelation, in which he has spoken and acted. As his epithets proclaim in manifold ways, he has made known in Israel his lordship, that he is lord in the reality of history. And whatever these epithets may be and whatever their origin, there is ultimately no analogy through which Yahweh's being, essence, and work as Lord could become accessible outside Israel, from some distant point of view. The Psalms speak of God in metaphors. They use the terms and epithets of the surrounding religious world in order to confess Yahweh's lordship and proclaim it polemically in the debates, struggles, and conflicts with the gods and spiritual powers. Thus, in hymns and liturgies, they reveal to Israel, in the language of the surrounding nations, new depths in Yahweh. But the epithets of Israel's religious environment do not serve as the basis for an accessible and understandable complex of ideas that could establish ''theism''; that is, they cannot fix clearly and unambiguously the concept and full image of a supernatural, personal, self-conscious, autonomous, and almighty king, creator, and ruler of the world. The language of the Psalms uses the various existing epithets in a highly flexible manner, and with and through them praises the God of Israel. The details of this situation can be drawn together and summarized.

With striking frequency the Psalms term Yahweh the God of Israel עליון (*'Elyon*). This term for God is correctly translated as ''Most High,'' because it is derived from the root עלה (''go up,'' ''ascend''). In this connection it is to be noted that in the Old Testament עליון (*'Elyon*) refers to places which are located at a higher level (2 Kings 15:35; Isa. 7:3; 36:2; Jer. 20:2; etc.). Similarly, in the sense of prerogative, the exaltation of Israel (Deut. 26:19; 28:1) or of the chosen king (Ps. 89:27) is expressed by the word עליון (*'Elyon*). In the Psalter עליון (*'Elyon*) is one designation of Yahweh among many others, an appellation, however, that obviously came to play a major role in the cultic observances at Jerusalem. If we examine the synonymous terms for God, it is striking that in the parallelism of members עֶלְיוֹן (*'Elyon*) corresponds to אֵל ("God") (Ps. 57:2; 107:11; but cf. Num. 24:16). The combination אֵל־עֶלְיוֹן ("God Most High") (Ps. 78:35; cf. Gen. 14:18-22) deserves special attention. Also, the synonymous use of עֶלְיוֹן ("Most High") and שַׁדַּי (*Shaddai*, "Almighty") should be noted (Ps. 91:1; cf. Num. 24:16). According to Ps. 47:2, the עֶלְיוֹן ("Most High") is מֶלֶךְ גָּדוֹל עַל־כָּל־הָאָרֶץ ("great king over all the earth") (cf. also Ps. 97:9 and Ps. 83:18). This identifies the realm over which the "highest God" exercises lordship. The seat of his authority is the sanctuary on Mount Zion (Ps. 87:5; 46:4), but he rules in "heaven" (Ps. 18:13), highly exalted above all gods (Ps. 97:9). More accurately, his throne is in heaven, and he is present on earth in the Zion sanctuary (cf. Metzger, 1970, pp. 139-158). All the אֱלֹהִים ("gods") are בְּנֵי עֶלְיוֹן ("sons of the Most High") and thus stand in the service of God "Most High" Ps. 82:6). Yahweh, as the שֵׁם עֶלְיוֹן ("name. . .Most High") is worthy of the praise of Israel (Ps. 7:17; 9:2); he is the refuge of the poor (Ps. 91:9), and vows are paid to him (Ps. 50:14).

On the basis of this initial survey the following conclusions can be drawn. (1) עֶלְיוֹן ("Most High") is a designation of Yahweh that is closely associated with the appellations אֵל (God), שַׁדַּי (*Shaddai*), and מֶלֶךְ (king), thus displaying traits of the so-called monarchical theology. (2) This term had its origin in the cultic life of Jerusalem. (3) "Monarchical theology," with its statements addressed to "God most high," gave witness to an absolute right to lordship and majesty over the entire world, in contrast to the claims of all gods and supernatural powers. It has long been well known that the divine titles עֶלְיוֹן ("Most High") and אֵל עֶלְיוֹן ("God Most High") passed from the pre-Israelite cult of Jerusalem, in which Melchizedek was the prototype of the Jebusite priest-king, into Israelite worship and were applied to Yahweh. That is to say, the epithet עֶלְיוֹן (*Elyon*, "Most High") originated in Canaanite-Syrian culture. Moreover, אֵל עֶלְיוֹן *El Elyon* (like אֵל עוֹלָם [*El 'Olam*, "Everlasting God"] or אֵל שַׁדַּי [*El Shaddai*, "God Almighty"], Gen. 21:33; 17:1) was originally a proper name designating the local deity of the Melchizedek-city of Jerusalem and served to legitimize his claims. Genesis 14:18-22 contains ancient traditions which substantiate the hypothesis of a prehistory of the divine name עֶלְיוֹן (אֵל) ([*El*] *Elyon*) in the pre-Israelite cult of Jerusalem. See Gunkel (1922, pp. 284ff.); Schatz (1972, pp. 207ff.); Della Vida (1944, pp.1-9); H. Schmidt (1955, pp. 168-197); Lack (1962, pp.44-64); Gese (1969, pp. 94-102, 116-134).

In reference to the nature of "monarchical theology," Paul Tillich wrote: "Monarchical monotheism lies on the boundary line between polytheism and monotheism. The God-monarch rules over the hierarchy of inferior gods and godlike beings. He represents the power and value of the hierarchy. His end would be the end of all those ruled by him." Later Tillich said, "Monarchic monotheism is too deeply involved in polytheism to be liberated from it" (vol. 1, pp. 225-226). These comments from the point of view of systematic theology need only to be refined and modified. In the monarchical statements about the deity (as remains to be shown in detail) there are three phases that can be distinguished. (1) The phase of the struggle and victory of a deity that leads to his enthronement (enthronement phase; cf. the elevation of Marduk to the supreme deity, to the "God-King" in the *Enuma elish*). (2) The phase of establishment and proclamation of specific hierarchies, in which the leading position and the absolute supremacy of the highest god is no longer in dispute (hierarchy phase; cf. the position of the god El in the Ugaritic pantheon, Gese, 1969, pp. 94ff.). (3) The phase of the modification of "monarchical theology" through a total stripping away of the power of the pantheon, as it occurred in the Old Testament, especially in the Psalms (loss of power phase; on individual questions, see below).

The God of Israel

It has already been shown that the epithet מלך ("king") directly accompanies the divine title עליון (*'Elyon*, Ps. 47:2). The Psalms glorify Yahweh as מלך גדול "great king," Ps. 47:2), as מלך רב ("great king," Ps. 48:2), as מלך הכבוד "king of glory," Ps. 24:7-10), and as מלך לעולם ("eternal king," Ps. 29:10; cf. Ps. 10:16; 145:13). The following characteristics of עליון (*'Elyon*) are also characteristic of God as אל (*El*): (1) lordship over all gods (Ps. 93:3; 96:4; 97:7, 9); (2) lordship over the entire world (Ps. 47:2, 7; 97:9). If we ask what is the situation in which Yahweh is king, the place where he is enthroned, we can derive three points from the formula ישב על־כסא קדשו (he sits on the throne of his glory"; Ps. 47:8). (1) יהוה למבול ישב ("The Lord sits enthroned over the flood," Ps. 29:10); this archaic expression points to the "heavenly ocean" above which the mythologically identified throne is to be sought (Begrich, 1964, pp. 39-54). (2) יהוה בשמים הכין כסאו, "The Lord has established his throne in the heavens" (Ps. 103:19). (3) ישב הכרובים "He sits enthroned upon the cherubim" (Ps. 99:1), or ישב ציון "dwells on Zion" (Ps. 9:11). Again it is strikingly evident that the God-king is seated on his throne in the heavenly world as well as in the sanctuary in Jerusalem. The concept of sacral reality found in the religious environment of which Israel was a part is evident here. The institutions of the sanctuary correspond to and are a copy of the features of the heavenly world that are seen by divination and through myth. The heavenly prototype is "portrayed" in its counterpart in the cult and the cultic sacral objects (cf. Exod. 25:9, 40; 26:30). On this problem see Metzger (1970, pp. 139-158).

There has been a degree of divergence in the attempts to determine the place which the divine title מלך ("king") occupies in the (cultic) history of Israel. Buber (1967, p. 130; see also pp. 22, 37, 108) advanced the position that the God of Israel was already regarded as "king" at Sinai and was so designated. Thus he termed the Sinai covenant a "royal covenant." Central to this explanation is the passage Deut. 33:5, as well as Exod. 15:18; 19:6; and Num. 23:21. However, this view and all other attempts to find the origins of the "kingship of Yahweh" in the early Israelite period must be weighed against Alt's thesis "that the concept of the kingship of Yahweh seems not to have been a constitutive element in the early form of Israelite religion" (1953a, 1:348). During the period of the Israelite monarchy the vision which Isaiah saw at the time of his call to be a prophet is the only firm and datable point for the use of the designation מלך (king) for Yahweh in the cultic history (Isa. 6:1ff.). In the eighth century B.C., the God who appears in the temple in Jerusalem and is surrounded by seraphim is seen as "king" and is so designated. There is only one comparable text in the Old Testament that goes back to an earlier time, 1 Kings 22:19. Micaiah ben Imlah recounted a vision along with his announcement of the word of Yahweh: "I saw the Lord sitting on his throne, and all the host of heaven standing beside him on his right hand and on his left." But this vision contains only the heavenly prototype, which, to be sure, may have corresponded in north Israel to a cultic copy. With the exception, however, of 1 Kings 22, there is no other strand which takes us back to a period earlier than Isaiah 6. In Ps. 99:1 it is said of Yahweh the God-king, ישב הכרובים ("He sits [enthroned upon] the cherubim"), a formula which clearly refers to the cherubim throne presupposed in Isaiah 6 (and thus to the tradition of the Ark of the Covenant). It also refers to the expression ישב הכרובים ("he sits ion] the cherubim") in 1 Sam. 4:4 and 2 Sam. 6:2, and thus also to the context of the Yahweh Sebaoth traditions (above pp. 17ff.). These oldest of all the extant materials handed down from the Jerusalem cult are found in the stories about the Ark (see Rost, 1926, pp. 4ff.; Eissfeldt, 1966b, pp. 417-425; Stolz, 1970). I want to advance the hypothesis that the designation of Yahweh as מֶלֶךְ ("king") first appeared in Shiloh, where he was first termed יֹשֵׁב הכרובים ("sitting [on] the cherubim"), and was then continued in the cultic tradition of Jerusalem.

In this context the designation of Yahweh as קָדֹשׁ ("holy") is of great significance. Yahweh is the holy one. In Psalm 99 Yahweh the king is three times glorified with the shout, קָדוֹשׁ הוּא ("holy is he!" Ps. 99:3, 5, 9). This corresponds to the trishagion in Isa. 6:3. Psalm 22:3 also proclaims that the one who is enthroned is holy. In any case, the designation קָדוֹשׁ ("holy") leads us once again into the world of the concept of God enthroned as king, where those around him are termed "the assembly of the holy ones" (Ps. 89:5-7; cf. Noth, 1957d). As עֶלְיוֹן ('*Elyon*) and מֶלֶךְ ("king"), Yahweh is "the holy one," "the holy one of Israel" (Ps. 71:22; 78:41; 89:18). On the problems from the point of view of history of religion see W. Schmidt (1966); Labuschagne (1966); Hanhart (1967); Wildberger (1972); and THAT, 1:802ff.

Köhler explained it well: "That God is holy means here that in His decision He is independent and free. Holy means superior, almighty. . ... God is free of considerations and conditions, absolutely free master of His own will, of His feelings, even of His wrath; mighty, not having any responsibility or requiring any justification, exalted over all, Lord absolutely of His resolutions and decisions and therefore to be feared absolutely. *Holy is at once exalted, supreme, and fearful*" (1957, p. 52). Karl Barth carried the discussion further. "The holy God of Scripture is certainly not 'the holy' of Rudolf Ott, that numinous element which, in its aspect as *tremendum*, is in itself and as such the divine. But the holy God of Scripture is the Holy One of Israel. That is the primary and fundamental thing to be said of him. But this does not mean first of all and decisively the God who is exalted over Israel, separated from it and confronting it, to be feared by it as the One to whom it has obligations. The holiness of God does mean this too, but only because it means primarily and decisively this—that God has adopted and chosen Israel as His child, has given it His promise, and has already conferred upon it His gracious help" (*CD* 2/1:360–361). In that the theological explanation of Yahweh's holiness as the one exalted, supreme, and to be feared points to a connection with the epithets עֶלְיוֹן ('*Elyon*) and מֶלֶךְ ("king"), the further explanation offered by Barth is reminiscent of the introduction above.

Once the designations of God as עֶלְיוֹן ('*Elyon*), מֶלֶךְ ("king"), and קָדוֹשׁ ("holy") are recognized as cultic traditions belonging to Jerusalem, then the questions pertaining to the history of religion can be stated more precisely. David established the sanctuary on Zion as the central sanctuary of Israel. At once two influences suggest themselves. (1) When the Ark of the Covenant and the priests attached to it came to Jerusalem they brought with them old Israelite traditions, but at the same time there also came sacral institutions and cultic traditions from the world of Canaanite and Syrian religion that had been incorporated into the tabernacle shrine at Shiloh and thus adopted by Israel. (2) The occupation of Jerusalem marked the annexation or adoption of the cultic features and the traditional theology of the old Jebusite sanctuary. In this way numerous concepts, terms, and concepts of Canaanite origin entered the cultic world of Israel.

In the light of these two streams of influence, the range of our investigation is to be broadened. Taking the terms עֶלְיוֹן ('*Elyon*), מֶלֶךְ ("king"), and קָדֹשׁ ("holy") as the starting point, we must investigate their relationship to the ancient world of which Israel was a part, as we have come to know it today. We need, however, a clear understanding of the possibilities and limitations of research in the history of religion. The "environment" of Israel, and especially of the cult in Jerusalem, is the culture of Canaan and Syria, which in turn was influenced by the culture and religion of the empires of Asia Minor, Mesopotamia, and Egypt. In any case we are to look for relationships to the immediate environment, Canaan and Syria, and the expressions of religion in the lives of these peoples. Such research must not overlook the fact that we cannot assume a unified religion for this area. Cultic practices and rites which, as is the case here, were oriented to the landscape of the immediate vicinity, to the specific features of climate, and to the world of nature and vegetation in each case, cannot be reduced to a common denominator, especially since the cultures of the great empires exerted their influence in a variety of ways. In addition, actual or incipient political structures that had influence on the cult are to be taken into account. Finally, historical developments and movements are factors that constantly warn us against ascribing too much importance to the rigid objects of parallel texts and available data.

At the same time, in any investigation into the history of religion in the Canaanite area considerable importance must attach to the Ugaritic texts. These texts provide us with the most extensive and clearest sources for the area we are studying, even though there are problems of decipherment and interpretation. The wealth of relationships illustrated by the Ugaritic texts is decisive. Today it is clearer than ever that certain points of view, terms, and basic concepts that can be found in the Ugaritic texts were the common possession of religions in the Canaanite and Syrian world. Consequently, insofar as it is possible to do so, the details of the data and evidence presented by the history of religion are to be examined and incorporated.

Genesis 14:18-20 led to the assumption that the god of Jebusite Jerusalem bore the name אל עליון (*'El 'Elyon*). In addition, the name *Melchizedek*, with the meaning "(My) king is (the God) Zedek," leads us to conjecture that the epithet מלך ("king"), even though it had already been used in Shiloh (see above) may have had great significance as a divine name in the pre-Israelite sanctuary of Jerusalem. There can be no doubt that as epithets עליון (*'elyon*) and מלך ("king") are equal concepts, analogous in meaning, and were used in the monarchical address to "God Most High." In the Ugaritic texts El appears as this highest God, and El is called *mlk* (W.H. Schmidt, 1966, pp. 23ff.). It is completely in accord with basic Ugaritic concepts when in the Psalter אל (*El*) and עליון (*'Elyon*) are used as synonyms. In addition, the corresponding designations and functions of the Ugaritic god Baal must be considered. In the mythological texts the title *mlk* is not used in apposition with Baal, but the texts do speak of a cyclic dramatization in the cult of the enthronement of Baal and of his death and resurrection (Schmidt, pp. 29ff.). Both the static traits of kingship exercised by the god Baal and the dynamic and dramatic traditions of Baal had their areas of influence in Canaan and Syria, and in Israel they influenced the divine titles of Yahweh. Two major points of view must be carefully considered in connection with divine kingship in Ugarit. The epithet *king* is first and foremost a designation of the relationship of the "highest god" in reference to the lesser gods. In Ugarit, monarchical theology displays two phases of this monarchicalism among the gods: a dramatic phase of enthronement, in which Baal is involved, and which was marked by a regular relationship to the annual rhythms and the cycle of the year, and a (static) hierarchical phase in which the chief position is given to the god El as the "highest god" who rules "for all time." In a continuing, unchangeable sense the position of honor as king of the gods is accorded only to El. The king of the Gods, however, had under him the pantheon of gods, "sons of gods," and "divine beings," which owe their existence to him as "father," usually in a genealogical sense. But whoever they may be they are subordinate to him as "king." The divine king sits enthroned in the "assembly of the gods" (Gese, 1969, pp. 100ff.). But the royal authority of the "highest god" extends not only to the world of the gods but to the entire earth. The עליון (*'Elyon*) is, as the Old Testament says, אדון כל־הארץ ("Lord of all the earth," Ps. 97:5). There must be a reason for this cosmic lordship. In Ugarit, El was called "creator of the creatures" (*bny bnwt*) or "creator of the earth" (*qn 'rṣ*) (Schmidt, pp. 58ff.). This content provides the explanation of how it can be said of the אל עליון (*'El 'Elyon*) in Jebusite Jerusalem that he is קנה שמים וארץ ("maker of heaven and earth," Gen. 14:19). Reference can also be made at this point to the ancient Babylonian myths in which Marduk, as the result of his cosmogonic deed of forming the world, becomes "king of the gods," "most honored among the great gods" (Pritchard, 1969). Consequently, not only is it necessary whenever the divine epithet of "king" occurs to think of the chief position in the pantheon as monarch, but the statements about the formation of the world and about cosmic lordship must also be kept in mind. One further element must be kept in mind. In the ancient Near East the earthly king usually also held the office of judge, and in the Ugaritic myths, judicial functions are ascribed to El and Baal (cf. Bauer, 1933, pp. 82f.; Eissfeldt, 1951, and 1966a, pp. 386-397). It is said of Baal:

mlkn.aliyn.b'l	Aliyan Baal is our king,
tptn.(w)in.d'lnh	our judge! (And no one is above him).

(See Schmidt, p. 36). This feature can also be traced in the Israelite cult, viz., Ps. 82:1-4; 96:13; 98:9.

In every attempt to establish relationships and dependencies in the area of Canaan and Syria, it must not be lost sight of for a moment that the basic features of a monarchical theology had long since been formulated in both Mesopotamia and Egypt, and that therefore phenomena such as those that have come to light in Ras Shamra cannot be viewed in isolation. Attention has been called to the elevation of Marduk to "king of the gods." In this connection it is interesting that the rise of a god to be "the highest god" reflects political and dynastic relationships of the specific city-state involved. When Babylon attained preeminence the city-god Marduk became king of the gods, took his place in the cosmic myth as the leader of the gods, and became creator and ruler of the world. In Egypt too there was worship of the "king of the gods" and his veneration in the cult (Sethe, 1929, p. 128; Kees, 1941, p. 468).

There are certain preliminary results that may be drawn on the basis of this overview in terms of the history of religion. (1) The idea of "monarchical monotheism," which is expressed in the designation of a god as "king" or as "highest god," and had widespread influence in the ancient Near East, was borrowed by Israel from the surrounding nations through the pre-Israelite cultic traditions of Shiloh and Jerusalem. (2) Cosmic universalism, which Old Testament scholars have long regarded as a late product of the development of the history of religion in the Old Testament, took shape early among Israel's neighbors. It entered the cult in Jerusalem in the appellations "Highest god" and "king."

Anyone who traces the course by which concepts in the history of religion are borrowed immediately becomes aware of the way in which Israel guarded against and rejected unacceptable elements in the thought of her neighbors. Such an investigator must seek to determine what transformations took place in the process of borrowing. A few general statements can summarize the specifics that can be established in the interpretation of the Psalms. (1) In Israel the borrowing of "monarchical monotheism" and its theology took place in such a manner that all the powers and deities were totally stripped of their power. The בני אלים ("sons of gods") were transformed into spirits in the service of Yahweh the King (Ps. 103:19-22), or their reality was totally denied (Ps. 96:5). The effect of the First Commandment is unmistakable (W.H. Schmidt, 1970). (2) Since the kingdom of Yahweh has passed far beyond mythological hierarchy into the phase in which the powers are stripped of their potency, it should be obvious that all features of the enthronement phase have long since been left behind. (This will be discussed more in detail in chap. 3, §C in the evaluation of the so-called enthronement festival of Yahweh. The Psalms stress again and again that Yahweh's kingdom is invincible and eternal (Ps. 10:16; 29:10; 74:12; 93:2). This is not a mere "El aspect" of Yahweh's kingship that is to be supplemented by a "Baal aspect," but it is the basic statement that is determinative for everything else. (3) In addition to the cosmic dimension, the political and historical aspect plays a strikingly significant role. Yahweh is king over the nations (Ps. 47:8; 99:2). It cannot be determined whether this represents a reworking of the mythical concepts of a battle among the gods in terms of a battle with the nations. In any case, however, the fact of the appearance of political and historical relationships is too significant to be ignored, for even the function of "king" Yahweh as judge extends to the nations (Ps. 96:10, 13; 98:9).

It has already been pointed out that the term קדש ("holy") belongs to the context of the מלך־עליון ("king"—'*Elyon*) tradition, and it is further to be noted that the designation "the Holy One" is an attribute of the deity El in Ugarit (W.H. Schmidt, 1966, pp. 28f.). The *bn qds* (as the "holy ones of the Most High") stand at the side of El (as the one who is *qds*, "holy"), Ps. 89:5-7. Consequently, it will no longer be possible to explain "holy" or "holiness" as a genuine Old Testament predicate of Yahweh (cf. W.H. Schmidt, 1962, pp. 62-66). Israel shared the declarations concerning holiness in common with its Canaanite-Syrian neighbors. The case is similar with the concept כבוד ("glory," cf. Ps. 29:9).

Yahweh is the Lord of Israel. The term בעל (*baal*) designates the Lord as the owner, and אדון (*adon*) designates him as the master. אדון (*adon*) is the one who is stronger, more powerful (Ps. 12:4); he is the master (Ps. 123:2), the ruler (Ps. 105:21, where אדון [*adon*] is synonymous with מלך ["king"]). The observations are based on the use of the term אדון where it does not refer to Yahweh. In reference to Yahweh the basic fact is that "God is the ruling Lord: that is the one fundamental statement in the theology of the Old Testament" (Köhler, 1957, p. 30). As אדון (*adon*) the God of Israel is the Lord and master in unlimited sovereignty and freedom. Therefore he is called אדני האדנים, "Lord of lords" (Ps. 136:3). He rules over the entire earth (Ps. 114:7), over the whole world (Ps. 97:5) as the אדון כל־הארץ ("Lord of all the earth"). Israel calls him "our Lord" אדנינו cf. Ps. 8:1, 9; 135:5; 147:5). The Lord of Israel is the creator; his name is majestic in all the earth (Ps. 8:1, 9). Israel's אדון ("Lord") is superior to all the gods (Ps. 135:5). He is great and full of power; his wisdom is beyond measure (Ps. 147:5). Accordingly the Psalms proclaim and laud the lordship of Yahweh. As the Lord of Israel Yahweh is also the Lord of the peoples and of all the world. For the theology of the Psalms this is a basic premise which colors the borrowed epithets עליון (*'Elyon*) and מלך (''king''), and includes above all the designation of Yahweh as judge. Concerning Yahweh as שפט (''judge'') we should note particularly the statements and declarations that God is the Judge of the nations (Ps. 7:8; 9:8, 19; 58:11; 82:8; 94:2; 96:10, 13; 98:9).

In contrast to the Ugaritic texts in which El is often called ''Father,'' the designation of Yahweh as אב (''Father'') can be found in only a few passages in the Psalms. In Ps. 103:13 there is the comparison, ''As a father pities his children. . . .'' And in Ps. 68:5 he is called ''Father of the fatherless,'' but this is not to be considered as a genuine predication, because it refers to the intervention of Israel's God on behalf of orphans. Only Ps. 89:26 is relevant for our understanding of the concept, where the king is reminded that he is privileged to address Yahweh with the words, ''Thou art my Father.'' The focus here is clearly on the father-son relationship that exists between Yahweh and his chosen king (2 Sam. 7:14; compare *Comm.* on Ps. 2:7 and the Intro. to *Comm.*, vol. 1 §9, 3.)

Israel acknowledges, praises, and proclaims the fact that Yahweh's lordship has shown itself as liberating, saving, and helping power. Yahweh is called אלהי ישענו (''God of our salvation,'' Ps. 65:5; 79:9; 85:4) or אלהי ישעי (''God of my salvation,'' Ps. 18:46; 24:5; 27:9). He himself and his name are symbols of liberation and deliverance, the prototype of which is the choosing of Israel and Israel's liberation out of bondage in Egypt (Ps. 78:12, 43, 51; 135:8, 9; 136:10; 80:8; 81:5, 10; 114:1). As the God who gives help, Yahweh is the one who shelters and protects. In the prayer song Ps. 18:1-2 the names given Yahweh are heaped one on another. He is חזקי (''my strength''), סלעי (''my rock''), מצודתי (''my refuge''), מפלטי (''my savior''), אלי (''my God''), צורי (''my Rock''), מגני (''my shield''), קרן־ישעי (''horn of my salvation''), משגבי (''my fortress'').

Yahweh is called ''my rock'' (Ps. 18:2; 28:1; 31:2, 3; 42:9; 62:2, 6, 7). This is not to be thought of as a metaphorical designation; rather, we are to remember that the temple sanctuary in Jerusalem was built on the ''holy rock'' (cf. Schmidt, 1933; Kraus, 1959). In connection with the metaphors ''refuge'' and ''fortress'' it should be noted that they bear a special relationship to the role of Jerusalem as the place where God functioned as the righteous judge. Those who were accused or persecuted fled to Yahweh for protection and appealed to his divine judgment (cf. Beyerlin, 1970). Reference may also be made to the work of Eichhorn (1972), even though his assumption that there was a ''prayer of the mediator'' is not convincing.

C. Yahweh's Revelation and Hiddenness

Our starting point is the fact that the Old Testament does not contain a specific expression for ''revelation'' (Rendtorff, 1968). We should not, however, expect to find in the Hebrew language a noun that would correspond to this English word. In the Psalms there is a variety of ways in which Yahweh's revelation is spoken of, and the events indicated by the concept are depicted variously. It is, however, appropriate to begin with the declaration that in the event which is called ''revelation,'' the God of Israel communicates something about himself, makes himself known, declares himself. Even though a certain skepticism has been expressed toward the concept of ''the self-presentation of God'' (Rendtorff, 1968) it cannot be denied that the intention of Yahweh's presenting himself is expressed in a verbal form. Above all, the already-discussed שֵׁם ("name") theology of the Psalms (chap. 1, §A) makes it clear that Yahweh has presented himself and made himself known in and by his name. "In Judah God is known, his name is great in Israel" (Ps. 76:1). Not for a moment is there any doubt that this event of self-disclosure is initiated and carried out solely through a free act of the divine subject. The recipient and the place to which he comes and communicates himself are of his own choosing. The Old Testament understands revelation as something that happens by the sovereign choice of Israel's God (Ps. 33:12; 65:4; 100:3; 132:13). God chooses to reveal himself. This shows that it is a real revelation, because it takes place in divine freedom and does not represent a possibility open to human choice. Israel is both the one addressed and the place that is chosen, and thus the place of Yahweh's revelation. In this way—and we must give this factor serious consideration—God's coming has become history, that is, an event that forms the basis of history. A basic relationship is established: Yahweh makes himself known to his chosen people. This people, his land, his history, the sanctuary in Jerusalem (Ps. 132:13) are the addressee, are the place of his choosing. Here it is that "our God comes, he does not keep silence" (Ps. 50:3). The event designated by the verb בוא ("come") is a harbinger of the cult celebrated in Jerusalem. Yahweh's revelation and presence are not at our disposal; they cannot be manipulated. They are not to be staged dramatically, reproduced through "creative drama" (Mowinckel, 1953, p. 78). Yahweh is the one who comes. Whether or to what degree he is the one who is present will be investigated later. In any case the goal of Yahweh's coming is not "a sanctuary" but Israel, the sanctuary Israel/Judah.

God comes to his people, and in the encounter they hear him and are called to respond (von Rad, 1962, pp. 355f.; Gross, 1967, pp. 248-256). Yahweh's revelation becomes the basis of communication, and this revelation, even though exclusively concerned with Israel, is still directed toward the world, the nations. Yahweh comes to judge the earth and to rule over the peoples (Ps. 98:9). Although the appellations of God (above, chap. 1, §B) already disclosed a "universalistic" tendency, it was especially under the influence of the message of the prophets, and, above all, that of Deutero-Isaiah, that the worldwide dimensions of the revelation of Israel's God became apparent. The God of Israel is the Lord of the peoples. It is noteworthy that the verb גלה ("reveal," *niph.*), which designates the act of self-revelation, occurs only a single time in the Psalter, in Ps. 98:2. That verse speaks of the revelation of Yahweh's righteousness before the eyes of all the peoples, and shows the influence of the message of Deutero-Isaiah.

Linguistic usage in theology and in the church has so narrowly defined the concept of "revelation" that it is difficult to establish the outlines of the Old Testament statements. The starting point, however, is the fact that it involves both the name *Yahweh* in a special manifestation of the God of Israel under distinctive conditions and God's intention freely to make himself known; not for a moment can we draw abstract conclusions from these basic data, which are dominant in the Psalter as elsewhere. This clearly expresses the idea that "For the knowledge of God as Yahweh a general ontology is not a sufficient basis. This knowledge demands the historical presupposition of the proclaimed name of God" (Knierim, 1971, pp. 223f.). The communication of the name and thus Yahweh's self-disclosure in Israel are not expressed in the Psalter in any other way than as the miracle of great and mysterious חסד ("steadfast love") and אמונה ("faithfulness"). Yahweh has said "I" and he continues to say "I" (Ps. 81:10). Thereby it became possible and remains possible to address him as "Thou." Yahweh is person. His name and his word (see below) are expression and demonstration of his personhood. The God of Israel is not some personified natural numen, but in the reality of his person he is the Lord, the king, the creator, and the judge of all being. The essential thing is "not that God is person, but the particular person he is" (Barth, *CD*, 2/1, p. 296). The being of this God is the being of the one who has always existed, who is without beginning (Ps. 90:1-2) and will exist for eternity (Ps. 93:2; 145:13).

The communication of Yahweh's name and word are the means through which the God of Israel makes himself known. "The basic connection between the revelation of the name and the revelation of the word is first of all the fact that in form the revelation of the name is a part of the revelation of the word. "The name is a word" (Grether, 1934, p. 159). Indeed, the שֵׁם ("name") could be termed the original word of Yahweh's self-communication. Grether characterizes the difference between שֵׁם ("name") and דבר ("word"): "The revelation of the name says who it is, that comes to humans in the revelation. The revelation in word says what the revealer shares with humans in the revelation" (p. 159). It is significant for the Psalms that the noun form "דבר ['word'] of Yahweh" (ignoring for the time being the synonymous usage of תורה [*torah*]) is found primarily in the historical Psalms and in retrospective views of history. Yahweh has "commanded" his word (דבר צוה ["word he commanded"], Ps. 105:8). His words were believed (האמין, Ps. 106:12, 24). He "remembered" the promise he made to Abraham (Ps. 105:42). From the pillar of the cloud the God of Israel spoke to Moses, Aaron, and Samuel (Ps. 99:7, verbal form). Israel praises Yahweh, because he has exalted his name and his word above the heavens (Ps. 138:2). Yahweh has spoken to Israel. This event formed the basis of history and accompanied history. Even more can be said. Through his creative word he called heaven and earth into existence (Ps. 33:9; 147:18). When he speaks, it happens; when he commands, then it is there (Ps. 33:9).

The basic experience of the Psalms is that Yahweh speaks in the sanctuary (Ps. 60:6; 108:7). Those who transmit his word (cultic prophets? priests?) seek to hear what he says (Ps. 85:8). When his word is heard, then the recipient of the message can proclaim, "I heard a voice I had not known" (Ps. 81:5). He has encountered the *verbum alienum*. In his prayer the sufferer, out of the depths of his troubles, waits for the דבר ("word," Ps. 130:5). He longs for Yahweh to speak to him and say, "I am your deliverance!" (Ps. 35:3). Yahweh's promise of protection is presented in Ps. 62:11. Those who are sick wait for the God of Israel to send his word and by it to heal them (Ps. 107:20). The king receives a divine oracle in the cult (Ps. 110:1). No one can escape when Yahweh speaks. Rebels and the wicked hear him speak in his wrath (Ps. 2:5; 50:16). Yahweh speaks and summons the earth (Ps. 50:1).

In the light of this survey the question arises of the concrete manner in which Yahweh spoke in the sanctuary. We may assume a threefold form in which his message was communicated. (1) It is clear that it was communicated by a (cultic) prophet in Ps. 81:5; 110:1; and 50:1; these texts indicate a prophetic message. (2) Begrich (1934, pp. 81-92) did research on the priestly salvation oracle. On that basis we may assume that when in a prayer song an individual gave voice to his lament and petition, the response was delivered with divine authority, usually with the characteristic introduction, "Fear not. . . ." (3) Within the scope of the institution of divine judgment (cf. Intro., Comm., §6, 2B) we find not only the promise of protection (Ps. 62:11) but also and especially Yahweh's pronouncement of his verdict, which concludes the legal dispute that has been brought before God at the holy site (Beyerlin, 1970).

God's revelation in word is found primarily in the Torah. It is worthy of the praise of all who pray (especially Psalm 19B and Psalm 119). For the singers of these Torah psalms the תורה (torah) is the "highest good," more valuable than gold and silver (Ps. 119:72). It is the epitome of what is reliable and abiding (Ps. 119:142). Wondrous things proceed from it (Ps. 119:18). In this connection three features should be noted. (1) in Psalm 119 the Torah is no fixed, static entity, but a power that is creative and life-giving. (2) Neither is the Torah an impersonal, absolute, given entity, but a דבר ("word") that goes out from Yahweh's majestic person, an אמרה ("utterance") that is addressed to humans. (3) All the healing, saving, creative powers of the Torah are contained in the fact that it is דבר פיך, instruction from the mouth of Yahweh, and that means spoken, purposive word (viva vox). A distinction between "law and gospel" in the manner of Luther's theology does not do justice to the events and realities to which the Torah psalms bear witness (cf. Comm., excursus to Psalm 119).

The question arises of what we are really to see as involved in the תורה (torah) that is praised in these above-mentioned Psalms. (1) The explanation has been repeatedly given that in the Torah psalms תורה (torah) is the "Sacred Scripture," the canon as it came to be in later times. Gunkel sees the situation in the following manner. "In this history of religion a phenomenon frequently observed is that a religion, after it has risen to powerful heights through noble prophets, forms a canon out of the writings of its great past and then honors it as the epitome of divine revelation. In such times an essential part of piety consists in inner familiarity with the letter of holy scripture." Is the Torah in this sense the basis of a religion of the letter? Is it the epitome of the γράμμα ("letter")? Now it cannot be denied that, for example in Psalm 1, the one offering the prayer has in mind a scroll in which he reads and meditates, but it is questionable whether this refers to the completed canon. It is certain, however, that we must not understand Psalm 1 as the expression of a religion of the letter. The scroll is an abiding power; it is like a stream of water that bestows life (Ps. 1:3). The singer is not confronted by a γράμμα ("letter") that kills, but by a power that brings life. (2) Under no circumstances should we translate תורה (torah) as "law," or introduce a corresponding understanding in legalistic terms. Buber stressed that תורה (torah) is instruction (cf. also Östborn, 1945).

While "law" is connected with the impression of something fixed, rigid, and static, instruction arouses the impression of something living, dynamic, in which directions, suggestions, commands, orders, and advice are imparted. The original meaning of תורה (torah) as guidance formulated and then orally transmitted by a priest remained preserved even where it refers to commands fixed in writing. In the word תורה (torah) the transition from oral transmission to a message fixed in writing is in flux, especially since it is to be assumed that even the commands and ordinances found in the written scroll were the object and medium of oral instruction. The Israelite, insofar as he was not a priest or one acquainted with the promulgated writings and scriptures, was dependent on having the scroll read aloud to him, and thus he received oral instruction (see Deut. 31:11). We may therefore assume that in the precincts of the sanctuary groups gathered around a priest for the purpose of hearing the Torah read and taught. The Torah psalms are also to be assigned to this setting.

Parallels to such instruction carried out in groups gathered at a sanctuary are common in the history of religions down to the present day, as for example in the study of the Koran in Islam. We must be careful, however, not to overlook the fact that in Israel the Torah instruction was not characterized by a strict and stern demand for obedience, but that the people praised it as a demonstration of the grace of Israel's God, who honored his people by imparting to them his commands that bring life and wholeness.

All these Torah traditions culminate in the Jewish celebration of *Simchat Torah*, which includes the words of a medieval hymn:

> This Feast of the Law all your gladness display.
>   Today all your homages render.
> What profit can lead one so pleasant way,
>   What jewels can vie with its splendor?
> Then exult in the Law on its festival day,
>   The Law is our Light and Defender.

(Translated by Israel Zangwill in Philip Goodman, *The Sukkot and Simhat Torah Anthology* [Philadelphia: Jewish Publication Society, 1973], p. 88.)

Yahweh also revealed himself in the history of his acts. As in the past, he still makes himself known in his "work" (פעל), in his "deeds" (מעשׂה), in his "wonders" (פלא). The historical psalms look back to the past. Ps. 106:2, 13, 22 speaks especially of Yahweh's mighty deeds for his people. The fathers saw his work (Ps. 95:9), but Israel "forgot" the wonderful deeds that had been done in their midst. The Israelites "did not believe" his wonders (Ps. 78:32). Yahweh's "works," "deeds," and "wonders" are mentioned in the Psalms not merely in historical retrospect. Yahweh "has caused his wonderful works to be remembered" (Ps. 111:4). In worship the great deeds of Israel's God are presented to the assembled cultic community as present reality. The people break out in joy and gladness over Yahweh's activities (Ps. 92:4, 5; 107:22). The fact that Yahweh has revealed himself in the history of his deeds, and is alone the one who does wonders, is the subject of neverending praise (Ps. 72:11). For Yahweh's works and wonders are not only presented, they are present. Yahweh has overcome the foes of the individual (Ps. 64:10). In the Psalms we find a remarkable correspondence between the wonders that are portrayed in the reenactment and the "works of Yahweh" for which the worshipers hope or which they experience. In the time of trouble they sing, "I will call to mind the deeds of the Lord; yes I will remember thy wonders of old. I will meditate on all thy work, and muse on thy mighty deeds" (Ps. 77:11-12).

It is probable that all the passages cited belong to a "specific cultic tradition and phraseology" (von Rad, 1973a). The people remember, or appeal to, or praise Yahweh's works and wonders through which he has made himself known to his people. It is in the history of his deeds that Yahweh has communicated and still communicates. We should not speak of "revelation in history," but speak concretely and precisely of revelation in the history of the acts of the God of Israel. Yahweh's works and wonders did not remain silent. They have spoken and do speak. They are not "plain facts" that are silently open to random observation. The quarrel over whether it is word or work that has the priority in the Old Testament has little meaning. It is only because Yahweh has "caused his wonderful works to be remembered" (Ps. 111:4) that these works are known.

In the Psalms, often in the same breath with the praise of Yahweh's acts in the history of his people, the works and wonders of Israel's God in the creation are praised. In Ps. 66:5-7 the "works" of Yahweh are his works of creation. The heavens are the works of his hands (Ps. 8:3; 19:1; 102:25). All the creatures were formed by his creative acts (Ps. 8:6). He made the sea (Ps. 95:5) and the heavens (Ps. 33:6) by his word. The distinctive term which in the Old Testament designates only Yahweh's acts of creation, the verb ברא ("create"), is found in Ps. 89:12, 47; 104:30; 148:5). In all this there are two traditions, two types of statements about creation, that are to be distinguished. Wherever Yahweh's creative acts or work are spoken, especially with the verb ברא ("create"), the created universe, heaven and earth, lies before God as his counterpart, and humans find themselves in the "theatrum gloriae Dei" ("theater of the glory of God," Calvin). They are to render laud, thanks, and praise. It must be kept in mind ". . .that Israel knew neither our concept of 'nature' nor the Greek one of a 'cosmos.' For her the world was not a stable and harmoniously ordered organism, including equally every datum, organic and inorganic alike, and so much to be regarded as a whole that the question of its ultimate determining principle ($\dot{\alpha}\rho\chi\dot{\eta}$) was legitimate" (von Rad, 1962, p. 426). For Israel the world was much more event than being. "Creation" in a static, substantive sense is foreign to the Hebrew language. "Creation" means not an object but an act. Still Yahweh's relationship to all that was created is determined by the fact that God as creator has established a reality which is distinguished from himself, that he is active in it (Psalm 104) and preserves it. God is not the creation, he is the creator. His hands formed everything. How can mankind, how can Israel know this? In the type of statements about creation to which we turn first, the name of Yahweh (Ps. 8:1) is the key to the secret of creation. It is Yahweh who made heaven and earth and whose name is majestic in all the world. Psalm 89:5-12 tells of Israel's conflict with the forces of creation that were honored in the surrounding nations. It is Yahweh, the one who revealed himself and made himself known through his name—he and no other god—who has overcome the primeval chaos and created the heavens and the earth. The statement that Yahweh created the world is not something obvious, but it is a confession of faith, based on the self-communication of Yahweh's name, and it becomes at once involved in the polemical arguments and debates against the religious claims of Israel's neighbors.

Yahweh created the world, heaven and earth, by his word (Ps. 33:6, 9). There are formal correspondences to Egyptian cosmogonies (cf. *Comm.* on Psalm 33). Nonetheless, Yahweh's word is not just any cosmogonic magical power. This word has shown itself as reliable in the acts which have been performed in Israel's history (Ps. 33:4) and called forth "righteousness" and "justice" (Ps. 33:5). So the earth is full of the חסד יהוה ("steadfast love of Yahweh," Ps. 33:5). The word, which in Israel displayed its power to establish and control history, is acknowledged as the only continuity between Yahweh and the world, and also as the only medium by which the creation can be known. In Israel the דבר־יהוה ("word of Yahweh") was experienced and believed in as the epitome of all creative power. And the same word that created the world is also the word that enables us to recognize that the world is the result of creation. All this makes it clear that "It is not the creator's own nature that he imparted to that which is living and life-giving; the living and creative is not the divine, but it is and remains creaturely, created, the work that is separated from the creator, and over which he has free reign'' (Bonhoeffer, 1959, p. 37). At this point a deep, unbridgeable chasm separates Israel's belief about creation from all cosmogonic myths and all deities who are manifested in nature. As the creation of God the world is truly worldly, not divine. It is true of the Psalms that ''the more consistently the world is seen as creation, the more consistently it is possible to speak of its worldliness'' (von Rad, 1973b, p. 151).

All these concepts and statements about Yahweh's creative work and the created world are to be clearly distinguished from another way of understanding creation. The created world, especially the heavenly sphere, imparts a message, a testimony to God, the creator (Ps. 19:1; 145:10). We thus find the concept that what Yahweh has created is not silent, but has a message which reaches out to all lands. The heavens ''are telling,'' the firmament ''proclaims'' (Ps. 19:1). ''All thy works shall give thanks to thee, O Lord'' (Ps. 145:10). Yahweh's righteousness is proclaimed by the heavens (Ps. 97:6). Elements of the created world are thus empowered to speak out and make the secret of creation known. The works of creation are thus direct mediators of revelation, that is, they do not speak of themselves or of the divine in the world, but they ''are telling the glory of God'' (Ps. 19:1). By examining the Old Testament psalms which belong to this group of themes shared by the hymns of the religions of Israel's neighbors, we can establish that the concept of a testimony which the creation brings to the creator and his majesty is found only in Israel (cf. von Rad, 1972, p. 175). But can we join von Rad in speaking of a ''primeval revelation''? Certainly it is not possible to do so in the sense of this concept as interpreted by Althaus (1966, pp. 37ff.). Karl Barth's explanation comes closer. '' 'The heavens declare the glory of God; the firmament showeth his handywork' (Ps. 19:1). To be sure, 'There is no speech,' nor 'language,' i.e., they have no power to do it of themselves. But they acquire this power. The final and trustworthy thing which they cannot say of themselves concerning their being and existence, they now say as they reflect the eternal light of God, as they answer His word and as they correspond to His truth. In other words, they speak of the meaning and determination of the creaturely world for what God is and does for man'' (Barth, *CD* 4/3: 164). This view is also supported by the New Testament. First Corinthians 1:21 is to be interpreted as saying ''that Paul sees the world as God's creation (in its origin and still today) mirroring the wisdom of God. God's creative wisdom speaks to humans, because the world as a work points to God, reveals God'' (Eichholz, 1972, p. 159). Those Psalms which speak of the self-declaration made by Yahweh's creation belong to the context in which חכמה (''wisdom'') was transmitted (cf. von Rad, 1972, pp. 144f.).

An additional observation must be made in reference to Psalm 19. Obviously this psalm, when viewed as a unit, was designed to express the view that the testimony which the created world gives about itself cannot be an adequate, sufficient word of Yahweh, since this statement is without speech or words (Ps. 19:3), and therefore cannot correspond to the event of the דבר יהוה (''word of Yahweh''). Therefore the manifest, verbal message of the תורה (*torah*) is specifically contrasted to the indirect and mysterious witness given by creation (Psalm 19B). This contrast by no means involves the idea that Old Testament salvation history supplements a general ''primeval revelation,'' as is made clear by the tone of the entire Psalm (see the *Comm.* on Psalm 19). Thus we should speak with caution and with reservations when referring to a revelation of God in the creation. What the created world says of itself is not a revelation of Yahweh, but is a testimony that points to the secret of creation, which is contained only in the name and word of the God of Israel (cf. Kraus, 1978).

In connection with the theme of revelation, the theophanies take on special significance. Jorg Jeremias has investigated the category of "theophany psalms" (1977). The portrayal of a theophany plays a particular role in the following texts: Psalms 18; 29; 50; 68; 77; 97; 144. It is beyond question that the concepts of Yahweh's appearing in storms, with thunder and lightning, shining splendor, and an atmosphere of fear were not only influenced by Israel's ancient neighbors, but were to a considerable degree directly borrowed from them (Jeremias, 1977, pp. 73ff.). Research into the texts from Ras Shamra has made a particular contribution to our knowledge of the history of religion. There are unmistakable parallels: Yahweh (like Baal) rides on the clouds (Ps. 18:9-11; 68:4, 33); his voice is heard in the thunder (Ps. 18:13), he scatters bolts of lightning (Ps. 18:14); his קוֹל ("voice") makes the earth tremble (Ps. 29:6; 46:6); and the noise of his chariot shakes the land (Ps. 77:18). It is difficult to find in the theophany psalms any connections to the theophany at Sinai (except for Ps. 68:8, 18). Nor are we justified in regarding the cultic festivals in Jerusalem as the Sitz-im-Leben of the portrayals of theophanies (*pace* A. Weiser) or as the place where an appearance of God was presented in a cultic drama (*pace* S. Mowinckel). The intention of the theophany psalms is too clear to be mistaken: In the language and the conceptualizations of Israel's neighbors they bear testimony to Yahweh's appearing to his people. Yahweh comes to his people, he appears to his own. This distinctive testimony to a relevatory event, unique in the language of the Psalms, occupies a central position. A precise explanation is essential here. The theophany psalms are a verbal witness, the content of which has the nature of a prophetic vision, of divination. The activity and the reality of the God who comes to his people are announced and described, but they are not left to the world of "theory," as was characteristic of ancient Greek religion (cf. Kerenyi, 1940). The elements of vision and divination of the theophany psalms find their expression in the verbal testimony to the reality of the God who appears to his people.

Pannenberg's thesis that "the self-revelation of God in the biblical witnesses is not of a direct type in the sense of a theophany, but is indirect and brought about by means of the historical acts of God" sets up a false dichotomy, in that it seeks to overcome the exclusive claims of a verbal testimony by establishing a contrast between "history" and "theophany." Pannenberg's view leads him to a highly problematical major thesis: "In distinction from special manifestations of the deity, the historical revelation is open to anyone who has eyes to see. It has universal character" (1968, pp. 125, 135). Revelation in history, which has in this manner become nonverbal, loses thereby its intense character as communication, as it is expressed in the portrayals of theophanies. Revelation becomes fully integrated into the "Klotzmaterie" ("raw material"; E. Bloch) of history and its supposed evidence.

The Psalms testify to the presence of Yahweh in the sanctuary and in the assemblies of God's people. In the cultic practices of the Old Testament, as we see them in the Psalms, there is no image of the deity. Anything that is visible is, by definition, a creaturely power, a cosmic element. "All worshipers of images are put to shame" (Ps. 97:7), and this applied above all to Israel, which made a molten image at Horeb and worshiped it (Ps. 106:19-20). To be sure, Ps. 17:15 speaks of the תמונה of Yahweh, that is, of his "form" or "appearance," but the synonym in the parallel line shows that this means the פנים, the "face" of Yahweh, which is turned toward the worshiper. For the language of the Psalms this is the characteristic expression for the secret of Yahweh's presence in Israel's worship. A survey of the material will indicate the significance of the statements about the "face of Yahweh." Israel is urged and exhorted to seek God's פנים ("face") continually (Ps. 24:6; 27:8; 105:4), to come before his face with thanksgiving (Ps. 95:2), and to behold his face (Ps. 11:7; 42:2). Help is to be expected from the face of Yahweh (Ps. 42:5; 44:4). His face "shines" (Ps. 31:16; 67:1; 80:3, 7, 19; 119:135). When Yahweh lifts up the "light of his countenance" over his own (Ps. 4:6), then gladness and joy reign (Ps. 21:6).

To be sure, in the religious world of Israel's neighbors, to speak of the "face" of a deity originally meant the face of the image of the god. "To seek the face of a deity" would then mean to go on a pilgrimage to the cultic place in order to look on the face of the sacred image. In Israel all these concrete, material aspects were eliminated. Whenever the "face of Yahweh" is spoken of, the reference is to the reality of his (invisible) presence in the sanctuary, in the assembly of the people of God. Those who "seek" this face are endeavoring to go to the sanctuary and participate in Israel's cultic assemblies, in order to "see" Yahweh, that is, to experience his presence, his help, and his grace. "The face of God is the revelation of the grace of God" (Köhler, 1957, p. 124). Most probably it was especially in connection with the processional ceremony involving the ark and the throne of cherubim that Yahweh's coming to his people and appearing to them was experienced, and those participating in the worship encountered the "face of Yahweh," the "face" that was then present in the *debir*. Adoration in the presence of king Yahweh (cf. chap. 3, §C below) was directed toward the face of God, the brilliant light of his glory (כבוד, "glory"). In the Psalms, כבוד is also an expression which refers to the revelation of the presence of Israel's God (see especially Ps. 26:8; but also Ps. 24:7-10; 29:3, 9; etc.).

But God can also hide his face (Ps. 10:11). This rouses fear and terror (Ps. 30:7). Many individual prayer songs speak of the hiddenness of Yahweh. They ask how long his face will remain hidden (Ps. 13:1; 88:14), they plead, "Hide not thy face from me" (Ps. 27:9; 69:17; 102:2; 143:7). Nevertheless, the hiddenness of God of which the Psalms speak is not to be understood in the sense of primeval fate, nor as a reference to an alien God, a "Deus absconditus." The Psalms speak of the hiddenness of Yahweh only in relation to the certainty of his revelation and his presence. It is only the God who reveals himself and is present with his people who can hide himself. Hiddenness is an aspect of his revelation. This is made especially clear in Ps. 22:3-5. That God "is silent" can be said only there where he has spoken and will speak again (Ps. 50:3). Therefore the certainty reigns that "he has not hid his face from him, but has heard, when he cried to him" (Ps. 22:24). Above all the Psalms make known the fact that Yahweh the God of Israel is not accessible in a permanent state of having revealed himself and being present, but that his self-disclosure is the result of his free and sovereign self-determination, and thus of his coming to his people. His presence is promise and assurance to the poor and helpless (Ps. 34:18; 145:18), but it is not constantly accessible through the cult.

"With that we come closer to what theologians call the hiddenness of God. They do not mean by that simply the abundantly familiar fact that God is amply hidden from natural man, the truism of human blindness with respect to God, but rather something much more exciting; namely, the fact that God, precisely where he reveals himself, where he personally encounters a man, conceals himself from the man in that very act. In his self-revelation God judges and destroys all our ideas about God, all the principal images and criteria of value that we accept about him. We can, on our own, imagine only idols, of course. Thus for Christian faith the cross of Christ is the place of God's most profound concealment, i.e., his impotence and shame, and at the same time the place of the revelation of his most exalted majesty. If there is any truth in that, then every revelation of the living God carries with it the temptation that follows as a shadow follows light. The knowledge of God's hiddenness does not, therefore, stand at the end of all thought like a great wall, but rather at the beginning of all knowledge of God'' (von Rad, 1980, p. 88).

''The Psalmists are aware of God's real absence. . .not although, but precisely because, they are in a position to confess and glorify His presence. On the contrary, all the denials of His presence, all the assertions of which we are masters respecting the hiddenness of God and our own incapacity to know Him without the Gospel, are only exercises. . .of no consequence compared to the limit really drawn between God and man. By their means we can but deceive ourselves as to the real position of things between Him and us'' (Barth, *CD* 1/2: 29; cf. also Michalson, 1957, p. 259). In any case we must understand the hiddenness of God as the content of a statement of faith. ''The assertion of God's hiddenness. . .tells us that God does not belong to the objects which we can always subjugate to the process of our viewing, conceiving and expressing and therefore our oversight and control'' (Barth, *CD* 2/1: 187).

In the background in all theological explanations of what the Psalms say about God and the revelation of God there is the question of the relation between the Bible and the history of religion. Many threads connect the prayers, songs of praise, and Psalms of the Old Testament with the religious statements about life found among the nations surrounding the people of God. However, any comparison of the testimonies expressed in the Old Testament with those in the religions prior to or contemporary with ancient Israel can no longer rest simply on details, that is, with the identification of analogous concepts, similar expressions, and parallel perceptions. Whole complexes must be kept in mind (cf. Westermann, 1964, pp. 189-218, esp. p. 192; Hempel, 1956, pp. 259-280. In this respect, the perspective which in the Old Testament, and especially the Psalter proclaims and waits for Yahweh as the God who comes to his people, is beyond doubt quite decisive. In the light of this theme which colors even the nuances, and in light of the reality to which this theme points, it may be said that ''the relationship of faith in Yahweh to the other religions cannot be expressed in purely conceptual or purely historical terms. It can be established only on the basis of the totality or the basic structure of faith in Yahweh or of that which takes place between Yahweh and his people'' (Westermann, 1964, p. 217). It must also be kept in mind that categories of development or explication in reference to the incorporation into Israel's faith of elements from foreign religions is problematical, if for no other reason than that every borrowing from the surrounding nations involves a basic intention that is antagonistic and polemical as well as confessional, and in detail is quite different in character. That which happened in those repeated encounters clearly takes precedence over the phenomenon of adaptation and development of the ''religion of Yahweh'' as demonstrable in the perspective of the history of tradition. For each confrontation reflects a basic debate with the religions and gods of the nations, or, to put it differently, the various and manifold confrontations determined the basic antagonistic and polemical character of the Old Testament and thus also of the Psalms. It can be affirmed that ''in His revelation God has actually entered a sphere in which His own reality and possibility are encompassed by a sea of more or less adequate, but at any rate fundamentally unmistakable, parallels and analogies in human realities and possibilities. The revelation of God is actually the presence of God and therefore the hiddenness of God in the world of human religion. By God's revealing of Himself the divine particular is hidden in a human universal, the divine content in a human form, and therefore that which is divinely unique in something which is humanly only singular'' (Barth, *CD* 1/2: 282). But what is the "distinctively divine," the "divine content," the "uniquely divine" in the Psalms? No theology will be able to find the formula in which this question could be answered in a comprehensive, easily understood manner. The reason is that even that to which there is no analogy, that which is unique, would be at once exposed to the "competition." Only by constant listening and paying attention to the nuances in the Old Testament texts can we hear the word that testifies to the God of Israel. A theology of the Psalms can only hint at this acute exegetical process, or perhaps, bring together observations and insights derived from the exegetical process, place them in relation to each other, reflect on them, and interpret them.

D. The Perfections of Yahweh

We will not discuss the distinctive features of Yahweh's being or his attributes, but his perfections. Any statement about the holiness, justice, mercy, truth, and faithfulness of Israel's God contains within it a testimony to his incomparable perfection. "In Deum non cadit accidens" (Augustine, *De trinitate* 5. 5. 6). Any attribute would be something mutable, replaceable. When we speak of Yahweh's "perfection," we mean the *proprietates Dei*, which in the Psalms tend to be incomparable and unalterable. In the light, however, of all that has been said above, especially on the theme of "the living God," our point of departure must be the conclusion that all Yahweh's perfections are attributes of his self-expression and his actions. Therefore the question of his "essence," the *essentia Dei*, is one that cannot be properly raised.

Yahweh is holy. His holiness is characteristic of his perfection. It has already been shown that the designation "holy" or "holiness" as applied to Yahweh was borrowed from the neighboring Canaanite and Syrian cultures. It entered the cultic theology of Jerusalem along with the epithets אל (*El*) and מלך ("king," cf. chap. 1, §B). We must now consider in what sense קדש ("holy") is a statement of perfection. The designation of holiness is seen most clearly in Psalm 99. Its relationship to the *trishagion* (Isa. 6:3) is unmistakable, and the *trishagion* was probably a part of the liturgy of the Jerusalem cult (cf. Wildberger, 1972, on Isa. 6:3). Wildberger trenchantly explains that קדש ("holy") does not involve contrasting extremes such as the polarity between God and world or creator and creation but, as is shown by the context, our attention is called to the way in which majesty permeates the whole earth. "Yahweh's holiness is a thoroughly dynamic entity, not a static 'property.' It expresses itself in crushing the resistance with which humans oppose God. It is God's absolute will to bring about the recognition of his kingly authority among his people, and among the peoples of the world. This is to say that the concept of holiness that is so widespread among Israel's ancient neighbors, as well as throughout the history of religion, was decisively modified by Israel's understanding of God" (Wildberger, 1972, p. 249). The holiness of Yahweh is his royal perfection as king, worthy of adoration (Ps. 99:5, 9), his divine power that shines forth in כבוד ("glory") and permeates the world. "Holy" is a statement about Yahweh himself, about his name (Ps. 33:21; 99:3; 103:1; 111:9; 145:21), about his word (Ps. 105:42), his arm (Ps. 98:1), his way (Ps. 77:13), and all his work (Ps. 145:17). In this context the essential factor is not that the God of Israel is the one who is "wholly other," separated from all earthly being, and exalted above all creatures, but the persistence of his self-expression and activity that overcomes obstacles and prevails over all. As the God who comes to his people, Yahweh is holy (cf. chap. 1, §C). His kingship will be acknowledged in the world of creation and in the world of the people.

Glory (כבוד) is the manifestation of Yahweh's holiness. It is the phenomenon of light that streams out in all the awesomeness of the majesty of God the king. The statement of the *trishagion*, that the whole earth is full of the glory of the holy God can be connected with Ps. 19:1 (Wildberger, 1972). The throne of Yahweh the king was placed above the מבול ("flood," Ps. 29:10). The heavens shine with the reflection of his כבוד ("glory"). When Yahweh the king is adored, כבוד ("glory") is ascribed to him. All the heavenly powers give up their own and present it to Yahweh (Ps. 29:1-8). And they all cry, "Glory!" (Ps. 29:9). The links with the Canaanite and Syrian cult of the god El clearly show that that was the original background of this psalm. But all the traditional and borrowed features now are in the service of the glorification of Yahweh, the God of Israel and of the praise of his incomparable perfection, his holiness. The explanation is not that the concept of holiness had extensive influence on the way the Psalms speak of God. But there is no doubt that this concept occupies a central place in the cultic theology of Jerusalem and is one of the sublimest, as well as most comprehensive designations that testify to Yahweh's perfection. Holiness connotes the will of Yahweh the king to attain to sole authority and to overcome everything that stands in opposition to his will. The considerable modification underwent by this concept of holiness which Israel borrowed from its neighbors is essentially due to the fact that Yahweh is a king who loves justice, who establishes a just order, and who has made justice and righteousness prevail in Jacob (Ps. 99:4). Yahweh is a God of justice and not a deity of being. The holiness of Israel's God is the power that makes justice and righteousness prevail. It is not an attribute of a numen, but the signature of a name (Ps. 99:3), that establishes justice.

Yahweh loves righteousness and justice (Ps. 33:5; 99:4). His perfection is his justice. Yahweh is just. An overview of the word צדיק ("righteous") as applied to Yahweh gives the following picture. Yahweh is the אלהים צדיק ("righteous God") because he judges righteously (Ps. 7:9, 11). He cuts the cords of the wicked (Ps. 129:4). He tests human minds and hearts, and therefore judges righteously (Ps. 7:10). Yahweh is צדיק ("just") in all his ways (Ps. 145:17). His judgments are just (Ps. 119:137). Those who are saved by Yahweh's work as judge, through his pronouncing of judgment, experience the graciousness and righteousness of Yahweh (Ps. 116:5), his compassion. Before investigating the nouns צדק ("righteousness") and צדקה ("righteousness"), we must first stress that Yahweh is צדיק ("righteous") because he judges righteously. In Old Testament theology, Luther's insight into Ps. 31:1 and the development of the communal aspects of the Hebrew concept of righteousness produced an extreme and one-sided explanation of Yahweh's righteousness as his work of salvation and the expression of his faithfulness to the community (cf. Luther, WA 3, 163; Fahlgren, 1932; Koch, 1953; von Rad, 1962, Koch, THAT 2: 507-530). To be sure, Yahweh's righteousness is a demonstration of his salvation and an expression of his faithfulness to the community. But the starting point must be God's work of judging. Yahweh is שׁוֹפֵט ("judge," cf. p. 31), but his judging consists in helping people get their rights. "God is the great champion of justice" (Köhler, 1957, p. 32). This justice has also the aspect of punishment (Ps. 129:4), but it is first of all, as its "proper work," the bringing of assistance, deliverance, and loyalty to those who are victims of injustice, persecution, and false accusations. But the statement that Yahweh is "just" is not fully exhausted by saying that he is "gracious." Yahweh is חַנּוּן וְצַדִּיק ("gracious and righteous, Ps. 116:5). In the execution of justice and the process of judgment he demonstrated his righteousness and, for the sake of his "proper work," his salvation, his grace.

In the usage of the noun forms, the masculine צֶדֶק ("righteousness") occurs more frequently than the feminine צְדָקָה ("righteousness"). "The difference in meaning is unmistakable, but not easy to establish and was probably not always felt the same in all periods of the poetry of the Psalms" (Koch, 1953, p. 158). But how can we describe the difference of meaning in those passages where it can still be recognized? Does צֶדֶק (*zedek*) refer more to a condition, while צְדָקָה (*zedekah*) has more the idea of an action? Koch believes that he can identify the distinction in meaning in Psalm 72 and Ps. 119:142, but the numerous other passages where the terms occur provide no clear basis for this. Even in the use of the noun forms, Yahweh's work of judging is involved. The worshiper comes before Yahweh with the petition, "Vindicate me [judge me]. . .according to thy righteousness" (Ps. 35:24). The righteousness of Yahweh is the perfection of the manner in which he sees through everything, evaluates, judges, and saves. It is the perfection of the one who, true to his responsibilities to the community, helps all who are oppressed, falsely accused, persecuted, or suffering, and reveals himself as their deliverer. Therefore those in peril can plead, "In thy righteousness deliver me!" (Ps. 31:2; 71:2).

In no case is it correct to understand the Old Testament concept of righteousness in the sense of an absolute, ideal ethical norm. Righteousness never stands above Yahweh. It is Yahweh who is righteous. He demonstrates *his* righteousness by helping people to get their rights, by displaying faithfulness to the community, and by rescuing his people when they are threatened by the law. It is also true that "ancient Israel did not in fact measure a line of conduct or an act by an ideal norm, but by the specific relationship in which the partner had at the time to prove himself true" (von Rad, 1962, p. 371). But it is still an essential part of the Old Testament concept of righteousness that it was not absorbed into the concept of salvation or subsumed under the concept of relationship in phenomenological terms. It primarily involves the establishment of the justice of Yahweh in the saving event of providing legal help for the deliverance of all those who were deprived of their rights. In the context of this explanation we can affirm the formulation, "Yahweh's righteousness was not a norm, but deeds, deeds that brought deliverance" (von Rad, 1969, p. 384).

In the Psalter the term חֶסֶד ("steadfast love") as an expression of Yahweh's perfection occurs 127 times (245 times in the entire Old Testament). חֶסֶד (*ḥesed*) can be translated as steadfast love, relationship, goodness, grace, mercy. It is clear that in the Old Testament it is in the Psalter that the statements concerning the "steadfast love of Yahweh" are truly at home. Throughout the Psalter we encounter the experience of Israel having seen proof of the steadfast love of their God. It is expressed in a variety of connections, with a multiplicity of synonyms

43

(see Stoebe, THAT 1:607). It is the nation Israel that experiences first of all Yahweh's steadfast love (Ps. 118:2-4; 136). "Yahweh remembered his steadfast love and faithfulness to the house of Israel" (Ps. 98:3). The king also received this steadfast love in that God stood by him and made him invincible (Ps. 18:50; 21:8). In the individual songs of prayer and thanks, Yahweh's חסד ("steadfast love") is spoken of again and again: he has delivered, helped, freed, or healed. Those praying cry out to Yahweh and appeal to his חסד (ḥesed). For example, "deliver me for the sake of thy steadfast love" (Ps. 6:4; 44:26); "save me in thy steadfast love!" (Ps. 31:16); "have mercy on me, O God, according to thy steadfast love" (Ps. 51:1; cf. Ps. 109:26). In the song of thanks (todah) and in the hymn the people sing of Yahweh's חסד (ḥesed) and rejoice over it.

How are we to understand the word חסד (ḥesed)? In what manner does it express the perfection of Yahweh? Prior to the work of Nelson Glueck (Das Wort חסד im altestamentlich Sprachgebrauch, 1927) it was customary to speak of Yahweh's spontaneous expression of his love for his people. Glueck advanced the view that חסד (ḥesed) was not such a spontaneous, essentially unmotivated love, but a relationship based on the rights and duties of basic human relations, such as husband/wife, parent/child, ruler/people. Glueck maintained that speaking of Yahweh's חסד (ḥesed) involves the affirmation of the declarations involved in the "covenant" and of the community of relationships established by the ברית ("covenant"). As a result of the studies of the root צדק ("righteous"), ideas involving faithfulness to the community were drawn on to help explain the concept of חסד (ḥesed) (von Rad, 1962, pp. 372ff.; Koch, 1961, pp. 72-90; other bibliographical references are found in Stoebe, THAT 1:600ff.). It is beyond doubt that the concept חסד (ḥesed) involves a community relationship and expresses the element of loyalty to community, as is shown with especial clarity by the combination חסד ואמת ("steadfast love and faithfulness," Ps. 25:10; 40:11; 61:7; 89:14; 138:2 etc.). Yet beyond this the Psalms proclaim "that חסד (ḥesed) means something special in a mutual relationship, something that goes beyond the obvious" (Stoebe, THAT, 1:607). This special element is clearly expressed by the idea of grace, unexpected and amazing goodness and kindness—not in the sense of a spontaneous, unmotivated friendliness, but on the basis and on the presupposition of a faithfulness to community that is manifested in the חסד (ḥesed) that is shown to Israel. Yes, this חסד (ḥesed) shown to Israel was and remains the special, unique element that is involved in the mystery of God's choice of the people. The perfection of Yahweh in his חסד (ḥesed) is proclaimed in the Psalms by reference to the greatness and fullness of his grace (86:5, 13; 103:8; 106:7; 108:4; etc.). Yahweh's mercy or steadfast love lasts "forever" לעולם: Ps. 89:2; 100:5; 106:1; 107:1; 118:1-4; 136; 138:8). It extends to the heavens (Ps. 36:5), and it fills the earth (Ps. 33:5; 119:64). Yahweh's חסד (ḥesed) is his liberating, saving, helping, healing mercy extended to Israel and to the poor in Israel. It implies action that changes destiny, that rescues, that constantly arises anew out of the perfection of Yahweh's grace and mercy. The sphere of its influence is as great as the whole of creation, as broad and high as the expanse of the heavens. Everything is permeated and filled with his חסד (ḥesed). Yahweh can send forth his חסד (ḥesed), like a hypostasis (Ps. 57:3). חסד (ḥesed) can pursue a person (Ps. 23:6), nevermore to forsake him. Thus חסד (ḥesed) is not only the perfection of Yahweh's readiness to help and save, but also the offer and assurance of the presence of his power over destiny in every situation and every place of distress and suffering. Therefore,

Yahweh's steadfast love is the object and constant ground of great trust (Ps. 13:5; 52:8). Yahweh's perfection is expressed in אמת (*emet*) and אמונה (*emunah*). The basic meaning of the root אמן (*aman*) is "to be firm, reliable" (cf. Michel, 1968, pp. 30-57; Wildberger, 1972, pp. 177-209, where further references are given). We might also begin from the connotations of אמת (*emet*) as that which is "firm, reliable, valid, true"; אמונה (*emunah*) is to be translated "constancy, reliability, faithfulness" (cf. Michel, 1968 p. 37). What do these results of research and study tell us about the texts under consideration? How do they help explain the theme of the "perfection of Yahweh" in the testimony of the Psalms? The petition in Ps. 69:13 is typical: "In the abundance of thy steadfast love answer me with thy faithful help (באמת ישעך)." We will return to the way in which חסד (*hesed*) and אמת (*emet*) are used as synonyms. It is clear, however, that אמת (*emet*) refers to the dependability of the help that Yahweh gives. We can rely on Yahweh's help; it demonstrates the saving faithfulness of the God of Israel, whose ישע ("deliverance") is constant and true. Therefore, in Ps. 31:5 Yahweh is called "faithful God" (אל אמת). אמת (*emet*) is the perfection of Yahweh, in which his חסד (*hesed*) is demonstrated and validated. Therefore, those who are surrounded by enemies can appeal to this saving faithfulness of God and pray for the defeat of the powers of destruction (Ps. 54:5). Just as the deeds of Yahweh are characterized by אמת (*emet*), so also are his words. They are dependable and true. "The ordinances of the Lord are true and righteous altogether" (Ps. 19:9). Everyone who relies on the teaching of the Torah, or on the word of Yahweh, walks in God's truth (אמת, *emet*; Ps. 25:5;26:3;86:11), which means that his or her way of life is under the banner of Yahweh's faithfulness and the truth that is demonstrated in this faithfulness. The formula חסד ואמת ("steadfast love and faithfulness") has already been referred to in the discussion of חסד (cf. Ps. 85:11; 89:15). Michel (1968, p. 56) says in this connection, "In the expression חסד ואמת (*hesed wᵉemet*) the אמת refers to the fulfillment of a promise, an oath, a blessing, or a sign." In Ps. 132:11, for example, this element of fulfillment is clear. A literal translation would read, "Yahweh has shown אמת (*emet*) to David, and he will not turn away from it." Here then, אמת (*emet*) is faithfulness to an oath. Beyond that, however, Michel (1968, p. 41) says, "It is clear that this involves the agreement of a (divine) word with events, specifically with future events." The correspondence between promise and future events is expressed in אמת (*emet*). The oath of faithfulness points towards its fulfillment. Yahweh is faithful, precisely in reference to the future fulfillment of his declarations, even though in the present everything seems to speak against the possibility of such fulfillment.

The word אמונה (*emunah*) also testifies to the perfection of Yahweh which is made known in his constancy and reliability. The synonymous parallelism in Ps. 33:4 is significant: "For the word of the Lord is upright (ישר), and all his work is done in faithfulness (באמונה)." A literal translation might run, "All his works express his reliability." Again it is a matter of the dependability of all that Yahweh says and does. In Ps. 96:13, the word בצדק ("in righteousness") is parallel to באמונה ("in truth"). Yahweh judges "with righteousness" and "with truth." There is nothing arbitrary in Yahweh. In his freedom he is the one who is reliable and true to his community. His promises concerning the future are sworn באמונה ("in truth," Ps. 89:49; cf. 132:11).

Whenever the Psalms speak in this way of Yahweh's dependability, steadfastness, and faithfulness, this involves not "attributes," but concepts of relationships which give concrete expression to the perfection of the faithfulness of Israel's God to those relationships. Yahweh shows himself to his chosen people as the one who is faithful. He comes in חסד (*ḥesed*) and אמת (*emet*) (אמונה, *emunah*) to the poor and helpless among this people, to those who call to him out of their distress.

Everything that Yahweh says and does, pronounces and accomplishes, takes place in the perfection of his might and power. Israel confesses, "Great is our Lord, and abundant in power (רב־כח)" (Ps. 147:5). His voice of thunder rings out with power (Ps. 29:4) "With mighty victories (גבורות) by his right hand" God helps his anointed one (Ps. 20:6). Yahweh's glorious deeds and his might are recounted in Israel (Ps. 78:4). Here is heard the praise of his mighty deeds (Ps. 21:13; 59:16). The individual, too, experiences the perfection of Yahweh's power. The song of thanksgiving proclaims, "The Lord is my strength (עזי)" (Ps. 118:14). Even among the nations, the God of Israel has displayed his incomparable might (Ps. 77:14; 106:8). Yahweh is mighty. "That little word 'mighty' does not mean here a quiet might, as it might be said of a contemporary king that he is mighty, even though he sits still and does nothing. No, it is an active might, and a constant activity that without ceasing goes forth and works. God does not rest but works without ceasing" (Luther, WA, 7, 574). God is "semper actuosus" ("always active"). His power is "actualis potentia" ("active potential") (Luther, WA, 18, 718). The Psalms speak and sing of the power of Yahweh's חסד (*ḥesed*) and of his רחמים ("mercy") (Ps. 79:8; 119:77; 119:156; 145:9).

E. The Heavenly World

Again and again the Psalms state that Yahweh is enthroned in heaven, that he is seated on his throne in the heavenly world (Ps. 2:4; 11:4; 103:19; etc.). Allusion has already been made (chap. 1, §B) to the relationship between God's heavenly throne or dwelling in heaven and God's presence in the sanctuary on earth, and in chap. 3 we will come back to this question. The concept of the divine king who is enthroned above the heavenly ocean (מבול) has its roots in mythology and in the rhetoric and metaphors of divination. "The Lord sits enthroned over the flood; the Lord sits enthroned as king forever" (Ps. 29:10; Begrich, 1964). God's throne rises, as it were, on columns out of the heavenly floods. These are God's "chambers" (עליות), where he reigns (Ps. 104:3). All these concepts contain rudiments of the ancient Near Eastern worldview, in which the blue of the heavens, from which the rain falls, is regarded as the heavenly ocean. God sits enthroned above this "flood" (Ps. 29:10).

Among Israel's neighbors the sky was considered to be a numinous realm, almost divine, but in the Old Testament we find a sharp distinction that is characteristic of Israel's belief in Yahweh as the creator. Psalm 89:11 still reflects the phase in which Israel had to assert Yahweh's claims to sovereignty over the heavenly world. The cry, "The heavens are thine, the earth also is thine," is both a polemic and a doxology, but it bears witness to the creator's sovereignty over heaven and earth. Yahweh created heaven and earth (Ps. 115:16; 121:2; 124:8; 134:3). The heavens are the work of God's fingers, or hands (Ps. 8:3; 102:25). The heavenly world has been called into existence by the creative word of the God of Israel (Ps. 33:6; 96:5; see *Comm.* on Ps. 33). This is why the heavens declare the glory of God (Ps. 19:1) and his righteousness (Ps. 50:6; 97:6). Heaven and earth await the Lord's command; he calls out to them (Ps. 50:4). The Psalms contain, free from tension, both dynamic and static, sovereign statements about Yahweh's sitting enthroned in the heavens. On the one hand, we read the statement that Yahweh rides in the heavens, or on the heavens (clouds), reflecting the influence of concepts now well known through the Ugaritic literature. On the other hand, the Psalms speak repeatedly of Yahweh's throne that is sovereign over all the world. He looks down from heaven (Ps. 14:2; 33:13; 53:2; 80:14; 102:19). On his throne in heaven he hears and responds to those who cry to him out of the depths (Ps. 20:6). He sends from heaven and saves (Ps. 57:3). When the Psalmist cries out, "Be exalted, O God, above the heavens!" he expresses a longing for the God of Israel to display his power that is greater than the world and that transcends all heavenly powers (Ps. 57:5, 11; 108:5). The one who is enthroned in heaven possesses unlimited and perfect power and sovereign freedom. "Our God is in the heavens; he does whatever he pleases" (Ps. 115:3). And this distinguishes him from all other gods and powers.

The greatest caution is required if we attempt to identify elements of a worldview in this survey of the material. The mythological aspects and the metaphors and concepts from divination which were borrowed from Israel's neighbors can scarcely be combined into a unified view even outside Israel. The attempt that has often been made to give a graphic presentation of the Babylonian worldview, for example, has been and remains something that is far removed from and strange to the ancient intentions expressed in those concepts. To be sure, there can be no doubt that the ancient manner of orienting the world was geocentric, concerned with what was up or down or distant. But even the explanation that the heavens were thought of as a "third story" involves static categories and an attempt to impose an order that can hardly do justice to the reality of the ancient worldview. In the Old Testament we encounter the statement, "Heaven and the highest heaven cannot contain thee" (1 Kings 8:27; cf. Deut. 10:14). The heavenly world is the world of Yahweh, the God of Israel, and not the realm of a numen that can be fitted into strata that form a worldview. Yahweh is enthroned in a realm that is superior to the world and is his and his alone. He is not immediately near to us, not identical with the forces of nature, not manifest in the phenomena of this world. But his throne in the heavenly world cannot be compared to the concepts of space with which we are familiar. This can be made clear by an examination of the concept מרום (*marom*).

The Hebrew word מרום (*marom*) denotes "the heights," "a prominent elevation." In terms of the history of religion this term is quite close to the concept which can be documented among Israel's neighbors, that the deities in heaven come down onto an Olympus, a divine mountain, a peak that rises into the heavens, and have their dwelling there. Thus מרום (*marom*) is the place that marks the transition between heaven and earth, where what is heavenly becomes earthly and what is earthly becomes heavenly. It is clear from Ps. 102:19 and Ps. 148:1 that מרום designates the heavenly height, in that מרום is used synonymously with שמים ("heavens"). Psalm 92:8 probably refers to the throne of God in the heavenly world, but alternative explanations are possible. It is unmistakable, however, that it is God who intervenes from the superiority of the heavens, reaches down from the heights, and rescues his servant from the great waters (Ps. 18:16; 144:7). Similarly, Ps. 93:4 declares that "the Lord on high is mighty," mightier than the thunder of the waters or the waves of the sea. Psalm 68:18, however, probably means the mountain of the sanctuary, since the preceding verse clearly states that

The God of Israel

Yahweh came from Sinai to the sanctuary. So too Ps. 7:7 probably refers primarily and in the foreground to God's being enthroned on the heights of the sanctuary, since where else could the "assembly of the peoples" be gathered about him? But what does it mean to say "primarily" or "in the foreground" of a concept? The vision of the God who is enthroned on the heights of the earth is not something in the foreground; it forms the background, and includes the heavenly perspective. This way of formulating the matter, "inclusion of the heavenly perspective," is more appropriate than the analogy introduced by the experts in Babylonian religion, "that which is above is also below." The mystery of the "inclusion of the heavenly perspective" is not a mythological analogy but a revelatory event. It is indisputable that mythological metaphors are involved. They must be recognized as such and be interpreted in terms of the history of religion. Nonetheless, these are merely rudiments that are involved and they must be explained in each instance in terms of their new context in the Psalms.

It is undeniable that the concept of Yahweh as the one who rides on the clouds is derived from the Baal mythology that has become better known through the excavations at Ras Shamra. In Ugaritic, Baal as weather God is called *rkb 'rpt*. It is significant for understanding the use made of this term when it was borrowed in the Old Testament that it did not include any reference to a fertility or weather deity. Rather, the metaphor and the term serve to proclaim Yahweh's majesty over the world, but especially his activity in hastening to the rescue and aid of those in distress.

In the heavenly world Yahweh, enthroned as God and king, is surrounded by powers who honor, praise, and serve him. Israel borrowed from the Canaanite-Syrian world the well-attested concept of a pantheon of gods and godlike beings who surrounded the supreme God, the ruler and monarch (cf. chap. 1, §B above). In Ps. 29:1-2 the בני אלים ("sons of God") give honor to Yahweh. They are subordinate heavenly beings stripped of their power, who are totally dependent on Yahweh and no longer possess any independent divine nature. In Job and the Psalter, powers of this sort are called אלהים, אלים, בני אלהים, or קדשים ("sons of God," "gods," "holy ones"; Job 1:6ff.; Ps. 58:1; 8:5; 86:8). But Yahweh alone is the highest God (עליון, *'Elyon*) and king. He has no rivals from the realm of polytheism. All heavenly or divine beings are servant spirits who glorify and praise him and carry out his will. In Ps. 82:1 we have a clear example of the idea of a "council of gods," borrowed from the religion and myths of neighboring cultures: "God has taken his place in the divine council; in the midst of the gods he holds judgment." The "highest god" is the judge (cf. chap. 1, §B above). The gods (אלהים) are his attendants. They are witnesses in the forum which Yahweh rules alone, and in which he alone possesses judicial authority. We might term the עדת-אל "Yahweh's heavenly court." All the gods and powers of the peoples are in his service. (For a fuller discussion, see below, chap. 5, §A.) The key issue is the description of the service rendered by the heavenly powers in the heavenly world.

In the Psalter the statements about the "messenger (angel) of Yahweh" are an integral part of the Old Testament traditions. מלאך יהוה ("angel of Yahweh") is a figure with clear contours in the traditions of the Old Testament. The angel of Yahweh is the representative of Israel's God in earthly transactions. We are to assume in the background of this concept two basic aspects that point to Canaanite influence (2 Kings 19:35; 1 Kings 19:7; Num. 22:22; Judg. 6:11ff.). First, the figure of the מלאך ("angel") originally was a member of the heavenly assembly of the gods. Second, manifestations of local Canaanite numina were borrowed by Israel and transferred to the "angel of Yahweh." At the same time a new understanding developed. The מלאך יהוה ("angel of Yahweh") is the messenger or representative of Yahweh. Von Rad (1962, p. 286) offers the explanation that the angel of Yahweh is "a being who helps, and who everywhere acts in Israel's favour, saving and protecting her; he is Jahweh's aid to Israel personalised almost in the way of a mediating official of the covenant relationship."

The situation in the Psalms is quite clear. In Ps. 103:20 and 148:2 the מלאכים ("angels") belong to the circle of heavenly powers around Yahweh who praise and honor him. But God also sends out "messengers" and "servants" (Ps. 104:4). He charges his angels to protect his servants in all their ways (Ps. 91:11). The ancient Israelite statements about the guidance that Yahweh has provided for Israel through his מלאך ("angel" or "messenger") have been applied to the individual. He experiences Yahweh's attentive nearness in the person of the מלאך ("angel"). Psalm 34:7 says, "The angel of the Lord encamps around those who fear him, and delivers them." Thus, the angels are heavenly beings sent to represent on earth Yahweh's ever-present help and protection.

All the statements in the Psalter about the heavenly world need to be demythologized and explained, because there is always the necessity of seeing and explaining the elements of metaphors from mythology or divination newly in the context in which they are applied to Yahweh. *The* mythological worldview as such is not found in the Old Testament, but there is a great wealth of mythic fragments which reveal in differing degrees their origin in the history of religion. "Demythologizing" then would mean translating and interpreting these foreign materials in such a way as to reveal their essential intention to make statements about Yahweh and to testify in varying, manifold form to his work, his sovereign being, and his transcendent majesty. The effect of this type of explanation can be illustrated by two examples.

"Statements that speak of God in heaven do not involve any boundaries of space or set limits on his vast majesty; no, they exclude any restrictions on his power and any need for human means or measures. They exclude his being subject to fate or fortune, but imply that the whole world is subject to his rule, and that he is superior to all obstacles that might stand in the way of his purpose" (Calvin on Ps. 115:3; CR 60:183f.).

"No philosophy, neither that of Aristotle nor Kant nor Plato can reach to the transcendence of God, for philosophers come only to the edges of the incomprehensible, of that which is higher than we are. All philosophy circles around heaven. Only the gospel tells us of what is in heaven, yes, beyond heaven. No spiritualist, idealist, or existentialist can lead us to the reality of God, to his transcendence, which is something other than spirit and invisibility. His transcendence is demonstrated, disclosed, made real in Jesus Christ, in the depths of his all-powerful compassion" (K. Barth, 1965, pp. 45f.). Barth's statement should be applied by analogy to the contrast between mythology and the Old Testament events of salvation.

2. The People of God

Yahweh is the God of Israel (Ps. 68:8). The designation אלהי ישראל ("God of Israel") binds Yahweh and his people together inseparably. Whenever Yahweh is spoken of, his people must also be mentioned, the people to whom he has made himself accessible, to whom he has communicated and revealed himself. Yahweh makes his appearance as the "Holy One of Israel" (Ps. 71:22; 89:18). As the קדוש ישראל ("Holy One of Israel") he is "our king" (Ps. 89:18). The metaphor of shepherd and flock is basic to the designation of Yahweh as the רעה ישראל ("Shepherd of Israel," Ps. 80:2). Another figure of speech is found in the term "keeper of Israel" (Ps. 121:3-5). These designations express the closest bonds between Yahweh and his people. Therefore, throughout the Psalms we must inquire which theology of Israel is expressed in them, what role is played by God's people, and what basic concepts and expectations, what prayers and expectations are involved? In answering these questions we will examine first the beginnings and basic relationships, then history and creation, and finally, the cultic community as present in worship.

A. Beginnings and Basic Relationships

Whenever the Psalms speak of Israel's beginnings or of the beginnings of Yahweh's coming to Israel, we find the theme of the exodus. The patriarchs, especially Abraham, are also mentioned (Ps. 47:9; 105:7, 9, 42), but in the Psalms the basic event is always the exodus, the deliverance from Egypt (Ps. 105:43; 114:1; 136:11, 14, 21; etc.). "So he led forth his people with joy, his chosen ones with singing" (Ps. 105:43). Thus the basic datum of God's choice of Israel is his rescuing them from Egypt. Israel did not engage in speculation about God's choice, but always saw itself in relationship to the event of Yahweh's liberating them and bringing them out of Egypt. The choice of Israel is the event that constituted the beginning, the basis, and the presupposition of Israel's existence as the people of Yahweh. This event took place, and the assembled people of God—in declarations, in narratives, and in praise—again and again reminded itself of the event. "For the Lord has chosen Jacob for himself, Israel as his own possession" (Ps. 135:4). The concept סגלה ("possession"), which originated in the Deuteronomic tradition, illustrates the basic relationship that was initiated by God's

51

choice of Israel: Israel is Yahweh's possession and belongs to him alone. A modern view might regard this as the end of any autonomy, but in reality this was liberation in an occurrence of immeasurable and unforeseeable dimensions. Israel was not the victim of a tyrannical theonomy. On the contrary, the chosen people were caught up in a powerful liberation movement. In addition, even the exodus as the basic datum of election is not to be confused with any act of self-liberation or as a process of "emancipation." Exodus means deliverance. Yahweh is the God who provided deliverance (cf. Kraus, 1972e, pp. 102-119). The joy that the exodus brought (Ps. 105:43) was due to the fact that those rescued from Egypt had been taken to the side of their deliverer and had entered into the incomparable realm of his might. This gave the people a completely new basis for their existence. Exodus and God's choice of Israel were not accidental features of a society that lived by the presuppositions of its folk culture and that constituted itself through the fate that befell a grouping of tribes with shared traditions. Instead, Yahweh had "made" Israel (Ps. 100:3; 149:2). "It is he that made us, and we are his; we are his people, and the sheep of his pasture" (Ps. 100:3). Israel owed its existence as the people of Yahweh to a free, creative act of choice. Thus election was and is a creative event. Israel's origin and foundation are contained in Yahweh's initiative and action alone. This was told to Israel in worship; this is the way the people of God understood itself.

Through the event of the exodus Israel became Yahweh's "sanctuary" (קֹדֶשׁ) and "dominion" (מֶמְשָׁלוֹת). This statement in Ps. 114:2 is to be understood in reference to synonymous parallelism. The Holy One of Israel (see above) destined Israel to be a sanctuary, a holy people (Bächli, 1962, p. 141; Kraus, 1972b, pp. 37-49). The holy people is the people to whom the holy God has laid claim, whom he has taken out of the context of their natural and historical life and separated and distinguished, just as a sanctuary represents an exceptional district that has been consecrated to and reserved for the exclusive claims and service of the deity. As "Yahweh's sanctuary" the people of God are the context in which God reveals himself and where his people give him their willing, obedient service in time and space. What this involves de facto is clearly expressed in the second part of the synonymous statement: Israel is Yahweh's dominion. Yahweh rules (מֹשֵׁל) over Israel; that is the basic feature in the earliest traditions (Judg. 8:23). Martin Buber correctly perceived "that the sentence: 'Jahweh (alone) shall rule over you' (Judg. 8:23), is axiomatic. God is the ruler, but He is ruler because He is Lord and not vice versa. The rule of God in the Old Testament is merely a corollary of His lordship" (Köhler, 1957, p. 31, referring to Buber, 1967). And yet the lordship of Yahweh in Israel is the lordship of the liberator. What the Bible says about God testifies that the God of Israel is the one who has the power of liberation (cf. Kraus, 1975, pp. 113ff.). In Israel, sovereignty does not depend on kings, political goals, or national interests, but on Yahweh. This is the basic nature of the people of God as determined by the exodus and by God's election, and it cannot be invalidated or abolished by any counterdevelopment that might arise among the people. Thus there is full certainty that everyone will acknowledge "that God rules over Jacob to the ends of the earth" (Ps. 59:13).

"In Judah God is known, his name is great in Israel" (Ps. 76:1). The entire mystery and wonder of Yahweh's name has been entrusted to Israel (cf. chap. 1, §A). The name *Yahweh* is, as has been shown, the assurance of the effectiveness of Yahweh's presence among his people; it is the gift and guarantee of God's call. Under the sign of his name, that is, his self-disclosure, Yahweh has made his gracious will known to his people. He has established his testimony in Israel (Ps. 78:5). "He declares his word to Jacob, his statutes and ordinances to Israel" (Ps. 147:19). So the hymn of praise says, "Thou hast executed justice and righteousness in Jacob" (Ps. 99:4). Yahweh's commands and ordinances are the expression of his saving will that reigns in Israel. For this reason the commands refer back to the basic event of the exodus (Ps. 81:10). Yahweh's commands stand under the sign of his liberating deed. They are his instructions in freedom. Joy over them echoes even in the late Psalm 119. As Yahweh's lordship in Israel prevails through "justice and righteousness," so too the people of God are destined to be the vanguard among all the nations of a new life together.

Israel is encompassed by Yahweh's majesty (Ps. 68:34). He is enthroned as the holy one, as the never-ending "praises of Israel" (Ps. 22:3). The content, center, and object of all the praise sung by the people of God is the God who chooses and rescues, to whom the "fathers" cried and were saved (Ps. 22:4-5). In the same way as at the beginning he laid hold on Israel, freed them, and spoke to them, so he has continued to show himself as the God who rescues and helps. The words and commands which he uttered at the beginning are spoken anew in the worship of the cultic community gathered at the sanctuary (Ps. 50:7; 81:9). The living God lets his living voice be heard (cf. chap. 1, §A). Thus the people of God are called on again and again to place their hope in God alone (Ps. 115:9; 130:7; 131:3). This appeal is all the more important and urgent, in that Israel continually resists their God and turns away from him. The sin of Israel functions as a constant hindrance against their realizing their basic destiny as the chosen people. (This will be discussed more in detail in chap. 2, §B.) The plea for forgiveness cannot fall silent, for every movement of repentance and penitence gains space for the lordship of Yahweh among his people. Their hope is directed toward the future: "And he will redeem Israel from all his iniquities" (Ps. 130:8). No prayer is uttered with so much anguish and longing as that for שלום על־ישראל ("peace upon Israel"; Ps. 125:5; 128:6).

When the Psalms speak of Israel as a people, the emphasis is always on the thoroughly distinctive nature of their role as the people of God. Israel became the "people of God" through Yahweh's word and work. He redeemed his people (Ps. 77:15; 111:9), and he made the בני ישראל ("children of Israel") into his own people, "the flock of his pasture" (Ps. 79:13; 100:3). After freeing them he led them through the wilderness (Ps. 136:16). He went before his flock like a shepherd (Ps. 77:21), leading his people like a king. (Ps. 68:8). He fed his people in the wilderness (Ps. 74:14) and let them flourish in the promised land (Ps. 105:24ff.). All these statements show clearly that Israel, chosen from among all the nations (see above) is distinguished by the fact that Yahweh wrought deliverance for Israel and announced to Israel his claims upon them. Israel is Yahweh's people, and it is this basic relationship that determines Israel's existence, its nature, and the course of its life.

Yahweh chose a land for his chosen people (Ps. 47:4). He drove out nations and "planted" Israel (Ps. 44:2). God's royal authority holds sway over the land from which the peoples have disappeared (Ps. 10:16). He gave to his people Israel the territory of King Sihon and King Og as their heritage (Ps. 135:11-12). Together with the gift of the land, Israel received "abundant prosperity," שלום רב (Ps. 37:11). They found the land enriched and well-watered (Ps. 65:10), and the land gave its increase, because "God, our God has blessed us" (Ps. 67:6). The blessing of Yahweh rests upon his people, and they constantly pray for it to be continued (Ps. 3:8). "God's acts of blessing the people, and the blessing itself are experienced in a manner entirely different from his saving deeds. They are not experienced in an event, but in a constant state—in growth and prospering, in good fortune and success, in increase and expansion. In terms of its origin, blessing has nothing to do with history. Its basic significance lies in the power of fertility, which throughout the world of that day was understood as divine or as a power of divine origin" (Westermann, 1964, p. 210).

At the same time, however, it must be added that Yahweh's blessing is bestowed as a consequence of an act of liberation and salvation. It is the blessing of Yahweh, the God of Israel. "This entire broad and manifold realm of blessing was coordinated with the activity of the God who saves, the activity of Yahweh, in such a way that the blessing itself became historicized or took on a historical aspect, because it was that which Yahweh had promised" (Westermann, 1964, pp. 210f.; cf. Keller and Wehmeier, THAT 1:353-376). Blessing is thus experienced in the natural processes of growth and prosperity, of fruitfulness and harvest, in success and achievement. "Precisely in these features of life faith sees Yahweh at work, without it being necessary for his activity to be always explicitly mentioned" (Keller and Wehmeier, p. 368). "Blessing in the Cult" will be dealt with specifically in chap. 2, §C.

The Psalms illustrate this with especial clarity. "Blessing," as the power that preserves and fosters life, is not something that one can "have," but must always be accepted and asked for anew. Anyone who "has" blessing experiences a superfluity that becomes excess and leads to a deadly satiety. The "flow" of blessing is interrupted when it is not channeled by giving and receiving, by thanksgiving and petition. In the Psalter the prayers for blessing never fall silent. They are not little liturgical flourishes, but expressions vital to life, in which Israel makes its needs known. In the prayers of the Psalter blessing is not primarily something that is given to an individual, but to the entire people (Ps. 3:8; 28:8; 29:11; etc.). Blessing is the bringing of שלום (shalom, Ps. 29:11). This leads to the expression of the content of ברכה ("blessing") in extremely complex formulations.

There is no doubt that the coordinated expressions, "Yahweh, the God of Israel" and "Israel, the people of Yahweh," are to be assigned a very early date. Wellhausen recognized this when he wrote, "Yahweh, the God of Israel, and Israel, the people of Yahweh—in every age that has been the most concise expression of Israelite religion. Israel's history began with the origin of this relationship" (Wellhausen, 1965, p. 73; compare also Smend, 1963). The question arises whether this "relationship" referred to by Wellhausen was known—even in early times—as a ברית (berit, "covenant"). Before the use of the theme "covenant" in the Psalms can be discussed, a survey must be given of the research in this area. The first problems arise in the translation of the term ברית (berit). In any case the German word *Bund* and the English word *covenant* are inadequate representations of the content of ברית. The question is, does ברית designate a community relationship between two unequal partners in the sense of the Latin word *foedus*, or must the Hebrew concept be understood in the sense of "stipulation," "obligation" (Lat. *testamentum*)? (Cf. Kutsch, THAT 1: 339-352 and the additional literature cited there.) For von Rad, ברית designates a covenant relationship which

Yahweh established by means of a covenant ceremony. ''Thus the making of a covenant is intended to secure a state of intactness, orderliness, and rightness between two parties, in order to make possible, on the basis of this legal foundation, a relationship in matters affecting their common life'' (von Rad, 1962, p. 130). In this way, according to von Rad, God's covenant on the one hand and the revelation of the divinely willed law on the other, are closely related. This mutual relationship is so close in the Deuteronomic and Deuteronomistic theology that the word ''covenant'' has become synonymous with the complex of commands and ordinances (p. 147). But this very Deuteronomic-Deuteronomistic theology confronts us with a further problem. No survey of the theological statements of the Old Testament on the theme ''covenant'' can miss the fact that a ברית (*berit*) theology first receives its specific expression in this body of literature (cf. Perlitt, 1969). The Deuteronomic view is that Yahweh swore to the fathers that he would establish a covenant (Deut. 7:9, 12b). *Covenant* thus ''stands for the promise Yahweh offers his people whom he has 'chosen' '' (Zimmerli, 1978, p. 50). The content of the promise is possession of the land. But the ''covenant'' includes, as von Rad has noted, the giving of the commandments at Horeb.

In the light of this concretely expressed covenant theology of the Deuteronomic tradition, the question arises of the existence and form of a pre-Deuteronomic covenant theology. Here we must take into account the ''silence'' of the prophets about the covenant (Perlitt), but we should not regard it as an argument against the validity of the question. Is it possible to agree with Zimmerli in assuming that ''the deuteronomic use of the term 'Horeb covenant,' too, as we would expect from the explicitly restorative nature of the deuteronomic movement, has historical antecedents in early tradition'' (1978, p. 52)? If so, it might be possible to contend with Zimmerli that ''if the people of Yahweh used the term ברית *b^erit* to describe their relationship with Yahweh even in the context of the events that took place at the mountain of God in the desert, the possibility cannot be eliminated that this crucial expansion of the people of Yahweh to include all 'Israel' took place once more under the rubric of a 'covenant,' to which the stone set up at Shechem was a 'witness' (Josh. 24:26b)'' (1978, pp. 54-55).

On the basis of that explanation we can construct the following picture: The relationship, the ''covenant,'' concluded between Yahweh and his people in the wilderness at the mountain of God was a relationship in community, characterized by commands and ordinances. This ברית was then extended at Shechem from the wilderness people of Yahweh to the Israel that was constituting itself, or was being founded, through the covenant with Yahweh. In other words, the establishment of the covenant at the mountain of God was repeated in Shechem. At once the question arises of whether this ''repetition'' brought with it consequences for the cult, and if so, what they were. The question is whether we may assume the possibility of a ''covenant renewal festival'' in the worship of Israel (cf. von Rad, 1971d, pp. 23ff.; Kraus, 1966, pp. 141ff., 197ff.). Reference to the disputed translation of ברית (*berit*) is an indication that the way in which this cultic hypothesis was arrived at has been brought into question at many points, and has recently become more and more problematical. We must also keep in mind something that can only be alluded to here, that what the Old Testament says about ברית shows varying accents, and that consequently ''covenant theology'' has been set in a variety of interpretive contexts—in the course of time, in the traditions, and in the theological formulations. Still the dominant feature of the ברית

is the basic concept of an order for life in community that is founded on Yahweh's faithfulness, and that is promised continuing life and uninterrupted duration.

What can the Psalms contribute to these briefly sketched questions? Before the major cultic problem of a possible covenant renewal festival can be explored, a few observations must be made. It is helpful here to start with a usage of the concept ברית (*berit*) that is not related to the relationship of God to people in the Old Testament. In Ps. 83:5 it is said of the foes of Yahweh and his people that "they conspire with one accord; against thee they make a ברית (*berit*)." The meaning of ברית in this passage is made clear by the context. The translation "agreement," "obligation" would be too weak. It involves an agreement to stand together and take joint action, on the basis of mutually declared, solemnly specified, legally binding ordinances. The ברית thus involves a common, mutually recognized, binding obligation that establishes a covenant. The alternative translations "covenant" or "obligation" would be a rational oversimplification of the complex nature of the relationship. In Ps. 83:5, ברית corresponds to the Latin term *pactum*, which denotes a mutual assistance treaty based on mutual agreement and obligation.

Yahweh's covenant, too, is such a mutual agreement, which has taken on a new basic nature through the initiative and the intervention of the sovereign divine partner. "He sent redemption (פדות) to his people; he has commanded his covenant forever (צוה־לעולם בריתו)." This statement in Ps. 111:9 makes it clear that Yahweh's redeeming and liberating intervention for his people which was announced the beginning was the self-identification of the divine partner—a self-identification by which and in which Yahweh drew an unmistakable distinction between himself and all other partners to covenant or mutual assistance, of whatever nature, human or superhuman. "Holy and terrible is his name" (Ps. 111:9). The divine initiative is termed פדות ("redemption"; cf. Stamm, 1940, pp. 13ff.). Accordingly the "covenant" that announces this "redemption" is in principle not a two-sided agreement, but a declaration valid for all times (לעולם) that God is on their side. It is Yahweh's declaration (צוה) that he is there for them, by which they are promised that through all the future he will intervene to redeem and deliver them. On the basis of this ברית (*berit*) Israel can call on Yahweh in times of trouble and distress and appeal to him with the words, "Have regard for thy covenant" (Ps. 74:20). But ברית (*berit*) cannot be understood as a mere one-sided obligation which Yahweh assumed in reference to Israel. A community has been established in which Israel has for its part taken on obligations, which beyond the possibility of doubt involve commands and promulgated laws. When it is said that the Israelites "were not true to his covenant" (Ps. 78:10, 37) the idea clearly is that the people had broken or turned away from the obligations of the covenant, that is, from its requirements of commands and ordinances. It is especially evident in Ps. 25:10, 14 that Deuteronomic theology is expressed in such concepts, because there "covenant" and "commands" ("testimonies") are synonymous. But all these preliminary conclusions are only preparatory explorations of the material. In the Psalms the relationships are difficult to determine, because a conventional cultic language affected expressions derived from the ברית (*berit*) theme, and in each instance these are to be explained in the context of prayer or song.

Psalms 50 and 81, however, which von Rad drew on for support of his hypothesis of a covenant renewal festival regularly celebrated in the cult, require particular attention (von Rad, 1971d, pp. 23ff.). Two features of Psalm 50 are to be noted especially: (1) The Psalm refers to a covenant that was established by a sacrifice (Ps. 50:5), and (2) Ps. 50:7-23 is a message (delivered by a prophet) in which law and righteousness are given concrete expression. Calvin suggested in his Psalms commentary that Psalm 50 refers to a cultic act during the course of which, in a solemn manner ("solenni ritu") the memory of God's covenant was renewed ("ac si Deus foedus sui memoriam renovaret").

Albrecht Alt, in the context of his research on ancient Israelite law, advanced the view that "apodictic law" was promulgated in the cultic act of a regularly celebrated renewal of the covenant, and that this ceremony had already been observed in Israel's early days (Alt, 1953b, pp. 278-332, esp. 327-332).

Alt refers to the scene depicted in Deuteronomy 27 and, based on Deut. 31:10ff., explains it as follows: "Because they were designated to be read aloud to the assembly of the people at the Feast of Tabernacles every seventh year, the category of apodictically formulated statements took its place in the context of characteristic concepts and institutions of specifically Israelite nature, and this affords us an even deeper insight into their significance. The connection with the Feast of Tabernacles is itself significant, because this celebration at the end of the agricultural year in autumn was for ancient Israel also the festival of the beginning of the year and was therefore filled with thoughts about the beginning of a new period in the life and work of the community as well as that of the individual. This holds true to a heightened degree and in a specific sense of the Feast of Tabernacles in the seventh year, because since ancient times this had been a time of rest from all agriculture, letting the land lie fallow, not for economic reasons but on sacral grounds. For the duration of this period the rights of the Israelite clans to the land assigned them by lot were set aside and Yahweh's own exclusive rights to possession were again clearly manifest" (1953b, p. 327). Alt assumes accordingly that there was a presentation of the apodictic law at the Feast of Tabernacles in the seventh year, which imposed duties on the entire national community. He designates this cultic occurrence as "a regularly recurring renewal of the covenant between Yahweh and Israel" (p. 328). Alt based this view explicitly on Psalm 81, "which, according to its hymnodic introduction was specified for the Feast of Tabernacles; it quickly moves into the style in which Yahweh speaks in the first person, and then becomes a recital of the first sentences of the Decalogue" (p. 330). Of course Psalm 81 cannot provide proof of this position, but this psalm displays the effects of the cultic event that has already been described.

Gerhard von Rad continued Alt's studies under a new perspective. His form-critical investigation of the entire Sinai pericope and the Sitz-im-Leben of this tradition led him to assume the existence of a covenant renewal festival, during the course of which the major events of the Sinai pericope were cultically "reproduced." Von Rad abandoned the connections that Alt had established with the sacral fallow and the year of release, which took place every seventh year, and instead assumed that there had been an annual celebration of a covenant renewal festival. Finally, Arthur Weiser in his Psalms commentary ascribed a central place to the "covenant festival" and a significance determinative for all of Israel's cultic life. Just as for Mowinckel the festival of Yahweh's enthronement was the great magnet which drew together and unified the most disparate cultic traditions, for Weiser the "covenant festival" was the key to almost all the Psalms.

To provide an absolutely necessary differentiation in terms of cultic history, it will be helpful to begin with a three-fold reexamination of this previous research.

1. Alt's hypothesis should be reconsidered, and indeed in the sense that there was in early Israel a cultic act of covenant renewal, an act that was connected

with the sacral fallow and the remission of debts that took place "every seven years."

2. All attempts to incorporate a covenant renewal festival into a festival of Yahweh's enthronement or into a complex "covenant cult" are to be rejected. The existence of an enthronement festival of Yahweh is questionable (cf. pp. 86f.), and a complex "covenant festival" as presented by Weiser flies in the face of all necessary differentiations in cultic history.

3. The history of ceremonial of covenant renewal is clearly difficult to establish in Israel's cultic life (cf. Kraus, 1966). In the Psalter there are only two witnesses to a ceremonial of covenant renewal—Psalms 50 and 81.

Recent research has made the assumption of a "covenant renewal festival" thoroughly questionable. For the arguments against it see Kutsch, 1955, Perlitt, 1969, and the exegesis of Psalm 50 in *Comm*. But in spite of all refutations, we should hold fast to the fact that, as Alt and von Rad have shown, Psalm 50 and Psalm 81 are witnesses that are to be examined thoroughly and carefully for a cultic renewal of the covenant. It therefore is incomprehensible that Perlitt does not mention these two Psalms (1969). According to Jeremias, Psalms 50, 81, and 95 belong to the type "great festival Psalms" (1970, pp. 125ff.; see the *Comm.*, Intro. §6). The three psalms are to be regarded as a special group within the Psalter. In each case the center is an address by Yahweh, dealing with the theme "law and righteousness." We are dealing here with a "judgment speech." Jeremias identifies the speaker of these first-person speeches of Yahweh by saying that these psalms are the expressions of circles which are similar to those behind Deuteronomy" (p. 126). This would lead to the assumption of Levitical authorship of these great festival psalms. It was probably Levitical priests who applied the commandments in these judgment speeches. Such "Levitical sermons" are to be dated relatively late. They have their counterpart in the speeches in the Chronicler's history (cf. von Rad, 1971a, pp. 248-261). On this basis we are to assume that Levites exercised prophetic functions in the late Old Testament period and displayed prophetic charisma, or "that in postexilic times prophets appeared in Levitical circles" (Jeremias, p. 127). All these findings still do not explain the Sitz-im-Leben, the cultic site and context of Psalms 50 and 81. Theophany, concluding of a covenant by sacrifice, and proclamation of the law, as they are seen clearly in Psalm 50, point to the context of a covenant renewal festival, the early history of which could be sketched only hypothetically by von Rad and Alt. A large number of questions must be posed, involving in particular the traditions restored in Deuteronomy. The Levites, of whose activity much has been said, are to be seen in the context of those traditions which are present in Deuteronomy in a form that was restored and made theologically normative, and is firmly fixed. What are the connections between the covenant renewal traditions that appear in Psalms 50 and 81 in a late form and those elements which can be identified in Deuteronomy or in the Sinai traditions and point to a cultic renewal of the covenant? Neither Kutsch nor Perlitt provides a thorough examination of Deut. 26:16ff. This passage shows that mutual ברית ("covenant") declarations and ברית ("covenant") obligations were undertaken and how they were formulated (for the literature and details of interpretation see the *Comm.* on Psalms 50 and 81). As far as the covenant renewal theme is concerned the case is not yet complete and the research has not yet led to a satisfactory conclusion. The two psalms mentioned above keep it an open problem. We would not be dealing fairly with the data if we eliminated the perspective of cultic history by appealing to the lateness of tradition and composition. In the last analysis it is only with the greatest difficulty that psalms can be assigned a firm historical setting, in the light of their complex history of transmission and their backgrounds.

According to biblical thought the concept of covenant is the culmination of the concept of God himself. The only way that Yahweh is known is in relationships—Yahweh is the God of Israel and Israel the people of Yahweh (Wellhausen). This covenant is not something that Israel discovered; Yahweh created Israel as the people of God (Ps. 100:3). "Covenant" means making claims on this people and taking them into God's service; it does not mean taking God into the service of the people. Everything that Yahweh accomplishes in Israel takes place in affirmation of the covenant and through its application, and without it Israel would not be what it is.

In the world of the nations Israel stands in total isolation, belonging only to Yahweh. "No person outside Israel knows Israel's secret" (Buber, 1963, p. 563). Israel's existence in the world of the nations and the course that Israel follows are a great mystery, of which also the Psalms speak as enigma and miracle. Yahweh creates a space for his people and for their history. He drives out nations before them (Ps. 44:2; 78:55). He displayed his power among the peoples (77:14) and is exalted on high above the nations (Ps. 99:2). In his sovereign might Yahweh frustrates the plans of the peoples (Ps. 33:10), who conspire and plot in vain (Ps. 2:1). As "judge of the peoples" (Ps. 7:8; 9:8; etc.) Yahweh assembles the foreign nations around himself (Ps. 9:8). Israel, however, has been selected from among all the national groups and chosen to play a role in God's history, to be Yahweh's road to the nations. Thus the people of God always stand in a prominent, exalted place. Israel has the task of telling Yahweh's deeds and miracles among the peoples and of bearing witness to them (Ps. 9:11; 96:3; 105:1). Israel calls the peoples to praise Yahweh (Ps. 66:8; 117:1), for the God of Israel is the lord and king of the peoples. It is through Israel that God comes to the world. All peoples will see his glory (Ps. 97:6). Israel "exists as a people only because this is the presupposition of the total human response to God." "There must be a people, so that the human response may be fulfilled in the whole of life, of which public life is a part. Not the individual person, but only the community in its totality and unity, in working and achieving together through its members with their different gifts and callings can lead the life that constitutes the human response to God (Buber, 1963, pp. 564f.). The Psalms are witness to the reality of Israel, even there where individual voices are raised. Israel is Yahweh's first partner, a people chosen, caught up in and enclosed in community and in faithfulness to the covenant. It is the first answer, the first witness. None other than the God of this people is the king of all peoples. The "meaning" of Israel's existence is the mission to the peoples.

B. History and Creation

Basic to the Psalms is the fact that Yahweh has revealed himself to his people. The stimulus to this did not come from the human side. "The fact that God has fellowship with man is due to His free and groundless will and is His first and fundamental deed" (Köhler, 1957, p. 59). But Yahweh does not reveal himself to just any individual on any occasion at all. He is no private God. The place where he reveals himself and communicates the mystery of his person is the history of his chosen people. The historical psalms, which deal with the beginnings and early events of Israel's existence, tell of this, and so too do the "prayer songs of the people" (*Comm.*, Intro. §6, 2aβ) which are related to the history of God's people in a twofold manner: to the present with its suffering and distress, and, in retrospect, to Yahweh's deeds in history that formed the basis of the people's life. The God of Israel revealed himself in the history of his acts. In these events he intervened fully for his people. In the Old Testament, history is that which it is and that to which it bears witness solely and entirely by virtue of the subject who acts in it. The great deeds of Yahweh are that to which Israel is constantly relating itself in the Psalms and on which Israel's life is based. In all these testimonies to history there is no doubt even for a moment that God's people are not relying on themselves, on their faith, on their accomplishments, but on Yahweh alone.

"For the people of the Old Testament, history is the thought-form of faith" (Seeligmann, 1963, p. 385). In what sense is this statement correct? The Psalms do not speak in a *thought*-form. In them Israel is *commemorating* everything that Yahweh has done and that has supported and determined the life and being of the people of God. In the prayer songs of the national community, looking back at the basic history has the structure of *memoria*. Israel "remembers" Yahweh's great deeds, which in this remembrance become present reality. God's history is the basis to which faith is related, the present basis of existence on which the people of God stand. This is thus not a concern for "history" as such, but for the history of God, for Yahweh in the history of his acts. The theological apotheosis of "history" is a highly questionable undertaking of Old Testament scholarship, in which frequently the singular nature of its object is validated as with a magic wand. The prayer songs of the national community appeal, on the basis of Israel's basic history, to Yahweh's faithfulness in saving and guiding his people, but not to a residue of history.

The extent to which the references in the Psalms to Israel's basic history are related to the Pentateuch must be carefully examined in each psalm. An unequivocal result is not to be expected in every instance, however, since the question must remain open whether it really was the "canonized" Pentateuch to which the historical statements of various psalms refer, or whether we must postulate a knowledge of traditions which later became part of the Pentateuch. When seen in this light, several hypotheses require further examination. This is especially true of the work of Jasper (1967, pp. 50-59), who holds the position that the following psalms refer to the Pentateuch: 44; 47; 60; 68; 77; 78; 80; 81; 99; 105; 106; 114; 135; 136 (see the *Comm.* on these psalms).

We must seriously and carefully ask where those who sing and pray in the Psalms got all that which they have expressed: the confession and testimony in their praise of God, their thankfulness, their comfort, their confidence; but also their cries of distress, their despair, and their hope. What is the source of their knowledge of God, of themselves, of the creation, the world, and the peoples, but above all, their knowledge of Yahweh's relation to them and theirs to him? The answer must always be that they got it from the history of God's actions with his people. "Israel found herself drawn by God from the start into a history. Indeed she found herself commandeered by God so inescapably that all attempts to elude this grip, of which there were more than a few, remained unsuccessful. This history—and now we go a step further—was, of course, no dumb, anonymous, fated course of events. Rather, God personally drew near to this history of his with Israel in his word that he addressed to Israel, and he chose her to be his partner in conversation'' (von Rad, 1980, p. 85). Anyone who suspects that Israel overestimated itself in the hybris of religious arrogance should reflect on the large extent to which it was always expressed that Yahweh's word was also constantly turned *against* Israel, and that God's history with his people was also a history against the people's religious and political self-assertion. This experience and knowledge are summed up in Psalm 78 and are portrayed in most of the historical psalms. Here is the end of all καύχημα (''boasting'') and the beginning of the exaltation in the faithfulness of Yahweh who resisted all opposition and insubordination, all apostasy and disobedience, in order to lead his people to its true destiny, that of being Yahweh's people, firstborn among the nations, bearer of all promises and the path and gate by which Yahweh comes to the world (Psalm 24).

It is worthwhile to reflect on what J. G. Herder wrote on the question of the uniqueness of Israel and its history. ''An artistic people, the idea of the earth in beautiful products, a heathen people, the ideal of human strength and conquest, a political people, the model of the contribution of the citizen to the common good—that is not what this people was to be, and therefore in these realms we are to look for other patterns. It was to be the people of God, that is, the image and pattern of the relationship of God to men, and of these to Jehovah, the unique one, the God of gods.'' To establish ''the adoration of the one God, the creator, the father of men on this earth, his influence on everything, his direct involvement in every detail of human concerns, hopes, troubles, how near he is to each of our sighs, our prayers, our failings, our forgetfulness of him, and how mild and forgiving he is to turn the evil to good, as soon as anyone is there to receive this good, and to let himself be clothed with a better raiment from heaven, however far man remains beneath God, beneath his human goals, promises, and commands, and where God's purposes are to lead—that, my friend, and much more in the bounds of such relationship is the spirit and purpose of this history and these writings'' (1780–1781, letter 12).

The historical perspectives that open before us in the Psalms make it all too clear that Israel was not a pious people, obediently following Yahweh. They always were open to serving other gods and powers besides Yahweh. How lightly the Israelites forgot their God, and ''turned away and acted treacherously like their fathers'' (Ps. 78:57). That Israel did not listen to Yahweh's voice or hearken to him (Ps. 81:11) is the shocking fact of their history, and Yahweh's anger burned against his people (Ps. 78:21, 31) and he utterly rejected them (Ps. 78:59). The terrible troubles in which Israel found itself again and again as described in the prayer songs of the people are always acknowledged as the consequence of apostasy and disobedience. The repentance which takes place in these prayers, the appeals to God's faithfulness and his undeserved intervention, as well as the self-knowledge that perceived the past and present depths of their troubles, show that each generation was confronted with the task that was always the same and always new, that of being Israel and of perceiving itself as Israel (cf. von Rad, 1962, p. 118). All these Psalms show clearly that Israel was not an already-existing entity, not a historical given, but always had to receive its identity anew from Yahweh and to be brought into being by him. Just as Yahweh's choice of Israel was the creative expression of his unrestricted sovereignty, so Israel's history was dependent on God's intervention and activity, which always made it possible for Israel to confront the moment and move forward. Thus it is one of the deepest mysteries of Israel's history that the presuppositions of the existence of God's people and of their course of life are based on the theme of ''creation.'' This is expressed most clearly in the confession, ''Our help is in the name of the Lord, who made heaven and earth'' (Ps. 124:8; 121:2; 115:15). Therefore, we must once again investigate, and do so in the realm of history, the theology of creation that is expressed in the Psalms.

In innumerable hymns and historical psalms in the Psalter the deeds of Yahweh in history and creation are recited and praised in close connection with each other. Psalm 136 is the clearest example of this. To be sure, their juxtaposition, as suggested by the pattern of the Pentateuch, its sources, and its preliterary traditions, is much more a case, properly speaking, of the one following the other. Creation is seen as a work of Yahweh in history, as the first, basic deed which brought into being the area of God's activity, of his choice of Israel and his establishing the covenant, of his leading and speaking with the people, and finally and above all Yahweh's coming to the peoples of the earth. In the Psalms this fact is worked out. ''But if the account of Creation stands within time, it has once for all ceased to be myth, a timeless revelation taking place in the natural cycle'' (von Rad, 1962, p. 139). Theologically, it is of great significance that Israel was able to bring the history of creation into relationship with that of election and covenant. It is God the creator who is at work in the history of his people, and history is carried forward and determined by the presupposition and the presence of the mystery and miracle of creation. These preliminary comments, however, must be followed out and clarified.

Israel knew Yahweh as creator, not in the numinous manifestations of nature or in cosmogonic myths, but only in that he himself manifested and communicated his name, and in the history of his speaking to his people and his saving them. ''O Lord, our Lord, how majestic is thy name in all the earth!'' (Ps. 8:1). ''The north and the south, thou hast created them; Tabor and Hermon joyously praise thy name'' (Ps. 89:12). The creator God, to whom the Old Testament and especially the Psalter give testimony and honor is not just any supreme being, but the Lord of Israel's history, Yahweh, who has revealed himself and made himself known in the history of his deeds and self-disclosures. In their encounter with the cosmogonic myths of the religions of Israel's neighbors, Israel perceived and experienced the creative power of their God on a universal scale, after the same creative power had been specifically encountered in election and deliverance. This universal discovery and experience, however, came about in the harsh battles and debates with the active claims of the cosmogonic powers of the world of the ancient Near East. Psalm 89 shows clearly how these debates took place. The statements about creation in this psalm are polemical, confessional, and doxological. But the psalm shows a clearly soteriological understanding of the creation, that is, a connection between Yahweh's activities in creation and in salvation history. The intention of Psalm 89 is to sing ''the steadfast love'' of Yahweh (v. 1). This makes it clear that the ''soteriological understanding of creation,'' that is, the relation of creation and salvation history to each other, was by no means a discovery of Deutero-Isaiah and a distinctive feature of that prophet (Isaiah 40–55; cf. von Rad, 1962, p. 138). Similar relationships are drawn in Ps. 74:12–17.

If we were to ask how Israel came to confess in hymns that ''The earth is the Lord's and the fulness thereof, the world and those who dwell therein'' (Ps. 24:1), our starting point must again be the distinctive event of the promise of the land and the occupying of it, in which Israel came to know Yahweh's right to a possession in the land of Canaan (Ps. 105:44; 135:12). The expansion to universal dimensions in creation theology is possible because of the particular history of Israel in its land, the land of Yahweh.

In the history of Yahweh's acts Israel experienced the absolute sovereignty of God, a sovereignty never in doubt, never involved in process of development. Yahweh's superiority in all activity, his power as the cause of everything, necessarily had its effect on creation theology. The Old Testament knows nothing of any theogonic speculations that precede the act of creation. ''Before the mountains were brought forth, or ever thou hadst formed the earth and the world, from everlasting to everlasting thou art God'' (Ps. 90:2). Even if in this statement there are echoes of rudiments of the mythological view of the procreative power of ''mother earth'' (cf. Job 38:4ff.), still there is clear testimony to the preexistence of the creator in the era before creation. God was there before the world. The world is not eternal like God. Existence in time is the basic characteristic of the ''form of this world.'' History is its beginning and its course.

The Old Testament does not explicitly speak of ''creatio ex nihilo.'' Even the Psalms do not speak in this way, although the concept ברא (''create''), as has already been shown, contains implicitly the idea of a ''creation out of nothing'' (Ps. 89:12, 47; 104:30; 148:5). It would perhaps be more appropriate to speak of a ''creatio contra nihilum,'' if *nihil* includes the abyss of chaos, the primeval chaotic power. Yahweh overcomes the primordial hostile powers (cf. Psalms 89; 93). Still it is remarkable—and explicable only in terms of the history of Yahweh's acts—that, unlike the mythologies of Israel's neighbors, there is no painful battle, no hard-fought contest between two powers out of which Yahweh emerges as the ''hero'' and the royal ruler of the cosmos. As is true of the history of his saving deeds of power, Yahweh's conquest of his foes is a sovereign event, only recently concluded, to which one now looks back (Ps. 89:1-4). ''Thy throne is established from of old: thou art from everlasting'' (Ps. 93:2). On the theme of the ''Foes,'' see chap. 5.

What has been said thus far about history and creation is in contradiction to what Claus Westermann has developed in his Genesis commentary (1984, pp. 25f.). His starting point there is the thesis that what is said about God's saving deeds cannot be applied directly to God's work of creating. He writes, ''The Old Testament does not speak of faith in the creator; there is no 'creation faith.' And more, the idea of revelation is not simply to be linked with God's creative action. One could not speak of a 'creation revelation.' The goal of creation is not a self-manifestation of God, so that God can be known from his work of creation (revelatio generalis)'' (p. 175). And in another place Westermann explains that the people of the Old Testament do not need to believe that the world was created by God, because that was a presupposition of their thought (p. 43). These statements are riddled with misunderstandings, because they involve a threefold polemical attack: first, against the soteriological understanding of creation or the relationship of salvation history and creation; second, against a dogmatic ''creation faith''; and third, against the involvement of the motif of faith in the Old Testament use of the creation theme.

Nevertheless, whatever judgment may be made concerning these problems, the starting point must be the fact that the Old Testament, and especially the Psalter, does not speak of Yahweh as creator, and thus that the creator is not known unless he communicate himself—his name, the manner of his activity and work, the power of his word, and the sovereignty of his being—in the encounter with Israel, and therefore specifically in the history of his acts. This self-communication and knowledge of Yahweh are the starting point and the hallmark of all that is said about the creator. And out of this self-communication and knowledge there develops the struggle to assert Yahweh's claims to lordship as the creator of heaven and earth. In the light of this fact, it is totally erroneous to assert that the people of the Old Testament did not need to believe that the world was created by God because this was a presupposition of their thought. To make the claim that the Psalter contains such "presuppositions of thought" would be to subvert the meaning of most of the statements. Rather the data show that the miracle of history and the miracle of creation are placed in direct relationship to each other (Psalm 136), and that faith in Yahweh's power and justice is equally determinative for both themes, "creation" and "history." Finally, belief in Yahweh as the creator was vigorously disputed. Foreign cosmogonic accounts and mythological statements about lordship over the world confronted Israel with other claims. The polemic, confessional, and doxological themes that can be identified in Israel's creation psalms (see above) have more than a little to do with what is called "faith." This applies specifically to faith in Yahweh, the God of Israel, but also to the universal lord and the creator of heaven and earth, and thus the one to whom the world belongs and who alone exercises power and establishes justice in this world. These facts did not come to constitute an obvious, self-evident presupposition of Old Testament thought. That the name of Yahweh, the God of Israel, is majestic in all the earth (Ps. 8:1) must have appeared ridiculous in the light of the vast dimensions of the empires of other ancient peoples and their cosmogonies.

Westermann is certainly correct in his assertion that neither a "creation faith" nor a "general revelation" can be found in the Old Testament. Creation as an anonymous act or as something that exists is not an object of faith, because "creation" as such does not communicate. Rather it is Yahweh, as creator and Lord of the world who is the "object" of faith, of laud, and praise, and trust—because (as Westermann so well shows) the goal of creation is not the self-disclosure of God. God's revealing of himself in history through his saving acts is the presupposition for and the medium of the knowledge and praise of God the creator. That the "language" varies from place to place is due to the fact that foreign elements were borrowed in connection with the theme of "creation." These elements differed considerably from the Israelite traditions of the mighty deeds of Yahweh; they were borrowed for use in speaking of Yahweh and not of an independent category "creation," which could have constituted a separate presupposition for Israel's thought. In his commentary on the first two chapters of Genesis, Westermann delved so deeply into isolated features of the text that he was unable to see and evaluate the internal and external relationships between creation and history. In dealing with the Psalms it is impossible to proceed in that manner.

H. H. Schmid also opposed the "prevalent tendency to accord priority and a central position to salvation faith in contrast to a secondary creation faith" (1973). He appeals to an "order of creation" that was basically understood as whole and wholesome, and in his book *Gerechtigkeit als Weltordnung* he reveals tendencies that have their counterpart in the theology of Emil Brunner. In the Psalms, however, there is no way in which statements such as the following can be substantiated: "History is understood as the completion of creation and the establishment of the order of creation" (H. H. Schmid, 1973, p. 9).

Once we accept the fact that creation signifies a radical removal of the world from the realm of the divine and the demonic, then the contrast that calls us to faith and trust can be recognized here as well. Under the absolute and unlimited lordship of Yahweh, who has authenticated himself in the history of his mighty acts, the biblical act of creation makes the world worldly. Only in terms of a secular historical context that is open to the world is the worldliness of the world understandable, as we find it set forth in the Psalms. There are no numinous remnants, no sacral islands. Psalm 104 is a striking example of this, especially in that the solar deity, the reigning god in the Egyptian original behind this psalm, is extinguished (v. 19). Only the lordship which Yahweh exercises in sovereignty and freedom is able to illuminate the reality of creation as it is found in the Old Testament, including the Psalms. This means, however, that only the encounter with Yahweh the Lord in the history of his acts can give us a proper perspective on the presupposition that is determinative for the biblical statements about the creator: He does not belong to the world, and he does not stand alongside the world in an ontological context that encompasses both him and it. He is its Lord. By this token the world is "world." Thus in the biblical meaning of the concept, creation does not imply a being and becoming with its own conditions for existence. The world—heaven and earth—have their reality only because of the unique activity and work of Yahweh (Ps. 65:6; 78:69). The belief that creation is an expression of God's grace, that in it the creator provides food as a father provides for his household (Ps. 104:27-28; 145:15-16), means that no one can lay claim to anything as a right.

And now it must be made clear that the creator of heaven and earth, to whom heaven and earth belong, the Lord of all creatures, is the Lord and king of Israel. The help and salvation of Israel are in the name of Yahweh, who made heaven and earth (Ps. 124:8; 121:2). All the creative activity of this God is directed toward his people. This is the point of view to which Deutero-Isaiah recurs, but which, as explained above, is by no means something that first appeared and became established in Isaiah 40–55. This point of view characterizes in explicit manner the historical activity of Yahweh, just as it is to be implicitly assumed in earlier statements. Thus we are to assume a reciprocal relationship between the themes "creation" and "history," because one and the same God is the liberator of Israel and the creator of heaven and earth. No exegesis centered in a tradition or a theme should be permitted to ignore, restrict, or bypass this fact. The Psalms bear unequivocal testimony to this point and show how the themes are interconnected and interwoven in Israel's worship.

In the prayer songs of the community the question of Yahweh's historical activity becomes acute. The new situation in which Israel finds itself, as expressed in these prayers, is a quite different one. Psalm 60 deals with the collapse of God's people in a wartime catastrophe and regards the collapse as the result of rejection (Ps. 60:1-3). Psalm 74 speaks of the destruction wrought by the enemy, but in Israel itself "an impious people" (עם נבל) cooperates with the foe (Ps. 74:18). The suffering that resulted is regarded as having been caused by God's casting aside his people (Ps. 74:1). Psalm 79 tells how the place where Yahweh is present has been shamed and defiled, and how God's servants have been killed. The community that gives voice to the weeping and lamentation of Psalm 137 is gathered by "the waters of Babylon," that is, in exile. Moreover, there may be inner causes for the plight of the people of God. Psalm 94:3-7 laments the corruption of the entire system of justice in Israel. The troubles which give rise to the prayer songs of the community are thus quite varied and will be discussed in detail in the commentary on this group of psalms.

The People of God

The question at once arises, Why have suffering, destruction, catastrophe, and corruption come upon Israel? While the realization of guilt and the confession of Israel's sin often find expression in the prayer songs of the community, Psalm 44, though by no means impenitent, has another starting point. The national community stood before Yahweh faithful and constant, offering praise and thanks (Ps. 44:4-8). They were never false to the ברית ("covenant," Ps. 44:17). Enmity and contempt have come upon them solely because of their relationship to Yahweh. In Psalm 83 the situation is seen in much the same way. The enemies want to destroy Israel and with it the witness to Yahweh's lordship and saving intentions. Their conspiracy is ultimately directed against Yahweh himself. Psalm 79:12 declares that Yahweh was taunted, and that his honor was attacked. Psalm 129 paints a dismal picture. From the very beginning the history of Israel has been lived under the sign of suffering and oppression. "Sorely have they afflicted me from my youth" (Ps. 129:1). But Israel's history with all its suffering is not the result of some fatal constellation, nor does it bear the mark of political and historical tragedy. Rather, it was and is the hatred of the enemy nations that Israel must bear, hatred against that people among whom God is present and to whom he discloses himself. Nevertheless, these aspects do not exclude the possibility that in other passages and contexts Israel confesses its guilt before Yahweh.

Reference has already been made to the manner in which the prayer songs of the community look back on the past. Now we must consider in more detail the nature of this looking back to the beginnings and foundations of Israel. The remembrance of the great, fundamental deeds of Yahweh in Ps. 80:8-11 is typical. Yahweh led his people out of Egypt and gave them the promised land. In Ps. 44:1-3 the praying community confesses that its existence is based on God's saving grace expressed in his gift of the land. Moreover, keeping in mind the fundamental saving acts and ordinances constantly inspires God's people to trust in Yahweh (Ps. 60:6-12). In this way the expectation is kept alive that he will again intervene, rescue, and help his people in the same way that he showed himself in the past as the God who rescues and helps. In the midst of the suffering caused by being forsaken and rejected by God the community affirms the reality of Yahweh's creative, saving deeds in the present day: "Remember thy congregation, which thou hast gotten of old, which thou hast redeemed to be the tribe of thy heritage!" (Ps. 74:2). The prayer song lays emphasis on the holiness of all God's ways (Ps. 77:13). This acknowledgment that all God's ways are holy does not spring from some consciousness of the distance between the people and the *Deus absconditus*, but from the encounter with the great miracles and deeds of the *Deus revelatus*, as these are brought to remembrance. It is striking that reference is made to Yahweh's activity and presence, though his "footprints were unseen" (Ps. 77:19), though there was no discernible evidence of his coming and manifesting himself. All the creative miracles of Israel's God bear the mark of concealment (Ps. 77:16-19). Yet when this aspect of Yahweh's activity is generalized we encounter problems. In the time of trouble Ps. 74:20 appeals to Yahweh's faithfulness to his covenant, his ברית. In addition the people look up to the complete and total power of Israel's God, who is "enthroned upon the cherubim" (Ps. 80:1). They called to the *Deus praesens* to appear and intervene. In Ps. 137:1, 5 Zion—Jerusalem—is called to remembrance, the place where God is present and where the community worships, and from which the exiles are now so far removed.

Through the confidence gained by remembrance, the people pour out their petitions and prayers, calling upon Yahweh and pleading with him to intervene once again for his defeated and scattered people (Ps. 74:2). Typical of these prayers is the cry "Restore our fortunes, O Lord" (Ps. 126:4). Psalm 80 not only prays that the God of Israel will come and appear to his people, but also that he will bring about a total restoration (Ps. 80:3, 7, 19).

In this context the call for vengeance takes on special importance (Ps. 79:10-12; 83:9-12; 137:7-9). It would be a superficial and emotional response to characterize the desire for revenge in the Psalms as something typical of the Old Testament, irreligious, unchristian, and repugnant. First, we must note that the cry for vengeance proceeds from the fact that Yahweh himself is being treated with contempt and his honor is defiled (Ps. 79:12). Then we must note that Israel does not set out to take revenge but prays to Yahweh and calls on him to do so (Deut. 32:35; Rom. 12:19). The "vengeance" for which Israel hopes is God's judgment in response to the scorn and mockery of the enemy nations. The prayer is that Yahweh will not allow his enemies free rein or let their rage go unanswered. It is expected that Yahweh will manifest his power in the world of the nations. Not alone in the Old Testament, but in the New Testament as well there is a certainty that this will not take place in an invisible, ideal realm of retribution, but in the reality of this world. Therefore there rings out a cry for revenge and for God's judgment in the face of the unbearable suffering and torment of God's people, on down to the Revelation of John (6:10). To set up a polarity of love and vengeance would involve a total misunderstanding of biblical truth. The cry for revenge that we hear in the Psalms is simply to be understood as the expectation of the oppressed people of God that Yahweh would bring the enemy nations to judgment for their scorn and contempt and that he would display his power in the world of the nations. In this perspective it is inappropriate to polarize the issue and appeal to New Testament love.

Psalm 123 involves quite other expectations than that of revenge. The community looks longingly to God, the ruler of the world and their helper. They wait expectantly for him and look up to him with patience. "Our eyes look to the Lord our God, till he have mercy upon us" (Ps. 123:2). It is in this atmosphere of expectancy that the cry "Have mercy upon us" has its place (Ps. 123:3). In the prayer songs of the community Israel always asks for and hopes for God's merciful intervention, the demonstration of his grace. This demonstration is the other side of the display of his might, for which the cry for revenge pleads.

The petitions of Psalm 85 stand between help that has already been given and future, final salvation. After God's people have experienced Yahweh's gracious intervention, they turn toward the coming fulfillment, the transformation of the whole world. This will occur when God's glory dwells in the land (85:9). It is then that "Faithfulness will spring up from the ground, and righteousness will look down from the sky" (Ps. 85:11). Then, together with the history of Israel, the creation will be complete.

C. The Cultic Community

The cultic community of Israel gathered at the holy place in Jerusalem. To go there on pilgrimage was "decreed for Israel" (Ps. 122:4). The various procedures and acts of worship on Zion will be dealt with in chap. 3. Here we are only con-

67

cerned with the people of God in the form of the cultic community. By what names is the cultic community that gathers at the holy place known? What expressions are used to identify it? The place to begin is with the word קהל (*qahal*) which has the meaning "gathering," "congregation." For emphasis the קהל עם ("congregation of the people") is called a קהל רב ("great congregation"; Ps. 107:32; 22:25; 35:18; 40:9-10). By this is meant the gathering of the community that takes place at the time of the three great annual festivals of Israel in Jerusalem. This festival community bears the name "Israel," the most common designation for the people when gathered for worship (Ps. 22:3; 50:7; 81:8; 115:9; 118:2; 124:1; 129:1; 130:7; 149:2). The בני ישראל ("children of Israel," Ps. 148:14) gathered together for the cultic festival observance can also be called בני ציון ("children of Zion," Ps. 140:2). Zion as the place where Yahweh is present and as the site of the sanctuary, is, at the same time, "Zion" the community that is called upon to sing praise (Ps. 97:8; 147:12). It is also "Jacob" (Ps. 14:7; 53:6), the posterity of Abraham, or of Jacob (Ps. 105:6; 22:23), who have gathered on Zion. This cultic community is the people of God in the presence of Yahweh ("my people," "thy people": Ps. 3:8; 28:9; 29:11; 33:12; 50:7; 79:13; 80:4; 81:8; etc.). They are an עם עצום ("mighty throng," Ps. 35:18), which praises and honors Yahweh and prays to him. The members of this people are called "saints" (חסדים), "just" (צדקים), "upright" (ישרים), "servants" (עבדים). The cultic community is the קהל חסידים ("congregation of the pious," Ps. 149:1). It is in this community that the priests function (Ps. 132:9, 12). In it the king appears in the presence of all (cf. chap. 4), accompanied by dignitaries (Ps. 68:27). Singers and minstrels intone the praises of God (Ps. 68:25), and choirs praise Yahweh (Ps. 68:26). They all represent the cultic community gathered at the holy place; the functions of the community will be discussed in detail in chap. 3.

The קהל ("congregation") that is gathered on Zion corresponds to the קהל קדשים ("congregation of the holy ones") in the heavenly world (Ps. 89:5). There Yahweh is praised by the angelic powers, his servants (Ps. 103:20), and by the *elohim* (Ps. 29:1). In Psalm 148 the heavenly and earthly communities function as an antiphonal choir, and the whole world of heaven and earth is caught up in the praise of God.

Israel as present in the cult before Yahweh is the community that is spoken to and that hears. The call goes out, "Hear, O my people, and I will speak; O Israel, I will testify against you" (Ps. 50:7; cf. Ps. 81:8). In the gathered community Yahweh makes "the power of his works" known (Ps. 111:6), because "he has caused his wonderful works to be remembered" (Ps. 111:4). The קהל (*qahal*) is a hearing community. In the expectation that a voice will be heard, a prominent (prophetic) speaker proclaims, "Let me hear what God the Lord will speak, for he will speak peace to his people, to his saints" (Ps. 85:8). Another transmitter of the word of Yahweh to his community designates the act of hearing the divine voice by saying, "I heard a voice I had not known" (Ps. 81:5). The *verbum alienum* in its new, acutely foreign form addressed the community. But the one empowered to speak also sees the frightening reality that Israel did not hear or heed the call of God and his words to them (Ps. 81:11). Therefore, the message to the cultic community is accompanied by the words of Yahweh in the first person, in an urgent, almost begging plea, "O that my people would listen to me, that Israel would walk in my ways!" (Ps. 81:13).

Israel as assembled in worship at the holy place is the answering community. They know that they are the people who are near to Yahweh (Ps. 148:14).

Therefore, as the result of being addressed by God the תפלת עמך, the prayer of God's people (Ps. 80:4), rises anew again and again. Priests and singers urge the people of Israel to speak to Yahweh and tell them what they are to say (Ps. 118:2-4; 124:1; 129:1). Note the fuller discussion of this theological outline in connection with the "prayer songs of the community."

On Zion Israel comes into the presence of Yahweh with joy and jubilation as the community that honors and praises God. "Let Israel be glad in his Maker, let the sons of Zion rejoice in their King!" (Ps. 149:2). Rejoicing and joy are heard in the gatherings of God's people (Ps. 48:11; 97:8), as illustrated by the cry, "Blessed are the people who know the festal shout, who walk, O Lord, in the light of thy countenance" (Ps. 89:15). Psalm 118:15 speaks of songs of victory "in the tents of the righteous." Joy and rejoicing accompany the praise of God. The חסדים ("saints," Ps. 30:4) and the צדקים ("righteous," Ps. 32:11) are called on to offer praise. God's praise is to sound forth in the קהל חסידים. When Israel appears before Yahweh on Zion, the people are exhorted, "Praise the Lord, O Jerusalem! Praise your God, O Zion!" (Ps. 147:12). In praise and adoration the cultic community is fully committed to Yahweh, looks away from itself, and fulfills its destiny as the "people of Yahweh" (Ps. 79:13; 95:7; 100:3). The praise of God is the highest joy, the fulfillment of life (Ps. 63:3-8), because those who praise God are "beside themselves," enjoying the happiness of God's presence. In praise the קהל ("congregation") is moving toward the consummation of creation: "Let everything that breathes praise the Lord!" (Ps. 150:6). "Praise is man's most characteristic mode of existence: praising and not praising stand over against one another like life and death: praise becomes the most elementary 'token of being alive' that exists: from generation to generation the hymns of the thanksgiving community flow on ('bubble'!) (Ps. 145:4-7). How one-sidedly praise had its home in life and in life alone can be seen in the fact that the people of God at praise regarded itself as standing shoulder to shoulder with the community of divine beings before the throne of Jahweh" (von Rad, 1962, pp. 369-370). Praise is not only a "category" within the Psalter; praise of God sounds through all the Psalms and rises even *de profundis*, out of the depths of tribulation. To praise God is the destiny of Israel, because praise includes the confession that God's people know that they are "absolutely dependent" on Yahweh and that everything which they have received or will receive is the result of his goodness as creator. Thus praise is Israel's appropriate response.

In the gathering of the "great congregation" the individual who has been rescued from trouble and distress brings his thanks and fulfills his vows. The one praying in Psalm 22 relies on the fact that Yahweh, the "praise of Israel," rescued the people's ancestors, who trusted in him and cried out to him (Ps. 22:3-5). From generation to generation Yahweh was the content, the "object," and the real meaning of praise, because those giving thanks brought their תהלה ("praise") as the תודה ("thanksgiving") to him as the God who liberates and saves. The individual in trouble and forsaken by God lays claim to the mystery and wonder of Yahweh's faithfulness to which the "great congregation" bears testimony. He speaks the prayer language of the קהל ("congregation"). If he experiences deliverance and help, then his praise begins with the words, "I will tell of thy name to my brethren; in the midst of the congregation I will praise thee" (Ps. 22:22; cf. Ps. 22:25; 35:18; 40:9-10; 107:32). Thankful testimony to Yahweh's help and his faithfulness in bringing deliverance is offered in the קהל ("congregation"). In this way the one expressing thanks in prayer and song becomes a part of the "cloud of witnesses," who were spoken of in Ps. 22:3-5. He too exalts the "Praise of Israel"—Yahweh, who is enthroned in holiness (Ps. 22:3). The participation of the individual in the language of prayer and praise of the קהל ("congregation") leads him back into the cultic community, and thus the individual adds his voice to the praise that Israel offers. The deliverance which he has experienced does not become a "theme in itself" but leads to an exalting of the name of Yahweh (Ps. 22:22). Thus the worshiper fulfills the vow of praise and thanks that was made in the hour of deepest need. It is fulfilled before Yahweh, "in the presence of all his people" (Ps. 116:14).

The cultic community expects and prays for blessing from Yahweh. We repeatedly encounter the prayer, "Thy blessing be upon thy people!" (Ps. 3:8; 29:11; 129:8). "O save thy people, and bless thy heritage" (Ps. 28:9). "Bless us!" (Ps. 67:1, 6, 7). ברכה ("blessing") is the comprehensive support of and stimulus to life, and to life in community in its growth, prosperity, happiness and well-being, in its success and its achievements. In the cultic realm blessing is in response to petition, but it is also a gift mediated to the recipient by the priest. We should remember "that the priest mediates Yahweh's blessing but does not himself bestow it" (Wehmeier, 1970, p. 147). This understanding of blessing is especially relevant to Ps. 118:26; 128:5; 134:3.

When we consider the way in which blessing is understood in the Psalter, its context in the history of religion should always be kept in mind. "The Old Testament knows that the experience of blessing did not have its origin in anything specifically Yahwistic. In order to express this phenomenon, the Old Testament used an expression that from all appearances did not originally have any theological nuances, but belonged to an animistic view of life and designated the power of multiplication and growth. The original concept of a power that dwelt in inanimate objects, living beings, and humans was, however, thoroughly transformed when it was brought into relationship with the activity of the God who is active in the history of his people" (Wehmeier, 1970, p. 227). Thus blessing is to be understood as the direct consequence of divine activity, but specifically as the consequence of *his* activity, *his* power that brings blessing. In this way Yahweh's "pancausality" is safeguarded in a comprehensive manner in relation to the concept of blessing. It is *Yahweh's* blessing that comes upon Israel (Ps. 3:8), not an anonymous manifestation of power. Anyone in the Old Testament who "blesses" is a mediator of Yahweh's power to bless. No human, but only Yahweh bestows blessing. Thus the priest's blessing is not a form of condescension proceeding from the office and enlivened with religious ceremony, but rather a mediating function, set forth at the command and with the full authority of Yahweh.

A distinctive feature of the Psalms is the fact that they speak of the blessing of Yahweh in such a way that Yahweh is the recipient, the object of human "blessing." For example, Psalm 34 begins with the statement, "I will bless the Lord at all times" (Ps. 34:1). Here and at other places in the Psalter ברך has the meaning "to praise." What does this mean concretely? Horst explained the significance as follows: "To recognize someone in every form of his power and of his innate majesty" (1947–1948, p. 31). Wehmeier, however, expressed more perceptively the meaning and intention of the concept of praise in בֵּרֵךְ. "Even when God is the object, *brk* is essentially a technical term. In daily usage the verb is characteristic of the well-known formula of praise, and in liturgical language of the recitation of specific prayers of praise (which originally began with *baruk Yhwh*). From there it took on the general meaning "to praise," "to thank," "to laud'' (1970, p. 171). Whoever praises Yahweh begins his praise with an (explicit or implicit) ברוך יהוה (''blessed be Yahweh''). Israel's response is therefore by no means an intensification of the power of God which could be accomplished through praise understood in a magical sense, as earlier interpreters thought on the basis of the meaning of ברך. Horst correctly objected to this method of interpretation, arguing that it involves primarily an acknowledgment of God's already existing, unlimited claim to might and majesty. Whoever ''blesses'' Yahweh praises and honors his sovereign might.

The gatherings of the cultic community are always concerned anew with the hope of Israel. The people who gathered for worship are again and again called on to hope in Yahweh (Ps. 115:9; 130:7; 131:3; etc.). The *piel* form of the Hebrew verb קוה (*qwh*) should not be directly equated with the English verb ''hope.'' It has two connotations that must be kept together. (1) The verb קוה (*qwh*) is close in its basic meaning and in its derivatives to the meaning of בטח (''trust''). It means to ''trust in,'' with particular emphasis on the future. ''Commit your way to the Lord'' (Ps. 37:5). Zimmerli wrote in this connection, '' 'Hope' is not in the first place a situation of tension toward the future, a wish or the indication of a goal that one awaits with tension—it is above all, and the Septuagint emphasizes this very strongly, a situation of surrender and trust, which naturally cannot be realized in a vacuum, but which requires one who stands over against us and calls us to trust'' (1971, p. 8). Israel in its hope is God's people in commitment and trust. (2) The verb קוה (*qwh*) is also directed toward the future, and is closely related (as is shown by its derivatives as well as its basic meaning) to the verb יחל (*yḥl*). It means ''wait,'' ''wait for'' (cf. Ps. 130:5-6; 131:3). Israel's hope looks expectantly toward God's future actions. The decisive factor is that ''according to the Old Testament faith, hope is legitimate only there where God remains the sole Lord, in activity, in gift and in promise, and where man anticipates the future in no other way than as the free gift of God'' (Zimmerli, 1971, p. 24).

The hymns that celebrate Yahweh as king show clearly that Israel's hope is ultimately directed toward the visible and fully real appearance and triumph of Yahweh's royal authority over all the world, that it includes a radical deliverance from and transformation of the present situation, and that it includes all peoples in its salvation (cf. especially Psalms 96; 98). The ''new song'' has as its content the new, future deeds and miracles of Yahweh; it is filled with the newness God will bring when he comes (cf. Ps. 96:1; 98:1; 149:1). In the perspective of Israel's hope, this is the final phase which, as present confidence, is related to the future path that the history of Israel will travel. Thus the cultic community is not involved in a realm far removed from or alien to history. The cultic community is the Israel of God's history, of which the Old Testament in all its parts speaks and testifies. It is the people of God preparing itself in worship to follow its course in the world of the nations and to survive, but which is also judged by Yahweh (Ps. 50:7) and established anew so that it will not fall short of its destiny and goal.

3. The Sanctuary and Its Worship

In the sanctuary in Jerusalem Israel gathered as a worshiping community. This chapter will discuss that sanctuary and its worship. First, certain concepts, expressions, and statements that are basic to worship will be examined (§A). Next, the Zion theology will be presented in detail (§B). Then we will look at the actual cultic practices (§C). And finally we will discuss problems involved in a theology of worship (§D).

A. The Sanctuary

The starting point must be the name of the city of God, Jerusalem. Psalm 125:2 describes its location: "The mountains are round about Jerusalem." The mountains that surround the "city of David," situated on the southeast elevation of the later city of Jerusalem, are higher than הר ציון (Mount Zion), the highest elevation of the city of God. "Jerusalem" is first of all the name of the city which functioned as the "property of the crown" of the Davidic dynasty and as the royal capital of Judah. In the Psalms there are references to the destruction of this city and to its rebuilding (Ps. 79:1-3; 51:18). But Jerusalem is also and especially the designation of the central sanctuary of the Israelite tribes (Ps. 122:3-4). In its "midst" is the "house of the Lord" (116:10). From his temple Yahweh shows his power over Jerusalem (Ps. 68:29). In other words, the city of Jerusalem lies within the sphere of the glory and might of the sanctuary. Thus "Jerusalem" can be used as a synonym for "Zion" (Ps. 102:21; 135:21) and also as a designation for the place where Yahweh dwells (Ps. 135:21).

    The distinctive designation of the Jerusalem sanctuary, however, is the name *Zion*. It is found predominantly in the form הר־ציון "Mount Zion" Ps. 48:2, 11; 74:2; 78:68; 125:1; plural: Ps. 133:3). It is here that Yahweh "dwells," or is enthroned (Ps. 9:11; 76:2; 99:2). הר־ציון (Mount Zion) is the הר־יהוה ("Mount of Yahweh," Ps. 24:3; 132:13). From Zion, God "shines forth," his theophany is manifest, help comes for the oppressed (Ps. 14:7; 20:2; 53:6), and Yahweh's blessing goes forth (Ps. 128:5; 134:3). On Zion, Israel's songs of praise ring out (Ps. 65:1; 147:12).

    As the הר־יהוה ("Mount of Yahweh"), Zion is Yahweh's holy mountain (Ps. 2:6; 3:5; 15:1; 43:3; 48:1; 87:1; 99:9), the "holy place" of the holy God

(מקום קדשו Ps. 24:3), the place where he is present and where he has his "holy habitation" (Ps. 68:5; 76:2). On this "holy mountain" the temple (היכל) stands, the "house of Yahweh" (בית־יהוה). The one praying in Ps. 5:8 proclaims "I. . .will enter thy house, I will worship toward thy holy temple." The worshiping community bows down before the temple, addressing its prayers to the house of Yahweh (Ps. 138:2; cf. chap. 3, §C), because in the temple, in the inner sanctuary (דביר) Yahweh is present, "dwells," is "enthroned." Therefore in prayer one's hands are raised toward the "most holy sanctuary" (Ps. 28:2). For the location and significance of the דביר ("inner sanctuary"), see 1 Kings 6:5ff.; 7:49; 8:6, 8 (Noth, 1968, pp. 95ff.). Temple and inner sanctuary are the "holy place" (קדש). There Yahweh communicates his word (Ps. 60:6; 108:7), and from there come help and comfort for those who are oppressed and needy (Ps. 20:2). The concept of the sanctuary includes the gates of the holy area (Ps. 9:14; 87:2; 100:4; 118:19-20; 122:2) and the outer courts (Ps. 84:2, 10; 92:13; 96:8; 100:4). The worshiping community assembled in the outer courts, and on the festival days participants in the cultic observances entered the temple itself.

The Jerusalem sanctuary on Mount Zion was in pre-Israelite times the sacred hill of the original Canaanite inhabitants, the Jebusites. In chap. 3, §B we will show that the cultic traditions of this Jebusite sanctuary were carried over into the Zion theology of the Old Testament people of God, and how this took place. The question to be considered here is how Israel's sanctuary received its legitimation, that is, how Mount Zion became the central sanctuary to which the tribes of Israel, in accordance with binding ordinances, were to make their pilgrimage (Ps. 122:4). Any attempt to answer this question must investigate the way in which the Ark of Yahweh came to be present there. Even though the Psalms speak only sparingly of this ancient Israelite sanctuary (Ps. 132:8), we still must reckon with the presence in the Psalms of concepts connected with the sanctuary of the Ark (especially in Ps. 24:7-10).

The first temple that can be identified in early Israelite times is in the sanctuary at Shiloh, and Shiloh traditions contain the first explicit statement that the Ark of the Lord stood in a "house." The destruction of this sanctuary sent shock waves through following centuries and had its echo in the Psalter as well (Jer. 7:12; 26:9; Ps. 78:60). The function and meaning of the Ark of Yahweh are attested to in a tradition that served as the *hieros logos* ("sacral tradition") of the Jerusalem sanctuary, where the Ark was kept (see Rost, 1926, pp. 4ff. and Eissfeldt, 1966b, pp. 417-425). This extensive account covers a period whose *terminus a quo* is the locating of the Ark in Shiloh, and whose *terminus ad quem* is the transporting of this holy object to Jerusalem. 1 Sam. 3:1ff. also contains references to the Ark. The sources provide us with a relatively clear picture. In Shiloh the Ark was the sign of Yahweh's presence and the place to which prayers and petitions were directed (1 Sam. 1:3, 9, 10). From the Ark there came the mysterious words of address and the prophetic message (1 Sam. 3:3ff.), for the Ark was the throne of יהוה צבאות ישב הכרבים ("Yahweh Sebaoth, enthroned on the cherubim," 1 Sam. 4:4; 2 Sam. 6:2; cf. above, chap. 1, §A). Above the most holy place the holy God was present with his כבוד (*kabod*, "glory"; 1 Sam. 4:21). The ark, however, was not only the throne of the God who in the cult was honored as present; it was also carried into battle as the palladium of the "holy war" (1 Sam. 4:3). The army welcomed this sign of Yahweh's presence with a תרועה, a great shout of joy (1 Sam. 4:5). Wherever the Ark made its appearance it was received with fear and joy (1 Sam. 6:13; 2 Sam. 6:9). Burnt offerings and sacrifices were presented before it (1 Sam. 6:14f.). The fate of the Ark can be summarized concisely. During the Philistine invasions, Israel's most holy object fell into the hands of the enemy army (1 Sam. 4:11) and was set up in the temple of the god Dagon as booty of war. Yet even in the land of the Philistines Yahweh demanded the honor due to him (1 Sam. 6:5). The Ark narrative stresses with particular emphasis that the God of Israel was always present above this his throne and that he displayed his might even in foreign lands. The Philistines had to return the Ark, and it came first to Bethshemesh (1 Sam. 6:12), and then to Kiriathjearim (1 Sam. 6:21; Ps. 132:6). A ceremony used when the Ark was transported can be recognized in 1 Sam. 6:7f., 14f. and 2 Sam. 6:3ff. It is not easy, however, to determine what significance was ascribed to this rite. Probably the people expected that Yahweh would choose to show the draft animals the way to go and would make the decision on the place where he would dwell. The "chosen place" was probably designated by a divine act of choice in a corresponding ritual.

After David had conquered the Jebusite city of Jerusalem, and this city-state, his royal possession, had been designated as the metropolis of the dual kingdom of Judah and Israel, the ruler had the double task of reviving the pan-Israelite central sanctuary that had perished when Shiloh fell and of giving it a new life in the form of a national cult. The events that were basic to and constitutive of the Jerusalem sanctuary are portrayed in the *hieros logos* ("sacral tradition") of the Ark narrative. The king rescued the holiest of ancient Israelite objects from its obscurity in Kiriathjearim and brought it to Jerusalem. This procedure was of decisive significance (Ps. 132:5ff.). By virtue of the presence of the Ark in the city of David, Jerusalem was raised to the rank of Israelite cultic center. In this way traditions and institutions of ancient Israel were transferred to the Zion sanctuary (cf. Noth, 1957e, pp. 172-187). Jerusalem was now the chosen place (Ps. 78:68; 87:1; 132:13). The *hieros logos* ("sacral tradition") of the Ark narrative thus clearly intends to announce that the history of worship in Jerusalem is a continuation of the Shiloh tradition, the previous site of the Ark. It is beyond question that the Ark narrative, as the basic documentary evidence of the choice of Jerusalem, had great significance. For pilgrims it was a demonstration of the central dignity and significance of the new sanctuary for Israel, and it instituted the ordinance that from then on the tribes were to make the pilgrimage to the Zion sanctuary (Ps. 122:4).

We may assume that the priests repeatedly communicated the *hieros logos* ("sacral tradition") of the Ark narrative to the pilgrims and dramatized it for them. At first there must have been significant difficulties. David had moved the Ark to the new metropolis by his own power and authority. Without question this act was an innovation in the realm of sacral law. Perhaps the explanation is that the ceremony mentioned in 2 Sam. 6:3ff. was intended to stress that in a free act of choice Yahweh, the God who was enthroned above the Ark, had chosen Jerusalem exclusively (1 Sam. 6:7ff.; Ps. 132:13). In the face of the conservative cultic ordinances and laws of ancient Israel the reference to the service which the king rendered by restoring the Ark to honor could hardly have had decisive significance.

The cultic significance of the final phase of the Ark narrative, in which the transfer of the Ark to the Jerusalem sanctuary is portrayed, will be investigated later (chap. 3, § C). Here it is important to consider the traditions and the settings in which the material concerning the Ark was preserved and handed on. For the meaning of the expression יהוה צבאות ישב הכרבים ("Yahweh Sebaoth, enthroned on the cherubim") see chap. 1, § A. The warlike concepts of Yahweh, "mighty in battle," which are connected with the Ark are clearly seen in Psalm 24:7-10. Even though the Ark itself is mentioned in the Psalter only in Psalm 132, we may assume that all the richness of the old traditions and concepts were taken into the Jerusalem sanctuary by the act that is recounted in 2 Samuel 6. More important than the borrowing and adapting of local cultic traditions from the Jebusite sanctuary was the bringing to the sanctuary of the ancient Israelite traditions and institutions connected with the Ark. Jerusalem became an Israelite sanctuary, not a cultic site that would be subject to new royal ordinances. Everything that has been said above fits this context and testifies to it.

In Jerusalem the "Shepherd of Israel" (Ps. 80:1) "dwells" and is "enthroned upon the cherubim," and he comes to be designated by and honored with the titles "king," "judge," "Mighty God," and "creator" (cf. chap. 1, § B). He dwells on Zion (Ps. 9:11; 132:13-14), and his throne is in heaven (Ps. 11:4; 103:19; 123:1). These two concepts, as has been shown in another context, are not mutually exclusive. Psalm 11:4 says, "The Lord is in his holy temple, the Lord's throne is in heaven." Our starting point is the following explanation. "The God who is enthroned (invisibly) in this place breaks through the limits of space. This is not to be understood as a spiritualized concept of God, but rests on a mythological understanding of space, for which the temple (mountain of God), the place where God is present, is the place where the categories of earthly and heavenly are abolished, since the sanctuary represents the entire cosmos" (Maier, 1965, pp. 66f.). "Psalm 24:7-10 shows that in the sanctuary the dimensions of space are broken through and transcended. The gates of the temple are exhorted to lift up their 'heads,' that is, their lintels, in order to provide room for the entrance of Yahweh Sebaoth, whom earthly space cannot encompass" (Metzger, 1970, p. 145). In Isa. 6:1ff. as well, the cube-shaped room is rent open, and above Yahweh's earthly throne the heavenly world is revealed in all its nearness, which at the same time includes the heights and majesty and holiness that transcend this world. The decisive factor is that Yahweh is present; and wherever he is present, the heavenly world is opened up. Thus the concept developed that "only Yahweh's feet rest on the Ark in the temple. God's 'high and exalted' throne above the cherubim reaches far beyond them into the heavenly heights" (Zimmerli, 1979, on Ezek. 43:7). And in Ps. 132:7 the Ark is called his "footstool."

It was עדות לישראל ("decreed for Israel") that the tribes went on pilgrimage to Jerusalem (Ps. 122:4). The pilgrimage to the Zion sanctuary always took place at the three great annual festivals. For the clans and families it was the high point of their lives. They looked forward to the days of festival with desire and longing, especially on occasions when a pilgrimage was not possible (Ps. 42:2-5). The pilgrim journey began with the exhortation to pilgrimage, "Come, let us go up to the mountain of the Lord, to the house of the God of Jacob" (Isa. 2:3). "I was glad when they said to me, 'Let us go to the house of the Lord' " (Ps. 122:1). In an expansion in eschatological terms, Isa. 2:2ff. describes the crowds streaming to the gathering place, as was customary in Israel before the start of the days of the festival. The pilgrims gladly took on themselves all the difficulties of the journey. They had to pass through arid regions (Ps. 84:6) with loads of gifts and animals to be sacrificed (Jer. 41:5). Their longing grew as they approached the place where the living God was present (Ps. 84:1, 7). The one offering the prayer in

Psalm 122 recalls the splendid moment of the arrival in the sanctuary, "Our feet have been standing within your gates, O Jerusalem" (v. 2). If the pilgrimage was accompanied by songs designated especially for it, then the "songs of Zion" were probably sung on the way, but especially when the pilgrims were standing immediately before the gates of the city of God (cf. *Comm.*, Intro. §6, 4). We can easily imagine that such songs as Psalms 46; 48; 76; 84; and 122 had such a Sitz-im-Leben. But the jubilation of the Zion songs fell silent when the pilgrims entered Jerusalem. Petitions and wishes for Zion were poured out before Yahweh (Ps. 122:6-9). Intercessory prayers were offered for the king as the proprietor of the temple (Ps. 84:8-9). Then began the cultic observance of the festival itself, which will be discussed in detail below.

The relationship of Israel and the clans and families of God's people to the sanctuary can best be made clear by examining the understanding which they had of time. The days and weeks of the year that were not times of festival passed by in the rhythm of work, as recounted in the peasant calendar from Gezer, a piece of writing inscribed on a limestone tablet from ca. 1000 B.C. The calendar begins with October/November, the start of the new year according to the ancient Canaanite calendar.

> His two months are (olive) harvest,
> > His two months are planting (grain),
> > > His two months are late planting;
> His month is hoeing up of flax,
> > His month is harvest of barley,
> > > His month is harvest and feasting;
> His two months are vine-tending,
> > His month is summer fruit. (Albright, 1955, p. 320)

The peasant calendar marks the natural order of the year and was organized around the great harvest festivals, which Israel borrowed and then made its own through adding Israelite traditions and cultic practices, without eliminating the elements of harvest festival and thanksgiving (Ps. 65:9-13; 67:6-7). The time of work passes with toil and trouble (Ps. 90:9-10). Thus the Sabbath, which in ancient Israel had no cultic significance, may well have been a distinctive symbol—a sign that all time belongs to Yahweh. Everyone who "sanctifies" the Sabbath by abstaining from all work is giving back to Yahweh that which belongs to him alone—time. But the Sabbath as a symbol of time was not able even to approach the great significance of the festival worship in the sanctuary, as far as the understanding of time is concerned. "For a day in thy courts is better than a thousand elsewhere" (Ps. 84:10). Time spent in the holy precincts, in the presence of the living God, is new time, qualitatively filled. It is different time, compared to the days and weeks at home. It is filled time. Thus in this connection God's people can confess, "Thy steadfast love is better than life" (Ps. 63:3). Joy and praise of God in the sanctuary have a tendency to permeate and fill all of life. "So I will bless thee as long as I live" (Ps. 63:4). "I will bless the Lord at all times; his praise shall continually be in my mouth" (Ps. 34:1). The statement, "I shall dwell in the house of the Lord for ever" (RSV margin, "as long as I live") (Ps. 23:6), is not merely a confession of faith uttered by the Levites, but an expression of the longing of all those who have "tasted" and "seen" the blessing bestowed by the holy place (Ps. 34:8). "Blessed are those who dwell in thy house, ever singing thy praise" (Ps. 84:4).

It would be erroneous to ascribe this exaltation and ecstasy to the influence of the holy precincts themselves. The life that is exalting and enobling, filling and fulfilling, which the ancient Israelites experienced in the sanctuary, is life that comes from Yahweh the אֵל־חַי ("God of life"). "For with thee is the fountain of life; in thy light do we see light" (Ps. 36:9). This is a key sentence for our understanding of Israel's cultic life. Fulfilled life is not the result of some magic power, but the result of the power of the *Deus praesens,* the gift of his steadfast love; it is blessing and *shalom* received from him. The personal relationship to the God who bestows these gifts is never clouded or brought into question by a power attached to some sphere or material object. Sanctuary and temple are signs of holiness only insofar as they are places at which the holy God manifests his presence and his gifts. Even when "traces of magic piety" appear, they are rudimentary formulas of foreign origin rather than relevant components of Old Testament faith.

B. The Zion Theology

In the same psalms which contain a detailed portrayal of the sanctuary on Zion, or Jerusalem, the city of God, we find also a remarkable Zion theology. The primary passages are the category "songs of Zion," where elements of this conceptual realm are found (cf. *Comm.,* Intro. § 6, 4; § 10, 2; Jeremias, 1971, pp. 183-198). Specifically, in Psalms 46; 48; and 76 the reader encounters remarkable concepts, descriptions, and expressions by which Zion or Jerusalem is praised and glorified. All the geographical, topographical, and other recognizable features indicate that these elements did not belong originally to the Israelite sanctuary. Rather they entered the world of the Old Testament people of God as secondary elements (as did the appellations of Yahweh, cf. above, chap. 1, § 2) and came to be applied to the holy city, a development that undoubtedly had already taken place in pre-Israelite (i.e., Jebusite) times. The problem that this poses could not be recognized by earlier Old Testament scholars and was obscured by inadequate explanations. For example, Gunkel attempted to understand the foreign elements in Psalms 46; 48; and 76 as "eschatological concepts," and consequently he "eschatologized" his overall explanation of these psalms. In recent decades, however, it has gradually become clear that in those psalms, and in other parts of the Psalter as well, we are dealing with quite ancient cultic traditions, which for the most part had already undergone a long history of transmission in pre-Israelite times in Syria and Canaan, a history which is no longer identifiable in detail and the phases of whose development can no longer be ascertained. Since we are still unable to understand the history of the transmission of these foreign concepts and terminology which came to be applied to the city of Jerusalem, any reconstruction must confine itself to major themes. This can be done by seeking with great caution for parallels in the history of religion and for hypothetical connections with Israel.

In Ps. 48:2 the location of Jerusalem is described as הר ציון ירכתי צפון ("Mount Zion, in the far north"). This "topographical" note cannot be explained in terms of the geography of the land of Israel. Therefore we must ask, What does it mean to call "Mount Zion" צפון, "north"? Within the Old Testament itself, Isa. 14:13-14 provides a clue. This text contains a taunt song directed against the king of Babylon. He himself speaks with arrogance and hybris: "I will ascend to heaven; above the stars of God I will set my throne on high; I will sit on the mount of assembly in the far north; I will ascend above the heights of the clouds, I will make myself like the Most High.'' Even though this song may have been composed in relatively late times out of various mythological elements, it still shows that Mount צפון (Zaphon) (quite apart from any reference to Jerusalem) was a mountain of the gods, soaring into the heavens, above clouds and stars. This sacred mountain was the throne of ''God Most High'' (עליון) and the place of the ''assembly'' of the gods (see above, chap. 1, § B). It is now possible to identify Mount Zaphon more closely in terms of the history of religion and to locate it topographically. In Syro-Phoenecia, north of ancient Ugarit (Ras Shamra), stood the holy mountain on which, according to ancient Syrian tradition the Baal of Heaven *(b'l spn)* was enthroned as the ''highest god.'' It is to be identified with the classical Mount Casius, the modern Jebel el 'Aqra. Zaphon was simply the mountain of the gods. In the culture of Syria and Canaan it was the equivalent of Mount Olympus, and was probably also thought of as being higher than all other mountains, rising above all elevations (cf. Isa. 2:2-3). This means then that universal preeminence was ascribed to Zaphon, as is appropriate for the place where ''God Most High'' dwells above, (chap. 1 § B). Otto Eissfeldt has shown how the name and the accompanying concepts, the mythological understanding of Zaphon, came to be transferred to other cultic sites that had been elevated to the rank of ''chief sanctuaries'' (1932; see also Albright, 1950, pp. 2-14; Savignac, 1953, pp. 95f.).

More recently there have been detailed studies of the concepts involved in Zaphon in the Ugaritic texts (see especially W.H. Schmidt, 1966, pp. 32ff.; Gese, 1969, pp. 119ff.). The name and the dwelling (throne) of the deity are closely connected in the Ugaritic texts. The ''highest god'' has his throne on the ''highest mountain.'' Baal is called *b'l spn, il spn, b'l mrym spn*, etc. (W.H. Schmidt, p. 32). Mount Zaphon is the cultic dwelling of Baal. When he overcame his enemies he reigned there as king. There is considerable evidence that in the Syro-Canaanite realm the name and the concepts connected with the divine mountain Zaphon were early transferred to other prominent cultic mountains. In any case, the cultic tradition known at Ugarit of the ''Mountain of the North,'' Mount Zaphon, came to be applied to Jerusalem, and this happened in the pre-Israelite (Jebusite) era. The following parallel to Ps. 48:2 is striking. Baal has his messengers announce, ''In the midst of my mountain, the divine in the sanctuary in the mountain of my own possession, in the beautiful place, on the hill of victory'' (cf. W.H. Schmidt, p. 34). In commenting on this quotation, Schmidt says, ''The concept of the mountain of god in the north, on which Baal resided as king, served to glorify the dwelling of Yahweh the King . . . . Israel took over for Yahweh and Israel that which the Canaanites said of their mountain of the gods'' (p. 34).

As the dwelling and throne of ''God Most High'' the ''mountain in the North,'' Mount Zaphon, was the center of the universe, the navel of the world'' (cf. Holma, 1915, pp. 41-43). If ''God Most High'' was also ''creator of the world'' (chap. 1, § B) then the place where his throne stood must be the center of all things. The religious universalism which is expressed in monarchical עליון (*'Elyon*)-theology finds expression also in the concepts of the cultic site. The influence which these borrowed traditions had for the theology of Zion can be seen most clearly in Ps. 48:2. As Zaphon, Zion can be termed משוש כל־הארץ (''joy of all the earth,'' Ps. 48:2). The majesty of the place where Yahweh sits enthroned shines out into all the world. Everywhere the beauty and splendor of the mountain of God are spoken of (Lam. 2:15). The splendors of paradise came to be associated with the concept of Mount Zaphon, and a great wealth of cultic and mythological concepts was transferred to Jerusalem, the city of God, and to Mount Zion. Yet all these concepts are merely the glorification of Yahweh, the God of Israel, or of the place where he is present. For Israel this quite early expansion of the belief in Yahweh in universal terms represented a breaking out of the limits of the older, particularistic tradition. Beginning with the first adoption of the Jerusalem cultic traditions, a knowledge of the world and a conquest of the world in light of the royal majesty of Yahweh as "God Most High" was set in motion and could not be arrested. In this connection the cult sanctuary on Zion exerted influences without which the "universalism" of the Old Testament prophets cannot be understood. The Zion theology wrought a cosmic expansion of unprecedented extent, but at the same time a consciousness of the central position of Israel, which both stabilized and intensified the old tradition of being the chosen of God. The consciousness of being at the center of the universe was not a postulate, nor was it determined by nature or mythology, but by divine election and by history. This consciousness enabled Israel to assimilate and subordinate the foreign cultic traditions.

In a passage that glorifies the city of God, Ps. 46:4 refers to streams which "make glad the city of God." In the light of the descriptions in the context it is obvious that the נהר פלגיו ("streams of the river") cannot refer to the Gihon spring at the foot of the hill on which the old city stood. Nor should we identify them with hidden (underground) streams, such as those mentioned in rabbinic mythology. It should be noted that Ps. 68:9 and Isa. 33:21 also speak of "streams" in Jerusalem and that Joel 3:18; Ezekiel 47; and Zech. 14:8 provide impressive parallels (on Ezekiel 47 cf. Zimmerli, 1979, ad rem). Gunkel (1921, pp. 48ff.) and Gressmann (1929, pp. 179f.) were the first to recognize that these texts contain mythical metaphors and concepts of a paradise, a garden of God, which were transferred to the city of Jerusalem. This garden of God is described in Genesis 2, where streams are also spoken of. By using the pattern primeval time/end time, Gunkel, in reference to Ps. 46:4, concluded that these were eschatological concepts. But all these explanations remain confused and indistinct. It remained for the texts from Ras Shamra (Ugarit) to provide new and highly concrete details and parallels. It became clear that the metaphors and concepts relating to the dwelling of God surrounded by streams have a direct relationship to the cultic tradition of the mountain of God as the dwelling of "God Most High." This refutes the relevance of the primordial time/end time schema. The Ugaritic texts present the god El, who dwells "at the source of the two rivers, in the midst of the waters of the two primeval oceans" (*mbk nhrm, qrb apq thmtm*). Gese (1969, p. 98) explains the Ugaritic formulation as follows: "The dual form (the two oceans) expresses the totality of the waters, and the mention of both primeval ocean and rivers must be interpreted as designating the totality of the primeval waters, at the springs of which, or in the midst of which he dwells. . . . El's dwelling by the primeval waters, which according to the ancient Near Eastern view of the world surrounded the earth, if not the entire cosmos, is an expression of the idea that El is the divine ground of being. The details can be compared with the dwelling of the god Ea who, at least as described by Berossos, shows many similarities with El in his nature as god of Wisdom, the wielder of divine powers. In metaphors and concepts that have been considerably simplified (as far as mythological complexity goes), the aspects of the "streams" (*nhrm*) which can be identified at Ugarit were transferred to the holy city of Jerusalem. What is said in other Old Testament passages, for example, about the "temple spring" (Joel 3:18; Ezekiel 47; Zech. 14:8) seems to fit into the context of these traditions. This may also apply to the "bronze sea" (1 Kings 7:23-26). Nevertheless, the complex of concepts that was applied to Jerusalem can be identified only through rudimentary relationships or mere allusions. It is clear that these deviations from and fragmentation of the borrowed materials involve the elimination of crassly mythological elements. But the application to Jerusalem of views that can be recognized in the literature from Ugarit undoubtedly took place in the ancient Jebusite sanctuary, specifically in the course of the borrowing of traditions of אל עליון ("God Most High," Gen. 14:18ff.). For detailed treatments see H. Schmid, 1955, pp. 187f.; Rohland, 1956, pp. 127ff.

The statement in Ps. 46:4, "There is a river whose streams make glad the city of God," is merely an embellishment in reference to Zion, but the context shows clearly that the concept of the primeval ocean (*qrb apg thmtm*), which is found also at Ugarit, has echos here, so that we are reminded of the powers of chaos (v. 5). All the metaphors and allusions are in the service of the declaration concerning the superior power of Israel's God, the protective might of the one who is enthroned on Zion and who intervenes for his people (Ps. 46:1, 3, 7, 11). This enunciates a further theme of the Zion theology.

Enemies threaten the city of God (Ps. 46:6; 48:4; 76:5-6). In Ps. 46:3 the tumultuous, chaotic primeval floods, aroused by an earthquake, threaten the mountains, symbols of all that is fixed and permanent. This cosmic motif probably represents the original form of the threat (cf. Ps. 93:3-4). In Ps. 46:6 the destructive powers of chaos make their appearance in a "historicized" form: "The nations rage, the kingdoms totter." It is noteworthy that these enemy powers are characterized as "kingdoms" (Ps. 46:6), "princes" (Ps. 76:12), or "kings" (Ps. 48:4; 76:12). The city of God is surrounded by hostile armies (Ps. 2:2; 48:4ff.). The foes threaten and roar like "many waters" (Isa. 17:12f.; Jer. 6:23). Obviously, the myth of the raging of the chaotic primeval waters has been applied specifically to Jerusalem in a historicized, political form, from which all mythological concepts and events have been eliminated. It is unlikely that this involves the cultic dramatization of a battle, as Mowinckel proposed (1921, p. 128). Rather, these are ancient cultic traditions that were appropriated by Israel, given new form, and stripped of their mythological significance. It is highly significant that the historicizing of the cosmic struggle against chaos first took place during the transmission of the material in Israel. This explanation also helps us to understand how it was that the ancient Israelite traditions of the holy war became a part of the motif of war among the nations. It is clear that Psalm 46 contains concepts and expressions drawn from the wars of Yahweh. The cultic site of Jerusalem was the place where Yahweh's power in battle and his supreme majesty were proclaimed and impressively depicted to the assembled nation of Israel. The foreign elements were the means for presenting the material in a vivid manner. In age-old categories they demonstrated the sovereignty of Israel's God and his superiority over all his foes and all the forces of ungodliness. On the theme "Foes" see chap. 5.

When the foes attack, it is shown that the city of God is unconquerable. This is supported by several factors. Jerusalem is the "city of God" (Ps. 46:4a; 48:1b; 87:3). Here is found the "holy habitation" of the Most High (Ps. 46:4b; 76:2; 87:5). The city of God is situated on Yahweh's "holy mountain" (Ps. 48:2;

87:1), on the summit of "Mount Zaphon," which, as has been shown, reaches into the heavens (Ps. 48:2). Here the earthly and the heavenly worlds meet. But the decisive reason for the invincibility of the city of God is the fact that Yahweh is "in the midst of her" (Ps. 46:5; 48:3). This is no area of taboo protected by magic; rather, "The Lord of hosts is with us; the God of Jacob is our refuge" (Ps. 46:7, 11). The theme of the invincibility of Jerusalem seems to rest on a very old tradition (2 Sam. 5:6; cf. Hayes, 1963, pp. 419-426). It was a firm certainty that Zion "cannot be moved," but "abides for ever" (Ps. 125:1; Isa. 26:1). When the foes attack they will be beaten back and destroyed (Ps. 76:3-6; 48:5, 6; Isa. 17:13-14; 24:21; 29:8). Yahweh himself shatters his foes with his thunder (Ps. 46:6), with his "rebuke" (Ps. 76:6; Isa. 17:13), and with the "terror" of God (Ps. 46:8; Isa. 17:14). He destroys their weapons (Ps. 46:9; 76:3-6). A careful analysis of all these factors shows that, on the one hand, such motifs as the "rebuke" had their origin in the stream of pre-Israelite mythological tradition, which assumed historicized form in Jerusalem. In the unconquerable city of God, Yahweh confronts his enemies as the creator God who "rebuked" the primeval waters (cf. Isa. 17:13; Ps. 76:6). On the other hand, the ancient Israelite traditions of holy war can be clearly recognized (Psalm 46). Two streams of tradition have merged. If we were to accept the hypothesis that the historicizing of the mythological concepts of the conquest of the enemy (chaotic) powers took place in the Israelite phase of the transmission of the traditions, then the motif of the "unconquerable city of God" should be assigned to the Jebusite tradition (cf. 2 Sam. 5:6).

Jerusalem, the city of God, is the abode of peace. In her the *shalom* of Yahweh reigns. In the Psalms the concept שלום (*shalom*) is used in four distinct meanings. (1) The people pray for, hope for, and await שלום for the land and for the whole earth. It will be manifested in the form of fruitfulness and undisturbed growth, prosperity, and life (Ps. 72:3, 7; 85:11; 147:14). (2) Israel prays for, hopes for, and awaits שלום (*shalom*) for the whole nation (Ps. 29:11; 85:8; 125:5; 128:6). (3) שלום (*shalom*) is the basic theme involved in the activity of the king (Ps. 72:3-7). (4) שלום (*shalom*) is a distinctive force that is available to the city of ירושלם (Jerusalem; Ps. 122:6ff.). The last of these four relationships sets the theme for this present discussion. The people should pray for the שלום (*shalom*) of Jerusalem (Ps. 122:6). The object for which they should pray is made explicit in Ps. 122:7, "Peace be within your walls, and security within your towers." The following verse makes it clear that שלום (*shalom*) does not involve the sphere of magic, but personal intentions: "For the sake of the house of the Lord our God, I will seek your good (שלום)." Men and women were to live in the שלום (*shalom*) of Jerusalem and find there everything good and wholesome that they could desire. The fact that שלום (*shalom*) is a concept so closely connected with ירושלם (Jerusalem) must involve the deity *Salem*, who had once been worshiped in the Jebusite city, and whose name was perpetuated in the name of the city (cf. Stolz, 1970, pp. 181ff., 240ff., 215 ff.; Steck, 1972, pp. 25ff.

We will not consider here the question of if and how in the Hebrew word שלום (*shalom*) a personal entity can still be recognized, who, as Stolz thinks, can be identified, for example, in Ps. 85:8-10 and Is. 60:17. Neither can we go into the question of the relationship between the terms שלום (*shalom*) and צדק (*zedek*), behind which there might have been deities who were so designated (Stoltz, 1970, pp. 181ff.). On the term שלום (*shalom*) see Stamm and Bietenhard (1959) , Eisenbeis (1969) , Westermann (1969) , Rost (1971) , and H.H. Schmid (1971). Finally, we should raise here the question whether in spite of the test of Ps. 122:6ff. we can follow Steck in saying that "the cultic tradition of Jerusalem is based, not on a world to which peace is to be brought, but on a world that already has been pacified" (1972, p. 27). We should draw a careful distinction: On the one hand there are the pre-Israelite שׁלום (*shalom*) traditions which depict the city of God in the light of complete happiness and prosperity and which, as fundamental elements of the glorification of the city, were borrowed by the Zion theology. On the other hand, there are the constantly renewed wishes, expectations, and petitions which are voiced less for the cultic site than for the cultic community gathered at the site, and beyond them for all Israel and its land. An investigation of the occurrences of שׁלום (*shalom*) in the Psalms leads to the realization that the word is used overwhelmingly in the context of petitions, wishes, and expectations.

In summary, we can say that the themes and motifs of the Zion theology have given us a profile of the cultic traditions of Jerusalem. As has been repeatedly stressed, these traditions stem for the most part from pre-Israelite times. Ancient Canaanite and Syrian motifs and concepts came to be applied to Zion, Jerusalem, the city of God. This occurred in part in the Jebusite period, and in part in Israelite times. It is highly significant that the themes and motifs of Zion theology are to be found especially in the prophecies of Isaiah, the prophet of Jerusalem, or in the prophecies most closely connected with Isaiah: Isa. 17:12ff; 24:21; 26:1; 29:7; 33:20f. The relationship of Jerusalem's cultic traditions to prophecy can be defined as one in which the cultic traditions were the primary element, and the prophecies contained in messages directed toward the future were secondary. In other words, the prophets took their declarations and concepts from the cultic traditions of Jerusalem. In addition to Isaiah and the non-Isaianic prophecies contained in the first part of the book of Isaiah, this holds also for Micah and Jeremiah, and later for Ezekiel, Zephaniah, and Deutero-Isaiah. Rohland has recognized and clearly presented the relations of the Jerusalem cultic tradition to prophecy and the future-directed messages of God's spokesmen (1956, pp. 145f.). In any case that tradition cannot be regarded as a genuine tradition of divine election. None of the themes and motifs that have been considered have any relationship to election, but they do involve a decided glorification of Zion as the place where Yahweh dwells and is enthroned. Therefore to do justice to the materials we should speak of the cultic traditions as involving the glorification of the city of God, and introduce the concept of election only when it can be shown that the election of Israel is a definite component of that glorification.

The explanations advanced above have been questioned and disputed by Wanke (1966). He has endeavored to show that "not only the Korahites and the Psalms ascribed to them, but also the theology expressed in a part of the completed Psalter belong to the postexilic period" (p. 108). Wanke's study pays special attention to the motif of the battle among the nations (pp. 70-99). The observation that in literature outside of Israel there are no parallels for this motif is correct, and much weight is attached to it. He denies the possibility of this motif having been derived from the struggle with primeval chaos (p. 77). This involves prejudgments that bring with them far-reaching consequences. By leaving aside the Psalms, he identified the battle among the nations as an "eschatological motif" in late prophetic passages, such as Zechariah 14; Zechariah 12; Joel 3; and Mic. 4:11-15. The origin of the motif is found in Jeremiah, or in the late preexilic period in general. This, however, reverses the relationship between cultic tradition and prophecy which has been propounded above. Wanke claims that the motif of the battle among the nations was formed in late prophecy and only then introduced into the Psalms (Psalms 46; 48) by the theology of the Korahites. Texts that stand in the way of this line of argument, e.g., Isa. 17:12ff., are assigned to the postexilic period (pp. 116f.) But more serious than all this is his failure to recognize the archaic traditions in Psalms 46 and 48 (and Psalm 78 as well). In addition, basic aspects of research in terms of the history of religion and the history of tradition were ignored from the outset. A methodical and critical discussion of our disagreements could cast light on the various details.

For a critical debate with Wanke's book, see Lutz, 1968, pp. 213ff. Here I will mention only the seven critical objections raised by Lutz. (1) "The texts which Wanke discussed briefly, Zechariah 12 and 14; Joel 3; and Mic. 4:11-13, cannot be automatically cited as examples of the motif of the rage of the nations." (2) "The concept of the 'Foe from the North' is not found in any original context with any of the three basic concepts of the theme—Yahweh, Jerusalem, and the nations." (3) "Even Ezekiel 38–39 can be included in the prehistory of the motif of the rage of the nations only in a limited sense." (4) "The only remaining representatives of the motif of the rage of the nations are Psalms 46; 48; and 78" (Wanke simply passed over the two inconvenient texts, Isa. 8:9-10 and Isa. 17:12-14). (5) "The well-rounded unity characteristic of the motif of the rage of the nations and of the songs of Zion . . . leads to the conclusion that this tradition must have had, even before Isaiah, but at the latest in his day, that fixed form which is represented in the songs of Zion." (6) "It is not the frequency with which a motif or a term appears that determines its age, but the assurance with which it asserts its place in early texts." (7) We must further take into account the assumption "that there was a Jerusalem cultic tradition." For additional criticism of Wanke's position see Metzger (1970, p. 147). (For further literature on the theme of Zion and Jerusalem see Porteous, 1961, pp. 235-252; Schreiner, 1963; H. Schmidt, 1966; Fohrer, 1969, pp. 195-241).

C. Worship in Jerusalem

The greatest danger in the study of Israelite cultic life is one-sidedness and the imposition of uniformity on the presentation of the procedures used in worship. This problematic trend was begun by Mowinckel's hypothesis that there was an enthronement festival of Yahweh. That hypothesis became a powerful magnet, drawing to itself all the cultic bits and pieces of Old Testament tradition and merging them into a unified picture. Since that time many scholars have followed in Mowinckel's footsteps, and the few critical voices that were raised went unheard. Instead, the tendency to impose uniformity on all aspects of the cult was intensified and consolidated phenomenologically through the "pattern" ideology (Hooke, 1958). The emphasis on the phenomenology of cult triumphed. It recognized no differences of place or time, but simply passed over the way the Old Testament cultic traditions, so rich in nuances, were related to history. The dominant factor was the ritual pattern of cult and myth that was believed to be in accord with the ancient Near Eastern cultic ideology, but even the differentiations that needed to be made within Near Eastern cultures were ignored. Noth's critique of the methods used in this approach was not heeded (1957c, pp. 188-229). The place occupied by the hypothesis that Old Testament cult was dominated by the enthronement festival of Yahweh was replaced by that of a "covenant renewal festival," advocated by Weiser in his Psalms commentary (1962), but this merely introduced into the study of worship a new but still one-sided way of forcing everything into a uniform whole.

Anyone who investigates the worship practiced in Jerusalem must not forget this highly problematic process which viewed the cult in a one-sided manner and reduced it to uniformity through a phenomenological approach. The task that confronts us is to identify the nuances of the cultic tradition and establish a careful differentiation. This task is all the more important in that the Psalms do not contain any accounts of ritual practices or any references to rituals, but, at best, fragménts and poetic reflections of individual phases of the ritual. The scholar is tempted to give his imagination free rein and indulge in adventurous reconstructions, stimulated by the rituals of Israel's neighbors in the ancient Near East (on the methodological problems involved, cf. Kraus, 1966, pp. 16ff.).

Pilgrimage to the Zion sanctuary was described (above, chap. 3, § A). The relevant statements were brought together from the individual psalms so that the concepts and expectations of the pilgrims could be identified. The clans and families traveled to Jerusalem, the mountain of Yahweh, with glad songs and the sound of flutes (Isa. 30:29). Their arrival is described in Ps. 122:2, "Our feet have been standing within your gates, O Jerusalem!" It is probably the city gates that are meant here, because the gates of the sanctuary had special significance. Who was worthy to pass through the gates which in Ps. 118:19 are called צדק שערי ("gates of righteousness")? "He who walks blamelessly, and does what is right, and speaks the truth from his heart . . ." (Ps. 15:2; cf. Ps. 24:3-4). In the "gate liturgies" (*Comm.*, Intro. § 6,6) the conditions for admission are made known to those who are arriving to take part in worship. The marks of the צדיק ("righteous") are proclaimed in the שערי צדק ("gates of righteousness"). This was clearly a liturgical act, in which the Torah was recited. We do not know whether or to what extent the conditions for admission were intended to prompt the worshiper's confession. Nor can it be determined whether the Torah statements were to call forth acts of confession and penance, or if so, how this was to be done. Nevertheless, it is possible that confessions of sin had their Sitz-im-Leben in the prayer songs of the individual, used when one was admitted to the sanctuary. It is possible to conclude from Psalm 5 that anyone who was unjustly accused and wanted to appeal to sacral justice in the holy precincts had to undergo a preliminary examination at the gate. No one who was boastful or an evildoer was permitted to come into the presence of Yahweh (Ps. 5:4-6). If the initial questioning was decided according to צדקה ("righteousness"), then the accused was granted admission, but since he had not yet been declared innocent he would affirm, "But I through the abundance of thy steadfast love will enter thy house, I will worship toward thy holy temple in the fear of thee" (Ps. 5:7). The "gates of righteousness" were opened to those who were righteous (Ps. 118:19). And they entered into the sanctuary (Ps. 118:20).

"Three times a year Solomon used to offer up burnt offerings and peace offerings upon the altar which he built to the Lord . . ." (1 Kings 9:25). This notice in the annals shows that the ancient Israelite festival calendar had now established its position as cultic law in Jerusalem. On Israel's cultic calendar (Exod. 23:10-19; 34:18-26; Deut. 16:1-17; Lev. 23:4-44; Num. 28–29) see Kraus, 1966, pp. 26ff. The three great annual festivals were celebrated at the sanctuary on Mount Zion and, as 1 Kings 9:25 indicates, their major feature was the great offering of sacrifices. As far as we can tell, in preexilic times the festival that was really the most significant was the Feast of Tabernacles, held in the autumn (1 Kings 8:2). Only during Josiah's reign did Passover attain preeminence (Deut. 16:1-8; 2 Kings 23:21-22). The Feast of Weeks probably played a subordinate role, at least in the early period. These few passages provide us with our only sketch of what took place in Israel's cultic history. In the Psalms there is hardly a trace of all this to be found. Psalm 81:3-4 is an exception. The (secondary) titles to the Psalms provide no authentic information. This shows how little interest the psalmists took in all the calendars, dates, seasons, and even the rituals. The content of the prayers, songs, and poems is the dominant factor. A sketch based on the cultic calendar can provide us only with an outline of background materials. It shows primarily that each of the three great annual festivals was limited to a single week, but it should be added that the autumn festival was later extended to a longer period. In the week of a festival the first and the last days were of particular significance. On the first day the entrance of the pilgrims must have taken place, followed by a ceremonial. John 7:37 still notes that the last day was the most important day of the feast. What took place during the course of the week can be determined only to a limited extent. In chaps. 4 and 6 we will return to the significance of the royal cult and the role of the individual in Israel's worship. In addition it should be noted that there is no indication at all in the Psalms that any of the songs or prayers had its Sitz-im-Leben anywhere except Jerusalem, or was preserved and transmitted in any other place. On the other hand, it can be established that older traditions or fragments of traditions were adopted in Jerusalem (see especially the exegesis in the *Comm.* on Psalm 68).

Immediately following the entrance ceremony of the ''gate liturgy'' in Ps. 24:1-6 we find the description of the entrance of Yahweh into the sanctuary (24:7-10). It is evident that these two events were directly connected. These were the events of the first day of a festival, perhaps the Feast of Tabernacles. Since Mowinckel's work (1921), Ps. 24:7-10 has consistently been explained in connection with those Psalms in which Yahweh is spoken of as king (Psalms 47; 93; 96; 97; 98; 99), and since the theory of the ''enthronement of Yahweh'' is connected with these psalms, it is necessary at this point to deal with the problem of Yahweh's enthronement and to take a position in regard to it.

The starting point is provided by those psalms in which Yahweh is acclaimed as king (see above). Even though a form-critical analysis of the question whether these psalms belong together raises serious issues (Crüsemann, 1969), it is clear that they belong together thematically (see *Comm.,* Intro. §6, 1bb). In the light of the theme and content of these psalms we may designate Psalms 47; 93; 96; 97; 98; 99 as psalms of Yahweh's kingship. Old Testament research has subjected them to a variety of explanations and interpretations. It was soon recognized that it was meaningless and inadequate to interpret them in terms of historical events, and the eschatological interpretation failed to answer innumerable questions (what *is* ''eschatology''?). Then Mowinckel's cultic interpretation carried the day and was widely accepted. (On the history of the exegesis of these Psalms, see Kraus, 1951b.) Mowinckel included in his cultic explanation various insights and discoveries from the history of religion in Mesopotamia. He constructed an Israelite parallel to the enthronement festival of Marduk, the Babylonian deity. (On the Babylonian festival see Zimmern, 1926; 1928.) Even before Mowinckel, however, Volz (1912) had demonstrated parallels in terms of the history of religion and had suggested the existence of an Israelite New Year's festival. Mowinckel too was of the opinion that the festival of Yahweh's ascension had been held on New Year's day—in his view, the greatest Israelite festival. He regarded the shout יהוה מלך ‎ (''Yahweh reigns'' as the central feature of this Israelite festival, and he interpreted it as an ''enthronement acclamation'' to be translated as ''Yahweh has [now] become king!'' This shout of joy was regarded as the conclusion of a cultic drama, an event with roots deep in the mythology of the change of seasons in nature (1922, 2:16ff.). Each year, as the old year gave way to the new, Yahweh, in Mowinckel's theory, was enthroned anew and acclaimed as king and creator (victor over chaos).

Gunkel (1933) had some reservations about this cultic interpretation, but he accepted it, although he understood the mythic and cultic-dramatic elements of these psalms as primarily eschatological, and assigned them a late preexilic date. It should be added that Mowinckel used the magnet of his enthronement theory to pull together numerous psalms, without first establishing clear criteria for evaluating the form-critical and thematic factors. Gunkel, on the other hand, undertook to limit the number of psalms under consideration to Psalms 47; 93; 96; 97; 98; 99.

In recent decades there have been studies that support or modify Mowinckel's hypotheses, but there have also been a number of critics who have disputed the entire cultic concept (see Stamm, 1955). For further discussion of what follows see *Comm.*, Intro. §10, 1b.

The decisive question for every interpretation of the psalms of Yahweh's kingship is the translation and explanation of the central formula יהוה מלך ("Yahweh reigns"). For many years it was generally accepted that it was an acclamation of enthronement, "Yahweh has (just) become king!" Now there are serious objections to that translation. The lexigraphical evidence is that the verb מלך (*malak*) has two meanings, "to be king," and "to become king." The meaning "be king" (occurring with על ["over"], ב ["in"], ל ["for"]) is found in Gen. 36:31; Josh. 13:12, 21; Judg. 4:2; 9:8; 2 Sam. 16:8; 1 Kings 14:20; etc. The meaning "become king," on the other hand, was assumed to be correct wherever the act of enthronement to the sound of trumpets must have been followed by a corresponding shout acclaiming the king, particularly in 2 Sam. 15:10; 1 Kings 1:11; 2 Kings 9:13. The syntactical relationship of the words, however, is of the greatest importance. 1 Kings 1:11 has מלך אדניהו ("Adonijah has become king"). This sentence beginning with a verb is clearly marked in context as a shout and informs us that a solemn act has just been completed. In translating it, however, there is some uncertainty as to whether emphasis should be placed on the action just concluded ("Adonijah has just become king") or on the state that has now been reached ("Adonijah is now king!"). Light is cast on the syntactic problem by 1 Kings 1:18, where the new situation is described with the significant word order ועתה הנה אדניהו מלך, "And now, behold, Adionijah is king." Since the shout מלך אבשלום ("Absalom reigns," 2 Sam. 15:10), which is raised at the same time as the trumpets sound, is directly connected with the act of enthronement or the ascension to the throne which has just taken place (cf. also 2 Kings 9:13), there seems to be good reason to translate the two-word sentence which begins with מלך as ". . . has (now) become king." On the other hand the reverse order of words depicts a circumstance in which the king in question now finds himself, "He *is* king." When the subject precedes the verb this indicates a circumstance in which the verb מלך functions to mean "to be king."

The significance of these syntactic observations for the psalms of Yahweh's kingship is that יהוה מלך in Ps. 93:1; 96:10; 97:1; and 99:1 is clearly to be translated as "Yahweh is king." Thus only Ps. 47:9 (cf. also Isa. 52:7) would refer to a proclamation of enthronement. It should also be noted that in reference to Israel's monarchical monotheism (chap. 1, §2) and the nations around Israel, the formula יהוה מלך ("Yahweh reigns") has a polemical and confessional ring, so that the sentence should be translated with the emphasis on Yahweh. *"Yahweh* (and no other) is king."* This rejection of the supreme deity proclaimed by Israel's neighbors must be kept in mind (cf. Michel, 1956).

Further literature on the translation and interpretation of the psalms of Yahweh's kingship: H. Schmidt, 1927; Frankfort, 1948; Mowinckel, 1952; Alt, 1953a; Bright, 1956; Gross, 1956; Maag, 1960; Buber, 1967; Lipinski, 1965; W. H. Schmidt, 1966, with further bibliographical references.

The Sanctuary and Its Worship

In addition to the syntactical considerations which rule out any understanding of the formula יהוה מלך ("Yahweh reigns") as an enthronement shout or any direct reference to a cultic enthronement of God, there are other considerations that indicate that it is impossible to conceive that a cultic enthronement of Yahweh took place in Israel's worship. First we must ask how it would even have been possible to act out the enthronement of Yahweh in Israel. There was never any picture or statue of God that could have been placed on a throne, nor is any other cultic emblem known which portrayed Yahweh. The Babylonian "parallels," which have been adduced since the publication of Mowinckel's *Psalmen-Studien 2* in 1922, have their own basis in the massive statues of gods and their ritual elevation to the throne of the temple where the deity was to appear. In Israel the conditions were lacking that would make possible any cultic enactment of the enthronement of Yahweh. In the aniconic Yahweh cultus it would have been absurd to establish processes that would have had to unfold at an abstract level. A second question must be raised. Is it conceivable that the ideology and mythology involved in the adoption of an ancient Near Eastern enthronement festival at the start of the new year (as were presupposed, e.g., in Mesopotamia or in the Baal cult of Syria and Canaan) could have been adapted, even in their rudiments, to the worship of the God of Israel? Anyone who posits an annual enthronement of Yahweh in the worship of Israel must assume—even regard as fundamental—the possibility that Yahweh could lose his lordship for a period of time, that is, that the God of Israel "functioned" in a manner analogous to the dying and rising deities. There is no basis for such an assumption in the psalms of Yahweh's kingship, indeed in the entire Old Testament. Moreover, to assume that the enthronement concept was adapted to the situation found in the worship of Yahweh is a last resort which ends in abstractions and lacks any relationship to the facts. Third, in reference to all the mythologizing involved in cultic drama that would have been introduced into the Old Testament with the ancient Near Eastern idea of enthronement, it must be stressed that the psalms of Yahweh's kingship had left far behind not only the phase of enthronement but also that of a hierarchy of deities (see above, chap. 1, §B). These two phases can be identified in the nations around Israel but are unknown in the Old Testament. Not only have all the hostile forces which could have threatened Yahweh's royal power been debased and stripped of their power, but also the gods and the mythological forces as well. Yahweh's kingship is eternal; it could not, can not, and never will be overthrown (Ps. 10:16; 29:10; 93:2). The psalms of Yahweh's kingship are filled with the pride expressed in the proclamation, "Thy throne is established from of old; thou art from everlasting" (Ps. 93:2). Nowhere can we find any tendency to waver on this point or to have a cultic renewal of the kingship of Yahweh. Thus, in the light of the data, the assumption of an "enthronement of Yahweh" is an impossibility.

The objection could be raised that Psalm 47 not only contains an "enthronement formula" (מלך אלהים, "God reigns") but also has all the marks of an enthronement procedure (cf. Ps. 47:5, עלה אלהים בתרועה, "God has gone up with a shout"). Moreover it can be pointed out that in characteristic passages in the Old Testament the Ark of Yahweh is regarded as the throne of Yahweh (Jer. 3:16-17; 17:12; 1 Sam. 4:4). Dibelius's book on the Ark of Yahweh (1906) was the pioneering study, and the idea it advanced was to be discussed again and again. Even if it could be shown that it was incorrect to regard the Ark as the throne of God, the existence of a throne supported by cherubim and attached to the

Ark must be taken into account (see above, chap. 1, §A). In any case we must bear in mind, as was pointed out at the outset, that a cultic entrance of Yahweh the king can be found in Ps. 24:7-10 and also in Ps. 68:24. This raises the question of whether, in spite of all critical arguments, it is not necessary to speak of a cultic enthronement of Yahweh and to put aside any reservations based on syntactical concerns and the available data. In dealing with this question it is helpful to begin by looking first at Psalm 47 in the light of other texts which speak unequivocally of a cultic process that brought the Ark into the sanctuary and the temple, or speak of an entrance of Yahweh as king (2 Samuel 6; 1 Kings 8; Psalm 132; 24:7-10; 68:24; cf. Kraus, 1951b, pp. 23ff. and Eichrodt, 1961, pp. 123f.). If the events in these passages and the settings in which they took place are examined, then it is quite clear that we cannot speak of an ''enthronement festival of Yahweh.'' At no place and at no time does Yahweh ascend a throne; nowhere can an enthronement, with the distinctive features that accompany it, be documented. Instead, Yahweh, acclaimed as king, present unseen above the Ark, enters the temple. Thus we are justified in speaking only of a cultic entrance of Yahweh, the divine king, an entrance that involved a procession with the Ark. It should be borne in mind that the tradition of Yahweh as king was connected with the concept of the Ark as a throne, probably as early as the Shiloh period (1 Sam. 4:4), but at the latest from the time of the adoption of the Jebusite cultic traditions in Jerusalem. The honoring of Yahweh Sebaoth as the ''king'' and ''God Most High'' (עֶלְיוֹן) was apparently connected with an entrance festival, the liturgical features of which were based on the cultic legend contained in 2 Samuel 6 (see above, chap. 3, §1, and the *Comm.* on Psalm 132). In all probability this entrance festival took place on the first day of the Feast of Booths (cf. 1 Kings 8:2). With this festive act the *hieros logos* (''sacral tradition'') of the Ark found its cultic expression on Mount Zion (chap. 3, §1; on the Ark narratives, see Rost, 1965, pp. 122ff.). Psalm 24:7-10 and Ps. 68:24 clearly are references to this festival. We may imagine that the worshiping community accompanied this entrance of Yahweh Sebaoth, whom they believed to be present with the Ark, with תְּרוּעָה (''shout''), that is with cultic rejoicing (2 Sam. 6:15) and, as is indicated in 2 Sam. 6:14, with dancing (Ps. 87:7). As the Ark entered the sanctuary, the people addressed a song to the gates (of the sacred area, or of the temple itself?). The community of the righteous wanted to go with the Ark into the שַׁעֲרֵי צֶדֶק (''gates of righteousness,'' Ps. 100:4; 118:19-20; Isa. 26:2). Yahweh, the king who entered the sanctuary, was thought of as ''high and lifted up''(Isa. 6:1); the heavenly king (cf. Ps. 29:9-10) far exceeds all limited concepts and descriptions. Visionary descriptions of a theophany probably accompanied the events in the sanctuary. Yahweh, whom heaven and the highest heaven cannot contain (1 Kings 8:27), was entering the temple to dwell there. We should not overlook the basic significance of Solomon's statement at the dedication of the temple:

> The Lord has set the sun in the heavens,
>   but has said that he would dwell in thick darkness.
> I have built thee an exalted house,
>   a place for thee to dwell in for ever.
>   (1 Kings 8:12-13)

On the translation and interpretation of this saying which is so important for Jerusalem's cultic life, see Noth, 1968, pp. 3, 168, 181f. The temple which

Yahweh the king has entered is the מִשְׁכָּן ("dwelling," Ps. 26:8; 43:3; 46:4; 74:7; 84:1; 132:5, 7). Schmidt (1963, pp. 91f.) called attention to the context in the history of religion as now understood in the light of the texts from Ugarit (Ras Shamra). We should keep in mind the transmission of those traditions, which were discussed in chap. 1, §B.

We must look once more at Psalm 47 (cf. also Isa. 52:7). Thus far we have proceeded from the assumption that for a large number of important reasons it is impossible to imagine, and certainly to prove, a festival of the enthronement of Yahweh. Further we have contended that the depiction of an entrance procession involving the ark in 2 Samuel 6; 1 Kings 8; and Psalm 132 can have a meaning other than that of an enthronement of Yahweh. These conclusions now lead us to some observations on Psalm 47. Four possible interpretations are to be examined: (1) It is conceivable that among Israel's neighbors there was celebrated an enthronement festival (of Baal?) involving concepts and cultic dramatizations which, in modified form, was adapted to the worship of Yahweh in Israel. (2) It is possible that the Southern Kingdom's political dependence on Assyria which, as is well known, involved the importation of novel cultic practices, may have led to the idea, and even the practice, of an enthronement of God in Jerusalem. This might produce speculation that in the period immediately prior to the exile there was introduced in Judah a cultic celebration of the enthronement of God, which—as a foreign element, to be sure—was then applied to Yahweh. Gunkel's comments (1933, pp. 84ff.) are relevant here, and it would be easy to relate Isa. 52:7, or Deutero-Isaiah's concepts of enthronement to this model. It should be kept in mind, however, that in Isaiah 40–55 there might be direct connections with experiences of the Babylonian exile. (3) We should consider whether or not Eissfeldt (1962, pp. 190f.) hit on the correct interpretation when he stated that the psalmist in Psalm 47 "means to say that Yahweh *is* king, but describes how he becomes king, because the meaning of the situation may best be portrayed through the splendor of the act that produced it." On this theory, Psalm 47 would involve a dramatic enactment based on the model of the enthronement of a human king. (4) The question whether Psalm 47 might not be related to the changed situation of the cultic practices in Jerusalem must be raised. The message of Isaiah 40–55 shows that the time in which the Davidic dynasty occupied the central position for God's people was at an end. Now Yahweh himself had become Israel's king. He ascends the throne: מָלַךְ אֱלֹהִים ("God reigns," Isa. 52:7). This transition in salvation history, which ushered in the eschatological kingship of Yahweh, would have led to the acceptance of the designation "king" for Yahweh and to the practice of enthronement. While the unknown prophet of the exile made reference to the traditions of Yahweh as king in the Jerusalem cult (see above, chap. 1, § B), these traditions, we must assume, were not absorbed into the proclamation of an eschatological transition. That is, the kingship of Yahweh became separated from the realm of hymnodic praise in the cult, and came to be a historical force in an eschatological sense. It is possible that Psalm 47 is connected with this prophetic message.

At this point it is necessary to examine the thesis proposed by Begrich (1938). He sought to show that the message of the unknown prophet of the exile presupposed the songs of Yahweh's enthronement. Not only was this thesis based on the as yet unrefuted assumption that the Psalter contains echoes of an enthronement of Yahweh, but it also ignored the difference between the formula יהוה מָלָךְ ("Yahweh reigns") and the shout at the enthronement מֶלֶךְ אֱלֹהִים ("God reigns"). Begrich's thesis is to be modified as follows. While Deutero-Isaiah knew the existing "hymns of Yahweh's kingship" in the Jerusalem cult, the "eschatological" proclamation in Isa. 52:7 was the acknowledgment of a transition which had no model in similar, older formulations in Israel's cultic life, unless the observations in reference to Psalm 47 in (2) above are accepted. The parallels to the Babylonian new year's festival, once considered so significant, and even their possible combination with an Israelite enthronement rite oriented to Baal worship, have received less and less attention in Old Testament research. All attempts to interpret Old Testament worship phenomenologically in general terms as forming a unity with worship in other ancient Near Eastern cultures are to be rejected. Nothing that was adduced under the alleged influence of an ancient cultic "pattern" can any longer be considered valid.

Psalm 95:6 contains the cultic cry, "O come, let us worship and bow down, let us kneel before the Lord, our Maker!" The verb נִשְׁתַּחֲוֶה ("let us worship") is significant here. It denotes bowing before Yahweh, falling down and praying "toward thy holy temple" (Ps. 5:7). Clearly, the goal of the procession of Yahweh and the cultic community was the great act of bowing down in the outer court of the temple before the divine king (Ps. 100:4). The community that was gathered there worshiped Yahweh "at his footstool" (Ps. 99:5) and praised, lauded, and honored him. In this act of worship the noble appellations of Israel's God were spoken—"king," "Almighty God," "creator," and "judge" (cf. chap. 1, § B above). It is in this cultic act that the psalms of Yahweh's kingship have their Sitz-im-Leben (cf. *Comm.*, Intro. § 6, 1bβ; § 10, 1b). Here the music of worship was performed (Psalm 150). Israel came into the presence of Yahweh in order to praise him and give him thanks (Ps. 100:4f.). The worship of God at the festival began with the call, "Serve the Lord with gladness! Come into his presence with singing!" (Ps. 100:2). Thus worship in Israel was characterized by joy. To serve God means in cultic terms to come before his face, to praise him, laud him, and honor him (Ps. 95:1-6). In the spirit of the universal nature of the appellations of Yahweh, Israel's adoration knows no bounds. All peoples, the whole of creation, heaven and earth, join in the praise of the divine king and creator (Psalms 96; 97:6-9; 98:7-9; 99:1-5; 100:1). As the people of Israel bow before Yahweh in adoration and praise, they fulfill the destiny that results from his choice of Israel to be his people. "We are his people and the sheep of his pasture" (Ps. 100:3b). "This is the day which the Lord has made" (Ps. 118:24a). Those who have already gathered in the temple precincts call out greetings and blessing to the crowds who are streaming in through the gates (Ps. 118:26). The praise of God knows no limits of time. All the Psalms are characterized by continual, never-ending adoration. Even during the night, praise rises up (Ps. 134; 8:3; Isa. 30:29).

During festival weeks, bowing in prayer must have taken place again and again. In terms of history of religion, this was comparable to the great throngs at prayer in Islam. In the course of the festival the clans and families probably took advantage several times of the opportunity to enter the temple and pray to the God who was present in the דְּבִיר ("inner sanctuary"). The prayers and the individual songs of thanks will be discussed in chap. 6. Psalm 48:12 informs us that solemn processions took place. The people moved around the sanctuary and the holy city. This was probably the occasion when the "songs of Zion" were sung (cf. *Comm.*, Intro. § 6, 4).

We do not know in detail what acts were performed during worship in Israel. It is, however, safe to assume that priests and temple singers instructed groups of worshipers, "put a song in their mouths" (cf. Deut. 31:19). The instruction probably dealt chiefly with two areas—the Torah and Yahweh's work in creation and history. Psalm 119 is the most impressive document of Torah instruction, and we may take it as an example of the study that was done in small groups. As for the theme "creation," we may wonder whether—apart from the praise of the creator as the people bowed in worship (it is here that the "creation hymns" had their Sitz-im-Leben)—the people may have been instructed on each of the seven days concerning the work which Yahweh did on that day (Gen. 1:1—2:4a). In any case, it is hard to imagine that a hymn like Psalm 8 would not have been accompanied by appropriate instruction. Yahweh's deeds in history were probably treated in similar manner. The "historical psalms" praise Yahweh's "mighty acts" (cf. especially Psalms 105; 135; 136). There was probably a recounting of Yahweh's great deeds and miracles in the history of Israel that corresponded to these psalms written in the form of praise and thanksgiving (Ps. 44:1-3; 78:3). Anyone who has experienced the manner in which stories are continually told and groups are instructed in mosques or in Hindu temples will be able to apply this living picture to his understanding of worship in Israel—not, however, in order to derive some "pattern" for the content, but merely to identify formal resemblances.

It is unlikely that the great basic traditions of Israel silently passed by the worship at the central sanctuary and then somehow at some time entered the canon. The echoes of these traditions in the Psalms show that they had a living relationship to the cultic community of Jerusalem. In other words, the historical traditions of Israel did not repose in fixed written form, cataloged and stored in the temple archives; they were the source of living narration and instruction. Israel's response as expressed in the Psalms cannot be conceived of without the ongoing message communicated and inculcated by priestly experts. This cultic proclamation, narration, and instruction had its counterpart in the handing on of the tradition in the clans and families of Israel. "Things that we have heard and known, that our fathers have told us—we will not hide them from their children, but tell to the coming generation the glorious deeds of the Lord, and his might, and the wonders which he has wrought" (Ps. 78:3-4; cf. Exod. 12:26-27; Deut. 6:7, etc.).

The question of what occurred in the worship at the festivals in Jerusalem in which "all Israel" took part must be once again explored. In chap. 1, § B the problem of the "covenant renewal festival" was discussed; here I will only refer the reader to that section. A few comments will suffice to supplement that material and give more detail. Our starting point is the prophetic message in Isa. 2:2-4, which specifically states that Zion, the "mountain of the house of the Lord," is the place from which the תורה (*Torah*) and the דבר יהוה ("word of Yahweh") go forth (Isa. 2:3). Here תורה (*Torah*) is to be understood in the sense of "instruction in the law" (Wildberger, 1972, p. 85), specifically, instruction which was received by all Israel, since the synonymous expression דבר יהוה ("word of Yahweh"), meaning the prophetic word, was addressed to the whole people of God. The basic concepts communicated by these two expressed in Isa. 2:2ff. in connection with the "pilgrimage of the peoples," now expanded in universal terms, are confirmed in striking manner in Psalms 50 and 81. In these two great festival psalms (cf. *Comm.*, Intro. § 6, 6), all Israel is addressed (Psalm 50:4, 7; 81:8-10). In addition, these psalms deal with the instruction given to God's people in reference to the laws and commandments of Yahweh (Ps. 50:16-21; 81:8-10). Finally,

it is a prophetic דבר ("word") that is addressed to Israel (Ps. 50:7; 81:5, 10b).
Even though there are many problems involved in the dating of these two psalms
(cf. chap. 2, §A and *Comm.* on Psalms 50 and 81), we can still recognize a stream
of tradition that was determinative for the Israelite cultus in the sanctuary in
Jerusalem.

Some questions remain. For example, it is uncertain whether, in the light
of Ps. 50:2f. a theophany is to be assumed in connection with the event of the
prophetic proclamation of law and judgment. If so, we immediately confront the
problem of how the cultic community was made aware of the manifestation of
God. The imaginative attempts of Mowinckel and others to explain the theophany
as presented in the form of a cultic drama have no basis at all. We might start from
a (cultic?) prophet's proclamation of a vision in which God appeared to him or
her. This is the simple meaning of the words in Ps. 50:1f. But the assumption of
such a proclamation of a theophany in the history of the cult, even though problems in the transmission of traditions remain open, is still problematic, especially
in the interpretation of Psalms 50 and 81. The concept of a *"rib* ('dispute') pattern" involves another question, which seems to defy solution. Was there a cultic
ritual of judgment in Jerusalem? And in such a ritual what meaning did Psalm 82
and its ancient background in the Middle East have? Finally, what might the relationship of a cultic ritual of judgment to the message of judgment in the great
prophets of Israel have been? These are all basically unanswered questions or at
least questions that have not been answered with unequivocal arguments. The
problems are apparent in the work of Whitelocke (1968).

The presentation of the sacrifice has constituted a special theme in the
cultic life of Jerusalem. It is, however, astonishing how little is in fact said in the
Psalms on this theme. Anyone who approaches the Psalter from the books of Exodus and Leviticus, with their differentiated and complex regulations governing
sacrifice, will have difficulty understanding how it is that there are so few references to the sacrifices, and that, as will be shown, these are so general. Do these
references correspond to reality? How are we to explain this when 1 Kings 8:5
says, "And King Solomon and all the congregation of Israel, who had assembled
before him, were with him before the ark, sacrificing so many sheep and oxen that
they could not be counted or numbered"? And is it not the case that the prophetic
criticisms of sacrifice deal with a situation that must be assumed to have existed in
the Jerusalem cult, namely, that whenever "all Israel" assembled for a festival
(but also in terms of sacrifices brought by individuals) innumerable sacrifices
were offered? Before we can describe and study these issues as they relate to the
Psalter we should examine the general explanation that has so often been advanced. It holds that in the Psalms one looks in vain for rituals or precise descriptions of the cult that was practiced on Mount Zion. Of sacrificial rituals in particular or even of fragmentary liturgical descriptions nothing is found.

It is appropriate to begin with the assured and generally acknowledged
data concerning the major types of Old Testament sacrifice, so that we may then
have a clearer grasp of the sacrifices that are mentioned in the Psalms. If we confine ourselves to the major types, the first significant fact is that in Israel two completely different types of sacrifices were offered. The first type is usually called
זבח (*zebah*), which etymologically means a "slaughtering." But it is not the mere
fact that the sacrificial animal is slaughtered that is vital, but the fact that a common eating of the flesh of the slaughtered animal establishes community. Simply

93

by the fact that they together eat the meat of the sacrifice, those who share in the meal become a community. The meaning, purpose, and effect of the זבח (*zebaḥ*) is the establishment of community among those who share in it. This human community is constituted by the basic community of the people with Yahweh, who is present as a participant in the meal. ''The fellowship formed creates not union; . . . it creates an offensive and defensive alliance; there is reciprocal acknowledgment ('I will be your God, and ye shall be my people,' Jer. 7:23; 'our God,' Ps. 95:7; 'thy people,' 79:13), one stands up for the other, those involved live together in a relationship of חזד ואמת'' (Köhler, 1957, p. 183). Thus זבח (*zebaḥ*) as a sacrifice that establishes community is distinctly a type of sacrifice that had a special role in relationship to covenant and to the process of establishing covenant. In this connection, Ps. 50:5 should be noted.

R. Schmid (1964) has given a detailed treatment of the ''covenant sacrifice.'' He dealt first of all with the sacrifice termed שלמים, (*šelamim*), since this term is distinctive of the prototype of a ''covenant sacrifice'' as depicted in Exod. 24:5-8. The concept שלמים (*šelamim*), resembles the זבח (*zebaḥ*) in its use as a designation of the sacrifice that establishes community, the nature of which Schmid explored in terms of ''covenant sacrifice.'' Schmid summarized as follows: ''Sacrifice originally consisted of a meal preceded by the slaughter of an animal and a ritual involving the blood (resembling the sacrificial meal of the Arabic nomads). After the Israelites settled in Canaan they adopted a sacrificial meal, along with various other cultic practices, in the form of the Greek θυσία (*thysia*), but retained the blood ritual. The officiating priests received their share of the sacrifices offered in the permanent sanctuaries. As sacrifice came to be more and more limited to the central sanctuary in Jerusalem, the rituals were specified in greater detail and more uniformly, until they reached the stage of the minute descriptions which became codified in the priestly document. It is still not possible to reach a final conclusion on the basis of the data that are available today . . .'' (p. 99). This cautious outline of the development of the שלמים, (*šelamim*) can be accepted with the one reservation that it still has not been proven that in the strictest sense it is possible to speak of a ''covenant sacrifice.'' It would be more cautious to say that the זבח (*zebaḥ*) and the שלמים (*šelamim*) could *also* be offered or celebrated in the context of the covenant.

Further literature: Gray (1925); Wendel (1927); Oesterley (1937); Dussaud (1941); Rowley (1950); von Rad (1962); Rendtorff (1967); W. H. Schmidt (1975:124ff.).

The other type of sacrifice is the gift offering. The best starting place is the characteristic expression מנחה (*minḥah*), which signifies something that is ''offered'' or ''presented.'' In a secular context it denotes a gift that is intended to win favor (Gen. 32:13-21; 43:11). ''Someone gives a gift to another person to show his respect for the other person. It is entirely his own affair and done of his own free will'' (Köhler, 1957, p. 184). It is not possible here to discuss the details of the ''gift offering'' or its history. More and more the term עלה (*'olah*) came to be the regular designation of this type of offering. It is usually translated ''burnt offering,'' and in fact the gift presented as an עלה (*'olah*) was usually to be consumed by fire. The smoke that ascended to heaven accompanied the homage, praise, petitions, and laments of the giver. The עלה (*'olah*), like the מנחה (*minḥah*), was designated for the exclusive use of Yahweh. In every case the shared offering and the gift offering are two totally different types of sacrifice. ''In the gift offering, man disposes of something which belongs to him for one reason or another. He gives. He surrenders his gift completely. He surrenders it by destroying it in the fire. He surrenders it because he seeks God's face, His forgiveness, His favour, His goodwill. In the gift offering he does not seek God's fellowship. The gift offering does not establish a relationship; it underlines in fact the distance between the two. It is an act of homage, a token of respect, submission, surrender to him who receives the gift'' (Köhler, 1957, pp. 184-185).

Investigation of the occurrence of the two types of sacrifice, or of the corresponding Hebrew terms in the Psalms yields the following picture. Psalm 50:5 is the only passage where זבח (*zebaḥ*) occurs in the relationship of God to his people, here specifically in connection with the act of establishing a covenant (כרת ברית). In Ps. 4:5 those enemies who are persecuting and slandering the worshiper are exhorted to present זבחי־צדק (*zebaḥe-ṣedeq*; cf. Ps. 51:19). The meaning of צדק (''righteousness'') in this context has been explained as follows: ''צדק means . . . Yahweh's saving gift that enables men and women to refrain from all wrong acts, to overcome any breach of the peace, and to restore the reputation (כבוד, *kabod*) of the one who has been unjustly accused. The sacrifices which are demanded are the means by which the צדק (*ṣedeq*) is transmitted. Through them, those who bring the sacrifices are thereby made partakers of the צדק (*ṣedeq*) and enabled to do their part in overcoming the injustice that has been done and to eliminate those things which work against a sense of community'' (Beyerlin, 1970, p. 87; see also the *Comm.* on Ps. 4:5 and 51:19).

It is significant that זבח (*zebaḥ*) usually appears in connection with the thank offering, and is a characteristic of that offering as the community meal that accompanies the offering (Ps. 27:6; 54:6; 107:22; 116:17). In Ps. 54:6 זבח (*zebaḥ*) is parallel to הודה (*hodah*). If we leave aside Ps. 106:28, which speaks of the illicit sacrifices for the dead, the following specific features of זבח (*zebaḥ*) in the Psalms can be identified: (1) In terms of Israel's relation to God, Ps. 50:5 refers to the ''covenant offering'' that establishes community; (2) זבח (*zebaḥ*) is found most frequently in the individual song of thanksgiving (*Comm.* Intro. § 6, 2ac) and refers to the fellowship meal celebrated as part of the thank offering (cf. Lev. 7:12-18; for a detailed discussion, see Rendtorff, 1967, pp. 63ff.). We will return to Ps. 50:8 and Ps. 51:16 later.

It is clear from Ps. 50:8 that it is ''all Israel'' that brings Yahweh the עלה (*'olah*) as a gift. When the prophet who speaks here addresses Israel he declares, ''Your burnt offerings are continually before me'' (Ps. 50:8). Even the individual says, ''I will come into thy house with burnt offerings,'' and ''I will offer to thee burnt offerings of fatlings'' (Ps. 66:13, 15). Nothing concrete is said about the עלה (*'olah*) and the data concerning מנחה (*minḥah*) are scarce. In Ps. 96:8 the nations are exhorted to honor Yahweh and to bring a מנחה (*minḥah*) to him. It is clear from the call to enter into his courts, that this involves a cultic act patterned on the offerings brought by Israel. In Ps. 141:2 the מנחה (*minḥah*) is referred to in a ''spiritualized'' sense (Rendtorff, 1967, p. 65). Thus it is clear that the assumption that the Psalms make only isolated reference to sacrifice in Israelite cultic practice is correct.

It should be noted that the piling up of sacrificial terms in Ps. 20:3; 40:6; 50:8; 51:16 provides no information on the individual expressions, but merely serves as a general designation of the entire sacrificial system. These passages, however, lead us to the problem of the criticism of sacrifice in the Psalms.

The explanations that have been offered of this criticism fall into two contrasting groups. Earlier explanations assumed that Ps. 40:6; 50:13; 51:16 reflected the prophetic critique of sacrifice. Mowinckel (1924, p. 51), however, advocated the view that these psalms do not reject sacrifice but rather shift the emphasis from the sacrifice itself to the presenting of hymns, especially of thanks (on the problems of interpretation, see Stamm, 1955, pp. 61f.). It may be asked whether strictly speaking these are really alternative interpretations. But first we must look at the three passages in context.

In Ps. 50:11-15 the prophetic speaker announces judgment and says that the earth with all its fullness belongs to Yahweh, creator and Lord of the world, and thus also all animals for sacrifice are his as well. No one can give him anything that he does not already possess. Israel's great guilt is not the result of offering sacrifices—that is made clear in Ps.50:8—but solely the result of their forgetting the majesty and the reality of their God (Ps. 50:22). Thus in the theophany Yahweh discloses himself anew to his people. All the näive, anthropomorphic concepts of God are rejected, such as that the God of Israel ate the flesh of the animals sacrificed or drank the blood of goats (Ps. 50:13). All magical manipulations are eliminated, including the expectation that those bringing sacrifices possibly would be able to influence Yahweh. The object of the critique is not the sacrificial system as such, but the fact that the people have forgotten and abandoned the reality of Israel's God and in the ethnic religion as expressed in the sacrifices reduced him to an anthropomorphic idol, dependent on humans and easily influenced by them. This component of the critique is closely related to the message of the prophets and corresponds to the message of Amos with its emphasis on the reality of the living God, "Seek Yahweh and live" (Amos 5:4, 6). In Ps. 50:11ff., however, the critique of sacrifice does not culminate in such an appeal, but rather in the exhortation, "Offer to God a sacrifice of thanksgiving, and pay your vows to the Most High; and call upon me in the day of trouble; I will deliver you, and you shall glorify me" (Ps. 50:14-15). This places the other component in the foreground, a positive concern with the act of זבח לאלהים תודה ("sacrifice of thanksgiving to God") with the thank offering. But was the psalmist thinking here of a thank *offering?* Must we not rather assume with Mowinckel that the concept זבח תודה("sacrifice of thanksgiving") has weakened and is to be understood only in the sense of presenting a *song* of thanks? Psalm 50:15 indicates that this question is to be answered in the affirmative. The verbal glorifying of Yahweh after the event of deliverance, which corresponds to the appeal to Yahweh in petitions and calls for help, constitutes the scope of the whole psalm. Yahweh is not in need of having anyone bring him nourishment by means of a sacrifice, nor is it possible to buy his favor. On the contrary, it is the human worshiper who in his need is dependent on Yahweh, whom Yahweh promises to hear and rescue, and who can bring to Yahweh no better sacrifice than his thanks for such help.

In Ps. 40:6 we have a similar example of the prophetic impact on a broken relationship to God and a sacrifice of praise that has become a song of thanks: "Sacrifice and offering thou dost not desire; but thou hast given me an open ear. Burnt offering and sin offering thou hast not required." The last line gives the impression of having been added. It underlines the verdict that has been pronounced on the cultic sacrifices with their various concepts. What is the reason for this clear rejection of sacrifice, which seems to refer to a declaration of disapproval made by a priest or a cultic prophet? Compare von Rad's statements on the declarative formula of the torah on sacrifice (1962, pp. 245f.). The question itself contains a part of the answer. We may assume that pointed, even thorough, declarations of rejection in the sacrifice torah motivated the criticism of the sacrificial system. It is not clear, however, whether these declarations actually had their Sitz-im-Leben at the cultic center and were proclaimed by priests or cultic prophets, or whether the prophetic rejections of sacrifice, found as early as the work of Amos, were responsible for this development in the prayers of the Psalms (cf. Würthwein, 1947, pp. 143-152; Wolff, 1977, pp. 262f.). The sweeping rejection in Ps. 40:6-8 points in the direction of the second explanation, especially the clause "but thou hast given me an open ear" (v. 6c). This signifies a contrast between sacrifice and obedience. It is not sacrifice that Yahweh desires, but attentiveness and obedience (1 Sam. 15:22). This is clearly a formulation of a prophetic demand, which is in agreement with the statement in Ps. 40:8, "I delight to do thy will, O my God; thy law is within my heart." This verse is similar to the message in Jer. 31:31-34 and Ezek. 36:25-28. Thus the influence which the message of the prophets had on Psalm 40 is unmistakable. At the same time Ps. 40:9 is related to the thank offering. The proclamation of Yahweh's righteousness "in the great congregation" refers to the element of confession and instruction that is evident so often in the song of thanks of the individual (*Comm.,* Intro. § 6,2a). This is additional evidence of the convergence of two strands of tradition, the prophetic strand and the strand which transformed the thank offering to a song of thanks, to a verbal offering.

The situation in Ps. 51:15 is similar. Here the element of praise is stated first: "O Lord, open thou my lips, and my mouth shall show forth thy praise." In terms of the object of prayer this petition is in full agreement with Ps. 50:14 and Ps. 40:10. An alternative to sacrifice is, as shown in Ps. 40:7-8, proclamation, the glorification of Yahweh's mighty acts, as presented verbally in the thank offering. The fact that Yahweh has "no delight" in sacrifices, and that he "would not be pleased" with burnt offerings (Ps. 51:16) is, like Ps. 40:7, the result of the impact which the sacrifice torah had in the form radicalized by the prophets. The exegesis of Psalm 51 shows the extent to which the entire psalm is dependent on Exod. 36:25-28 (cf. also Jer. 24:7; 31:33; 32:39). In this respect the situation is similar to that in Ps. 40:8. But in Ps. 51:17 the expression takes a distinct turn that is unique in the Psalter: "The sacrifice acceptable to God is a broken spirit." The one who offers the prayer is not bringing a substitute sacrifice. Even the song of thanks is not to be thought of as a substitute. In prayer the worshiper presents to God a broken, contrite heart in the certainty that this sacrifice will not be declared unacceptable, but that it is pleasing to Yahweh (cf. Ps. 34:18; Isa. 57:15; 61:1). Humans in all their inadequacy, helplessness, and poverty are the recipients of the promises of the God of Israel (Ps. 50:15). They can "present" themselves in all their misery and not be rejected (Ps. 51:11). The fact that the severe critique of sacrifice in Ps. 51:16-17 was later modified (v. 19) merely shows that in a general sense and as a matter of principle sacrifice occupied a firm place in the worship of Israel. The one who speaks in v. 19 gives voice to a continuing loyalty to the sacrificial system as a component of worship. Even in the Psalms the criticism and rejection of sacrifice remains the exception, a hint and a partial anticipation of that which receives a final formulation in the New Testament in the Letter to the Hebrews.

In addition to the regular festivals and feasts of the Jerusalem cultus, we must also consider the cultic practices in response to particular occasions. The prayer songs of the national community (*Comm.,* Introduction, § 6, 2aβ) call our attention to times of national mourning, and we may begin by considering what provoked this response and what practices were involved. In the Hebrew language the cultic observance of such mourning was called צום, "fasting." The call went out to observe such a fast whenever a severe national crisis made it seem necessary. The threat that was faced and the call to cultic lamentation were to be proclaimed throughout the land (Isa. 22:12; Joel 1:14). The decision to do so was made by the elders, and the priests convened the gathering at the sanctuary. The קהל ("congregation") gathered together (Joel 2:16; Jer. 36:6, 9; 1 Kings 8:33, 35). This was the custom even in earliest times (Judg. 20:23-26; 21:2-4; 1 Sam. 7:5-6). The "fast" was "sanctified" (Joel 1:14; 2:15). The worshipers who gathered in Jerusalem refrained from all food and all rejoicing (Isa. 58:3-5). The participants took off or tore their clothes (Isa. 32:11; Mic. 1:8; Joel 2:13), and dressed themselves in coarse sackcloth (Isa. 22:12; 58:5; Jer. 4:8; etc.). They shaved their heads (Isa. 15:2; 22:12; Mic. 1:16). As a sign of their repentance they threw themselves on the ground and rolled in the dust (Ps. 44:26; Mic. 1:10; Jer. 6:26) and strewed ashes on their heads (Neh. 9:1). These were acts of self-humiliation which testified to their pain and sorrow and to their readiness to repent. Under the leadership of the priests, who were also dressed in sackcloth, the assembled congregation spent day and night in the sanctuary (Joel 1:13). Lamentation, wailing, and crying arose from the dust (Isa. 29:4; Mic. 1:8; Jer. 14:12; Joel 1:5, 8; 2:1). From 1 Sam. 7:6 and Lam. 2:19 we learn of a ritual of pouring out water as the people mourned and wept.

It was in such assemblies where the people pleaded with God that the national songs of prayer had their Sitz-im-Leben. The priests and the singers were the ones who recited the petitions and songs of penitence (Joel 1:9, 13; 2:17). They described their plight and held it up in prayer before Yahweh—the collapse of the nation in the disasters of war, drought, plagues of locusts, and, above all (as will be shown), the destruction of the sanctuary in Jerusalem. In the Psalter it is principally war and the destruction of the temple that come to expression in the prayer songs of the nation.

The destruction of Jerusalem and the desecration of the sanctuary constituted a particular crisis. The events of the year 587 B.C. gave rise to the regular observance of a ritual of mourning which was observed amid the ruins of the sanctuary. The book of Lamentations (Kraus, 1968, pp. 8ff.) and, in addition, those psalms which have the destruction of the temple as their central feature are songs and prayers reflecting this particular occasion and its effects over a long period of time. Ancient Middle Eastern parallels to the "lament for the destroyed sanctuary" are impressive witnesses to the fact that throughout the ancient world it was customary to sing songs of lamentation amid the ruins of a sanctuary which had been destroyed by foes. Portions of the lament over the destruction of the sanctuary in Ur help us to gain a picture of the situation.

> The Lord of the lands has forsaken (his house) . . .,
>   Mullil has forsaken the sanctuary of Nibru . . . ,
>   Baba has abandoned the "Holy City" . . .
> O city, bitter is the lamentation made for you,
>   Bitter, O city, is the lamentation made for you.
> For the goodly city that has been destroyed
>   Bitter lamentation is made . . . .
> An evil day has been decreed for me, its lamentation
>   imposed on me,
> That I might feel the sorrow of this day . . . .
> At night bitter lamentation is my fate . . . .
> (Falkenstein and von Soden, 1953, pp. 187f., 192f.)

From Zech. 7:5 it can be seen that the mourning over the destruction of the city of Jerusalem and its sanctuary was observed not only in the fifth month in remembrance of the date of the catastrophe, but also in the seventh month, that is, at the time of the great autumn festival (cf. also Zech. 8:19, where there is in addition mention of a lamentation in the tenth month). To keep the "fast," the clans of God's people made a pilgrimage to Zion (Jer. 41:5) in order to remember the great disaster with confession and petitions, asking Yahweh to reverse the fortunes of the nation. Such times of fasting and worship were most probably observed among the exiles as well.

For further literature on the national songs of lamentation, see Gunkel and Begrich, 1933, chap. 4, and Wolff, 1977, p. 21, and the bibliography given there.

The first characteristic of the prayers of confession of the cultic community is the portrayal of the plight of the nation. They bring the catastrophe in all its aspects to Yahweh's attention. The destruction of Israel means not only the fearsome experience of encountering the wrath of God (Ps. 80:4) but also the feeling of being forsaken and rejected by God (Ps. 60:1-3; 74:1). In Ps. 60:1-3 we find the cosmic dimensions of the result of Israel's destruction. The foundations on which the earth rests have been shaken. This signifies that God's people, with their certainty of having been chosen by God, see their destiny and their mission among the nations of the world as forfeited. This is expressed clearly in some of the prayers. The destruction that the foes have wrought has profaned Yahweh's honor, his holy name. But the confession of guilt is not toned down or restricted by this insight. The nation confesses its guilt, which is so deeply rooted in the events of past generations. From the very beginning Israel avoided carrying out Yahweh's saving purpose—or even was in opposition to it (Psalm 78). Thus the judgment of God is justified. The well-deserved punishment is accepted.

Isolated passages in the Psalms mention rites and rituals which were customary in the lamentations described above. Self-abasement and confession of guilt open a new approach to the activity of Israel's God in the history of his people. The worshiping community looks back to the basic historical events: the miracle of deliverance from Egyptian slavery, the wandering in the desert, and the occupation of the promised land (Ps. 80:1, 8-11). The ancient, inviolable ordinances are called to mind again (Ps. 60:6-8). In Ps. 74:12-17 a hymnodic interlude glorifies Yahweh as "king" and creator of the world. The remembrance of the miracle of creation and the conquest of the primordial forces of chaos strengthens the people's confidence in the limitless might of Israel's God, especially in the face of which they were confronting. There is absolute certainty that Yahweh Sebaoth, who is enthroned above the cherubim, possesses power in the highest degree (Ps. 80:1-2). Thus the petitions of the national community are not uttered in a vacuum, but they appeal to Yahweh's great deeds and miracles "Restore us, O God" (Ps. 80:3, 7, 19); "turn again, O God of hosts!" (Ps. 80:14). The distinctive themes of petitions and cries for help are the restoration of God's people and Yahweh's return to Israel (against the background of divine election and of covenant history). The distant, hidden God is called on to appear. "Let thy face shine" is the request in Ps. 80:19.

Alongside the petition for the restoration of Israel there are cries that demand revenge and the destruction of the nation's enemies. Here it is significant that the demands for revenge are voiced in the specific context of the prayer songs of the national community. It should be stressed that the longing for vengeance is bound up with the request and expectation that Yahweh's honor be restored (Ps.

74:22-23). The heathen nations are no longer to ask scornfully, "Where is their God?" (Ps. 79:10). But it should also be noted that these passages, often felt to be offensive, have been influenced by traditional cultic language and are the consequence of ancient execration formulas which were customary at the establishment of a covenant and other occasions (cf. Ch. Barth, 1961, p. 56; Noth, 1957b, pp. 155-171).

Psalm 83:18 expresses an insight with far-reaching consequences: In Israel עליון, God Most High, has revealed himself. Wherever and whenever Israel's enemies triumph, it is evident that the nations are seeking to destroy those who bear witness to Yahweh's will to provide deliverance and to reign as Lord. That is how far-reaching the implications are. And so the judgment on the enemy nations is swallowed up in the mystery of divine election and God's activity in the history of the world. Luther recognized this when he wrote, "God must be known and honored by all nations, whether in his grace or against their will in damnation . . . . It is a fearful thing to fall into the hands of the living God . . ." (WA 31/1, 33).

Finally, a few comments on regular worship. It began with the pilgrimage and the entrance into the temple precincts, and it concluded with the benediction in the closing ceremony. Psalm 67 could be termed a "psalm of blessing." In the form of wishes and petitions all the statements center around the theme ברכה ("blessing"). Psalm 67:1 is clearly based on the Aaronic blessing in Num. 6:24-26. The unusual form of the psalm is probably the result of a cultic situation that can no longer be identified (cf. Crüsemann, 1969, p. 200.) Even though Ps. 67:6-7 is a clear reference to thanksgiving for the harvest, it is still conceivable that the wishes for blessing belong to the concluding phase of the cultic event. The transition from v. 1 to v. 2 is remarkable. "May God be gracious to us and bless us and make his face to shine upon us, that thy way may be known upon earth, thy saving power among all nations." Note also v. 5, "Let the peoples praise thee, O God; let all the peoples praise thee!" The blessing for which Israel prays and which has been promised to the nation is not a power restricted to the boundaries of God's people and active only there, but it is a light shining on Israel which is to shine forth into the world of the nations and move all the ends of the earth to fear Yahweh and to praise him. The religion of Israel is set within a universal framework, in its beginning, in all its festivals and observances, and in its conclusion. God's people never celebrate their own glorification, but understand it as the consequence of divine election, destiny, and mission in the world.

The ceremony that marked the end of worship is reflected in Psalm 121 and reaches its climax in the assurance, "The Lord will keep your going out and your coming in from this time forth and for evermore" (Ps. 121:8). The worshiper takes leave of the sanctuary and enters the realm where he faces danger in rugged mountains, under the burning sun, and from the threat of many perils. As he sets out for home he asks, "From whence does my help come?" (Ps. 121:1). "My help comes from the Lord, who made heaven and earth" (v. 2). On his travels his foot will not slip and no dangers will overtake him by day or night. It is the creator of heaven and earth himself who watches over those returning home. The one who keeps Israel "will neither slumber nor sleep" (v. 4). He watches over each individual who leaves the sanctuary ("the source of life") in the same way that he watches over his people. "The Lord will keep you from all evil; he will keep your life" (v. 7). The pilgrim leaves Jerusalem with this promise and this assurance.

D. The Theology of Worship

Worship (עבדה) means first of all the cult that is practiced and celebrated in the precincts of the sanctuary. But in Israel to "serve Yahweh" does not merely mean to encounter God in the cultic festivals, honor him, praise him, and be ready and willing in various ways to listen and to act in the context of the festival. In the Old Testament, God is not restricted to the limits of the cultic. At the gates of the sanctuary all who enter the temple are asked about their conduct in everyday life (Psalms 15; 24). That which is said to the cultic community of Israel in worship is also to be observed outside the sanctuary (Ps. 50;81). From the beginning it was clearly shown that in Israel worship is not something nonpolitical, far removed from history. There are many features of the Psalms that reflect the criticisms voiced by the prophets. Israel's worship is to result in "justice" and "righteousness" (Ps. 37:28; 50:16-21; 82:3; 98:9; 99:4; 103:6; 119:5-7; 146:7; 147:19). "False worship reduced God to passivity. True worship activates community life through justice and righteousness" (Wolff, 1979, p. 54; cf. Kraus, 1972a, pp. 195-234).

At the same time, worship in the sanctuary was a special event. The service of Yahweh, which God's people were chosen to perform, occupied a central position in the cult. The festivals were the high point of life, the sources of all life and activity. Israel existed on the basis of the filled, meaningful time of the cultic gatherings. "For the Israelites 'time' was not an empty concept, a mere line, as it is for us. Time is filled with content; it consists of that which occurs in it" (Mowinckel, 1953, p. 58; cf. Pedersen, 1926, pp. 461ff.).

Although it is essential to keep in mind a general phenomenology of worship, the distinctive nature of worship in Israel should be stressed. The following passage can be the starting point for a basic phenomenological understanding of what is meant by cult. "The festival always signifies the return of a world time, when that which is oldest, most honorable, and most splendid returns. It is a return of the age of gold, when the ancestors were intimately involved with the gods and the spirits. That is the meaning of the sublimity of festivals, which—wherever there are actual festivals—is to be distinguished from everything else that is serious or joyful. This is the reason for the splendid forms of genuine cultic events that verge on the extravagant and whose style cannot be at home in the realm of practical concerns. It bears witness to a holy fullness, an excited delight of the soul that belongs to the uncommon, the primeval-eternal, the divine. A person stands on a height to which the return of the world hour has raised him" (W. F. Otto, 1955, p. 255). Eliade (1959, pp. 68-69) expresses it similarly: "By its very nature sacred time is reversible in the sense that, properly speaking, it is a primordial mythical time made present. Every religious festival, any liturgical time, represents the reactualization of a sacred event that took place in a mythical past, 'in the beginning.' Religious participation in a festival implies emerging from ordinary temporal duration and reintegration of the mythical time reactualized by the festival itself. Hence sacred time is indefinitely recoverable, indefinitely repeatable."

Israel's worship is to be explained in sharp, decisive distinction from this basic understanding of cult. (1) The return to the mythical primeval time has no validity in the Psalms or anywhere else in the Old Testament. Nowhere do the Psalms speak of a "return of a golden age" or of a "reentry into mythical time." Israel did not think of itself as primarily determined by a primordial age of myth or periodic natural events. (2) the Old Testament people of God were primarily related to the history of God's mighty deeds, which included the events of creation, "Israel's belief that she was not bound primarily to the periodic cycle of nature but to definite historical events, was the expression of a faith that was probably at the time still completely unaware both of its absolute difference in kind . . . and of its own vigour. While, therefore, it is perfectly correct to say that Jahwism is founded in history, this does not, of course, involve any thought of the modern concept of history which, as we know, lays great stress on the idea of relativity and of the transitoriness of all events. The historical acts by which Jahweh founded the community of Israel were absolute" (von Rad, 1965, p. 104). Even Mowinckel (1953, p. 77), who consistently ascribed great significance to a general phenomenology of cult in the study of worship in Israel, stated, "Israel may have borrowed much from the common Near Eastern 'cult pattern' and its concepts and rites, but Yahweh is 'the living God,' 'the holy God, who does not die,' and who 'reveals himself,' who, in creative, victorious activity demonstrates who he is. Israelite cultus was an encounter with the all-powerful God who is well known through the experience of history." This clearly indicates the distinctive features of Old Testament worship. (3) Worship in Israel, because it concerns the God who is to come, possessed an unmistakable orientation to the future. Waiting for Yahweh, hoping in him, and above all the expectation of the universal fulfillment of the divine election and destiny of Israel in the world of the nations—these are the things that determined the nature of worship in Jerusalem.

In Israelite worship Yahweh himself spoke to the assembled people of God. "Let me hear what God the Lord will speak" (Ps. 85:8). This readiness to hear a prophetic message shows the significance attached to the word of God in Israel's worship (cf. also Ps. 50:7-15; 81:8, 10). In addition to the priests who prepared Israel—and the individual within Israel—for an encounter with Yahweh in praise, song, prayer, and sacrifice, there were the prophetic figures who had responsibility for transmitting the word of Yahweh (Mowinckel, 1953, pp. 57f.). We still have no clear picture of cultic prophecy and of the role of the prophets in Israel's worship, but Israel's response as expressed in the Psalms is inconceivable without Yahweh's speaking to the people, the central fact of Old Testament cult. To be sure, we should guard against projecting onto the world of ancient Israel any "Protestant concepts" of the role of the Word in Old Testament worship. In our search for an understanding of ancient cultic practice we must continue to rely on the general features and definitions known to us from Israel's neighbors.

Mowinckel (1965b, pp. 120f.) felt that the decisive factors in the cult were "the visible and powerful forms ordained and established by society, through which the religious experience of community between the deity and the people was established and by which it exerted its influence." This general definition produced a conflict with the thesis which had been advanced by Wellhausen that the cultus was originally the ethnic element in Israel's religion. He wrote, "It is clear that such pecularities of the cultus of ancient Israel did not make it better than that of other peoples and did not constitute a significant difference. If there really was a difference, it did not involve the nature of the worship but the deity toward whom it was directed. Israel dedicated its worship not to Baal but to Yahweh. In the earliest period this was not done so exclusively as it was later. In certain respects Yahweh was even more tolerant" (1965, p. 79). Is that really the way it was? Is the only difference the one to whom the worship was directed? It has already been shown how significant history was for Israel's worship, and in addition certain basic distinguishing features were pointed out. There can be no doubt that Israel elaborated its worship in the framework of ancient Near Eastern cultic festivals and served its God in the categories, and in terms of the principles, of cultic practices. What influence then did this fact have on the theological understanding of Old Testament worship?

"In cult, revelation becomes institutionalized" (Mowinckel, 1953, p. 46). What does that mean? Mowinckel explains that "the deity continues to reveal himself at the same place through the same means to the 'God seeker.' This can occur in various ways—through regular cultic practices or through special means such as the giving of oracles, the pronouncing of sacral judgments (the ordeal), in dreams, or through ecstatic experiences" (p. 46). Institutionalization means regularity. Regularity, however, presupposes that, or produces the result that, certain happenings will occur and are to be expected. In the cult, revelation becomes institutionalized. Does this mean that the institution known as "cult" controls the revelation of Israel's God, that it regularly brings it to pass according to the expectations of the cultic community? Are the cultic practices means by which priests and other cultic functionaries bring about—according to the regulations—the presentation of revelation as a reality? These are questions that a theology of worship will always have to raise.

The "autonomy" of the world of cult demands clarity as to whether, and if so, to what degree, the God of Israel permitted himself to be conformed to the categories and laws of cult as it was shaped in the ancient Near East. We know too little of the mystery of theophany to be able to answer these questions. Moreover, our knowledge of the details of what actually happened in Israelite cult, of how the festival rituals were introduced and regularly carried out, is all too limited. Only certain general statements can be made. (1) Nowhere in the Psalms is there the slightest hint that Yahweh's freedom was restricted by the institutional law of the cult, much less that it was abrogated. That is, there is no hint that the sanctuary officials controlled the occasions on which Israel's God could appear or that they could regularly bring such an appearance about. (2) It is instead the case that the powerful historical factors operating in Israelite worship had the result that neither the people of Yahweh, nor any individuals among this people regularly felt themselves to be in control. On the contrary, they were pleading and waiting in the sanctuary, in their troubles crying out for deliverance. They felt that Yahweh was far from them, that he was silent, so that the people had to cry out, "Where art thou?" Thus in the Psalms the human task is to wait and hope, while on God's part there is the secret of his freedom to come whenever he chooses.

But was not the Ark of Yahweh regularly carried into the temple? And did not this event involve the palpable demonstration of Yahweh's coming to the temple and the certainty of God's presence? Wasn't all worship in Jerusalem offered to the God who was present, Israel's God, who was enthroned on Zion and dwelt there? Was it not true that the worshiping community constantly, regularly acted on the assurance that they found fellowship with Yahweh in the sanctuary and were able to pray to him, knowing that he was present there? All these questions are to be answered with an unequivocal yes. This does not, however, indicate any sort of mechanical worship. That Yahweh "comes" and is present on Zion is understood everywhere in the Psalter as an expression of the חסד ("steadfast love") of Israel's God and as a proof of his אמת ("faithfulness"). This gives the central position to a personal element that is decisive here. That Yahweh "comes, he does not keep silence" (Ps. 50:3) is a constantly new manifestation of his grace, and that he appears again and again, and thus demonstrates his living presence, is the proof of his faithfulness. Manifestation of his grace and proof of his faithfulness are, however, as has been shown, based on Yahweh's actions in history by which he chose his people and made himself accessible to them. The entire cultus in Jerusalem harked back to these actions and drew from them God's assurance and promises.

Although the expression "community with God" is a general designation of the goal of the cult, a more precise and detailed definition is desirable. What is "community with God"? How was it expressed? Mowinckel (1953, p. 60) indicates the problems involved: "Men and women of ancient times had a tangible proof that an encounter with the deity actually took place in the cult—the experience of being filled with exalting, overwhelming feelings of power, which was expressed externally in ecstatic behavior." To be sure, we cannot deny the presence of ecstatic behavior in the cultic life of Israel. The תרועה ("festal shout") and many other acts of joy, excitement, dancing, and happiness accompanied the experience of God's presence in Jerusalem and of community with the *Deus praesens*. But they were secondary expressions of the assurance given by Yahweh's declaration, "I am your God, and you are my people." The God of Israel is not the stimulus to ecstatic possession as were the Baals of the nature cult of Canaan, but he is the one who through his deeds in history revealed himself, who rescued and liberated his people, and whose blessing on his people cannot be separated from his work in history (see above).

Those who gather for worship expect to receive life and blessing. This expectation is universal. Blessing could be termed the truly fundamental power of life. In the everyday world life is vulnerable, always threatened. "Men and women seek God in order to live, and God encounters them in order to give them life . . . . To gain life and to preserve it is the most elemental requirement of life" (Mowinckel, 1953, p. 61). Are we to assume that such elemental needs, expectations, and satisfactions were features of worship in Israel? Beyond any doubt. Mowinckel's portrayal, however, is to be corrected in two respects. First, we must make a deeper and more precise inquiry into the understanding of life in the Old Testament, and especially in the Psalms. This will be done in chap. 6, § A, where the anthropology of the Psalms is discussed. Here it must suffice to say that in the Psalms the understanding of life is permeated by the reality of Israel's relation to Yahweh their God as the people of God. Second, Yahweh is the living God. As the creator of all living beings he is the content and source of life. His divine, creative power over life does not decrease and can never be extinguished. This fact constitutes a new and basic aspect of our understanding of that which occurs in the cult.

Mowinckel clearly discerned the cultic pattern of the ancient Near East in its relation to the natural world, and he then endeavored to apply this to Israel's worship. During the dry summer in Palestine and Syria life dies, and the deity also dies. All life declines and approaches death. But the new year's festival brings a turning point in the cycle of the seasons. The deity "revives." "The cultus increases the deity's power to bless" (Mowinckel, 1953, p. 64). In the worship offered at the new year's festival the renewed life of the deity is made available to the cultic community. The cult effects a renewal of the life of nature. Mowinckel postulated an analogous procedure for Israel, with the specific modification that the world of myth and nature was "historicized." In Israel it was "an important part of the festival that history came alive again. Yahweh came again and renewed his covenant with his people, thus giving them new life. During the festival the community relived the ancient history of salvation—the exodus from Egypt, the miracle at the Sea of Reeds, the revelation at Sinai, experiencing it all as new and living reality. In this way Israel's religion is stamped with features that distinguish it from all the other cultic systems in ancient Near East" (Mowinckel, 1953, p. 73). Yet the distinctive and decisive nature of Israel's religion as determined by Mowinckel remains indistinct, because the concept of renewal seems to remain tied to nature, imprisoned by the rhythm of the seasons. The fundamental features of the ancient Near Eastern new year's festival are accorded too strong and uninterrupted an influence on the understanding of Old Testament worship. It was also held that, through history, worship in Israel brought about the renewal of the life of nature. The problems involved in these explanations have their roots deep within the explanations that Mowinckel advanced for the kingship of Yahweh and for the enthronement festival of the deity (see above chap. 3, § C). In the cult it was necessary that the kingship of Yahweh (which had been temporarily lost and was without authority) be renewed in an act of cultic enthronement in order to become effective (*renovatis renovandis*). This interpretation, however, does not agree with the statements that are dominant in the Psalter concerning Yahweh as king and creator, as Lord and source of life, as the God who is "immortal" (Hab. 1:12 NEB; cf. Kraus, 1972d, pp. 16ff.).

The concept of cultic renewal is in need of a thorough and comprehensive examination. What was the significance of renewal in Israel's cult? Is it at all possible to speak of renewal in reference to this cult? Is it even relevant to speak of a renewal of the covenant, for example? "Many writers speak of a covenant renewal festival. This concept presupposes a previous abrogation of the covenant, but that does not fit the case. 'Covenant festival' or 'covenant remembrance' seem to me to be more relevant terms" (R. Schmid, 1964, 106 A 16). But in Schmid's critical reflections is not the concept of renewal thought of in too rational and sequential a manner? In the Psalms the response to the "new" is a "new song" (Ps. 33:3; 96:1; 149:1). But what does "new" mean in biblical language? This is not the point hastily to introduce the concept of eschatology. One thing, however, can be asserted with certainty: that which is new is what Yahweh brings about, in contrast to all that is done by humans, supernatural powers, and deities. Newness and renewal derive their nature from Israel's God. At the same time the concept of renewal requires a comprehensive explanation in terms of its role in the cult.

Also belonging to this context is the question whether and, if so, how renewal is dramatized in the cult. To quote Mowinckel again, "The cultic rites and objects are never mere symbols." "In the cult something always happens. The cult is an event, a reality that occurs, a saving event that is self-realizing" (Mowinckel, 1953, p. 73). "Cult therefore bears a more or less dramatic nature; it is a cultic drama" (p. 74). Do these explanations apply to the worship of Israel? In what sense could they apply? What kind of event is it that takes place in the cult? What does it mean to say, "a saving event that is self-realizing"? What is the qualitative difference between what happens in the cult and what happens in history? It is clearly inadequate to assert that in Israel salvation history becomes reality through cultic dramatization. The understanding of time which is presupposed in every concept of actualization begins with the idea that historical events belong to the past. "History presupposes the past and what is past is what has lost its reality. In this sense the Hebrew mind hardly knows the past or history . . . . Past and present are one single act of God" (Köhler, 1956, pp. 118-119). In these terms everything that once happened belongs not to the past but to the present. The mighty deeds of Yahweh are a reality that brings life today. In that case speaking and acting can only testify to, bring near, and apply in the present that which Yahweh has done. That which is active in Israel's worship is not the presentation of cultic drama, but an application in speaking and acting that bears testimony to and communicates what Yahweh has done. Cultic drama stages a "representation," it brings back from the past that which is in danger of losing its living power. According to Mowinckel cultic drama is "creative drama" (1953, p. 78), in which magical, creative power inheres. This category, while it may be relevant to the representation of the mythical primeval time of the nations around Israel, does not do justice to worship in the Old Testament, because it ascribes the carrying out of the event and the creative, renewing powers to the cultic operation as such (*opus operatum*), while in the worship of Israel Yahweh alone is the one who is at work, who creates, who is present. Word, action, and gesture relate to what God does, relate to what God is accomplishing, and involve the worshipers in the event (cf. Exod. 12:11ff.). There is hardly anything of this sort to be found in the Psalms. The category of cultic drama is not really applicable to any of the Psalms. And yet the message addressed to Israel (in the most comprehensive sense) has preceded Israel's response which is proclaimed in the Psalter.

In all the explanations and presentations of Israel's cultic life, we must not leave out for a moment the broader theme of Yahweh's universal kingship. Yahweh is glorified as king and creator, as judge of the nations. Heaven and earth are his, and the nations must worship him. Israel's worship always involves the whole world and its history. The meaning of this often discussed aspect of Israelite worship must not be overlooked.

"Yahweh on Zion is seen in relation to the whole world in cosmic terms, as well as in relation to the world of the nations in political and social terms, and he is at work as creator of a world order that is life-preserving, and as guarantor of a life-sustaining course of the world. Even though at a somewhat earlier time Israel borrowed various similar statements from surrounding Canaanite sanctuaries and used them to describe Yahweh, these concepts as a whole represent a development toward a new Israelite knowledge of God. The traditional forms of the veneration of Yahweh in the period of the early Israelite state and the preceding period thereby took on new nuances and emphases because of the openness of these concepts to the universal dimensions of the work of Yahweh" (Steck, 1972, p. 21).

4. The King

Several songs in the Psalter celebrate the king. In Ps. 45:2 they are called מַעֲשַׂי לְמֶלֶךְ(maʿaśay lmelek). Hermann Gunkel (1933, § 5) called them "royal psalms." They include Psalms 2; (18); 20; 21; 45; 72; 89; 101; 132; 144:1-11. Concerning the group into which they fall by form, see the *Comm.*, Intro., § 6,3. It is not possible to identify a linguistic form common to all these psalms. The only distinctive feature of the royal psalms is the central figure of the king, which establishes the theme of kingship and sets a boundary. It is not legitimate to extend the concept of "royal songs" to psalms that contain no royal motifs or only weak allusions to such a motif. This means first of all that the title לְדָוִד ("of David"), which refers to a king, does not justify including the psalm that follows in this category, if the figure of the מֶלֶךְ ("king") does not clearly appear at any point.

Mowinckel began by interpreting kingship in Israel in terms of the examples from the ancient Near East, especially Babylon. He described the king's divinity as follows: "The king is holy, he is overwhelming in power. This means that he is divine, because holiness and power are specifically divine attributes. Whoever possesses them is more than human. Deification of the king is not foolishness, nor courtly flattery, but living religion" (1922, p. 302). What began with a leveling out of distinctions in terms of the history of religion was methodologically developed in the "pattern school." A "cultic pattern" and a "ritual pattern" were developed that were assumed to be common to the ancient Near East. And since, in the opinion of those who followed this line of research, death and resurrection, suffering and exaltation were elements of such a "pattern," a large number of psalms in the Psalter which Gunkel had designated as songs of lamentation and thanks were included under this pattern and thus regarded as "royal psalms." Special note should be taken of the collection of essays edited by S. H. Hooke under the title *Myth, Ritual and Kingship* (1958). Even writers such as Aage Bentzen (1948, p. 20), who considered the "ritual pattern" to be an abstraction and not something that could be positively identified, interpreted such psalms as 3; 11; 12; 13; 14, etc., as "royal psalms of lamentation." So extensive were the effects of the suggestion of a pattern! Most scholars assumed that a "democratization" of earlier royal psalms had taken place, but they still did not doubt that royal motifs were determinative for these psalms. It is easy to see that the dissolution of the boundaries of clearly distinct categories with the help of the pattern principle was an inappropriate measure which permitted speculation to go beyond all bounds.

In the criticism of the pattern principle it was of great importance to establish that there were differing concepts of kingship in the ancient Near East. In particular, Egypt and Mesopotamia had sharply different concepts, and in both areas a historical differentiation is to be assumed (see H. Frankfort [1948]; and C. J. Gadd [1948]. In addition it is important to point out that kingship in Israel had a distinctive origin and a particular history. It would be totally false to blur the contours of this origin and this history by subjecting them to a "pattern of divine kingship." For the criticism of this pattern see especially Noth (1957c, pp. 188-229).

In seeking to understand the royal psalms of the Old Testament it is extremely important to discover their Sitz-im-Leben. We should begin in an appropriate and concrete manner with a clear and well-differentiated consideration of the specific situation in Israel, and thus avoid confusing the issue by a cultic pattern derived from the ancient world of Israel's neighbors.

On what occasion were the royal psalms sung or recited? Psalm 110 provides a good starting point. It contains accounts of the situation and of messages connected with the coronation festival of a king in Jerusalem. Ancient privileges of the Jebusite king of the city of Jerusalem are transferred to a ruler from the Davidic dynasty. Psalms 2; 72; and 101 could also be regarded as songs that were part of the coronation ceremony. This, however, raises the question of whether the ascension to the throne corresponds to an annual festival of king and temple, a festival which dramatized the fundamental presuppositions of worship in Jerusalem—the choice of David and the choice of Zion—and was connected with the opening ceremonial of the chief annual pilgrimage festival. Gunkel was the first to call attention to this "annual festival" and its Egyptian parallels (1933, p. 141). Psalm 132 would then provide vital information about the festival. On the basis of this psalm it is possible to assume a cultic procedure that commemorated the choice of Jerusalem (Ps. 132:13) by a solemn procession with the Ark and the recitation of 2 Samuel 7 in commemoration of the choice of David and his dynasty (Ps. 132:11-12). It would also be possible to ascribe Psalms 2; 17; and 101 to this annual festival that opened the Feast of Booths, and call it a "royal Zion festival" (cf. Kraus, 1951b, pp. 50ff.; 1966, pp. 183ff.).

A totally different situation could be assumed on the basis of Psalm 45, which reflects a royal wedding. Thus it would still be necessary to determine in detail the situation in which the divine oracles, prayers, and songs of thanks of the king fit. In any case, the petition for the king is a significant element in the theology of kingship in the Old Testament, and so are the wishes for blessing on the king and the expressions of praise which show the influence of the phraseology of ancient Near Eastern courtly style.

Literature on the royal psalms: K. R. Crim (1962); S. S. Patro (1976); W. H. Schmidt (1975, pp. 180ff., where further references are to be found).

A. Terminology

In the overwhelming number of cases the central figure in the royal psalms is called מֶלֶךְ ("king"): Ps. 2:6; 20:8; 21:1, 7; 45:1; 61:6; 63:11; 72:1; 89:18. Here are to be included petitions for the king that are found in other psalm categories. In Ps. 144:10 the plural מלכים ("kings") is found, and there it refers to the rulers from the dynasty of David. A distinctive feature is the use of the term "anointed" (משׁיח) for the king of Israel: Ps. 2:2; 20:7; 84:9; 89:38, 51; 132:10. The use of possessive suffixes is interesting. The king is Yahweh's anointed: Ps. 2:2; 20:7; 84:9; 89:38, 51; 132:10. Psalm 89:20 even declares that Yahweh himself has anointed him with the holy oil (cf. Ps. 45:7). W. H. Schmidt (1975, p. 199) has summarized the research on the act of anointing as follows: "It is by no means obvious that the anointing constituted an essential part of the coronation ritual. It occurred from time to time in the installation of high Egyptian officials, and a Syrian vassal prince was made a king, according to an Amarna letter, by Pharaoh Thutmose III, who poured oil on his head. Still there are no clear instances of the anointing of a king himself, either from Egypt or Mesopotamia. It would thus seem that the practice was unknown in both these empires. The Hittite king, however, was anointed by the people or the nobles, as was often the case in the Old Testament. Thus it would be easy to assume that the rite in Israel and Judah goes back to Hittite custom, probably mediated through Canaan" (see also E. Kutsch, 1963, p. 56). In Israel anointing assumed great importance. It placed the ruler under Yahweh's protection and signified that his person was not to be violated (Ps. 105:15; 1 Sam. 24:6; Ps. 89:20-28). The משׁיח (*messiah*, "anointed") was also equipped with the charismatic gifts which his office required, and given full power to fulfill his office as Yahweh's king. At this point it should not be overlooked that in ancient Israel the charismatic leaders and deliverers of the age of the judges were equipped with the רוח יהוה ("spirit of Yahweh"). Since this רוח ("spirit") was transmitted by anointing (1 Sam. 10:1ff.; 16:13f.; 2 Sam. 23:1f.), the רוח ("spirit") came to be spoken of as "resting" or "remaining" on the anointed one (Isa. 11:2; 61:1). In any case anointing is an act that transformed and renewed the recipient. Calvin rightly termed this a creative process ("creare," CR 59:42). Anointing might be understood as belonging to the realm of magic and taboo if it were not always remembered that it is Yahweh's act and choice that gave the king in Israel his dignity and office. The God of Israel *chose* David and his dynasty (Ps. 89:3, 20; 132:11). Therefore the king is called Yahweh's "chosen one" (Ps. 89:3, 20). It is not the ideal of the establishment of power but the secret of divine choice that upholds and directs the monarchy. Yahweh's anointed is the chosen king of the chosen people.

In Babylon it was held that the kingship came down from heaven in mythical prehistory (AOT, 2d ed., p. 167), but in Israel the concepts are quite different. It is not possible to speak of kingship as such. "The striking historical aspect of kingship in Israel is that Israel established this institution only late in its history" (Noth, 1957c, p. 216). Kingship was introduced in the face of strong opposition, and it rested on different presuppositions in Israel compared with Judah (cf. Alt, 1959b, pp. 116-134). In the Psalms, what is said of the king always involves the name David. David is the first one to be chosen (Ps. 89:3, 20, 35; 132:1, 10, 17; 144:10). The kings in Jerusalem (Ps. 144:10) are the "seed," the descendants of David, and therefore the heirs of the promise given through Nathan (2 Samuel 7), which promised David and his family an everlasting kingdom. In order to carry out this promise, Yahweh chose David and, as later expressions put it, established a "covenant" with David and his descendants. That is how deeply the kingdom in Jerusalem is anchored in the history of Israel, and therefore in the mighty deeds of Yahweh! Here any mythological exaggeration or generalizing in phenomenological terms is excluded.

It is necessary to show that such foreign religious terminology as calling the king the "son of God" has been brought under the influence of the theology of divine choice and thus has been "demythologized." In Ps. 2:7 the ruler is declared to be the son of Yahweh. We must examine in detail how this expression is related to the father-son relationship indicated in Ps. 89:27. Since in the act of coronation the ruler is called to Yahweh's side and is invited to take his place, "Sit at my right hand" (Ps. 110:1), he can be called "the man of thy right hand" (Ps. 80:18). As the one enthroned at the right hand of God, the ruler shares in Yahweh's dignity and power as עליון ("highest"), and he can be acclaimed as "the highest of the kings of the earth" (Ps. 89:27). Many expressions must be understood as part of the ancient Near Eastern court style. Filled with awe, a cultic speaker calls the king "my lord" (Ps. 110:1), accords to him the divine designation "shield" (Ps. 84:9-11; 89:18), and even addresses him as אלהים ("god," Ps. 45:6). The correctness of this reading has been disputed. Noth offers the explanation that "It is beyond doubt that the Jerusalem monarchy, and even more, the monarchy in the states of Israel and Judah, was never regarded as divine." He adds, "When this statement is made, it should at once be added that even in Ps. 45:6 the king is not addressed as 'God'. . . ." He goes on to suggest that the sentence should be translated as, "Thy throne is [like] that of God, enduring for ever and ever" (1957c, p. 225). The principle that Noth established should be firmly maintained: in Israel the king was not regarded as equal to God, and thus was never consciously addressed in theological terms as אלהים ("god"). Of course, the exaggerations of the court style make it seem otherwise. The bold hyperbole is unmistakable when the ruler is then described as "the fairest among the sons of men" (v. 2), and when the epithet "divine" is added (v. 6). In the exaggerated praise of a wedding song the term אלהים ("god") is not a reliable indication of apotheosis, but a bold stroke of the court style in praise of the "divine." The context makes this clear. Moreover, it is quite possible that such hyperbole developed in Israel out of the Canaanite traditions of the cultic center, as did the office of the "priest-king" ("priest for ever after the order of Melchizedek") in Ps. 110:4, part of the heritage of the pre-Israelite, Jebusite traditions.

Striking, but still not well explained is the fact that in a Psalm of petition (Ps. 80:17) the king is called בן־אדם (ben adam, "son of man"). This is terminology that belongs to the complex of ideas found in Deut. 7:13-16 and in apocalyptic writings. This raises the question of what role the myths of the primeval man played in Israel's theology of kingship. Apparently they exerted only a peripheral influence on the Old Testament traditions, since they are found only in rudimentary form. It is only in apocalyptic that they can be clearly identified. Thus it would be a serious mistake to engage in a hasty and stereotyped application of the אדם (adam) traditions (as seen for example in Ps. 8:4-8) to the monarchy and to indulge in speculations about an ideology of the primeval man as king. In this area the Old Testament is quite sober in its approach. In the statements concerning creation, אדם (adam, "Adam") is a real man and not a "primeval royal figure." Thus the בן־אדם (ben adam) in Ps. 80:17 belongs to the (hidden) prehistory of the theology of the son of man that appears in apocalyptic.

The insignia and symbols of the king's authority are found in the context of the portrayals of the king in the Psalter. The ruler wears a crown, a diadem built around a golden circlet (נצר, *neṣer*, Ps. 132:18, and also in Ps. 89:19; see *Comm.*). This crown can also be called עטרת (*'aṭeret*, Ps. 21:3). In addition the king holds a "royal scepter" (Ps. 45:6; 89:44; 110:2). He sits on a throne with his feet on a footstool (Ps. 110:1; 89:4, 14, 29, 36, 44; 132:11-12). There is still a question of where the throne stood. On the problems involved, see the *Comm.* on Psalm 110.

Section 2 below examines the role of the king in worship and section 3 his charismatic gifts and his duties as ruler. A basic orientation toward these aspects has been done most clearly by Bernhardt (1961, p. 225): "According to the evidence of the historical books of the Old Testament, the Israelite understanding of kingship was quite distinct from the ancient Near Eastern royal ideology at three crucial points: (*a*) the identity of God and king; (*b*) the king as an object of cultic worship; and (*c*) the power of the king over the forces of nature . . . . There is no evidence of any of these three elements in the Psalter."

B. The King in Worship

It is beyond doubt that in Israel's worship the king was not the object of veneration. Not even rudiments can be found of any veneration offered to him. At the same time the reigning king in Jerusalem exercised cultic functions. According to Ps. 110:4 the office of priest (כהן) was conferred on him. Following the ancient Jebusite order, the Davidic kings were priest-kings, "after the order of Melchizedek." They were responsible for performing mediatorial functions, such as offering prayer for all cultic institutions in the royal sanctuary in Jerusalem (1 Kings 8:22-26), blessing the assembled people of the nation (1 Kings 8:14), and, on special occasions, offering sacrifices (1 Kings 8:62-63). In Jer. 30:21 the technical term that describes the access of the king to the Holy of Holies is קרב, "draw near." Thus, it is to be taken as established that the king exercised cultic functions of the type described.

In the annual celebration of the royal Zion festival, however, and in the act of enthronement the king was at the center of the cultic event, as can be deduced especially from Psalm 132. Since motifs from the enthronement at the beginning of a reign and those from the regularly celebrated festivals overlap, it seems best to discuss the cultic features of enthronement in the light of all the available texts, and then on the basis of Psalm 132 to seek to identify aspects of the annual festival.

Psalm 110 contains the most clearly recognizable descriptions and texts of an enthronement festival. The solemn rites of initiation and consecration and the oracles present the picture of an enthronement in a fragmentary, but still impressive, form. There have been attempts to reconstruct the program of such a ceremony. The attempts of L. Dürr and G. Widengren deserve mention. Dürr (1929) compared Psalm 110 with the Egyptian Rameses papyrus and thought he could identify the following ceremonial order: (1) enthronement, (2) investiture, (3) adoration, (4) installation as priest, (5) and (6) victory over the foes, (7) sacramental drink from the holy spring. Widengren (1955) proposed a different order: (1) divine oracle, with the proclamation of divine sonship, (2) ascension to the throne, (3) taking possession of the scepter, (4) presentation of gifts to the king, (5) putting on the robes, (6) presentation of the king, (7) drink from the spring.

Such reconstructions always overlook the fact that the Psalms of the Old Testament do not contain any complete rituals. This is also the case in Psalm 110.

The King

We have only excerpts from the ritual, rudimentary descriptions of the situation and of the texts taken out of a larger cultic context, which it is not possible to reconstruct as a whole. Thus in Psalm 110 we have primarily the pre-Israelite, Jebusite royal traditions, related particularly to the Melchizedek traditions and concentrated on the investiture and consecration of the ruler as priestly king "after the order of Melchizedek" (Ps. 110:4). Drinking from the well (the Spring of Gihon) was probably an ancient rite in the enthronement ritual in Jerusalem (Ps. 110:7). In view of these specific citations from the ritual it should not and cannot be forgotten that the ruler enthroned in Jerusalem united several offices in his person and, therefore, that in the act of enthronement several assumptions and traditions concerning his office had to be taken into account and their authority conferred on the ruler. This king is not only the heir of the old Jebusite city kingdom (Psalm 110; Gen. 14:18f.), but he is also and above all the successor to the Davidic dynasty (2 Samuel 7; Psalm 132). He was also crowned king of Judah (2 Sam. 2:4), and in him the traditions of all Israel are present (2 Sam. 5:3), as they related to the Ark sanctuary (Psalm 132). Finally, he is heir of the "crown" of Jerusalem, the "city of David" (2 Sam. 5:9). All these individual traditions came to expression in the cultic ceremony of enthronement in Jerusalem and will now be portrayed, to the extent the royal psalms permit us to do so. It is of great methodological significance that research into the cultic practices of the Old Testament be characterized by study of tradition history in a manner that differentiates and draws distinctions and is not distorted by phenomenological stereotypes. With this understanding and with care in observing rudimentary distinctions, we may turn to Psalm 110.

At the beginning of the sacred ritual of enthronement a message is proclaimed (Ps. 110:1; cf. 2:2, 7-8; 110:3, 4). This involves the actual transferral of authority, the basic legitimation. Parallels are found in the Egyptian royal procedures, in which the conferring of authority and the bestowal of the regnal name are constant elements (cf. von Rad, 1971b). In the Old Testament these procedures are called עדות (ʿedut, 2 Kings 11:12) or חק (ḥoq Ps. 2:7). Outside the Psalms the promulgations of the regnal name is found in Isa. 9:6. That it is not found in the royal psalms is evidence of the fragmentary nature of the selected parts of the ritual in the Psalter. In any case we may assume fixed procedures in documentary form, as mentioned in Ps. 2:7 by the term חק (ḥoq). Attention should also be called to the fact that such procedures of fundamental legitimacy in the Old Testament are called "decree of Yahweh" and thus are shown to involve a prophetic communication. To put it differently, the conferring of sovereign authority in Israel is from the outset recognized in prophetic proclamation as a basis of law. The oracle of Yahweh in Ps. 110:1 is introduced by the word נאם (neʾum), which is characteristic of prophecy. This is not the place to go into the whole problem of cultic prophecy, but we are justified in assuming that prophetically inspired speakers were involved in the cultic act of enthronement in Jerusalem.

If we begin with a consideration of Psalm 110 and Ps. 2:7 we can establish that there were three distinctive features in the official conferral of authority according to protocol, features which must have had primary significance in the tradition. First, there was a solemn declaration that the king was the "son of God" (Ps. 2:7; 110:3). Second, there was the exhortation to ascend the throne at the "right hand" of God (Ps. 110:1). And third, the one who ascended the throne was declared to be the legitimate heir of the normative royal tradition of Jerusalem (e.g., the Melchizedek tradition, Ps. 110:4). Here too we should recognize that the identifiable elements are only selections from the ritual.

Since the ruler is solemnly proclaimed the ''son of God'' we can speak of a throne name, in correspondence with Egyptian royal procedures. The decisive factor, however, is the transformation of the king's essential nature which is made known in the declaration (clearly announced by a prophet) in the important passage Ps. 2:7: ''You are my son, today I have begotten you.'' This fixed, official statement of the sacral royal law was communicated at the enthronement of the king, whether it was an enthronement reenacted annually or one that had just taken place. The king lays claim to this statement and makes it known. It is also possible that the actual making of the statement was as such an arcane event.

In the ancient Near East it was a common concept that the king was the ''son of God.'' In contrast to those ancient interpretations of divine sonship of a ruler, careful distinctions must be drawn. The main question here is that of the context and presuppositions with which the title ''son of God'' in Ps. 2:7 is to be understood. We must begin with Ps. 2:7, because the parallels in Ps. 110:3, which reflect the enthronement procedures more clearly, present us with problems which can be clarified only if the question is first answered in reference to Ps. 2:7. In recent scholarship it has frequently been assumed that in the Old Testament, as in the ancient Near East as a whole, a mythological, physical relationship is to be assumed, in which the king is the son of God. But it must be kept in mind that we cannot assume a single, unified concept in the ancient Near East. In the Egyptian traditions the Pharaoh can be termed ''son of God'' in the sense of an incarnate deity, begotten by the God Amon and born of the queen mother. But such mythological, physical concepts of the king's divine sonship are totally foreign to the Old Testament. The king in Jerusalem becomes the ''son of God'' by being called to that status and installed in a ceremony that confers power and authority. More specifically, the king's sonship is based on an adoption formula. By adoption the ruler is declared, through a prophetic announcement of a legal act, to be the son of God. For the legal act of adoption outside the royal procedures, see Gen. 30:3; 50:23. Here we see the true depths of the conferral of power and sovereignty that is expressed in the חֹק (*ḥoq,* ''procedure''). The prophetic and procedural declaration, ''You are my son, today I have begotten you,'' is disclosed as a creative word that establishes a new existence. The divine choice is reflected in adoption. The chosen king is placed at God's side by adoption. He is elevated to the position of representative of God's sovereignty and of heir to his power (Ps. 2:7-9). Thus it is that in the Old Testament ''the king was not 'son of God' by nature, nor did he by his ascending the throne necessarily enter into the sphere of the divine, but by a decision of Israel's God he was *declared* to be son at his entry into the office of king'' (Noth, 1957c, p. 222).

Thus the king in Jerusalem did not become ''son of God'' in mythological prehistory or in a mysterious event in which deity and humanity were united. He became ''son of God'' *today,* the day in which he was declared God's son through adoption and enthronement. The decisive factors were conceptions drawn from the realm of family law, not foreign myths (cf. Gese, 1974). In this context it is appropriate to note that Calvin himself recognized that the statement in Ps. 2:7 did not point to a ''perpetual act outside of time,'' but to the concrete ''time in which it was enacted'' (CR 59:46). The simple meaning of the text is falsified not only by interpreting it in terms of foreign mythologies, but also by Christological speculations imposed on the Old Testament.

The father-son relationship between Yahweh and his king, which is seen in Ps. 2:7, requires further explanation. It is clear that in Ps. 2:7 the ruler's sonship was constituted by the authoritative declarations of adoption, just as the statement in the Code of Hammurabi § 170f., "You are my children," involves the legally valid incorporation into the family group. In 2 Sam. 7:14 and Ps. 89:27-28, however, we find another basis for the father-son relationship between God and his regent. Yahweh's statement, "I will be his father, and he shall be my son" (2 Sam. 7:14), has a parallel in the covenant announcement in Jer. 31:33, "I will be their God, and they shall be my people." Such a formulation of the father-son relationship involves the "covenant with David." The Davidic covenant is spoken of in a manner analogous to statements about the covenant with Israel. Just as the covenant with Israel has its basis in Yahweh's choice, so the Davidic covenant goes back to God's act of choice (cf. especially Ps. 89:3-4). On the Davidic covenant see Ps. 89:3, 28; 132:11; Isa. 55:3; 2 Sam. 23:5; Jer. 33:21. On the choice of David, see 1 Kings 8:16; Ps. 89:3. In the Davidic tradition, the divine choice of David and the covenant with him are based on the promise of Nathan (2 Samuel 7) and extend to the entire Davidic dynasty as the חסדי דוד ("pious ones of David") Ps. 21:7; 89:24, 28, 33). This requires a more detailed discussion in the context of the explanation of the essential statements in Psalm 132.

Parallel to the declaration of divine sonship in Ps. 2:7 is the mysterious statement in Ps. 110:3, which is difficult to understand and is accessible only through text-critical emendation (see the *Comm.* on this passage):

> On the holy mountains,
> out of the womb of the dawn
> have I begotten you like dew.

It must of course be asked whether the reconstruction of the original text, as attempted in the above translation, is successful. It remains in any case hypothetical. If we attempt a provisional justification, we note the difference between Ps. 2:7 and Ps. 110:3. In Ps. 2:7 the transformation into "son of God" takes place through the declaration of adoption, while in Ps. 110:3 the begetting of the king is described in mysterious figures of speech. It took place "on the holy mountains," out of the "womb of the dawn," and "like dew." There are possibilities of interpretation by association with other figures in the Old Testament and the ancient Near East. In Isa. 14:12, for example, the king of Babylon is termed "son of dawn." But reference to the *hieros gamos* ("sacral marriage") does not advance our understanding. Neither will it be fruitful to look for a connection with the Ugaritic deity *šḥr*. On the contrary, Ps. 110:3 is to be interpreted by archaic metaphors. In Josh. 8:20 and Isa. 58:8 the dawn is a symbol of hope and a turn for the better, comparable with the star that arises out of Jacob (Num. 24:17). The intention of the mysterious statement in Psalm 110 seems to be to ascribe the location and process of begetting to the heavenly sphere. The king comes forth from heights beyond this world, from the world of God. His appearance is like something that will "dawn upon us from on high" (Luke 1:78). Thus in Ps. 110:3 on the day when the ruler ascends the throne he is ascribed miraculous origin from on high and the hope of a dawning light, birth from the "heavenly world." In the archaic metaphors there are fragments of a mythology that we are no longer able to interpret. It is thus quite possible that elements of an old Jebusite royal ideology lie hidden in this text. Only the intention to interpret the metaphors in the light of their context will enable us to decipher the archaisms. Once again we emphasize that this can be only an attempt.

Gese (1974) translates and interprets the text of Ps. 110:3 quite differently, and reference to his interpretation should at least be made here. Gese begins by looking at the first lines of v. 3: " 'There are nobles with you on the day of your power.' This day of power . . . is clearly the then-present day of enthronement; it continues in analogy to Ps. 2:7, 'In the holy mountain land, out of the mother, out of the dawn have I borne you.' The 'holy mountains' are Zion (as in Ps. 87:1 and also Ps. 2:6; 3:4; 15:1; 43:3; 99:9), where this birth takes place, which is formulated here with special concreteness as birth 'out of the womb.' The immediately following word explains the womb as being dawn. In contrast to the attempt to see demythologizing in Ps. 2:7, one should not fall into the opposite extreme and see in this reference to womb the Canaanite goddess *šḥr*, because *šḥr* is a god and not a goddess and thus cannot at all be what is meant here."

Therefore, more significant for understanding the content of the basic legitimation of the ruler in the act of enthronement is the declaration that he is "son of God." This signifies transformation of his being to that of a man who is fully committed to God's side, as God's representative and heir, as the administrator of God's lordship over Israel. More is to be said about his role as heir (see § C below). First we must consider the consequences of his being declared to be the son of God. Psalm 110 draws a bold conclusion with the exhortation, "Sit at my right hand." Yahweh himself speaks to the king with a prophetic message (Ps. 110:1). This points to the Holy of Holies, where Yahweh's presence is made known in Jerusalem. The ruler is to take his place beside Yahweh. This makes it clear what position and office he now undertakes. The one enthroned is exalted, and he takes part in Yahweh's glory. As the "man of thy right hand" (Ps. 80:17) he sees the demonstration of God's power: his foes lie stretched out like a stool for his feet. Like Yahweh himself he is now the king עֶלְיוֹן (*'Elyon*), "the highest of the kings of the earth" (Ps. 89:27). It is a logical development of all these acts of conferring power and authority that in the Chronicler's history it is declared that the king sits on Yahweh's throne (1 Chron. 28:5; 29:23; 2 Chron. 9:8; 13:8). Yahweh's lordship over Israel and over the nations gains concrete human form in the one who is enthroned.

The one who in this manner is exalted to the throne is declared to be the heir to the royal traditions which have their home in Jerusalem. In Psalm 110 this occurs in the installation into the office of priest-king "after the order of Melchizedek" (Ps. 110:4). As has already been mentioned, the Davidic king entered into the ancient functions of the Jebusite royal city-state, whose founder was Melchizedek. Genesis 14:18 tells how this Melchizedek exercised his priestly office in ancient Jerusalem. As priest of God Most High he offered bread and wine; as royal representative of the "maker of heaven and earth" he had at his disposal the power to bestow blessing (v. 19). In this manner, then, the descendants of David were also installed as priest-kings.

To be sure, this installation was not a part of the genuine and primary tradition of Israel. It received secondary acceptance from the cultic traditions of Jerusalem. Everything which is found in Psalm 132 is a genuine and primary part of the Israel tradition. The cultic Sitz-im-Leben of this psalm has already been alluded to. Two events portrayed in it were represented in a living and impressive manner: the choice of Zion and the choice of David and his dynasty. Therefore, the corresponding festival can be identified as a "royal Zion festival," a cultic festival which annually called to remembrance the presuppositions and origins both of the sanctuary on Zion and David's dynasty. At the same time, in this structure of remembrance, it gave visible expression to the currently valid fundamental principles of the cultic community. It is naturally to be expected that such a Yahweh festival would include themes and protocol texts from the cultic enthronement. Thus, for instance, the question of the Sitz-im-Leben of Psalm 2 cannot be answered unequivocally.

But what was the form of the royal Zion festival which we infer from Psalm 132? What ideas and concepts motivated it and gave it form? Before these questions can be answered we must first remind ourselves of the limited possibility of reconstructing the festival. Even Psalm 132 does not provide us with a ritual. We find only isolated scenes and excerpts. But these scenes and excerpts are so clearly related to cultic observances that any interpretation that ignored the clear relationships of the psalm to a festival will fall into highly problematical reconstructions. It is beyond dispute that Psalm 132 is a representation of the events of the transfer of the Ark of the Covenant to Jerusalem. There are clear and specific references to the events of David's reign which are preserved in the traditions contained in 2 Samuel 6. In addition, the psalm is a reminder of promises made to David, to that significant encounter with the prophet Nathan, in which "the Lord swore to David a sure oath from which he will not turn back: 'One of the sons of your body I will set on your throne' " (Ps. 132:11). That is, it involves a reenactment of the divine choice of David and of his whole dynasty. This remarkable double theme is found also in 1 Kings 8:16. God had chosen Jerusalem as the place where his name would dwell, and David as the one who would rule over God's people, Israel.

Without going into the details of scholarly investigation of this theme, the following points may be used to summarize the results. (1) 2 Samuel 6 is the conclusion and climax of the *hieros logos* (sacral tradition) of the ancient Israelite sanctuary of the Ark in Jerusalem. Such a *hieros logos* is retold over and over, making the past come alive again. It is even probable that the account of the conclusion of the transfer of the Ark to Zion found in 2 Samuel 6 points to a cultic repetition of this significant event, a vivid and moving presentation of the divine choice of Jerusalem and one which makes itself effective through the remembrance of the original event. (2) Just as David had earlier moved the Ark to Jerusalem and in so doing constituted the Zion sanctuary the cultic center of Israel, so too in the cultic reenactment of that event each successive heir to David's throne could repeat the moving of the Ark and assume the position of his ancestor. The cultic relevance of assuming David's role is shown by the petition in Ps. 132:10, "For thy servant David's sake do not turn away the face of thy anointed one." (3) In reference both to David and to his successors there is the question: who authorized David and his dynasty to transport the Ark to Jerusalem, to reign as king in Zion, and as the "son of God" to be the representative of Yahweh's sovereignty? The answer is contained in the promise given through Nathan, which is preserved in 2 Samuel 7, but whose original form is not readily recognizable there. In Ps. 132:11-12 the choice of David and his dynasty is depicted as follows:

The Lord swore to David a sure oath
  from which he will not turn back:
''One of the sons of your body
  I will set on your throne.
If your sons keep my covenant
  and my testimonies which I shall teach them,
their sons also for ever
  shall sit upon your throne.''

    The cultic reenactment of the promise given through Nathan which is expressed in these lines makes clear the intention of the original prophetic oracle: a continuing, eternal kingdom was promised to David. It is this fact which constituted the fundamental, genuinely Israelite royal tradition in Jerusalem in all the ages through which the kingdom endured. How could there be any doubt that the recurring reference to the Nathan oracle was given cultic dramatization and was regarded as the basis of the legitimacy of the royal sanctuary on Zion? We must bear in mind how close the relationship was in the ancient Near East between kingship and sanctuary. The king was lord of the temple. As the central figure, he stood in the middle of cultic life, especially when in the rhythm of the year the cult began anew and had to make visible once more the basis on which it rested. In Jerusalem, however, within the framework of the Zion cult as determined by Israel's history, that could take place only if the basic events recorded in 2 Samuel 6 and 7 were made present reality in worship.

    For the details of the scholarly research, which cannot be presented here, consult L. Rost (1926), M. Noth (1957e), and H. J. Kraus (1951a, 1966).

    If we bear in mind that no rituals are preserved in the Psalter, and that we can by no means count on there being a complete reflection of cultic life in the texts, then we must rest content with what is communicated to us from the royal cult. Hypotheses concerning the role of the king in worship are to be kept within bounds, the bounds drawn by each of the texts and by the form in which they have been preserved. Yet beyond what has already been said, we must consider the significance of prayer in worship, especially in relationship to the king. The ruler as ''son of God'' could claim an inexhaustible παρρησία (''freedom'')—the right freely to voice petitions. In the historical books of the Old Testament two texts show what is involved. In 1 Kings 3:5 Yahweh himself tells Solomon, ''Ask what I shall give you.'' The rights of the ruler as son include the privilege of free and comprehensive petition. In case of a transgression the king could even choose his own punishment (2 Sam. 24:12). In the light of such boundless παρρησία (''freedom''), which in Ps. 2:8 is directly connected with the divine sonship of the one being enthroned, it was the expression of the desires of the cultic community in worship during the enthronement: ''May he grant you your heart's desire, and fulfill all your plans!'' (Ps. 20:4). The community is concerned for the continual validity and efficacy of the royal privilege to voice petitions freely. Psalm 21:2 testifies to the actual fulfillment of the divine promise and the granting of the petition. God had heard the wishes and desires of the king. He asked God for long life, and the request has been granted (Ps. 21:4). This evidence from Psalm 21 shows that ceremonies of worship concerned with the demonstration of God's grace toward the monarchy accompanied the entire life of a king.

117

The King

Therefore, it is easy to understand how petitions for the king, which are expressed in the Psalter in various literary categories, play so large a role. In Ps. 20:1-5, a royal psalm, petitions for the king are presented in the form of wishes and urgent hopes. On the day of peril may Yahweh hear and protect the ruler, be present with him, remember the sacrifices he has offered, and fulfill all his desires. Another royal psalm, Psalm 72, is introduced by a petition, the content of which is still to be discussed: "Give the king thy justice, O God, and thy righteousness to the royal son!" (Ps. 72:1). Petitions are also found in Ps. 132:1, 10. Moreover, there are other psalm categories in which petitions for the king are expressed. In the תפלה Ps. 61:6-7 an individual prays,

> Prolong the life of the king;
>   may his years endure to all generations!
> May he be enthroned for ever before God;
>   bid steadfast love and faithfulness watch over him!

The heart of the one offering the prayer is always concerned that there be full and joyful realization of the relationship between God and the king (Ps. 63:11). The content of the petition is that Yahweh would look with mercy upon the king (Ps. 84:9).

The wedding festival of the king, which we see depicted in Psalm 45, was a part of the wider realm of the royal cult. The question naturally arises as to why such a psalm was included in the canon. Certainly the occasion and the text cannot simply be considered as secular. It involves an event in the royal cult. In this respect the Psalm differs from the collection of love songs in the Song of Solomon. On the other side, however, Psalm 45 cannot simply be subsumed under the mythological theme of the *hieros gamos* (sacral marriage). What significance should then be ascribed to such a psalm? How was the song understood at the time it was canonized? The monarchy was at an end. Other psalms could be included under a "messianic motif" (which still remains to be discussed), but a wedding song can hardly be placed in this category. Was the whole song interpreted "spiritually"? To be sure, allegorical explanations are common in the history of Jewish interpretation. For example, they interpret the bride as the community. This type of interpretation was continued by the exegetical tradition of the church. Still this was a false path. In consideration of the actual content of the statements of Psalm 45 we must look at the simple meaning of the words of the text. It is immediately obvious that the numerous attributes of perfection ascribed to the king transcend empirical reality and are designed to portray an ideal figure (H. Gunkel). It could even be said that we have here a visionary portrayal of primeval beauty and splendid humanity that borders on the divine world (Ps. 45:6). "The royal psalms reveal the kingdom and the office of the anointed one according to his still hidden divine *doxa* [glory], which they already have, and which might be made manifest at any moment" (von Rad, 1940–1941).

Psalm 45 praises the full glory of shining beauty, the fragrance of incense, the splendor that points to that which is more than human, and the amazing richness of the scene. All the available oriental coloring is used to present to the eye the military might and the imposing form of the ruler. The music of stringed instruments accompanies the portrayal. So we must affirm that this wedding song has at least the tendency to portray a messianic picture of perfection. The king who has received his authority from Yahweh (and that would be a cautious, provisional definition of the concept ''messiah'') is the most splendid human figure of them all, a divine prince among rulers. The splendor of all the peoples pales before this manifestation of glory. God's chosen king, in the great earthly felicity of marriage, is being honored. Foreign nations too are included (Ps. 45:10-12). The theme of Isa. 60:3-7 also characterizes Psalm 45. The wedding song written for a king in Israel is the epitome of homage and veneration, of joy and celebration, of beauty and complete good fortune. It may tentatively be asked whether it is not the case that in such a psalm of adoration the messianic metaphor of marriage is being expressed, a metaphor that plays such a great role in the New Testament: Matt. 22:2-14; 25:10; 9:15; John 2:1-11.

C. Charisma and Commission

In the act of enthronement and of basic legitimation, the anointed of Yahweh received the royal charisma and the concrete commissions which he was to carry out as representative and administrator of the splendor and glory of his God. The inner significance of charisma and commission involved right and righteousness. Prayers were offered that the ruler would receive the gift of rendering helpful judgments and dispensing justice (Ps. 72:1). It was his commission to judge the people in righteousness, but above all to be the advocate and support of the weak and oppressed (Ps. 72:2, 4, 12ff.). As the one who defended the divine will for justice against men of violence, the king was to carry out the office of judge—on behalf of those to whom justice had been denied. He loved righteousness and hated wickedness (Ps. 45:7). He was to intervene for the oppressed when there was no longer any other voice raised on their behalf. In Jerusalem there were ''thrones for judgment . . . the thrones of the house of David'' (Ps. 122:5).

To be sure, it is nothing unique in the ancient Near East that the ruler should function as the highest judge and the advocate of the poor. What is probably most noteworthy in Israel is the twofold basic relationship of the royal office of judge in Jerusalem. First, the kings who pronounce judgment on Zion are successors of an ancient Israelite institution, which was embodied in the office of ''judge of Israel.'' This ''judge of Israel'' had the responsibility to ''know and explicate the law and to give information about it,'' to watch over its observance, and to be responsible for its application to new situations and thus see to it that it is further developed and validated (Noth, 1969). When the monarchy became established in Israel, the old system confronted a crisis. There is no doubt that the Davidic kings rendered the final verdict in legal cases and in the framework of their royal charisma and commission continued the old tradition and institution (cf. 2 Sam. 15:1-6; 1 Kings 3:16-28; Jer. 21:12; Isa. 16:5; 11:3). Second, the judicial activity of the kings in Jerusalem is to be seen in its consistent reference to Yahweh, the God of righteousness and justice. Righteousness and justice proceed directly from the God of Israel (Ps. 72:1). The king must submit himself fully to the righteous will of God. As צדיק (''righteous'') he stands in a right relationship to his God, a relationship in which Yahweh's own righteousness and his own justice will be able to find expression.

The influence of the monarchy operating under the authority of Yahweh went beyond the sphere of justice and the pronouncement of verdicts. It involved the שׁלוֹם (*shalom*) of the land and the people. The ruler, of course, had no power over the forces of nature; he did not participate in the creative power of God or in God's power that sustains the world. And yet the effects of Yahweh's saving presence with his king as felt in the life of the people and in the world of nature are themes of the royal psalms: "Let the mountains bear prosperity for the people, and the hills, in righteousness!" (Ps. 72:3). Life, bounteous harvest, good fortune and blessing in boundless measure—these are the expectations connected with Yahweh's presence with his king, and they are not to be thought of as due to the immanent power of a "divine monarchy." Thus the petitions and hopes that look toward שלום (*shalom*), in the most comprehensive sense of the word, are closely connected with the monarchy in Jerusalem.

In external affairs the charisma and commission of the king are characterized by war and the conquest of all foes. Yahweh himself arms his anointed when he goes to war against the foes of his people (Ps. 18:39). God intervenes for his king and aids him (Ps. 2:5, 8-9; 21:8-9; 110:2-3, 5; 144:1-2). With Yahweh's help the king defeats and destroys all his enemies. They are made a stool for his feet (Ps. 110:1). Just as in matters of justice so too in reference to the military activities of the ruler in Jerusalem we must note a twofold relationship which sharply distinguishes Old Testament kingship from lust for world conquest and the search for power. For one thing, in the Israelite monarchy the tradition of the charismatic deliverers of the period of the judges was still alive. The spirit which suddenly overpowered the men of God in olden times, and for a time enabled them to perform great works of deliverance, was at work also in those who were the anointed of Yahweh, the kings. The Spirit empowered them and authorized them to perform deeds of valor by which Israel was liberated and brought into a life of שלום (*shalom*). In the second place, it is Yahweh himself who is involved in the battles of the kings. Just as in the holy wars of ancient Israel it was Yahweh alone who intervened for his people, led them into battle, and overcame their foes, so now the entire divine power to overcome the enemy is lodged in the chosen king. The decisive factor is not trust in one's potential for waging war, but the invoking of Yahweh, his involvement, and his aid (Ps. 20:7-8). Yahweh himself declares, "I will crush his foes before him and strike down those who hate him" (Ps. 89:23). Yahweh himself will strike down the king's foes before him (Ps. 110:1). Here it is clearly seen that the institution of the holy war was active in Israel's history, and it is made clear to what extent this was the case (von Rad, 1969).

Other issues are raised by the observation that in Ps. 2:1-3, for example, the authority of Yahweh and his anointed is assumed, and that the kings of the earth have joined in revolt to break free of this lordship. In the ancient Near East this motif is connected with the events of enthronement. When there is a change of rulers, when a great king dies and a new ruler is enthroned, then the subjugated peoples seize this opportunity, this brief breathing space during the reorganization of the empire, in order to free themselves, if possible. It is this motif we find in Psalm 2, but from the outset we must note that it has an entirely new dimension. The starting point is not the claim of the king in Jerusalem to a position of imperial might, but the lordship of Yahweh and his anointed (Ps. 2:2), against whom the revolt is directed. In any case it is important to explore more in detail this theme of the worldwide authority of Yahweh and his anointed.

It must be noted that the royal psalms speak of the worldwide authority of the king in Jerusalem in extravagant language and with surprising boldness. Aside from Psalm 2 there are also such relevant texts as Ps. 18:43-47; 72:8-11; 89:25. In discussing these texts the commentaries again and again begin by saying that such language of universal sovereignty as ascribed to the Davidic dynasty never corresponded to the actual situation and thus was in stark contrast to the whole of historical reality. To be sure, it is possible to take refuge in the explanation that the passages mentioned from the royal psalms are examples of exaggerated poetic flattery, imitations of the praises that exceed the bounds of reality in the ancient Near Eastern "court style," which can be illustrated in many ancient texts (cf. Gressmann, 1929, pp. 1-64). More recent interpretations view the exaggerated statements about the worldwide authority of the ruler in Jerusalem as examples of the "patterns" of the ancient Near Eastern "royal ideology" and its mythic-sacral bases (I. Engnell, G. Widengren, and others). These methods of interpretation, however, touch only the periphery, the external form of the sayings. No access is gained to the message itself. It is of greater importance to bear in mind the following three points.

(1) In Israel there undoubtedly were concrete historical situations that could lead to a wide and extensive concept of sovereignty. At this point Gunkel and the older commentaries are to be refuted. Above all, Alt (1959a) has shown that David ruled over a kingdom that played a not insignificant role in the history of the formation of empires in the ancient Near East. Alt stated, "You may call it 'court style' when the songs used at the accession to power of a new king from the house of David wish the king 'dominion from sea to sea, and from the River (Euphrates) to the ends of the earth,' or when with similar words a universal empire is spoken of (Ps. 72:8). But even though such formulations sound exaggerated in comparison with the actual power or lack of power of the Davidic kings following Solomon, they were not chosen without thought or simply borrowed from the phraseology of other empires. No, from the outset they were brought into relationship with the historical reality of David's empire, with its universal aspirations, which were held before the eyes of the epigones as an ideal and a program" (p. 75). Noting this historical situation gives us an important point of departure. The empire of David and Solomon is the model of the empire of David's followers. We will need to return to Alt's statement of "an ideal and a program."

(2) It must not be overlooked that the concept of David's empire has been expanded in the royal psalms to the concept of a world empire. We may leave aside for the moment whether the tendency toward expansion and exaggeration is bombast (or "court style"), ideal, or postulate. In any case we must note that a conventional, fixed metaphorical language expresses this gigantic expansion. It cannot be denied that the Jerusalem monarchy makes use of concepts and descriptions of an ancient oriental "royal ideology," though with differences in detail. The emperor stands at the center of a universal view of the world. He finds himself at the intersection of sacral enthronement and mythical cosmology. As divine king the ruler must acknowledge the universal right to dominion belonging to the deity who leads the world in his triumphal train. Mythical cosmogony is the root of the claim to universal dominion. Therefore, it must never be abstracted from the relationship of God and king, however this relationship was portrayed in detail in the religions of Israel's neighbors.

(3) If the oriental emperor, through the events set in motion by the enthronement, is "God's regent" in the sense of the then accepted cosmogonic myths, the king in Jerusalem is to be understood exclusively in terms of his relationship to Yahweh, which determines the nature of his office, his charisma, and his responsibilities. The universal authority of this king is determined by his relationship to the universal sovereignty of Yahweh, the creator and judge of the peo-

ples of the world. Therefore, the statements about the universal authority of the Davidic kings are ultimately neither bombast nor court style, neither an ideal nor a postulate, but they are the reflection of a comprehensive mandate which Yahweh, as creator and Lord of the world, has entrusted to his chosen king. The peoples and the "ends of the earth" (Ps. 24:1-2; 47:2, 8; 89:11; Isa. 6:3) belong to Yahweh, the God of Israel, the אדני (Lord, Ps. 2:4; 8:1). Therefore, he can give them over to his anointed (Ps. 2:8). Even though the conventional language used to exalt the worldwide authority of the Davidic kings may bear a close resemblance to the language common to the ancient Near East, the decisive question concerns the right with which each ruler asserts that he has assumed universal sovereignty, or inherited it, or been commissioned to receive it. To whose authority does the king in Jerusalem appeal? In the course of Israel's history it may well have been that a king of Jerusalem, with his decimated, threatened territory, sounded ridiculous when he still dared to speak of his "universal sovereignty." And yet, behind him stands Yahweh, the creator and Lord of the world, the Most High over the nations.

A statement by O. H. Steck (1972, pp. 19f.) may serve to summarize what has been said: "Yahweh's work on every hand throughout the cosmos, from its center in Jerusalem, employs, according to the conception of the Jerusalem cultic tradition, not only heavenly instruments (the official court), but also the king of the city of Jerusalem. The Davidic kingdom, in this view, is the regency of the universal kingship of Yahweh. The king guarantees and brings to fruition the activity of the creator God in providing blessing and fertility in nature. He has received from Yahweh lordship and power over the world of the nations. He is the agent of divine law. The king in Jerusalem is thus not simply the king of a tribe or of a people. In this light he is the central earthly figure of the cosmos, the administrator serving the heavenly King who is enthroned on Zion, who brought forth this cosmos, watches over it, and, in the concrete realm of his sovereignty that involves Jerusalem, has installed his king."

This broadens the perspective. It becomes more and more evident that the charisma and task of Yahweh's anointed bring Yahweh's own work, his perfection of power, the full scope of his sovereignty, to realization. Everything that the chosen king is, does, and attempts, has its basis in Yahweh himself. Through this the mystery of the Messiah is made known. In the nonidentity of person (the anointed is "son of God" by adoption, and *not* God) expression is given to the deliberate identity of the work of the king and Yahweh's own work. This identity is supported and determined by God's choice and promise, and therefore it points beyond itself and has as its goal the final fulfillment.

Psalm 45 has portrayed the *doxa* of the chosen monarchy in bright colors, and the entire psalm has a tendency to glorify it, but it should not be overlooked that in the Old Testament there is increasing attention to the humanity of the king (W. H. Schmidt, 1971). The laments over the decline of the monarchy and the dissolution of the covenant with David (Ps. 89:38-45; Lam. 4:20) show the true situation more clearly than does Psalm 45 or Psalm 2. Emptiness and death cast their shadow over the often acclaimed "long life" of the ruler (Ps. 89:45, 47). The "eternal covenant" which was sworn to David and his dynasty is darkened by the signs of the end (Ps. 89:39). The deeply human side of the king becomes evident. And the question voiced in Ps. 89:48 is totally new in the royal psalms, "What man can live and never see death? Who can deliver his soul from the power of

Sheol?'' The psalmist is looking for a man whom death will not overcome, for a king whose office will not become the prey of decline and and decay.

Yet another perspective opens before us. ''While the king already has the duty of helping the poor (Ps. 72:12-14; Isa. 11:4), the Messiah himself has now become one of the 'poor' who must 'be helped' (cf. Ps. 33:16; 20:6, 9: Num. 12:3; Isa. 53:4)'' (W. H. Schmidt, 1975, p. 205). It is not only his frail humanity, but also the poverty of the anointed that becomes obvious here. The ruler, who is always accompanied by the help which Yahweh gives, now is characterized by total helplessness. He has become poor among the poor of his people.

The picture of Yahweh's anointed given by the tradition is characterized by both these aspects, that of glorification, and that of abasement. The themes of the royal psalms outlasted the age of kings and took on new significance for God's people of Israel and for Judaism. The royal psalms were no longer applied to the earthly rulers but were understood as prophecy and promise of the messianic king of the end-time. Such an understanding cannot be explicitly found in the Psalms. And yet the intention of the statements implicitly goes beyond the historical context and its relation to worship. The charisma and task of Yahweh's anointed do not attain their final fulfillment in the Old Testament. The identity of the activities of the king and those of God can be recognized only in terms of their intention, and that identity is obscured by humanity, decay, and poverty.

5. The Enemy Powers

Much attention has been given to the identity of the foes in the Psalms. Scholarly study has primarily concentrated on the "foes of the individual," whose identity and activity are especially problematic. However the problems are attacked, the decisive issue will be whether or not the question of form criticism is faced. The various form groups must be carefully examined in reference to the specific information they provide concerning the foes. Such investigation must be kept free from any hastily imposed schema, whether it be historic in nature, or related to some "pattern" or other, or based on some convenient hypothesis.

We need no more than mention the view which Bernhard Duhm advanced in his commentary on the Psalms, but which is hardly noted or discussed at all today. Since Duhm dated the Psalms to the period of the Maccabees, he regarded the foes of the saints as "members of the pro-Hellenistic party," enlightened and contemptuous modernists, who rejected the antiquated teachings and way of life of the pious Jews. This explanation is entirely dependent on the late date to which Duhm assigned the Psalms.

If, however, we approach the problem in terms of form criticism, then in the first overview of the material we must be ready to assign specific themes to specific forms and to approach the problem in this framework. It is then unavoidable that we inquire first of all about the enemies of the nation of Israel. The royal psalms and the prayer psalms of the people are then the two categories that come into consideration. Naturally the investigation should not be limited to these two psalm categories, because the hymns (songs of praise) and other psalms also speak of Israel's foes. First of all, we must note the way in which Israel's foes are regarded as Yahweh's foes. In this context the songs of praise must also receive attention, because the hymns speak in a remarkable manner about the foes who confront or work against the powerful activity of Israel's God. Only then will it be possible to speak of the foes of the individual. Here too it is necessary to investigate the appropriate categories of the Psalter—the prayer songs of individual psalmists in Israel and the songs of thanks of the individual. It is here that the main emphasis will be placed in this investigation.

Finally, it is undeniable that the foes, whether they are the foes of Israel, of God, or of the individual, are more than human. Although they are seen as mythic powers, this does not introduce an explicit mythology into the Psalms. Rather, these are rudiments of mythology which speak especially of the threat posed by the foes and their uncanny nature.

This procedure is in direct opposition to any approach that blurs the features of form-critical data, for example, any approach that does not distinguish between the distinctive royal psalms and the prayer songs of the individual. "Ritual pattern," that net of statements belonging to a generalizing royal ideology, has been imposed on all the Psalms. This produces from the outset a mythologizing of concepts of the foes that is not at all justified. A wide-ranging phenomenologizing accords a priori validity to the category of myth. It fails to recognize that the differentiations and relationships that can be identified through form criticism introduce transcendent and cryptic exaggerations into the realm of myth. That is to say, we encounter here a situation which has already been thoroughly discussed and analyzed critically in the context of the royal psalms. See the references to the problematic methodology of the "pattern school" in chap. 4, and the bibliography cited there.

A. Enemies of the Nation

Our starting point should be the royal psalms, which provide us with a clear picture of the enemies of the people of Israel. In Ps. 45:5 we find the expression אויבי המלך, "the king's enemies." These enemies of the king, which are of course the enemies of Israel or of Judah, are called אויב ("enemies," Ps. 18:40; 21:8; 72:9; 110:1, 2; 132:18), or משנאים ("haters" Ps. 18:40; 21:8; 89:23, 42), צרים "foes," (Ps. 72:9, emendation; 89:23, 42), and קמים ("adversaries," Ps. 18:39, 48). It is possible to draw a more concrete portrait of these foes. They are the peoples who wage war against God's people (Ps. 2:8; 18:47; 45:5; 72: 11; 144:2) or the kings and rulers of these peoples (Ps. 2:2, 10; 110:5). They are designated by general and stereotyped terminology. Psalm 72:11 speaks of "all kings," and Ps. 2:10 of "kings" and "rulers of the earth." The background of these comprehensive terms is the universal authority of the kings in Jerusalem, which points to the universal sovereignty of Yahweh, as was set forth above in chap. 4, §3. The hostile powers, "kings of the earth" and "rulers" (Ps. 2:2) rise up against Yahweh and his anointed. The total picture is dark. Denounce and destroy—that is the determined will of the peoples and their rulers. These foreign forces are guided by their reliance on armed force ("chariots" and "horses," Ps. 20:8). The threatened or oppressed people of God and their king, by contrast, know only one path, the path of appeal and petition to Yahweh to intervene and rescue them. May Yahweh bring into play the power which he displayed in the holy wars of ancient Israel, and come to the aid of his anointed.

Especially important for the king in Jerusalem are the promises which were made to him on the day of his enthronement and on other festive occasions. Yahweh will make the king's enemies a footstool for his feet (Ps. 110:1). He will crush the foes and "strike down those who hate him" (Ps. 89:23). Yahweh's incomparable ridicule falls upon the rebellious powers (Ps. 2:4), and his wrath upon the foes (Ps. 2:12; 110:5). But it is the king of Jerusalem who brings all this to pass. He defeats his opponents (Ps. 2:12; 21:8-9). His foes must flee from him and a judgment of destruction falls upon them. It must, however, also be noted that Yahweh can stir up the people's enemies against them (Ps. 89:42). Then the superiority of their enemies is a warning for God's people, a stimulus to make them ask the "why" of history, concerning the verdict which has been rendered de facto.

If in defeating his foes the king acts as the representative and agent of Yahweh, the situation is the same for the execution of punishment which the domestic ruler metes out to "the wicked in the land," and to those who do evil in the city of Yahweh (Ps. 101:8). The identity of these רשעים ("wicked") in one's own land will be investigated in the section "Enemies of the Individual."

An aspect similar to that involved in the group "enemies of the king" can be found in the prayer songs of the people. On this psalm category see *Comm.* Intro., §53. Clearly the king is not the subject here. The foes of God's people are the object of fear and lamentation, of petition and vehement utterances. The range of the vocabulary is similar. אויב ("enemy," Ps. 44:16; 74:4, 10; 80:6; 106:42); צרים, צררים ("foes," Ps. 44:7, 10; 60:11, 12; 74:4, 10); משׂאנים ("haters," Ps. 44:7, 10). These foes are described as "proud" (Ps. 123:4); "taunters and revilers" (Ps. 44:16; 79:4; 123:4); they are "avengers" (Ps. 44:16). The concept of the "nations" (גוים) is clearly defined in Ps. 79:6 as those who do not know Yahweh, that is, do not know God's decisions and sovereignty in the world of the peoples. "Kingdoms" fight against the people of God (Ps. 79:6), kingdoms that have overcome Yahweh's people. In general we may assume this situation: The hostile powers have overthrown Judah and have committed the sacrilege of laying waste the sanctuary. This is stated in several of these psalms (Ps. 74:3-4, 7; 79:1). Only seldom are the hostile foreign nations identified. In Ps. 137:1 we clearly see the situation of the Babylonian exile. In prayer to Yahweh the psalms of the grieving national community depict their horrible plight, not least of all to move Yahweh to intervene, to awaken his mercy, and to call forth his aid. The victorious peoples mock and shame those they have defeated, and ask provocatively, "Where is their God now?" (Ps. 74:10; 77:7; 80:6).

In the prayers of the national community much insight and knowledge is expressed. The question of the "why" of the historical catastrophe is answered in the assumption of the divine judgment. Under Yahweh's wrath the people of the covenant, the chosen people, were defeated and crushed (Ps. 60:1). Thus the enemies have been the executors of a historical judgment which Yahweh has pronounced. They mete out to God's people the suffering which it was theirs to bear from their youth up (Ps. 129:1-2). The answers vary. Yet wherever the ambitions of the hostile powers are voiced, the enemies of the people become Yahweh's enemies (Ps. 83:2). It is Yahweh's land that the opponents wished to conquer (Ps. 83:12). The war which they wage and the oppressive might with which they rule are directed ultimately against Yahweh himself. The foe "reviles *thy* name" (Ps. 74:10, 18). This certainty is based on the strength of divine choice. It enables them to pray that Yahweh would intervene for the sake of his own name and his honor. Impatiently they ask, "How long?" (Ps. 74:10; 79:5). And now the petitions are presented, "Have mercy upon us, O Lord" (Ps. 123:3). "Restore us, O God" (Ps. 80:3, 7, 19). "O grant us help against the foe" (Ps. 60:11; 79:9; 80:2). "Arise, O God, plead thy cause" (Ps. 74:22). "Rise up, O judge of the earth" (Ps. 94:2). It has been explained above how at this point even the revenge motif has its place and how it is to be understood in this context (chap. 2, §B).

When we consider the deep, far-reaching effects of the hostile actions against Israel in the context of God's choice of Israel, then it at once becomes clear that the extent of the hostile destruction exceeds the dimensions of history.

The Enemy Powers

Nature itself is involved. The earth is cracked and torn open, and it quakes. The descriptions indicate an earthquake, a cosmic catastrophe of unprecedented extent (Ps. 64:2). The concrete, historical events are not played down, and certainly not transformed into mythological visions. Events that took place in the history of Israel form the subject of the descriptions of the hostile powers, with the terror and prayers of the people. But the scene is enlarged. All that has happened affects the foundations of the earth. Enmity toward Yahweh and his people has a seriousness that extends beyond the historical events. It is this aspect that requires closer examination in the songs of praise in the Psalter, but which also leads into new dimensions.

Israel's songs of praise laud Yahweh's power and grace in creation and in history. They praise and exalt the creator of heaven and earth, who is also the king and Lord of the world of the nations. In this context, however, the theme of the "enemies" also occurs. Hostile powers set themselves in opposition to the creator and Lord of the peoples. אויבים ("enemies," Ps. 66:3; 68:1, 21, 23); צרים, צררים ("foes," Ps. 97:3); משנאים ("haters," Ps. 68:1). The creation psalm speaks of Yahweh's "foes" (Ps. 8:2). It is seen especially in Ps. 104:35 and Ps. 145:20 that the presence of those who oppose Yahweh and treat him with contempt is felt as an incursion of disharmony. How is it possible that in the magnificent realm of Yahweh's lordship over all the creation which he has called into being, there is still the dark presence of selfish, vengeful, destructive powers and elements? This is the question which provokes thought. Therefore, Ps. 8:3 sees a way of putting these hostile powers to shame (cf. *Comm.*). In Ps. 104:35 the sweeping wish is uttered, "Let sinners be consumed from the earth, and let the wicked be no more!"

At issue is the completion of creation as the "theatrum gloriae Dei" ("arena of God's glory," Calvin). When will the world be free and no longer under the threat of destructive powers? When will the glory and the name of Yahweh alone fill heaven and earth (cf. Ps. 8:2; Isa. 6:3)? Israel's praise is not free from threats and contradictions posed by the hostile powers that rage through nature and history. In praise the antitheses are voiced aloud. They involve not only history, but creation as well. At this point their aspect broadens in the way already elaborated on.

Since the songs of praise honor the Lord and judge of the peoples, we must reflect on the fact that—and the manner in which—the hostile powers are spoken of in this context. Yahweh's foes make their appearance (Ps. 68:1). They are "the nations" (Ps. 66:7; 68:30; 96:7-10; 98:2, 9; 99:2; 135:10) and their "kings" (Ps. 68:12, 14; 135:10). These foes are overcome and their overthrow is described directly and vividly. Yahweh himself arises and scatters his foes (Ps. 68:1). Fire consumes his adversaries (Ps. 97:3). The direct effects of the theophany are depicted. The end and purpose is that all, including his foes, will "cringe" before Yahweh (Ps. 66:3). The praise songs raise to lasting validity the liberation and rescue by Yahweh that Israel experienced in history. It is even possible to speak of "eschatological" perspectives, since in actuality the goal and end of the history of all peoples is involved.

The peoples and their kings, that is, the political and historical powers, are not Yahweh's only enemies. "Floods lift up their roaring" against him (Ps. 93:3). By drawing on the myth of the primeval conquest of the waters of chaos, a fragmentary element is employed as a basic symbol of hostility. The enemy powers are the floods of chaos which threaten the order of creation and strive to destroy it.

It cannot be overlooked that here and elsewhere in the Psalter there are tendencies toward transcendence that draw on the field of mythology. But they have no function of their own that would revive and employ the total myth. They are only metaphors that express the breadth and depth of Yahweh's superiority and power over all hostile powers (Ps. 93:4). The primeval powers are used to show by comparison how great Yahweh's power is.

References to mythology are found also in the praise that speaks of the overcoming of the gods. The gods of the peoples are as nothing before Yahweh (Ps. 96:5). Scorn is heaped on the idols (Ps. 135:15-18). In all these allusions it is astonishing that Yahweh, in contrast to the gods of the surrounding nations who had to overcome the chaos, did not have to wage a toilsome war with the primeval powers, and that there is not a single word about a victory in battle against the foreign gods. The God of Israel reigns over the hostile powers in unchallenged sovereignty. They have been stripped of all power. It is only as relics that they make their appearance.

B. Enemies of the Individual

In the prayer songs of the individual, in which songs of thanks are embedded, the "foes" are designated by well-known Hebrew terms. In singular or plural the following terms are found. אויב ("enemy," Ps. 3:7; 6:10; 7:5; 9:3, 6; 13:4; 17:9; 31:8, 15; 41:5; etc.), צר or צרר ("foe," Ps. 3:1; 7:6; 13:4; 23:5; 27:2; 31:11; etc.), מרעים ("evildoers," 26:5; 27:2; etc.). The term מרעים ("evildoers") assumes a perceptive insight into the manner in which such persons act—they do "evil." The case is similar with the descriptive terms רשעים ("the wicked," Ps. 3:7; 9:17; 10:2ff.; 11:2, 6; 12:8; 17:9; 26:5; etc.) and רדפים ("pursuers," Ps. 7:1; 31:15; 35:3; etc.). The foes of the individual are "godless" and "persecutors." Both concepts must undergo careful investigation. As a "godless" person (רשע) the foe of the individual is not only one who denies God in some sense yet to be defined; he is above all a person who has no shame before God or humans when he carries his evil, deceitful, deadly murderous plans into action. The godless person is, as the wisdom theology saw it later, a "fool" (נבל) in that he says in his heart, "there is no God" (Ps. 14:1). This assertion is not the expression of an atheistic theory, but the summary of a practical attitude. As one who denies God, the רשע ("wicked") discloses himself in his deceptive activity that brings death and destruction. In the mouth of the רשע ("wicked") there is "no truth," they are filled with destruction, and "their throat is an open sepulchre" (Ps. 5:9; 9:6).

The statements which are placed in the mouth of the רשע ("wicked") are significant. He says, "I shall not be moved" (Ps. 10:6). With unshakable confidence he goes his way. He relies on the destructive power of his words and asks in his hubris and sense of superiority, "Who is our master?" (Ps. 12:4). That God is not his Lord means concretely for the רשע ("wicked") that God does not intervene, show his existence as significant. "Why does the wicked renounce God, and say in his heart, 'Thou wilt not call to account'?" (Ps. 10:13). The godless sees the victim of his persecutions as completely defenseless. "God has forgotten, he has hidden his face, he will never see it" (Ps. 10:11). This is then the way the רשעים ("wicked") think and live.

They are also persecutors. On the basis of all that we know of the Psalms, the deceitful and persecuting activity of the godless works out so that the innocent are made to appear guilty by lies and malicious gossip, and those who are sick are "analyzed" in terms of the guilt of their earlier life. This calls attention to two institutions in which the foes of the individual are active according to the Psalms: the institution of the divine judgment, and that of the cleansing of the sick. These will be discussed later. Here we will consider only the efforts of the foes. They are "dissemblers" (Ps. 26:4). They plot, and plan, and grumble (Ps. 4:4; 35:20). Their goal is the ruin and destruction of the defenseless and "poor." They are deceivers (Ps. 5:6; 12:2; 26:4). They lie (Ps. 4:2; 5:6; 12:2). They utter unheard-of accusations (Ps. 7:3-5). They encourage false witnesses (Ps. 27:12; 35:11). The רשעים ("wicked") "love violence" (Ps. 11:5). In their arrogance they despise and ridicule their victims (Ps. 22:6; 35:16; 39:8). They are the strong who trample on the weak (Ps. 35:10). The רשעים ("wicked") seek accomplices for their murderous deeds. Proverbs 1:11-13 gives a vivid picture of their seductive enticements:

> Come with us, let us lie in wait for blood,
> > let us wantonly ambush the innocent;
> like Sheol let us swallow them alive and whole,
> > like those who go down to the Pit;
> we shall find all precious goods,
> > we shall fill our houses with spoil.

Murder and robbery are what the godless are planning. The "poor" and those who lack influence are defenseless against their corrupt acts. We should not think that the רשעים ("wicked") are isolated evil and criminal elements in Israel. They were "respectable" (Ps. 4:2, emendation), influential, and, above all, strong (Ps. 35:10), those who oppressed the weak. They are characterized by insolence (Ps. 53:3; 86:14) and ruthlessness (Ps. 86:14). All their thoughts and actions are filled with hatred, and they are known as "haters" (Ps. 35:19; 38:19; 41:7; 69:4; 86:17). Their strongest weapon for carrying out their murderous intentions is slander (Ps. 5:9; 27:12; 56:2; 59:6-7). Everything that these enemies do is the result of such perverse and dark motivation that terror is the only possible response to these evil powers.

Three metaphors illustrate the uncanny and gruesome assaults of the foes. (1) The foes of the individual are often compared with a hostile army that attacks the helpless and surrounds them with overwhelming forces (Ps. 3:6; 27:3; 55:18; 56:1; 59:1-3; 62:3; etc.). The situation is that of war (Ps. 35:1). "Many" (Ps. 4:6) have swarmed out in order to cut off the "poor" without any hope and to overcome them. Is it possible to speak of a "democratizing" of such concepts and say that they actually belong to the world of the king and are speaking of the ruler as commander of the army? Does the "poor" man, by entering into a royal context and making it his own, find himself in a "messianic" situation? Does he share with the anointed of Yahweh the privilege of divine deliverance when he cries out in his troubles to the God of Israel? We can only pose the questions and take care to avoid speculation. For it is quite conceivable that these are the metaphors which the prayer songs make use of when they use a powerful army to illustrate the might of the enemy. (2) The enemies of the individual are compared with hunters or fishers who seek their prey (Ps. 7:15; 9:15; 31:4; 35:7-8; 57:7; 59:7; 64:4; 140:5). The hunter sets traps, digs hidden pits, sits in the dark, and aims and shoots his deadly arrows. The fisher sets his nets in order to take a catch. The focus of the metaphors is on lurking and lying in wait. (3) The enemies of the individual are compared with wild, ravenous beasts which suddenly spring on a person (Ps. 7:2; 22:12-13; 27:2; 35:21). The comparison becomes clear when the psalm reads that the enemy has behaved "like a lion" (Ps. 7:2; 10:9; 17:12; 22:21). The teeth with which the beasts of prey tear the flesh of their victims merit special mention (Ps. 3:7; 22:12-13, 21).

The designation of the enemies of the individual as פעלי און (*po'eley awen*, Ps. 5:5; 6:8; 14:4; 28:3; 36:12; 59:2; 92:7, 9; 94:4, 14; 101:8; 141:4, 9) constitutes a particular problem. The translation "evildoers" is too weak. און is the (abyss of) viciousness, the dark counterpole to צדק (cf. פעל צדק, "doer of righteousness," in Ps. 15:2). Should the expression make us think of magical practices, or of occult practices which the enemies use to persecute their victims? The issue was first raised by Mowinckel (1921, pp. 1ff.). We will return to this problem later. Here we can at least assert that the phrase פעלי און (*po'eley awen*) is clearly a specific characterization of the enemies of the individual. It occurs together with the word רשעים ("wicked"), and beyond any doubt is intended to express the primeval uncanniness of the enemy powers.

The basic picture of these evil and murderous beings stands in contrast to the picture of those who are just and weak. The contrasts in the prayer songs are unmistakable. The opposite of the פעלי און (*po'eley awen*) are the פעלי צדק ("doers of righteousness"). The strong are in contrast to the weak (Ps. 35:10). The ones who are weak and vulnerable, however, are the poor (עני—אביון). It is significant that in the prayer songs of the individual the contrasts are drawn so sharply and clearly. The enemy powers threaten, persecute, and destroy the poor (Ps. 9:18; 10:2, 9; 22:24; etc.), those who have no one to help them and can take refuge in Yahweh alone. The enemies slander and harrass the צדיק ("righteous") who can look to no one but Yahweh for justice (Ps. 7:11; 11:5; etc.). The force of the contrast is a dark, demonic portrayal of the enemy. But the question must be asked once more, especially with reference to research, Who are the foes of the individual? How are we to understand their thoughts and deeds?

For the literature on this subject see the following: H. Schmidt (1928); H. Birkeland (1933b); P. A. Munch (1936, pp. 13-26); H. Birkeland (1955); K. Schwarzwäller (1963); G. W. Anderson (1965, pp. 16-29); L. Delekat (1967); O. Keel (1969); W. Beyerlin (1970); L. Ruppert (1973).

When such questions have been formulated and posed (Who are the foes of the individual? How are we to understand their thoughts and deeds?) then, in reference to recent research, we must investigate those institutions in the context of which the enemy powers make their appearance. As has already been mentioned, there are two sacral institutions which require attention: the rendering of God's judgment and the cleansing of the sick. H. Schmidt and W. Beyerlin have called attention to the divine decision in judicial cases. It is there that the enemy powers appear as accusers and persecutors, accusing their victims of breaking the law. They stoop to lies and slander and even summon false witnesses. In Israel normal judicial procedures had their Sitz-im-Leben in the "city gate" of a locality (Deut. 16:18; 21:19; 22:15; 25:7; Ruth 4:1; 2 Sam. 18:4; Amos 5:15; etc.), but all difficult and complicated cases in which the testimony was not unanimous were to be handled at the central sanctuary in Jerusalem (Deut. 17:8-13). The defendant, together with his accusers and persecutors, had to submit to the sacral institution of divine judgment. The related psalms clearly show that the accusers and persecutors had tried to slay their victim before they came to the sanctuary, either in fulfillment of blood vengeance or through a murderous attack. In view of such threats the function of the holy place as a sanctuary for those who were persecuted had decisive significance. The defendant, on entering the sanctuary, can take refuge in God's protection. This situation is seen especially in Psalms 3; 17; 27; 57; 63. In the holy precincts, the place of "refuge" under the shelter of the wings (of the cherubim), the place where Yahweh is present, the hostile powers can do nothing. The one persecuted can pass the night in safety and quiet (Ps. 3:5; 4:8). But God's protection in the sanctuary is only the prelude, the beginning of the sacral process of judgment proper, for which the accused prepares himself with petitions, sacrifices, and rites of purification (cf. the oath of purification in Ps. 7:3-5) through a night of "incubation" in the temple. In the morning of the next day (Ps. 5:3) the divine verdict was to be pronounced. In the prayer songs, the petition is uttered, "judge me, O Lord" (Ps. 7:8; 26:1-2; 35:22-24; etc.). The one who is unjustly accused submits to the verdict rendered by God through the priest. He hopes for a declaration that he is righteous and for acquittal. When we recall all these concrete features of the institutional context, the activity of the foes comes into sharper focus. The hostile powers are accusers who disrupt the צדקה ("righteousness") and the כבוד (kabod) of their victim. By lies and slander they endeavor to place him in the wrong so that they can see him condemned, but if possible they would prefer to lynch him before the trial. In the light of God's protection of the temple precincts and of the institution of the divine judgment the eerie nature of the activities of the hostile powers becomes manifest as having a decidedly demonic character. The one who belongs to God, who relies on God, is to be destroyed. The murderous impulse threatens the servant of God, the one who is weak and poor.

A similar situation is present in the institution of the purification of those who are sick. In the Old Testament the unbreakable causal connection between guilt and sickness is seen as a basic element of general folk religion. Reference may be made to Ps. 32:1-4; 38:3-11; 39:8, 11, for example (cf. von Rad, 1962, pp. 274f.). In the sickness, guilt is made manifest as the cause of ruin and as the target of God's wrath. The enemies of the sick person are eager to focus on the causal relationship between guilt and sickness by analyses, accusations, and slander. They pursue the weak and the poor. They want to put them in the wrong and thus show that the sickness is well-deserved punishment. The hostile powers are determined to make obvious to the sufferer and all his relatives and acquaintances that the sickness is a sign of being forsaken by God. The sick person is to be marked as separated from God, as helpless and lost. These procedures in which the hostile powers want to separate and alienate the sick person from God have a threatening significance in the practice of retribution in the precincts of the sanctuary (see K. Seybold, 1973). Restitution, the sacral cleansing of the sick, was accompanied by acts of atonement. Here, however, the (slanderous) accusation would have a threatening outcome, in that the sick might not be restored to life. In other words, restitution might be denied. In the light of this institution the activity of the foes is disclosed in clear contours. The accusers of the sick are powers that want to separate the sick from God (Rom. 8:38-39).

The contextual situations illuminated in research in form criticism and the history of institutions forbid any hasty mythologizing of the hostile forces that appear in the Psalms. It must be stressed above all that the foes of the individual are human (Ps. 9:19; 10:18; 12:8; 56:1; 76:10; etc.). These humans are פֹּעֲלֵי אָוֶן (*po'eley awen*)—beings that commit abominable acts and therefore can be brought to justice, judged, and condemned (Ps. 7:12-16; 9:15-16; 35:7-8; 141:10). Nevertheless, in contrast both to the sacral institutions of the sanctuary and to the poor and weak existence of their victims, but especially in relation to the God who judges and saves, the hostile powers have eerie, demonic attributes. They want to cause separation between God and the poor, the just, and the sick. They raise accusations and set out to sever the bonds that unite Yahweh and his servants. Here the human features of the picture of the foes are constantly transcended. Archetypes of evil and eerie powers become evident. These are powers that are hostile and destructive of life, that cause separation from Yahweh and that corrupt the creation. Therefore we often have the impression that "the Psalms do not appear to portray a reality that is present to the eyes of the just, but, it would seem, a picture of maximum godlessness and evil expansion of power, as portrayed in the tradition" (Ch. Barth, 1961).

In his commentary on Romans, Karl Barth poses the question of the identity of the enemy." He answers: "The Psalmists . . . saw in the enemy not merely a rival or an unpleasant person, an opponent or an oppressor, but the man who to my horror is engaged before my very eyes in the performance of objective unrighteousness." Therefore it is thoroughly justified that "in the passionate language of the 'Psalmists the enemy attains BEFORE GOD a stature which is almost absolute, and why it is that they cry unto God that they may be avenged of him." "The *enemy* shows me the known man as finally and characteristically evil. He shows me, moreover, the evil freely running its course without let or hindrance, without obstacle or contradiction from within or from without. He lets loose in me a tempestuous, yearning cry for a higher—non-existent—compensating, avenging righteousness, and for a higher—non-existent—judge between me and him." "Then it is that the last, supreme temptation to Titanism lies so strangely near at hand. Shall I take the matter into my own hands? Shall I undertake to battle for the right? Shall I become myself the invisible God? Shall I, as an enemy, set myself against the enemy? Shall I, as a Titan, war against the Titan?" (K. Barth, 1933 [1968], pp. 471-472).

There can be no doubt for even a moment: the prayer songs of the individual which speak of the deceitful work of the enemy powers are motivated by the petition and the goal of overcoming the enemies. All who pray know that this depends on Yahweh alone. "Enemies" are not some unavoidable destiny, some fate, to which the weak must submit. Even when the threat posed by the enemy powers appears terrifying and uncanny, or even inescapable, all lament and petition is directed toward putting an end to these powers. The victim of persecution is "cast" upon Yahweh alone (Ps. 22:10). God's mercy and intervention are his only hope. Therefore the plea is raised, "Be gracious to me, and hear my prayer" (Ps. 4:1). "Arise, O Lord! Deliver me, O my God!" (Ps. 3:7; 7:1, 6; 10:12; 22:19; etc.). The one persecuted pleads for Yahweh's reassurance, "Say to my soul, 'I am your deliverance!' " (Ps. 35:3). Since Yahweh is under attack and has become involved through the activity of the enemies, the one praying calls out for God's vengeance (Ps. 17:9). The result which the victim prays for can be seen on the periphery of the prayer songs, and especially in the songs of thanks. Shame and disgrace, terror and destruction are the lot of the foes (Ps. 6:10). They are "put to shame." Their advantages disappear. They stumble and vanish (Ps. 9:3, 6). The mischief they planned returns upon their own heads (Ps. 7:16). The "immanent nemesis" that is evident in such statements can be understood only as the external side of a final event—Yahweh himself destroys the advantage of the enemies, pronounces his verdict over them, and carries out his judgment. Hidden within the mystery of their doom the judge of peoples and of each individual is at work (Ps. 7:6-8; 17:13-14; 96:10-13). His judgment is also at work where an "immanent nemesis" seems to hold sway. Those who have been persecuted can look back with thanks and joy at the defeat of the enemies when it occurs (Ps. 3:7; 23:5; 138:7). As far as the theme of the "enemy forces" is concerned, the Psalter is no "book of failure," but a testimony of thanks, of assurance, and of newly established promises.

C. Mythical Powers

The question of the nature and work of the enemy powers involves in all psalm categories again and again the transcendent element, the intention to move beyond what is earthly and human and to give visibility to supernatural powers. This tendency to see mythical powers in the enemies must be considered once again by way of conclusion.

It has been shown that the Psalms of the Old Testament know of powers of resistance and enmity which are still active in the created world. Primordial contrasts that are presented in mythology were taken up by Israel. The floods of chaos, which Marduk overcame in the Babylonian epic, are the epitome of the hostile forces of destruction. That these floods have "lifted up" (Ps. 93:3) is known also to the Old Testament. By his power, however, Yahweh has set boundaries for the seas. In mythological terms, he broke "the heads of the dragons on the waters" (Ps. 74:13). Israel was not ignorant of the threats of the hostile primeval powers, whose destructive force is depicted in fragmentary metaphors drawn from myth. But hymns praise the incomprehensible activity of Yahweh "on high" (Ps. 93:4), and Ps. 29:10 tells how he sits enthroned "over the flood" (מבול). "The voice of Yahweh is upon the waters; the God of glory thunders, Yahweh, upon many waters" (Ps. 29:3).

It is not the hostile powers, but Yahweh alone who is ruler, he who overcame the primeval powers of chaos in sovereign lordship over the world. This was known to those who sang hymns and offered prayers. But they also knew that the hostile powers have traits of transcendence, not only in the created world, but also in history. The "tumult of the peoples"—the enemies of Yahweh and his anointed—is directly compared in Ps. 65:7 with the roaring of the primeval sea. "Cords of death" and "torrents of perdition" (Ps. 18:4) are on the loose wherever the peoples are in tumult. "Cords of Sheol" and "snares of death" lie in wait (Ps. 18:5).

The motif, derived from mythology, of hostile primeval powers that are at work, bringing chaos and destruction, has entered into the concept of Israel's foes. All opponents who rise up against Yahweh, his anointed, his people, and his servant are powers of Sheol and forces of death. The foes of the individual are humans, but their nature and work are surrounded by an eerie darkness that has come from the mythological tradition. This insight does not create myths, but it uses mythical metaphors to depict the reality of that which exceeds human understanding. In this attempt to express transcendence, the various pointed statements in the Psalms about the enemies come together, but in the process the historical and human attributes of the hostile peoples and the persecutors of the individual are not obliterated or even weakened.

When it is said that the primeval foe is a power from Sheol, it is quickly pointed out that Sheol and the enemy have in mind one and the same goal, a single result, to separate from their God those who cry out to him. Sheol is the place that is far from God, the diametrical opposite of the life that has its source in Yahweh (Ps. 36:9). The hostile accuser separates his victim from God. He draws on all the weight of lies and slander, of accusation and persecution, in order to destroy the covenant of life and help, which Israel and the individual in Israel have received. To that extent Martin Buber was right when he wrote: "The enemy about whom the psalmist showed so much concern is not a human being or human powers, but the primeval tempter, the one who in history hinders redemption" (Buber, 1966, p. 169). But we must be careful not to take such interpretations in an absolute sense. Our task is to follow the intention of the text and to explicate it in the context of tradition history. From the perspective of biblical theology, however, it will be significant in every case not only to ascribe the New Testament statements concerning demons to the contemporary understanding of reality, but also to take seriously the Old Testament statements about the hostile powers and to place them in a larger context.

We must look once again at the designation of the foes as פעלי און (*po'eley awen*). Mowinckel (1921, pp. 1-58) held that און (*awen*) was magic practiced by the enemies. Birkeland (1955), too, believed that the enemies were magicians who by means of magic manipulations and occult practices wished to conjure up destruction for the poor. This position can be based on the fact that in the Mesopotamian world there were portrayals of enemies in those realms in which depictions of magic predominated. It would then be difficult to deny that the word און (*awen*) designates something "dark, uncanny, that shuns light" (Gunkel and Begrich, 1933, p. 201). But the deeds of און (*awen*) performed by the enemies in the Psalms cannot be identified concretely. Therefore we should not too quickly believe that analogies have been confirmed. The פעלי און (*po'eley awen*) were therefore—to state the matter cautiously—"doers of uncanny deeds." Only in a few passages in the Psalms can the magic and occult sense of און (*awen*) be perceived. For example, Ps. 10:9 indicates that the פעלי און (*po'eley awen*) made use of the dangerous power of the curse in order to destroy a person (cf. also Isa. 59:13). It is possible to explain the designation of the enemies as פעלי און (*po'eley awen*) in certain passages in terms of the efficacy of pronouncing a curse. They pronounce over the one they are persecuting a magic word that separates the victim from Yahweh and his blessing. In the light of such occult practices the plight of the individual takes on uncanny aspects.

But it is possible that in explaining און (*awen*) we can go even further. From the Egyptian execration texts we know that the shattering of an earthen vessel on which the names of foreign nations were written had magical significance. The act of shattering not only symbolized victories in coming battles, but also magically produced the realization of those victories. Compare Ps. 14:4 and the interpretation in the *Comm.* on that passage. We can assume that the פעלי און (*po'eley awen*) performed similar symbolic actions. When we read in Ps. 14:4 that they "eat up my people as they eat bread," there could be behind that "as" (just as there is in Ps. 2:9) an actual magic act. The enemy swallows a piece of bread on which is written the name of the one to be attacked and harassed. Or perhaps a specific sign of identification pointed to the victim. Finally, we may ask what the psalmist means in Ps. 141:4, when he says he does not want to eat the "dainties"

The Enemy Powers

of the פעלי און (po'eley awen). It cannot merely involve some bait which appears to be desirable but lures one to destruction. Perhaps it was poisoned food in a disguised form that was offered to the intended victim.

However all this may be, alongside the mythic powers, in whose garments the foes in the Psalms are clothed, there stand פעלי און (po'eley awen), who go about their work with the help of magic powers. They too belong to the realm of the uncanny which hovers about those who act perversely in the Old Testament.

6. The Individual
in the Presence of God

Three categories of psalms comprise the primary material for consideration under the theme "The Individual in the Presence of God." They are the prayer songs, the songs of thanksgiving of the individual, and the wisdom poems (in which problems of human existence are considered).

The structure of the prayer songs of the individual may be sketched briefly. These psalms usually begin with an invocation of Yahweh (in the vocative). This invocation may be repeated several times. It is accompanied by cries for help, statements in which the one offering the prayer describes his needs. Elements of the main body of the prayer can also occur in the introduction, especially descriptions of troubles, petitions, and wishes. In the main part of the prayer the one praying says that he wants to "pour out" his נֶפֶשׁ (*nephesh*, "soul") before Yahweh. Then there is a narration or description of the troubles being suffered. They mainly involve legal problems (persecution of an innocent person), sickness, the feeling that one has been abandoned to the powers of destruction (שְׁאוֹל, *Sheol*), or has been abandoned by God, or the feeling of guilt. The prayer song is permeated by pressing questions, "Why?" "How long?" These questions often border on being reproaches and complaints against God. Then the sufferer pleads for Yahweh's gracious intervention and a turn for the better in his destiny. Alongside the petitions, there may be wishes, expressed in the jussive of the third person. A basic note of trust and confidence can often be heard through the petitions and wishes. Also, reasons are given why Yahweh should intervene. The prayers appeal to God's mercy, honor, or faithfulness. In detail, the statements are characterized by motifs drawn from the specific situation. The conclusion may include a vow of thanks. The one praying vows that he will bring Yahweh a thank offering and praise his name.

At this point we can begin to understand the song of thanksgiving of the individual (תּוֹדָה). The one praying finds himself in the situation toward which he was looking when he made the vow of thanks. That is the Sitz-im-Leben of the prayer song of the individual, as it looks back and makes the troubles seem present reality again, with the accounts of suffering and the petitions. But the turning point has been passed. The one who has been rescued praises the grace of the God who comes to our aid. The point of view is made clear in Ps. 22:22, 25: "I will tell

of thy name to my brethren; in the midst of the congregation I will praise thee.''
''From thee comes my praise in the great congregation; my vows I will pay before
those who fear him.'' Thus there is in the great congregation room for the descriptions of trouble, for the petitions and the expressions of thanks offered by the individual. When Israel is gathered for the annual festival in Jerusalem (Ps. 122:1-5),
individuals raise their voices in prayer. They bear testimony to the great deeds
which God has done in their lives, and they proclaim the name of Yahweh (Ps.
22:22). They do not speak with biographical exactness of their ''own experience,'' but speak of that which the God of Israel has brought to pass.

In the prayer songs and thanksgiving songs of the individual, the situation
of men and women before God is revealed. Two important aspects must be especially noted. One of these is the formation of a literature of prayer, in which conventional formulas and traditions of prayer borrowed from earlier times are employed. Second, there are didactic poems in the tradition of wisdom literature,
which, among other things, reflect on the aspects of human destiny that are mentioned in the songs of prayer and thanksgiving, and which are now interpreted in
terms of new insights. The reflections contained in these didactic poems can then
become problem-centered poems, which demand special attention.

On the form-critical problems of the songs of prayer and of thanksgiving of the individual, and also of didactic poems in the sapiential tradition, see Gunkel and Begrich,
1933, §§6, 7, and 10; see also the *Comm.*, Intro. A special section in this chapter is devoted
to problem-centered poems in the Psalter (§F, ''The great problems of life''). It may be
noted here that this group of didactic poems has a distinctive parallel in the Egyptian debate
literature (cf. E. Otto, 1950).

A. The Individual in Israel

The subject is not the ''Hebrew individual'' (L. Köhler), but ''the individual in Israel,'' because special interest attaches to the specific problem of how the individual is related to Israel, the people of God. In the Psalter this question takes on
dominant proportions. We encounter ''formulations of incomparable personal
fervour and earnestness: but form criticism long ago showed that, as far as phraseology goes, even the wholly personal prayers of lamentation move with few ex-
ceptions in an obviously completely conventionalised body of formulae. In spite
of the entirely personal form of style in these prayers, the exegete will hardly ever
succeed in discerning anything like an individual or biographically contoured fate
behind the details given by the suppliant. Rather the suppliants express their sufferings in a few typical and often very faded concepts'' (von Rad, 1962, pp.
398-399). Thus the question of the relationship of the individual to Israel, the people of God, is first to be considered by looking at the texts in terms of form criticism and tradition criticism. The problems presented by these texts cannot be
solved either by the extreme explanation that individual destinies of a biographical
nature are reflected, or by the equally extreme explanation that the texts point to
the existence of set rituals. The assumption that they are lyrics reflecting personal
depths of feeling is just as inappropriate as the hypothesis, based on Babylonian
examples, of an impersonal ritual literature. Von Rad speaks of the ''conventional
phraseology'' of the prayer songs and thanksgiving songs, but this explanation is
to be subjected to a careful and full investigation, taking as the starting point the
date of Israel's language of prayer. Documents in the form of agendas and formu-

las could be found within the temple precincts. The difference can be best understood if we keep in mind that in the songs of prayer and thanksgiving in which the people of Israel expressed themselves the reader encounters living and powerful expressions, great vitality, and a wealth of relationships, while the Babylonian rituals are stiff, formalistic, and monotonous. This striking vitality, however, cannot be explained as flowing from the springs of creative individuality. Rather, the ''I'' of the Psalms, who speaks, sings, laments, prays, and offers praise and thanks, is participating in all the fullness found in Israel's language of prayer. This participation is not a simple borrowing of stiff, stereotyped ritual formulations, but participation in the tradition of Israel's prayer language:

> Yet thou art holy,
> > enthroned on the praises of Israel.
> In thee our fathers trusted;
> > they trusted, and thou didst deliver them.
> To thee they cried, and were saved;
> > in thee they trusted, and were not disappointed.
> > > > > > > > (Ps. 22:3-5)

The prayers and praises which the fathers uttered were taken up by their sons. How did this come about?

We must begin with the assumption that the vast majority of the Psalms were the work of priests and temple singers. They established the agendas and formulas. It may also be assumed that the prayer songs and thanksgiving songs of the individual were composed by cultic personnel at the sanctuary in such a way that, on the one hand, the experiences of those suffering and those who had been rescued were heard and, on the other hand, use was made of the conventional expressions of prayer language. In any case the priests and temple singers were the instruments that enabled the worshipers to formulate their prayers. They incorporated into the traditional lanugage of prayer the descriptions of suffering and earnest expressions of thanks. They also transmitted to the worshipers the agendas and formulas in which one could voice prayers, even though that individual was not able to articulate the suffering that had been endured or the manner in which the turn for the better had taken place. It may even be assumed that most of those who offered prayers in Israel adopted to their own use psalms that were available in the sanctuary, and whose wording they learned from priests and temple singers who were responsible for teaching them. In Deut. 31:19-22 this activity of the cultic functionaries is expressed in two terms: לִמֵּד, ''to teach'' the song, and שִׂים בפיהם, ''to put [the song] in their mouths.'' That is how the worshipers came to use the prayer language of Israel. That is how they learned to give voice to their troubles and thanksgiving in language that was able to express their situation fully because it transcended each person's own destiny, but which yet, with the use of archetypal expressions of suffering and deliverance, could portray concrete events vividly, reflect their reality, and give a full summation. But the archetypes by no means indicate mythological or rigid ritual categories. On the contrary, the archetypal statements of suffering and deliverance in the Psalms of the Old Testament had become in the history of Israel a rich and well-constructed whole. They had become that ''conventional phraseology'' to which von Rad referred. In this respect the already cited passage in Ps. 22:3-5 is significant for characterizing the transmission process.

The Individual in The Presence of God

We must also consider the other process. An Israelite who has been rescued from trouble and the threat of destruction lets his tale of suffering and his expression of thanksgiving be transformed into a psalm through the skills of the priests and temple singers, who write the text down and perhaps display it on a stele. In the Old Testament this process—and even its terminology—can be clearly identified. The priest writes the song (כתב את השיר, Deut. 31:19-22). In Ps. 102:18 we read תכתב זאת לדור אחרון ("let this be recorded for a generation to come"; cf. also Job 19:23-24). This leads to the act of which Ps. 40:7 speaks, "Then I said, 'Lo, I come; in the roll of the book it is written of me.' " The context gives the following picture. In the precincts of the sanctuary the worshiper has dedicated to Yahweh the psalm that expresses his suffering and thanks, probably as an offering, and possibly with a dedication such as that recorded in Ps. 19:14. The "records" accepted by the priest, that is, the narrations which had been put into poetic form according to the rules committed to the cultic personnel, and the variations of the formulas that had been handed down, were "published" by being written on a stele. In the act of giving thanks the worshiper could appeal to what had been written down, without the necessity of reciting the entire content of the prayer. We must also take into account the contemporary level of culture. At the level of education in the ancient world, reading, writing, and composing poems were the privileges of priests and temple singers and corresponded to the privileges of the "scribes" (ספרים), that is, the officials and secretaries at the royal court. Therefore, each act of reading, writing down, and preservation in the temple archives is to be credited to the corresponding temple personnel trained in that specific skill. As far as the privileges in the sacral realm and in the political realm are concerned, the "correspondence" which we may assume existed between כהנים and ספרים provides an important insight into the process through which the Psalms came into being. Since scholarly research has established that the secretaries of the royal court were the ones who transmitted the wisdom poetry, we are justified in assuming that the influence of the sapiential movement on the poetry of the Psalms, which was at work especially in the didactic poems, is to be traced to the culturally significant relationships between priests and scribes at the court.

All that has been said thus far leads us to see the men and women of Israel, not in isolation, not as individuals, not as personalities, or whatever other categories of western anthropology might be thought to apply, but rather in unrestricted participation in history and the transmission of tradition, specifically the tradition of prayer in Israel, the people of God. The Old Testament preserves the secret of human life in Israel, and therefore the secret is understandable only by looking at Israel. This has nothing at all to do with a "primitive collectivism." The individual expresses himself by using the prayer language of God's people as the vehicle for expressing his own destiny. By means of this prayer language, and thus in the language that expressed the tradition of suffering and how suffering is overcome in Israel's history, the mystery of humanity as the counterpart to God is disclosed. The counterpart of this God is first and foremost Israel, and then the individual man or woman in Israel, speaking, praying, and singing in sentences and songs that developed among the "fathers" in the transmission of the tradition. In this highly differentiated occurrence the phenomenon is overcome which is customarily designated by the deprecating term "primitive collectivism," and it is overcome in a distinctive and quite lively manner. Therefore it will be necessary to review thoroughly the well-known and currently accepted "developmental phases" which are alleged to have led from primitive collectivism to a slowly developing individual consciousness.

On the other hand, the ancient Near Eastern concept of a mythological superman (in Sumerian, *lugal*), is foreign to the Old Testament. This figure arose out of the dull gray of the masses to become king. Humanity is not concentrated in the representative figure of the ruler, who would be the only example of the category "human" worth mentioning. Herein lies the serious error of the ideology of divine kingship, which assumes a priori the absolute, anthropologically superior position of the king as the "primeval man," in order then a posteriori to assert the existence of a "process of democratization," in which those who offered the prayers of the Old Testament laid claim to the privileged humanity of the ruler as the "text" for their lives. No worse distortion and misunderstanding of the content of the Old Testament is possible.

Yahweh himself calls to the men and women of Israel and invites them, "Seek ye my face" (Ps. 27:8). Yes, it is the individual to whom the words are addressed, "Call upon me in the day of trouble" (Ps. 50:15). The call and invitation are accompanied by God's promises, "I will deliver you" (Ps. 50:15); "Fear not, I will help you" (Isa. 41:13). Yahweh's word opens the way to petition and thanks. The one who comes to pray comes in the assurance of God's help. Therefore the institutions of worship bear the sign of God's accessibility.

The biblical material indicates four institutions in which the individual in Israel comes into the presence of Yahweh. (1) The thank offering. This is the institution which we are to regard as the Sitz-im-Leben of the prayer songs and thanksgiving songs of the individual. Here, as has already been noted, the threatening situation is described, and then the תודה ("song of thanksgiving") is offered. Sacrifice and psalm come together. (2) The sacral judgment. This has been discussed in chap. 5, §B. Denial of justice and unjust persecution drive their victim to seek safety in the sanctuary, where he hopes to be vindicated by God. (3) The act of restoration of one who has recovered from illness. Rites of cleansing and confession are carried out in this act. The sins of the one who has been sick are also mentioned, so we may assume that some of the prayers of confession had their Sitz-im-Leben in this institution. (4) The gate liturgy. This has been discussed in chap. 3, §C. The individual is questioned at the gate of the sanctuary (Psalm 15; 24:3-6). It is possible that some of the prayers of confession were used here.

In these institutions in which the individual steps forth from the cultic community, the Israelite man or woman can be perceived. This individual suffers troubles and perils, and faces extreme danger of persecution and slander, of deadly disease and the questioning of his righteousness. The institutions and the psalms that belong with them make it plain that the individual man or woman is helpless, needy, subject to attack by hostile powers. Yahweh is the only hope for better things.

Comprehensive, general concepts and metaphors indicate the extent to which the individual is hard beset. The suffering continues endlessly. Especially significant is the question that rings out in many psalms, "How long?" (Ps. 6:3; 35:17; 62:3; 74:10; 119:84). Yahweh is "silent" (Ps. 28:1; 35:22; 109:1; etc.). The worries become threatening. Has Yahweh "forgotten" the sufferer (Ps. 9:12; 10:12; 13:1; 42:9; etc.)? Has he "hidden his face" (Ps. 10:1; 27:9; 30:7; 55:1; 104:29)? Is he "asleep," like the dying vegetation deities of Israel's Canaanite neighbors (Ps. 44:23; 78:65)? When will he awake (Ps. 7:6; 44:23)? For the one who is praying, God's hiddenness becomes an intolerable burden (cf. chap. 1, §C. No manipulation of any sort whatever can overcome this hiddenness of God. Only Yahweh himself can step forth out of the hiddenness and reestablish communication with the one who is suffering, only he can break his silence and let his face shine.

Exegetes have always been fascinated by the remarkable "swings in mood" which can be seen in some psalms. Lament breaks off and praise and thanksgiving ring out. How can this transformation be explained? When this question is directed to the specific psalms, four explanations present themselves as possibilities. (1) Yahweh's silence has been broken and the worshiper has received an answer from God. Such an answer transmitted by priests or by cultic prophets could be, for example, "I am your deliverance" (Ps. 35:3). The announcement that Yahweh will intervene to save is decisive. (2) Assurance that the prayer is heard (cf. the *Comm.* on Ps. 22:22; Ps. 34:4) could also be the result of a change in the fate of the individual. (3) A theophany in the sanctuary assured the individual at prayer that Yahweh is present and has the power to save (Ps. 18:9-15). From the context of the explanations of the theophany it is never possible to conclude what may have accompanied it (cf. chap. 1, §C). The fact to be noted is that the individual finds in Yahweh's appearance in the sanctuary concrete consequences for his life. (4) The sufferer who is praying has received a sign from Yahweh that he will be helped. This indication that something good will happen is called in Ps. 86:17 אות לטובה ("a sign of thy favor"). Thus the conclusion may be drawn that the "swing in mood" is the result of Yahweh's intervention, described in various ways.

The explanations advanced here should not mislead anyone into thinking that there can be a thematic interpretation of the Psalms. Not every psalm is comprised of two elements, one of which is the description of the troubles and the other the rescue that has occurred. Neither should anyone postulate a "mixed category" in which the two elements mentioned are found mingled. Christoph Barth (1961, p. 24) has stated it well: "To explain this situation by saying that here a lament and a song of praise had been combined would be just as unsatisfactory as the assumption that we were dealing with a 'mixed category'! Strictly speaking, all laments of the individual contain expressions of trust and assurance; they contain within themselves the transition to praise. Israel did not know of any lament for the sake of lament, and even the songs of praise of the individual are not sharply separated from the laments. Lamentation and thanks, petition and praise contrast like two foci of an ellipse. The individual psalms stand somewhere between the two, related to both." Thus we must investigate the common Sitz-im-Leben of the prayer songs of lament and petition and also the songs of thanksgiving of the individual. Among the prayer songs that suddenly break out in praise and thanks are the following: Psalms 6; 13; 22; 28; 30; 31; 41; 54; 55; 56; 61; 63; 64; 69; 71; 86; 94; 102; 130.

Thus we see that the description of trouble and the giving of thanks are intimately connected with each other. The turning point has been passed. The time of trouble is vividly recalled in all its seriousness and threats. In the approach to the prayer itself any dramatic or tragic components are excluded. The individual Israelite is one who has been delivered from trouble. He or she did not remain the prey of the hostile powers with their slanderous accusations, persecutions, sicknesses, and disruptions. Therefore thanks can be offered for the great deeds of Yahweh. It is significant that this thanks is proclaimed in the presence of the "great congregation" gathered at the great festivals as the people of God (Ps.

22:22, 25; 35:18; 66:16; 109:30). That which came forth from the assembly (קהל) is rendered back to it again. Tradition and inspiration meet. The תודה ("thanks-giving") becomes embodied in the tradition. On the one hand, it can be shown, even in terms of form criticism, that the תודה ("thanksgiving") shares in the language of prayer of Israel, but on the other hand it is striking how much emphasis the one giving thanks places on the power of inspiration (Ps. 40:3; 51:15; 116:13, 18-19). Yahweh must open the worshiper's lips so that the mouth can proclaim his glory (Ps. 51:15). Only a "new song," not something handed down from the past, really praises Yahweh. But the "new song" is a psalm that Yahweh has placed in the singer's mouth (Ps. 40:3). In praise it becomes clear how great is the power of the new, which is able to break through the traditional elements of the language of prayer and praise. In the Old Testament the singer is not without initiative, not locked into the tradition. Within the tradition there is space and freedom. Still more, the freedom of praise will break through the bonds of tradition. This is made clear by Ps. 40:3. Therefore it would be a mistake to speak too hastily of an "eschatological song." The explanation is to be sought in the area where tradition and inspiration meet. The one who prays in the Psalms is not constricted by the language of tradition, but is free to sing a "new song." He is destined to praise God in the breakthrough of that which is new.

B. Aspects of Anthropology

In the entire Bible, Old and New Testaments, there is hardly any group of texts so well suited for the study of aspects of anthropology as the Psalms. The methodology, however, must be carefully considered. A study of concepts that was exclusively oriented to lexicon and concordance would be based on the assumption that an abstract world of concepts lies behind the texts. Great care must be taken in referring to the Hebrew terms, and constant attention must be paid to the special relationships and situations. Under any circumstances we must avoid constructing, with the aid of an abstract and superficial investigation, "a variant of the understanding of man generally common in the ancient East" (von Rad, 1962, p. 356). From the outset, therefore, anthropology must have a theological orientation, that is to say, it must investigate how man in Israel is seen in the presence of God. Concentrating on man himself can only lead to erroneous conclusions. Any attempt to discover "the eternally unchanging human," the one picture of humanity, must be avoided at all costs. If in the Old Testament the secret of man is preserved in Israel and therefore disclosed in Israel, we must consider the great movements of history in which the aspects of anthropology are involved. We must especially note the creative transformation as it finds expression, for example in Ps. 51:10-12. Movement, brokenness, and new creation—these key words are reminders that static constructs must be avoided under any circumstances. In all this it must be kept in mind that "it is simply an illusion to consider man as the established and given fact and God as the doubtful one. On the contrary, man is man only before God and with God, and where he loses this connection, he becomes immediately and without fail a monster. For a life without God is a life that God no longer defends" (von Rad, 1980, p. 109).

At this point I must state my opposition to any phenomenology that is based on the "religious human" and that thereby imports certain dominant motifs into the anthropology of the Old Testament. The following can be taken as an expression of a general phenomenology. ''Religious man assumes a humanity that has a transhuman, transcendent model. He does not consider himself to be *truly man* except in so far as he imitates the gods, the culture heroes, or the mythical ancestors. This is as much as to say that religious man wishes to be *other* than he is on the plane of his profane existence'' (M. Eliade, 1959, pp. 99-100). At this point it must be stated that in the Old Testament the thing on which all else depends is that individual in the presence of Yahweh (and therefore *not* the ''religious human'' in a general sense) is not following a superhuman, transcendent model. On the contrary it is in one's life and walk in the presence of Israel's God that the human truly becomes human and discovers his true being. It is not possible here to go into the inappropriateness of the distinction between ''religious'' and ''secular'' (cf. von Rad, 1962, pp. 205ff.).

A striking feature of the Psalms is that they speak of the ''human'' in an absolute sense. ''What can man do to me?'' asks the one praying in Ps. 56:11 and 118:6. ''Man'' here is in absolute contrast to God, his power, and the help that he gives. ''Men'' are hostile powers, but without capacity (cf. Isa. 31:3). It is significant that there are these two sides to the question. They are adversaries (Ps. 56:1; 66:12; 124:2), but at the same time they are weak, vulnerable beings (Ps. 9:19; 18:17). In the presence of Israel's God all human capabilities, powers, and instruments of war are stripped of their strength. Men are worthless beings. They puff themselves up, but they are unable to carry their plans through to completion. This is true also of the assembled human might in the world of peoples and nations, with their armies and their aggressive acts. ''Let the nations know that they are but men!'' (Ps. 9:20). They have no godlike ability, even when they arrogantly act as if they did. Yahweh, superior to the world in all his power, confronts the armed hosts that have assembled in their hubris (Ps. 2:4). ''The Lord looks down from heaven upon the children of men'' (Ps. 14:2). But these contrasts are not based on a view of a transcendent God, who stands over against a correspondingly feeble view of man. Yahweh has made his power and his grace known in Israel, in the history of his chosen people. The assertions grow out of the authority of prophecy (cf. Isa. 31:3) and represent the working out of prophetic charisma.

An examination of the anthropologically relevant terminology can take place only in the context of what has been said here. The terms by themselves say very little. It would be easy for them to merge into the realm of ancient Near Eastern anthropology and no longer be capable of expressing anything distinctive. Each of the Hebrew concepts in the Old Testament must be examined and understood in its literary and intellectual context.

Human beings are ''flesh'' (בשׂר, *baśar*), that is, the substance of their physical existence is subject to attack, injury, damage, and decay. It is not that humans have flesh, they *are* ''flesh.'' בשׂר (''flesh'') is the form of the physical body. In Ps. 16:9 בשׂרי can be translated ''my body.'' The skeleton of the body is covered with בשׂר (''flesh,'' Ps. 102:5; 38:3). The human body is vulnerable and perishable. The hostile powers want to ''eat up the flesh'' of their victims (Ps. 27:2 KJV), the way beasts devour their prey. The body (''flesh'') is weak and feeble when trouble and sickness befall it. Then the בשׂר (''flesh'') faints ''as in a dry and weary land where no water is'' (Ps. 63:1; 42:2; 143:6). Without Yahweh's protective power the human בשׂר (''flesh'') is subject to insecurity and decay (Ps. 16:9-10). Humans are pitiable in their perishable existence in בשׂר (''flesh,'' Ps. 78:39). On the other hand, it must be remembered that humans who act arrogantly are only בשׂר (''flesh,'' Ps. 56:4), weak, stumbling beings. Indeed, all humans are united to each other in that they share the common substance ''flesh'' (cf. H.

144

W. Wolff, 1974, p. 29). "All flesh," that is, all human beings, come into the presence of Yahweh and praise him (Ps. 65:2; 145:21). "He gives food to all flesh" (Ps. 136:25). In addition to the concept of "flesh," human frailty in its terrifying vulnerability is represented by two other metaphors. There is the metaphor of green, flourishing vegetation, which springs up in the morning, but at evening has withered and dried under the searing wind (Ps. 103:15-16; 90:5-6; 102:11; Isa. 40:6-8; Job 14:1-2). Then there is the metaphor of הבל (*hebel*), the feeble breath that can scarcely be perceived and that quickly passes away (Ps. 39:5, 11; 62:9).

The concept נפש (*nepeš*) characterizes human existence and self-expression in a distinctive manner. Old Testament scholarship recognized early that an important component of the meaning of נפש (*nepeš*) involves its concrete localization in the human "throat." Thus נפש is the organ through which nourishment is taken (Ps. 107:5, 9). This also calls attention to human need (Wolff, 1974a, pp. 10ff.). Humans need nourishment; they are eager to satisfy the hunger and thirst of the נפש (Ps. 42:1-2; 143:6). The נפש is the seat of all the tumultuous longing and desire, seeking and yearning of humanity (Ps. 24:4; 35:25; 42:1-2). It also represents the seat and the process of spiritual feelings and inner conditions. In matters of this sort it is appropriate to translate נפש "soul" (Ps. 31:7; 35:9; 42:5-6, 11; 43:5; etc.). There is a significant nuance of meaning in that "the human *is* נפש, and it is not the case that נפש belongs to him" (H. W. Wolff, 1974, p. 21). In such cases the Hebrew term approximates the meaning of "person." This is the presupposition for the view which is so important in the Psalms, that נפש (*nepeš*) can be translated as "I," "I" in the totality of my unsatisfactory life (Ps. 54:3; 84:2; 103:1; etc.). Wolff (1974, p. 25) writes that it must be noted that נפש "points pre-eminently to needy man, who aspires to life and is therefore living." When this inadequate individual addresses himself and says, "Hope in the Lord" (Ps. 42:5, 11; 43:5), this shows where the inadequate, dependent, and needy נפש (*nepeš*) of the vulnerable individual seeks and finds life and hope.

The center of human life is the "heart" (לב, לבב). This "heart" is the site of all thought, planning, reflection, explanation, and ambition (Ps. 4:4; 10:6; 15:2; 20:4; 33:11, 21; etc.). It is the place where the whole person experiences or suffers the full weight of joy (Ps. 4:7; 19:8; 33:21; 64:6; 105:3; etc.), sorrow, anxiety, and fear (Ps. 25:17; 55:4; 61:2; 27:3; etc.), bitterness (Ps. 73:21), and hope (Ps. 28:7; 112:7). What the heart thinks and plans does not lie at the surface of human existence. The process of reflection, planning, and deciding takes place in hidden depths. No one is able to penetrate to the final depths of his or her own heart. Yahweh alone can try the "hearts and minds" (7:9; 17:3; 26:2; the word translated "minds" by the RSV in this instance is rendered "reins," i.e., kidneys, in the KJV; in the ancient world the "kidneys" were regarded as the seat of secret feelings). Yahweh alone knows the depths of the human heart (Ps. 44:21). He is the one who has "fashioned" the heart and notes all its movements (Ps. 33:15). Deep within the heart, guilt is found (Ps. 36:1). לבב (*lebab*, "heart") can be the location of evil (Ps. 28:3; 112:7). The whole heart can be characterized as "perverse" (Ps. 101:4, לבב עקש). We should not overlook the general statements that are made about the לב ("heart") in the Psalms. Human petitions, divine promises, and divine renewal involve the "pure heart" (Ps. 24:4; 51:10; 73:1; etc.). Yahweh can "incline" the human heart to good (Ps. 119:36, 112; 141:4), so that the Torah may dwell in the heart (Ps. 37:31; 40:8), and so that it becomes possible to speak of those who are "upright in heart" (ישרי־לב, Ps. 7:10; 64:10;

94:15; 125:4). With an urgency that grew out of the Deuteronomic-Deuteronomistic theology, the question of wholeness of heart is raised (Ps. 9:1; 86:12; 119:2, 7, 10, 34; 138:1). A "double heart" (Ps. 12:2) would be a heart that was "not steadfast" (Ps. 78:8, 37). Thus we see that the formulas that point to a total characterization of the לב ("heart") are noteworthy. The wholeness and integrity of a person are dependent on the clear direction and the wholeness of the "heart."

In the relationship of life and death this finds expression once more. The sorrowing person has a "broken heart" (Ps. 34:18; 51:17; 102:4; 109:22; 143:4; 147:3). His "heart" has become like wax, melted within him (Ps. 22:14). The center of human existence has collapsed and dissolved. In view of this weakening and dissolving of life at its center, it is the wish of everyone who has experienced Yahweh's saving intervention, "May your hearts live for ever!" (Ps. 22:26). Both the body and the heart fail (Ps. 73:26), but the hearts of those who seek God can revive (Ps. 69:32). The "heart" is not subject to human control; it can err in every direction. The heart can be set on riches and fall victim to them (Ps. 62:10). The belief that Yahweh has the human heart in his control is not a late teaching of wisdom poetry, but is an insight that is involved in the motif of the hardening of the heart. He can turn the hearts of the nations to hate his own people (Ps. 105:25). He can "harden" the heart. But we should note that in Ps. 95:8 it is human perversity and stubbornness that bring about hardness of heart, meaning that the "heart" is totally closed and inaccessible to Yahweh's word and instruction. Perhaps—Wolff (1974, pp. 40ff.) notwithstanding—we should not hold that the "heart" is the representation of "rational man." In the Psalter the statements that qualify the לב ("heart") and sum up its attributes are dominant. It is astonishing how rare are statements that deal solely with the anthropological aspects (e.g., Ps. 38:8; 19:3; 40:12; etc.). The crucial texts are those in which the "heart" with its dimension of "depth" is characterized and interpreted in relationship to Yahweh. It is precisely in the hidden depths and at the center of life that the individual in Israel confronts first and last, without interruption, Yahweh his God.

The occurrences of רוח (ruaḥ) in the Psalter in anthropological contexts are not easy to interpret. Here too H. W. Wolff's undifferentiating explanation (1977, pp. 57ff.) is not adequate for an understanding of the Psalms. Our starting point should be the literal meaning. רוח (ruaḥ) is the wind, the breath of life, the life-giving power. Both רוח (ruaḥ) and נשמה (nišmah, "breath") are to be understood in this basic sense (cf. Gen. 2:7). The divine breath that enters into the material world makes the human being into a "living being" in unity and wholeness. "When his breath (רוחו, ruaḥu) departs he returns to his earth (Ps. 146:4). In the human "heart" רוח (ruaḥ) is that which moves and is moved (Ps. 78:8), but לב (leb, "heart") can also be understood as synonymous to רוח (ruaḥ, Ps. 32:2; 77:6). Like the "heart," the רוח (ruaḥ) also in man can be "faint" and "fail" (Ps. 142:3; 143:4, 7). This identification in content of רוח (ruaḥ) and לב (leb), however, does not extend to a clearly marked context such as Gen. 2:7 and Ps. 146:4, when one who faces the threat of death cries out, "Into thy hand I commit my spirit; thou hast redeemed me, O Lord, faithful God" (Ps. 31:5). When facing the threat of death, the one praying commits his or her life breath and therefore the life forces in their totality to Yahweh. He yields up his life, which through the redemption (פדה) wrought by God has passed into the power and possession of God.

But we must return to the synonymity of רוח (ruaḥ) and לב (leb). In Ps. 51:10 there is a petition for a "clean heart" and a "new and right spirit." Clearly this involves a creative renewal of the human רוח (*ruaḥ*), that is, of the active and passive powers that hold sway in the "heart." But this creative renewal (cf. ברא ["create"] in Ps. 51:12) can be brought about only by a new intervention and activity of the רוח (*ruaḥ*, "Spirit") of Yahweh. His "holy Spirit," which is a "spirit of obedience," must sustain (Ps. 51:11-12) the broken human spirit (רוח נשברה, Ps. 51:17). רוח (*ruaḥ*) as a revivifying element of creation corresponds here to רוח (*ruaḥ*) as the divine power of new creation, or of its effect on the human spirit. The person who has been renewed in her or his רוח (*ruaḥ*) through God's "holy spirit" is the counterpart to the person who as God's creature has been given life through רוח (*ruaḥ*) or נשמה (*nišmah*). Both aspects, however, are intimately related, because it is the will of Yahweh the Creator to renew his creation (Ps. 104:30; 96:10-13; 98:8-9; 146:6-9). This will is, however, first active in human beings in Israel. Here the human רוח (*ruaḥ*) is in need of God's protection and guidance through the divine Spirit. "Let thy good spirit lead me on a level path!" (Ps. 143:10).

The "openness" of human existence which is spoken of in modern anthropology, has in the Psalms a different, more profound and comprehensive meaning. Human life is open before God. God alone searches out and knows the depths and abysses of human existence. The most detailed and concentrated statement on this theme is found in Psalm 139. It is possible that motifs from the realm of sacral judgment provided the initiative to comprehensive reflection on the theme, "O Lord, thou hast searched me and known me!" Those who are persecuted and unjustly accused pray, "Prove me, O Lord, and try me; test my heart and my mind" (Ps. 26:2; 7:8-9). In terms of Israelite institutions, such an openness of the depths of the heart before the *Deus praesens* was customary during the night of incubation in the temple. It was done in the assurance that Yahweh tests the "heart and mind" and that therefore a just verdict will be pronounced (Ps. 7:9-11). But in Psalm 139 all these relationships and motifs are raised to the level of urgent reflection, and their light falls not only on the one who is unjustly accused, but on man in the totality of his life and activities. It is appropriate to this psalm, with its astonished expressions of divine knowledge and human trust, that they are spoken (or proclaimed) by an "I" in a form adapted for use by every person who confronts the reality of Yahweh, and is thereby ready to acknowledge the truth of his or her own life. Yahweh tests and knows the individual. "Before him no creature is hidden, but all are open and laid bare to the eyes of him with whom we have to do" (Heb. 4:13). The place of waiting, the path of wandering, the movement of thought—all are known to Yahweh (Ps. 139:1-6). Human life is surrounded by Yahweh's presence and care. This insight is not to be reduced to the dogmatic formula of the omniscience and omnipresence of God. It is alive and discomforting: "Such knowledge is too wonderful for me; it is high, I cannot attain it" (Ps. 139:6). No one can flee away and hide in some distant place or secret abyss (Ps. 139:7-12).

What is the basis of this unlimited knowledge that Yahweh has of humanity? How is it to be explained? Yahweh created men and women, including their most intimate aspects and capacities (Ps. 139:13). On the basis of creation all human life is open and transparent to the creator (Ps. 139:16). But there are no uncontrolled speculations about the determination of the days of one's life. The one offering the prayer gives thanks for the gift of life which he has received (Ps. 139:14). Amazed and overwhelmed, he or she contemplates the immeasurable greatness of Yahweh's knowledge and thoughts (Ps. 139:17-18). The one who prays does not attempt to penetrate them or to encompass them with the net of speculative reflections. For humans the appropriate expressions, indeed the only meaningful expressions in the presence of God, are thanksgiving and astonishment. The reality of God discloses the truth about mankind.

The following two explanations of Psalm 139 deal with the theme "faith and knowledge," but also touch on that of "being and nonbeing."

"This whole psalm, indeed, is a paradigm of that intermingling of faith and knowledge. The desire for knowledge is so pressing that, at the limits which are imposed upon it, it becomes itself a witness to God's inscrutability. The fear of God not only enabled a man to acquire knowledge, but also had a predominantly critical function in that it kept awake in the person acquiring the knowledge the awareness that his intellect was directed towards a world in which mystery predominated" (von Rad, 1972, pp. 108-109).

"There can be no real secession to a realm hidden from God, the realm of a being of non-being independent of Him, the kingdom of another God. For there is no such kingdom. Even the non-being to which we turn, and into which we can fall, actually is before God even though He turns away from it. In the form of His turning away from it, it is no less the object of divine knowledge than that which is before Him. Our escape fails because being an escape from God, it has no goal. Every goal that can be reached lies within the realm of the one God and therefore within the realm of his knowledge. At every one of these goals we again stand before God. We are seen and known by Him. We are no more inaccessible to Him than He is to Himself. We may fall into sin and hell, but whether for salvation or perdition we cannot fall out of the realm of God's knowledge and so out of the realm of His grace and judgment" (K. Barth, *CD* 2/1: 554).

The inclusion of Psalm 139 in the "aspects of anthropology" should make it clear how and to what degree that view of mankind fits into the relationship of life and being of mankind in the presence of Yahweh. It must again be emphasized that truth about mankind is totally dependent on the encounter with the reality of God. This applies also to the deep mystery of the nature of mankind as God's creation, which, in the context of the question of a "first cause" by no means constitutes anything like an introit to biblical anthropology. On the contrary, this mystery is to be seen in the light of Yahweh's self-revelation in Israel. In the Psalms the *locus classicus* is Ps. 8:4-8. After this passage is studied and explained, other statements in the Psalter about mankind as the creation of God will be considered.

The words "What is man" should be followed not by a question mark but, in keeping with the context, by an exclamation point (Ps. 8:4). The attempts to derive a Christian anthropology out of מה־אנוש ("what is man?") are not justified by the context. The exclamation introduced by מה ("what") expresses boundless astonishment. In heaven and earth the creation bears witness to Yahweh's greatness and majesty, and through this the psalmist becomes aware of the ultimate depths of his humanity. The statement in Ps. 8:1 is decisive. Just as Yahweh's creative power and majesty are knowable in all the world only through the medium of the revelatory power of the "name" (שם), so too the mystery and miracle of mankind's origin and destiny can be perceived only through the self-disclosure of Israel's God. Concretely, this means that Yahweh is "mindful" (זכר) of humans and "cares for" (פקד) them (cf. Ps. 8:4). Where except in Israel, among the people to whom Yahweh has disclosed his "name," have this mindfulness and care become reality (Ps. 8:1)? It is not through insights that are immanent in the world, or through spontaneously perceived, intuitive knowledge of a humanistic type that the biblical human knows the destiny of his or her being; it is solely through the act in which Israel's God manifested himself to his people, in which, *pars pro toto,* all that is אֱנוֹשׁ ("human") or בֶּן־אָדָם ("son of man") learns his or her future and destiny. Basic to אֱנוֹשׁ (*enosh,* "the human") is the concept of a weak, vulnerable humanity. Thus the dialectic is stretched to the utmost. Weak humanity, sinking and disappearing under the high, glorious heaven of God (v. 3), as if it were nothing, is incomprehensibly the mankind acknowledged and accepted by Yahweh (Ps. 144:3; Job 7:17; 14:3).

The singer of this psalm then speaks at once of a fundamental law of the creator, according to which man has his place in the order of creation: "Thou hast made him little less than the heavenly beings" (מְעַט מֵאֱלֹהִים, Ps. 8:5; RSV, "little less than God"). In this passage, אֱלֹהִים (*elohim*) has beyond doubt the meaning "heavenly beings," "*elohim* beings" (ἄγγελοι ["angels"] in Heb. 2:5, 7, following the Septuagint of Ps. 8:5). Immediately below the heavenly beings which surround the throne of Yahweh (1 Kings 22:19; Job 1:6; Isa. 6:1ff.) the human has the place accorded to him by the creator. The origin and being of mankind are to be understood in this manner. The mythologizing expressions rule out any placing of mankind in a direct relationship with God. In relation to the higher, divine world, mankind is to be seen and understood, not through presumptuous and mythologically motivated assertions, but in a manner that corresponds to the ordinance of Yahweh (Gen. 1:26-31). When Yahweh is mindful of man and cares for him (v. 4), then the relation of man to God consists ultimately in the reaction of the בֶּן־אָדָם to this initiative of Yahweh. It is significant that Psalm 8 does not speak of man in terms of the "image of God." Therefore the interpretation must be made with care. "Thus man is a creature that can be understood only from above . . . and that can regain and preserve his humanity only by hearing the word of God, in conversation with God" (von Rad, 1980, p. 72). Only in continuing coexistence and partnership with God do humans become aware of their origin and destiny. Only if they persevere in this basic relationship do they take their place in the order of creation, where they exist as מְעַט מֵאֱלֹהִים ("a little less than *elohim*").

The relationship depicted in Ps. 8:7 does not depend on human possibility or capability. The origin of human life and the form of its meaning are given in relationship to God, the God who has a concrete name (Ps. 8:1). Only in this face-to-face relationship does the glory of God's world shine into the depths where mankind stands, and only thus does the "*elohim* nature" of mankind find tangible expression, and only thus do splendor and beauty, like a royal crown, adorn and honor mankind. By Yahweh's decision and ordinance, humans, though miserable and vulnerable, have come to belong to God's world. Just as the name of Yahweh is manifest on earth, and God's majesty is reflected in the creation of the heavens, so now from mankind, as beings incorporated into the "*elohim* world," the reflection of God's majesty shines forth. Humans, in the nature of "*elohim* beings," are destined to rule over God's creation (Ps. 8:6-8). The psalm calls the roll of the realm of the creator's dominion, which has now become the realm over which mankind rules. In contrast to the portrayal of the human's pitiable nature and worthlessness in Ps. 8:4, his position as one of the "*elohim* beings" and as sovereign is an indescribable miracle, comprehensible only in the context of Israel's destiny and related solely to the name of Yahweh. Therefore the human is ordained to praise God, to renounce all self-glorification and arrogance, and instead to see himself or herself in lowliness and in the status of "*elohim* being" bestowed on him or her.

If we look at the whole world of humanity, we see that the gifts of majesty disclosed in the Psalms, as well as human happiness and joy for being created and rescued by Yahweh, are all threatened and questionable. Humans are hostile powers, destroyers of God's creation and of their fellow human beings. This anxiety can lead to the conclusion that "all men are liars" (Ps. 116:11 KJV). Immediately, darkness and fear spread over the bright world of creation. The darkness can increase so greatly through mutual condemnation and hostility that every positive aspect is disrupted. And Yahweh's חסד (*hesed*) shines out only in contrast to the fallen world of humanity. Therefore it is appropriate for humans to express humbly the humanity which they have discovered in the presence of Yahweh—not arrogantly, but in complete dependence on Yahweh (Ps. 131:1ff.).

Thus we see that the Psalms do not present a "type of Adam" as a timeless entity or metaphor. History and the experience of human suffering in the presence of Yahweh disclose the final developments of the form of human life. Life cannot be grasped by means of a theory, not even the best biblically derived theological theory. Humanity discovers its unity and nature only through history, the history guided by Yahweh, the God of Israel, in which this God brings to light the origin, destiny, and truth of mankind. This does not take place in disclosures that could lead to abstract expressions of knowledge, but in the concrete testimony of biblical texts, whose fullness, manifold nature, and specific relationship to situations and constantly new contexts make it possible to construct an approximation of a "theology of the Psalms."

C. The Poor

There are various characteristic self-designations of those who pray in the Psalms. Those who are suffering from poverty and trouble call themselves עני ואביון, "poor and needy" (Ps. 40:17; 70:5; 86:1; 109:22). A survey of terminology in this area yields the following: עני ("poor") in Ps. 9:18; 10:2, 9; 14:6; 18:27; 68:10; 72:2; 74:19; etc.; ענו ("afflicted") in Ps. 9:12; 10:17; 22:26; 25:9; 34:2; 37:11; 69:33; 147:6; 149:4; אביון ("needy") in Ps. 40:17; 70:5; 72:4; 86:1; 109:22; דל ("weak," "poor")in Ps. 41:1; 72:13; 82:3-4; חלכה ("hapless") in Ps. 10:8, 10, 14. In each case these are designations or self-designations of those who out of the depths of their need come into the presence of Yahweh and plead with him to intervene and save.

In Old Testament scholarship the identity of these "poor" has continued to be a subject of discussion. The stimulus to detailed investigation of the concepts and their range of meaning was provided by the studies of A. Rahlfs (1892). Rahlfs held that the "poor" were a specific group among the Old Testament people of God, a party of committed followers of Yahweh. This interpretation of ענוים ("poor") influenced the work of B. Duhm, R. Kittel, W. Staerk, and H. Gunkel. Causse (1922) introduced a modification in this line of thought. He believed that the "communauté des pauvres" ("community of the poor") was a spiritual family and brotherhood with specific ideas and traditions, and that they were united in their worship and inspired by common ideals. According to Causse, the Psalter is the book of Israel's "poor" (1922, pp. 81ff.). But the interpretation of the poor as a party or a group did not win continuing acceptance. H. A. Brongers and J. van der Ploeg, in particular, opposed that widely held position (cited by J. J. Stamm, 1955, pp. 1-68). Mowinckel also rejected the explanation of the "poor" as a party or group. Scholarly attention was rightly attracted to the contrast between the "poor" and the "enemies" in many psalms. The tendency to interpret the work of the פֹּעֲלֵי־אָוֶן (*po'eley awen*, "evildoers") in terms of magic resulted in a narrowing of the focus of interpretation. It was held that originally the "poor" were the victims of magic practiced by their "foes" (cf. Mowinckel, 1921, pp. 113ff.; 1924b, p. 61). H. Birkeland (1933) advanced a different interpretation. He too rejected the explanation of the "poor" based on the view that they were a party and contended that the "poor" were those who were "currently suffering," but left it open how "currently" was to be understood and explained.

Additional literature: P. A. Munch, 1936, pp. 13, 26; A. Causse, 1937; A. Kuschke, 1939, pp. 31-57; J. J. Stamm, 1946; J. von der Ploeg, 1950, pp. 236-270; H. Brunner, 1961, pp. 319-344; P. von den Berghe, 1962, pp. 273-298; R. Martin-Achard, 1965, pp. 349-357; L. E. Keck, 1966, pp. 54-78; O. Bächli, 1966, pp. 385-395; J. M. Liaño, 1966, pp. 117-167.

One can only applaud the stimulus to fresh interpretation provided by Mowinckel when he rejected the view that the "poor" were to be understood as a party or a religious order in Israel, and at the same time called attention to the polarity between the "poor" and the "foes." In the Psalms the "poor" are the victims of their "enemies." The essential feature of this situation of "poverty" is the attack by hostile forces and the resulting state of helplessness and need. It can be shown that the "poor" are above all those who are persecuted, slandered, and falsely accused, who are not able to defend themselves against the superior power of their foes. They flee to Yahweh for refuge and in the sanctuary present their lost cause to Yahweh, the righteous judge. The "poor" are therefore those who appeal to Yahweh for mercy and for help in obtaining justice (Ps. 9:18; 10:2, 8-11; 18:27; 35:10; 74:19). Thus the Hebrew terms listed above have almost consistently the meaning, "helpless," "miserable," "depressed," "oppressed," "insignificant," "weak," "powerless." In their trouble the "poor" flee into the temple precincts, plead with Yahweh to intervene, and pray that their "foes" will be defeated. The use of these contrasting expressions, however, is not limited to the situation of persecution and the denial of justice. Wherever hostile forces make their appearance in their various forms, there the "poor" are to be found as the victims of that nefarious activity.

Parallels from ancient Egyptian religion show that the concept of the "poor" was also current in the worship of other cultures. A prayer to Amon reads, "Amon, incline your ear to one who stands alone in court, who is poor, but whose enemy is mighty. The court presses him, 'Silver and gold for the scribe! And clothes for the servants!' But he finds that Amon has transformed himself into the form of the vizier so that the poor man may escape" (A. Erman, 1934, p. 140). It is interesting that in this text also the contrast is clear. The "poor" man is oppressed by a "mighty enemy." He is not able to offer bribes. In such troubles the deity is the refuge of the oppressed. The understanding of the situation of the "poor" leads also in Egypt from the situation of the courtroom out into the whole of religious life (cf. H. Brunner, 1961, pp. 319-344).

The Individual in The Presence of God

We should not too quickly lose sight of the concrete situation of the court-room. The Old Testament stresses again and again that Yahweh is the defender of those who are denied justice and who lack influence. He takes the part of widows and orphans, foreigners and outcasts. It is significant that in Ps. 82:3 the "weak," "the fatherless," the "afflicted," and the "destitute" are mentioned in the same breath. "Poor" are those who are denied justice, who possess no influence or status, who are at the mercy of opponents with unlimited power. These features of social justice should not be transformed too readily into a religious or spiritual interpretation. The "poor" are those who lack social status, who are underprivileged, whose inability to obtain justice comes to light in the place where justice and help before the law are promised—where Yahweh is present in the temple. The "poor" are those without bread (Ps. 132:15), those who have been robbed (Isa. 3:14), those without land or possessions, the dispossessed, the strangers. The extent of the suffering caused by social problems becomes clearer when the prophetic books and the wisdom poetry are included in the investigation. The "poor" are those who are disadvantaged and helpless in the struggle for existence. No one comes to their aid. They have, as it often says in the Psalms, "no help." Yet in Yahweh they find comfort and support. They hope that he will bring about a turn in their fortunes. Not only does Yahweh intervene as the advocate and deliverer of the "poor," but the king does so as well. Once again it is the concrete situation of being brought to trial that is the focus of the wish, "May he defend the cause of the poor of the people, give deliverance to the needy, and crush the oppressor!" (Ps. 72:4). "Yahweh's anointed" is the one who provides justice for the "poor." These expectations involve the ruler in other areas of the ancient Near East as well. But the Old Testament stresses the direct correspondence between the help provided at law by God and that provided by the king. "The conviction that those whose legal standing was weak and who were less privileged in the struggle of life were the objects of Jahweh's particular interest reaches far back into the history of the people of Jahweh. This conception of the poor practically contains a legal claim upon Jahweh; and it was precisely this which later made it a self-designation of the pious before Jahweh" (von Rad, 1962, p. 400). This claim • to a right to justice, or to the divine provision of legal help is involved in the basic meaning of the term "poor." This basic meaning does not justify us, however, in moving too quickly to the religious or spiritual self-designation of "pious." Rather, we must first take into account all the types of need and of threats from one's foes that are included in the term "poor."

The "poor" are those whose troubles drive them to rely on Yahweh alone. This reflects their inner attitude. These persons who seek refuge in Yahweh are being persecuted and ridiculed. They are oppressed and abused. Injustice is done to them. They wrestle with death, with the accusation of sin, and with evil powers. In all this they rely wholly on God and wait for his judgment, for his aid and for improvement in their lot. The "poor" are those who wait, who have nothing in themselves, and hope to receive everything from God.

Full of longing and expectation, the "poor" make the pilgrimage to Zion, fleeing to the precincts of the sanctuary. With great intensity they turn to God, who is their help and salvation. They can be designated as יוֹדְעֵי שְׁמֶךְ, "those who know thy name" (Ps. 9:10), because, full of confidence and aware of all God's promises and assurances, they call upon the name of the one who is present in the sanctuary. For, above all, the עָנִי ("poor") is assured of the miracle in which

Yahweh brings salvation. Thus, in Jerusalem the "poor" are the conspicuous recipients of salvation (ישועה). They become witnesses to God's gracious presence, to his transformation of their destiny, and to his effective provision of justice (Ps. 9:18; 10:17; 18:27; 22:26; 25:9; 37:11; 69:33; 147:6; 149:4). On Zion the "poor" have a claim to justice, which can involve the high privileges which are promised to the needy who seek help and have been denied justice. The God of justice and right reveals his living presence. "The Lord has founded Zion, and in her the afflicted of his people find refuge" (Isa. 14:32). Thus we see that the distinctive manner in which the Psalms speak of those who are "poor" and "needy" is not to be traced to the existence of a party or a group, but to the privileges of justice and salvation that are granted to helpless men and women. It must, therefore, be firmly maintained that the "poor" do not represent a religious party in Israel. Nor does the term refer in a spiritual sense to a type of persons whose piety is to be considered as the ideal. Rather the term "poor," as the contrast to the superior hostile powers, points to those who are helpless and abandoned, who lay claim to the privileges of justice and salvation which Yahweh, the God of justice and assistance before the law, promises and guarantees to those who unreservedly trust him and hope in him alone.

We can clearly observe in the Psalms the way in which testimony is given to the deliverance experienced by the "poor." In Ps. 34:6 a witness utters the words, "This poor man cried, and the Lord heard him, and saved him out of all his troubles." The help which Yahweh gives extends to "all troubles," but especially to the troubles of those who suffer injustice. In Ps. 10:17-18 the "poor" man identifies with the widows and orphans who have no rights. Experiencing deliverance brings knowledge, a clear recognition: "I know that the Lord maintains the cause of the afflicted, and executes justice for the needy" (Ps. 140:13). This statement also reveals the outline of the help that Yahweh gives to those who are deprived of their rights. Their firm assurance and knowledge is proclaimed: Yahweh gives hope to the poor (לדל תקוה Job 5:16); he is a "stronghold" for the oppressed (Ps. 9:9). Even when the troubles seem to continue without end, "The needy shall not always be forgotten (Ps. 9:18). They have hope, for Yahweh "is near to all who call upon him, to all who call upon him in truth" (Ps. 145:18). He is praised in the hymn in Psalm 113, "He raises the poor from the dust, and lifts the needy from the ash heap" (v. 7).

The self-description "poor and needy" includes more than it seems at first glance. Complex experiences of suffering accumulate. The individual comes into Yahweh's presence simply as "poor." By identifying with the עני ואביון ("poor and needy") he or she is coming to God in the truth of his human condition. The declaration "I am poor and needy" is not a formula of pious phraseology and religious humility, but has reference to a wide range of concrete reality. In spite of its complexity the term does not become vague, but the original significance remains alive in it. The "poor" are concerned with denial of their rights and with help in obtaining them. Because of the privileges which Israel's God has promised to all who are helpless, deprived, and oppressed, the "poor" have a claim on Yahweh's assistance. Paradoxically, the claim to rights is not based on what one "has" but on what one does not have. The "poor" have a claim to God's assistance only because they are the have-nots, because their poverty is what is significant. This basic feature runs through all the Psalms. It is characteristic of the human situation before God, which finds its theological expression in the New Testament in the doctrine of justification.

The "poor and needy" are the ones who in the Psalms speak of the brokenness of their hearts. We find the נשברי־לב ("brokenhearted") in Ps. 34:18; 51:17; 145:3; and Isa. 61:1. Who are these "brokenhearted"? First, it should be said that they are persons whose troubles have affected the center of their lives, the "heart." But the biblical context can be specified more precisely. "The 'brokenhearted' are those who have been overcome by a deep despair about themselves" (von Rad, 1973c, pp. 80f.). This brokenness of one's natural self-confidence is a symptom of deepest "poverty." It is "a condition of a profound sense of defeat and despair in one's relationship to God, and for this very reason, according to the understanding of biblical and reformation theology, is the sign of especial nearness to God" (von Rad, 1973c, p. 81). It speaks of those who no longer regard themselves as having any worth, and have no desire to do so. They are convinced that God will accept them. Thus they stand in the mystery of a still hidden, but soon to be manifested, fellowship with God, and the turning point in their fortunes.

D. The Faith of the Righteous

Among the characteristic expressions for those who have experienced Yahweh's help and who belong to him, there is the term צדיק (ṣadiq, "righteous"). In explaining it, the two nouns צדקה (ṣedaqah) and צדק (ṣedeq) must be taken into account from the outset. It has been emphasized repeatedly and has already been set forth in this book that "righteousness" in the Old Testament can be understood neither as a norm nor as an absolute ideal. "Ancient Israel did not in fact measure a line of conduct or an act by an ideal norm, but by the specific relationship in which the partner had at the time to prove himself true" (von Rad, 1962, p. 371). Because righteousness is not a norm but a relationship, it involves the faithfulness to community which must be preserved in a covenant relationship and a legal relationship. The צדיק (ṣadiq) lives "true to the covenant," "faithful to the community." Therefore no one is "righteous" on the basis of an accounting of his moral accomplishments, but solely because he works to promote שלום (shalom) and does not disrupt or hinder it; he lives in a "covenant" community, that is, community with Yahweh.

The Psalms make it clear that the "righteousness" of the "righteous" takes on its distinctive character only through opposition and temptation. Just as the negative counterpart to the term "poor" is "enemy," so the term "ungodly" (רשע) stands in contrast to "righteous." רשע can also be translated as "wicked." "The wicked (רשע) plots against the righteous (צדיק)" (Ps. 37:12). "The wicked watches the righteous, and seeks to slay him" (Ps. 37:32; 94:21). This clearly indicates an antagonistic situation. In the first place, the רשע ("wicked") is determined to act as an "enemy" and bring doubt on the faithfulness of the צדיק ("righteous"), to accuse him of concrete misdeeds and to bring formal charges against him. The "righteous" is cast into the fire of these suspicions and charges. Since specific accusations are brought against him, as Ps. 7:3-4 shows, the "righteousness" of the accused must be made manifest as innocence. This aspect is enormously important. Concrete accusations sharpen our understanding of צדקה ("righteousness"). Through contradictions and temptations the "righteousness" of the "righteous" takes on its distinctive nature. The "righteous" person is the one who is innocent. This is anything but self-righteousness. The person is suffering through slander and false accusations. A profoundly human problem with all its unpredictable burdens unfolds before us, first in the trial before God in the sanctuary of Israel, and then in a continuing, complex sense.

That person is "righteous" whose innocence has been demonstrated by Yahweh's verdict of not guilty, which refutes all accusations and shows that they are baseless. The one who has been persecuted by the רשעים ("wicked ones") is certain that Yahweh's eyes "are toward the righteous" (Ps. 34:15). Yahweh "tests the righteous" (Ps. 11:5). He alone knows and probes the depths of the heart (Ps. 17:3). He intervenes. He establishes the "righteous" again (Ps. 7:9) and "upholds" him (Ps. 37:17). The innocence of the צדיק ("righteous") is made evident by Yahweh's pronouncement. The "righteous" person is the one whom Yahweh's verdict has declared innocent. With Rom. 8:33 he can proclaim, "Who shall bring any charge against God's elect? It is God who justifies." It should be pointed out once again that the Psalms are concerned with concrete accusations and therefore with concrete verdicts of innocence. The "righteousness" of the "righteous" has been established in spite of all the verbal attacks and all the questions that have been raised.

Since it is said of Yahweh that he is "righteous" and acts "righteously," it is one of the inalienable privileges of the צדיק ("righteous") that he or she enter into the sphere of God's צדקה ("righteousness") and participate in it—thanks to the verdict of not guilty—and thus enter into intimate fellowship with Yahweh. He or she experiences the goodness of God. Yahweh loves the righteous (Ps. 146:8); God is "with the generation of the righteous" (Ps. 14:5), blesses them (Ps. 5:12), and restores their joy (Ps. 32:11; 58:10; 68:3). "The righteous shall possess the land, and dwell upon it for ever" (Ps. 37:29). In these last-cited passages the term צדיק ("righteous") has taken on a more complicated meaning which is not entirely expressed in the term "pious." The person who is צדיק in Israel is open to the activity of Yahweh's צדקה ("righteousness") and has been accepted into the sphere of the divine "righteousness." In this context it should be stressed that the "righteousness" of Yahweh is not fully expressed in the idea of assistance and salvation. The forensic situation of judgment is always present. "Neither in the Old Testament nor in the New can the concept of justice ever be interpreted in such a way that there is no longer any true or serious question of the Law, of the Judge and His judgment" (K. Barth, *CD* 2/1: 382).

The acquittal is not always the event that marks the transition from the accusation to the proof of innocence. The "righteousness" of Yahweh can also be seen when the harm that has been set in motion by the hostile powers falls back upon its instigators, e.g., Ps. 7:13-16. It was widely believed in the past that such concepts were expressions of the dogma of retribution, sharpened by the "legalism" of the Old Testament. K. Koch (1955, pp. 1-42) has refuted this view. Koch began with the observation that in the Old Testament it is regarded as certain that every evil deed rebounds to the detriment of its perpetrator. The Hebrew language does not have a word for "punishment." In the worldview of the ancient Near East the two factors that exist separately in the dogma of retribution, act and punishment, or act and reward, consititute a unity in which the action brings its own results for the fate of the actor. Thus there is an "immanent nemesis" at work. And this "immanent nemesis" is incorporated into the Old Testament view that Yahweh is the cause of everything. We must, however, immediately ask whether the merging of these two concepts does not require the drawing of theological distinctions. What is the relationship between God's personal action and reaction, on the one hand, and, on the other, the ontological sphere of actions that bring their own retribution? Franz Delitzsch said that Ps. 7:13-16 is an example of the self-punishment of sin, under the principle that God has "given them up" to do evil (Rom. 1:24). We should not think abstractly of the way in which the working out of Yahweh's צדקה ("righteousness") is to be explained. The legal decision which Yahweh renders has its effect on the "immanent nemesis." The prayers of the Old Testament bear witness to this certainty. If this really involves the rejection and the nullification of the hostile accusations and, at the same time, the "righteousness" of the innocent, then everything that takes place in that sphere where actions bring their own retribution is highly symbolic with highly personal consequences for the justification of the innocent. These procedures cannot be banished to the realm of magic and subsumed under that theme.

Everything that has been presented above involves the theme that the "righteous" person is innocent. In the realm of interpersonal relations this innocence is disputed, ultimately in the presence of Yahweh in the act of sacral judgment. But nowhere does anyone assert innocence before God. Especially in the psalms of confession we see how far-reaching the consciousness of guilt can be. To be sure, in the presence of Yahweh concrete offenses are confessed, as seen especially in the "guides to confession" in Psalm 15 and Psalm 24, or in the causal relationship of sickness and guilt presented by those who bring accusations. In Psalm 51, however, an ultimate dimension opens up. The one making confession declares that he knows his transgressions and that his sin is always before his eyes (Ps. 51:3). He continues, "Against thee, thee only, have I sinned, and done that which is evil in thy sight, so that thou art justified in thy sentence and blameless in thy judgment" (Ps. 51:4).

How is this statement to be understood? Did the psalmist sin against Yahweh by worshiping idols (so F. Baethgen)? Or is an offense against humans seen as an offense against God? Gunkel rejected both views. He wrote, "The frequent attempt to explain the words as meaning that all sin, even that against humans, is ultimately only an offense against God, is a distortion of the text." Gunkel's conclusion is not correct. Very early in the Old Testament offenses against other humans were regarded as sin against God himself (Gen. 39:9). In 2 Sam. 12:13 David confessed after his sin with Bathsheba, "I have sinned against Yahweh." The similarity of these confessions must not be overlooked. Whoever transgresses against Yahweh's commands is sinning against Yahweh himself. This is an allusion to the fact that sin is a violation of the First Commandment. Note, however, the form and intention of the "judgment doxology" in Ps. 51:4. Anyone who sins is urged to give Yahweh the glory (Josh.7:19). F. Horst (1929, pp. 45-54) identified this psalm category as "judgment doxology." This confession of guilt is intended to put God in the right (*Deum justificare*). In a confession of guilt against God himself, the worshiper submits to the righteous judgment of Yahweh. To give God the honor, to put him in the right, is, acccording to Luther, the way of faith.

The prayer in Psalm 51 speaks of the original, primeval tendency to sin, "Behold, I was brought forth in iniquity, and in sin did my mother conceive me" (Ps. 51:5). Statements of this sort cannot be understood either causally as biologically inherited sin, nor in terms of sexual morality. They have no didactic tendency that would lead to dogmatic formulations. Rather, they recognize the power of evil to corrupt humans from the very beginning (cf. Gen. 8:21; Job 14:4; 15:15f.; 25:4; Ps. 143:2; John 3:6). Human sin not only contains a component of sinful actions that place responsibility on us; it also has a component of fate, which weighs on all that is human. Genesis 3 speaks of this primal sin.

The context of Ps. 51:4-5 makes clear what the psalmist means in Psalm 143, "No man living is righteous before thee" (v. 2). In the context of the theme, "The 'righteous' is the innocent one," this statement is unintelligible. All claim to righteousness is denied to every human being (cf. Ps. 14:3; 130:3; Job 4:17; 9:2; 25:4; Rom. 3:20; Gal. 2:16). This view is not an expression of pessimism. It gives voice to the profound insight that all humans are fallen and guilty. A final limit is placed on all protestations of innocence. The justification of the ungoldly is made known. The sacral demonstration of the צדקה ("righteousness") of the innocent becomes questionable, and it points beyond itself to a final solution.

When those who are termed צדיקים ("righteous ones"), who are open to and caught up in Yahweh's צדקה ("righteousness"), are spoken of in the Psalms in descriptive contexts, additional terms are used which require consideration. First, there is the term עבד ("servant"). Those who belong to Yahweh are his servants, and the one who prays calls himself "thy servant" (Ps. 19:11, 13; 27:9; 31:16; 69:17: 86:2; 116:16; 119:17; 143:2). When the king is called "the servant of Yahweh" (Ps. 78:70; 89:3; 132:10; 144:10) he is accorded a place of honor and a role of service, and the same is true of those "men and women of God" who are called "servants." Their whole life is committed to the Lord; the Lord is "ever before them" (Ps. 16:8; 25:15; 26:3; etc.). They are the ישרים ("upright," Ps. 11:7; 19:9; 33:4; 37:14, 37; 111:8; 119:137). They are those who are "upright in heart" (Ps. 7:11; 12:1; etc.). תמים ("wholeness") is a synonym that refers to life with Yahweh that is complete and intact (Ps. 37:18; 101:6; 119:1). The fact that these terms do not imply any ideal of piety is seen in the highly characteristic term חסיד (*ḥasid*, "pious," Ps. 30:4; 31:23; 37:28). The חסידים (*ḥasidim*) are aware of their special relationship to Yahweh, "that they belong to the congregation, that is, they live in the realm where the grace of God is bestowed" (Stoebe, THAT, 1:619). The חסיד (*ḥasid*, lives in the sphere of divine חסד (*ḥesed*, "steadfast love"), which creates community and trust. To translate the word as "the pious" would only distort the focus. We do not have terms in English that could reproduce the loyal, intimate, and trusting relationship of life and service, the commitment and devotion of those who are faithful to God.

The most frequent expression in the Psalms for this relationship is "those who fear Yahweh" (Ps. 22:23; 25:12, 14; 31:19; 34:7, 9; 61:5; 66:16; 85:9; 103:11, 13; 112:1; 128:4; 130:4; 147:11). Those who fear Yahweh live in obedience to God's will, in permanent attentiveness and submission. What is involved here is a never-ending commitment to the God of Israel and to his commandments, an always present "knowledge of God" (H. W. Wolff). For those who fear Yahweh, God is a living reality. They look for the self-disclosure of God and are always alert to receive him. Undoubtedly, the phrase "fear Yahweh" became less vivid with the passage of time and occasionally it became a mere formal designation. But the basic meaning of real fear never disappeared, fear that knows that God is the judge and is aware of his incomprehensible sovereignty and freedom (Ps. 119:120). Fear does not exclude love. "We should fear and love God," said Martin Luther. Yahweh's people turn to him in love (Ps. 5:11; 18:1; 31:23; 40:16; 69:36; 97:10; 122:6; 145:20). They are constantly attentive to God and always long to be near him. Therefore they love the temple as the place where they meet God (Ps. 26:8; 27:4; 84:4).

Those whose prayers are found in the Psalms were full of hope and expectation. Their eager openness to Yahweh their God is expressed primarily in the verbs יחל ("wait") and קוה ("wait for"). In Ps. 69:3 the situation of waiting is vividly described. "Waiting" (יחל) is not a silent expectation that there will be a turn for the better, but involves calling and crying out, being constantly on the lookout. The one who is praying is "weary" from crying, his "throat is parched," his eyes "grow dim" with waiting for God (Ps. 69:3). Beneath the sufferer's troubles a yet deeper sorrow lies hidden—the sorrow of restless, tense waiting and crying out for Yahweh to intervene. In the Psalms "to wait" means not giving up, not growing tired, not surrendering to overwhelming grief, but persevering expectantly. The distinctive feature is the certainty that the eyes of the Lord are upon those who "hope in his steadfast love" (Ps. 33:18). The hope of those who wait is based on the conviction that Yahweh is gracious, that he will bestow on them his חסד (*hesed*, "tender mercies"). Yet, wherever trust and certainty based on Yahweh's help in the past are the dominant attitude, the one praying does not reach a place of calmness or of stagnant belief. Israel and the men and women of Israel remain those who wait. Trouble and suffering have no end. Thus the frequent exhortation, "O Israel, hope in the Lord! For with the Lord there is steadfast love, and with him is plenteous redemption" (Ps. 130:7). A basis is given for this exhortation. Steadfast love and redemption are to be found in Yahweh, and only in him. "Waiting" is not a sign of capitulation and weakness. Those who "wait" (יחל) on Yahweh will wait for him with strength and courage of heart (Ps. 31:24).

Like יחל ("wait"), the verb קוה also connotes incessant, expectant looking forward on the part of those who suffer, looking forward with their whole life to Yahweh, the "God of help." It is to him that they cry out again and again with the words that are full of promise, but by no means possessive, "my God!" Our starting point is the explanation given by Walter Zimmerli (1971, p. 24): "According to the Old Testament faith, hope is legitimate only there where God remains the sole Lord, in activity, in gift and in promise, and where man anticipates the future in no other way than as the free gift of God." In the Psalms the waiting and the hope of those who suffer represent an orientation of life toward Yahweh alone, which nothing can shake. Those who persevere in their hope experience God's answer and intervention (Ps. 40:2). In the נפש (*nephesh*), the seat of all need and all desire, hope is alive and active (Ps. 130:5).

The hope of those who wait is directed to Yahweh's word ("and in his word I hope," Ps. 130:5). The decisive feature is the confidence and strength of the heart (Ps. 27:14) that so easily gives up and sinks in the undertow of darkness. Biblical hope, however, is no "militant optimism" (Ernst Bloch), but is anchored in Yahweh's faithfulness, in a confidence that moves forward into the unseen. The hope of those who pray has a direction. Those who "hope" in Yahweh do not call out to or run after other gods and powers. Nothing can cause them to despair of God's eventual help, of his coming to their aid. Those who pray are certain that what is coming, future help and deliverance, is more sure than what is present. "Thus hope is not a subsidiary theme in the Old Testament. On the contrary, it is indissolubly linked with Yahweh as the God of the patriarchs and prophets, the God of the threats and promises that he has proclaimed, the God of great changes and of final salvation; but equally with the God of all who pray and with the God of the wise. Just as hearing and speaking are man's specific characteristics, so the expectation of the future is the distinctive mark of human life in time. In so far as it is a well-founded hope, the expectation of the future is for the Old Testament inseparable from obedience to the God who has promised himself to Israel and to the nations" (H. W. Wolff, 1974, pp. 153-154). The hope of the psalmists belongs in this larger context. It must be emphasized that this hope of those who pray in the Psalms is a well-founded hope. But "well-founded" does not mean accessible, visible, tangible. Only the promise of Yahweh's faithfulness and the testimony to the experience of the חסד ("steadfast love") of Israel's God are adequate grounds for a hope that is not misplaced. For faith is "the assurance of things hoped for, the conviction of things not seen" (Heb. 11:1). Thus, the one who hopes walks in the faithfulness of the God of his salvation (Ps. 25:5). Hope means to "keep to his way" (Ps. 37:34), not to be distracted into following other paths that do not lead to the goal of divine help and salvation.

Trust does not replace hope. On the contrary, all hope, all waiting for Yahweh is based on trust (בטח). And all trust awakes new hope. The psalmists trust in Yahweh's חסד (*ḥesed*, Ps. 13:5; 52:8). They rely on his faithfulness as the demonstration of his friendly, gracious condescension and assistance. Because Yahweh is known as one's "strength and shield," it is possible to say, "In him my heart trusts" (Ps. 28:7). In this confidence the rejoicing over God's help can already begin (Ps. 13:5). Bright prospects open up for future: "I trust in the steadfast love of God for ever and ever" (Ps. 52:8). In trust something permanent, inalienable, is received—the strength to hope. It is significant for the Old Testament that trust is not limited by any restrictions of cultic practice, that it is not restricted to the place where God is present. Psalm 23 expresses the certainty, "He leads me in paths of righteousness" (v. 3). Yahweh is the God who travels the road with us, who leads us. Therefore, the one who is threatened by hostile powers (v. 5) does not fear harm, even in the dark valley, "for thou are with me" (v. 4). It is not only in the temple that Yahweh is near to his people; in the "valley of the shadow of death" he is present with those who suffer, and his goodness leads and guides them. This holds true for the future as well. The psalmist expresses the confidence that "goodness and mercy shall follow me all the days of my life" (v. 6). This statement shows us how greatly that confidence influences the future. Finally, it says, "I shall dwell in the house of the Lord for ever" (v. 6). This introduces a theme that must be explored in detail.

Our starting point is the function of the holy place as a sanctuary. Those who are persecuted and oppressed "hide" themselves with Yahweh. They seek refuge in the temple, under the shadow of Yahweh's wings. The institution of sacral sanctuary involves the divine judgment to which those who are persecuted and oppressed commit their cause. But it should be noted that in the Psalms the trust that is expressed in the protection afforded by the sanctuary frees itself from the concrete institution and blends the institutional relationship with the symbolic language of prayer. In reference to this process there is no reason to speak of a "spiritualizing" of the relationship to God, as von Rad does (1962, pp. 402-403), because the symbolic language is designed to preserve the concrete nature of institutional images, while removing them metaphorically from the specific sacral context. "Spiritualizing" is not a term that can be applied to this process. What is involved is a transposing into an analogous, but no longer institutional, destiny of the individual. This is the case in Psalms 16 and 62. Here we find the old "confessions in the sanctuary" in a changed situation (cf. also Ps. 27:1, 5; 36:7). The protection offered by the sanctuary becomes the epitome of all divine protection. In this confidence time stretches out into dwelling in the house of the Lord as long as one lives (Ps. 23:6) in order "to behold the beauty of the Lord" (Ps. 27:4).

It could, of course, also be assumed that the wish to remain in the Lord's house all the days of one's life refers to the priestly life, so that what is intended is joining the ranks of the priests. In that case it must have been a transposed Levitical confession. Once again in reference to this process von Rad speaks of a "spiritualizing," and of the development of a "sublime cultic mysticism" (von Rad, 1971c, p. 432). Quite apart from the problems involved in this explanation (see above), it can be shown in Ps. 23:6, for example, that the one praying had been persecuted by his foes and is now experiencing how Yahweh prepares "in the presence of my enemies" a table for the one they had victimized (v. 5). These factors indicate that the wish to remain in the house of Yahweh as long as one lives relates to the experience of protection in the sanctuary. (This interpretation differs from that offered in the *Commentary*.)

Expressions of deep confidence include the statements of the psalmist, "The Lord is my chosen portion (חלקי)," and "I have a goodly heritage (נחלתי)" (Ps. 16:5, 6). The two Hebrew terms belong to the context of the traditions of the occupation of the land and the distribution of portions by lot (cf. גורלי ["lot"] in Ps. 16:6). The details are found in Josh. 14:4; 15:13; Num. 16:55; Josh. 17:5; Num. 18:21; Deut. 4:21; Josh. 13:23. What does it mean when the psalmist proclaims his trust in Yahweh in terms borrowed from the ancient tradition of the occupation of the land? Does it involve "primitive, almost childish metaphors" (H. Schmidt)? The context indicates deeper levels of meaning. When the land was divided among the tribes, the Levites were left out, according to the traditional account. In preference to all the other tribes, they received from Yahweh a unique privilege, which is expressed in the statement, "Yahweh is his inheritance (נחלתו)" (Deut. 10:9; Josh. 13:14). Yahweh declared, "I am your portion (חלק) and your inheritance (נחלה)" (Num. 18:20). Von Rad offers the explanation, "This prescription simply contains a regulation for the maintenance of Levi, and is consequently to be understood in a perfectly material way (Deut. 18:1): Levi does not maintain itself by work on the land; it does not in fact hold any land but lives from the shares in the sacrifices and other cultic payments" (1962, p. 404). It thus involves a Levitical prerogative, the meaning of which was probably extended far beyond the material sense at an early period. In Israel the נחלה ("inheritance") was more than a mere "portion of land for one's maintenance"; it was the basis which Yahweh had given for life. It was now the distinctive privilege of the Levites that Yahweh himself was the basis of their life and thus the נחלה ("inheritance") and חלק ("portion") of the priests. When in prayer Israelites who are not priests take as their own the confession, "You, Yahweh, are my portion," they are making the prerogative of the Levites their own. They enter into it without occupying foreign territory. For one thing, we must assume that those who speak here are the "poor." For them Yahweh alone is their hope and the basis for their life. In addition, the Levitical prerogative contains within itself a tendency to complexity, in that it incorporates the living expressions of trust which both correspond to the status of the "poor" and also bear witness to a place of security for more than the individual. This again contradicts the attempt to explain the concept as a "spiritualization" (von Rad). Indeed, the concept of "spiritualization" always introduces an inappropriate polarity of matter and spirit in the Old Testament. This distorts the data.

In addition to the terms and metaphors for confidence, the Psalms use, though relatively seldom, the Hebrew verb that is usually translated as "believe." האמין ("believe") contains the root אמן (*'aman*), which means "to be firm," so that the *hiphil* of the verb could be translated as "make oneself firm," "have unshakable certainty" (cf. Ps. 27:13). Whoever has "remained firm," has "believed," can say in retrospect how horrible the despair was which he or she suffered (Ps. 116:10). In what can the believer make himself or herself secure and find an "anchor"? Using negative statements as a foil, Ps. 78:22 declares that it is in Yahweh, and in his "wonders" (v. 32). In Ps. 78:22 the expression בטח בישועתו ("trust his saving power") is synonymous to האמינו באלהים ("believe in God"). Actually, faith has as its object God's "words" (Ps. 106:12) and "promise" (Ps. 106:24). In a Torah psalm the verb האמין ("believe") is used in reference to the "commandments" of Yahweh (Ps. 119:66). This introduces a new realm, which is identified by the term תורה (*torah*).

Psalms 19 and 119 show with especial clarity that men and women in Israel loved the Torah of their God and were faithful to it, that joy over the "instruction of Yahweh" filled their lives, and that they carried the Torah in their hearts (Ps. 40:7-8). We must pose the important question of how this relation to the Torah is to be understood, and the prior question of the meaning contained in the term תורה. From the outset the issues are stated wrongly if תורה (*torah*) is translated "law." Martin Buber pointed this out again and again. תורה (*torah*) is "instruction." This must be clarified in detail. The false trails that scholarship has followed are amazing. Without a qualm, B. Duhm ascribed the statements in the Psalms about "the law" to the Pharisees and scribes of the late Old Testament period. There is hardly an exegete who does not talk about "legalistic piety," or rigid religiosity, or even of "legalistic Judaism." Martin Noth explored the relationships between "covenant" and "law" in the Old Testament. In Psalms 1; 19B; and 119 he ascribes the basic of תורה (*torah*) to the presuppositions of the covenant. According to his view, the "law" became an absolute entity, unconditionally valid. Of Psalm 19B he says, "In these and similar cases the formulations show how 'the law' had become an object of a personal appraisal to be made by an individual, how individuals were expected to take such a position toward 'the law,' and how each individual then had to bear the consequences of his position" (Noth, 1957a, p. 127).

The misunderstandings, however, begin, as has been said, with the translation of the term. התורה (*hatorah*) is not "the law," but "instruction," the gracious expression of the will of Yahweh as experienced by the individual. This defines for him a path from which he is not to deviate, either to the left or to the right. From the human side the expectation and petition is expressed, "Make me to know thy ways, O Lord; teach me thy paths" (Ps. 25:4). With his Torah Yahweh guides a person's steps (Ps. 37:23), so that his way will be wholesome. The word of the Torah is a lamp for the feet and a light on the path of the "righteous" (Ps. 119:105). Above all, Psalms 1; 19B; and 119 are in total agreement that תורה (*torah*) is no rigid, lifeless entity which can be elevated to absolute validity only by an individual's acceptance of it. On the contrary, in the תורה (*torah*) we encounter a living and active word. If God can be heard to speak through the "instruction," then one's life is "revived" (Ps. 19:7) and one's heart rejoices (Ps. 19:8). Light shines forth from the Torah (Ps. 119:105, 130). Thus the relation of individuals to the תורה (*torah*) is characterized by joy, love, and eagerness, and does not display the traits of a rigid religiosity, or legalistic observance, or of an unconditional obligation. No, the תורה (*torah*) is the stream of life which makes human existence fruitful in wholesome, successful activity (Ps. 1:2-3). Thus it would be a serious error to introduce the theology of Paul as the criterion for our understanding of "the law" in the Old Testament. If it is necessary to identify a theological category, it may be said that the idea of the *tertius usus legis* ("third use of the law") provides the best possibility for explaining the data.

Whenever the relationship of the individual to the Torah is spoken of in the Psalms, we are dealing with texts that belong to a relatively late period (post-Deuteronomic). Thus it is worthwhile to ask what meaning texts such as Deut. 30:11-14 and Jer. 31:31-34 have for our understanding of the תורה (*torah*). It cannot be denied that Ps. 40:7-8 and Ps. 37:30-31 refer to the effects of the "new covenant" which had been promised, especially in Jer. 31:31-34. Gunkel regarded the connection as distant when he said of Ps. 40:8, "Even under the dominance of the law . . . the spirit of the prophets lived on in certain pious circles among the laity, and these were uninhibited enough to unite the veneration of the law with the thought of the prophets. They read the Torah in the light of the prophets." Two questions may be directed to this statement from Gunkel's Psalms commentary. (1) How is it possible that Gunkel, who in biblical-theological questions acted with such caution and reserve could, without reflecting at all, apply the theologically highly volatile concept "dominance of the law" as his characterization of a "period" in religious history? (2) How can we give concrete expression to the indefinite references to "spirit of the prophets" and "the Torah read in a prophetic sense"? In this instance Karl Barth certainly saw the connections more clearly when he raised the question in reference to Ps. 40:7—"Who is the man who can take to himself the words of Ps. 40:8f.: 'Then said I, Lo, I am come; in the roll of the book it is written what I must do. I delight to do thy will, O my God: yea, thy law is within my heart'? To be sure, this was said by a member of the later Jewish Church, but in what dimension was he thinking, in what hidden sense—pointing up and away from himself—was he speaking, unless we are to take it that he was most strangely puffed up and self-deceived? . . . The Psalmist was no doubt speaking of himself, but in so doing he obviously did not focus his gaze upon the place to which he finally addressed that prayer. In these verses we have an almost verbal reminiscence of the well-known promise of Jer. 31:31ff. concerning the new covenant of the last day. When and as God establishes this new covenant, it will come to pass that 'I will put my law in their inward parts and in their heart will I write it.' The subject is obviously what Jer. 32:39 speaks of as 'another heart,' and Ezek. 11:19; 36:26 as the promised 'new spirit'—the future I that lives and works only by the grace of God and that is promised to the Israelite by the grace and Word of God" (Karl Barth, *CD* 2/2: 604). If we leave aside the problems of translation involved in Ps. 40:7-8 (cf. the *Comm.*), Barth's explanation points up the concrete context with all the clarity that could be desired. The promise of the new covenant was a source of strength for the times that followed, and in that light and under its influence individual Israelites began to participate in the mystery of that which was new. The joy in תורה (*torah*) is ultimately to be seen in this light, which also gave new effectiveness to the Deuteronomic correlation of "covenant" and "instruction." For the specific questions involved see Kraus, 1951a, pp. 337-351; 1972f, pp. 179-194.

E. Life and Death

The confession of faith expressed in the prayers of the Old Testament is concentrated in the exclamation, "With thee is the fountain of life!" (Ps. 36:9). Yahweh is the origin of all life. He is "the God of my life" (Ps. 42:8). Life is not a power

162

that proceeds from itself or is grounded in itself. Those who offer their prayers in the Psalms know that they are "absolutely dependent" on Yahweh. All life comes from him. The place where Yahweh is present is designated as the "source of life." Neither of these beliefs—that all life comes from the deity and that the cultic site is the "source of life"—is a distinctively Israelite concept. Throughout the ancient Near East people believed that all life comes from God. "All life flows from thee" is a confession that belongs to the basic beliefs of every religion (Christoph Barth, 1947, p. 36). The deity allows that which in all its fullness belongs to the deity to flow down to the creaturely world. Among the Sumerians and Babylonians the god is the "lord of life" (cf. Ps. 42:8). Thus prayers for protection or for restoration of life are offered to the particular god being worshiped. "Life of whatever sort has its origin in God and is therefore to be found where God appears and shows that his presence is near. Whoever is in need of life will strive to go into God's presence. There he knows that he is in the atmosphere in which life flourishes" (Christoph Barth, 1947, p. 48). It is in cultic practices that life can be preserved or restored (Mowinckel, 1953, pp. 63ff.).

Nevertheless, the extensive correspondences are limited by the fact that the deities of the nations around Israel were caught up in the dualism life/death. Yahweh, however, stands in contrast to the gods of death and life, especially those of Syria and Canaan" (Mowinckel, 1953, p. 68). Baal "lives" and Baal "dies." The deity is a power that dies and rises again. All life shares in the rhythm of the changing seasons, but Yahweh "never dies" (Hab. 1:12 JB). "Yahweh lives" (Ps. 18:46). He is not subject to the sleep of death. He "will neither slumber nor sleep" (Ps. 121:4). The life that he imparts is not primarily—as it was among Israel's neighbors—the natural fullness of vitality and vegetation, from which the power of being emanates. It is rather, transcending all seasonal rhythms, the power of blessing that is active in the history of the chosen people and in the created world that "shall never be moved" (Ps. 93:1). The God of life is Yahweh, and his name is not interchangeable with any other.

Thus, all statements about life are to be seen and understood in the primary context of Israel's Psalms, without losing sight of the fact that the Old Testament shared in the expressions and concepts of the religious world of the peoples around them. Life is a gift and a trust, like the land that was given in trust to God's people in the Old Testament. Humans have a "portion in life" (Ps. 17:14). Yahweh satisfies them with good (Ps. 103:5). Thus in relation to all the world, Yahweh is gracious, the one who bestows life. God opens his hand and satisfies "the desire of every living thing" (Ps. 145:16). The giving hand is a sign of personal activity. Yahweh is not some impersonal life power, the solar deity, of whom it is said in the Hymn to Aton, "When thou hast risen they live; when thou settest they die. Thou art lifetime thy own self, for one lives (only) through thee" (ANET[2], p. 371). Psalm 104 does not deal with a static deity. The concept of an emanation that can be influenced by magic is also alien to the Old Testament. Israel's understanding of nature is totally different from any other that is known. "Israel was not familiar with the concept of nature, nor did she speak about the world as a cosmos, i.e., about an ordered structure that is self-contained and subject to definite laws. To her the world was primarily much more an event than a being, and certainly much more a personal experience than a neutral subject for investigation" (von Rad, 1980, p. 116). Psalm 104, which was so strongly influenced by the language of the Hymn to Aton, shows that the entire world is supported and ruled by the activity of Yahweh. His activity involves all the elements and creatures of the created world. Like the father of a family, Yahweh stretched out the tent of the heavens (Ps. 104:2). Like a master builder he "laid the beams" of his chamber (v. 3). Like a wise manager he takes the fertility-bringing, life-giving water to the fields (Ps. 104:13-15). Like the head of a family he portions out the goods and gifts needed in daily life (vv. 27f.). Therefore all creation turns expectantly to Yahweh. It is dependent on him and dies without him (v. 29). It lives by his creative acts that continue their work of renewal (v. 30).

For the individual, the life which he has received from Yahweh is the epitome of his honor (כבוד [kabod], Ps. 3:3; 7:5). A person's invaluable reputation, the dignity of his appearance, stands or falls with life. Every diminishing of life (this will be discussed later) brings totally into question the life and thereby the honor of the individual. Therefore the "poor," those who are needy, join in with the chorus of those who pray, "Give us life" (Ps. 80:18). Whenever anyone's life is threatened, that person is concerned that Yahweh will turn to him in mercy and do good for him so that he will be revived again (Ps. 119:17, 77, 116; 22:26; 69:32). In the face of attacks and persecution Yahweh is the "stronghold" of his life (Ps. 27:1). Life is protected and renewed by Yahweh. Yahweh shows the "path of life," in which "fullness of joy" is to be found (Ps. 16:11). Since life—not in its immanent power, but as the gift of Yahweh, life in the presence of Israel's God—was for the people of the Old Testament the highest good, they prayed for and waited expectantly for "long life" as the most precious gift and the most marvelous blessing (Ps. 21:4; 61:6; 91:16; 133:3). Decisive, however, is the direction of one's life, its openness to Yahweh. The proper way of life for the men and women of Israel is one in which they call on Yahweh and praise him. Indeed, "praise becomes the most elementary 'token of being alive' " (von Rad, 1962, p. 370). Whoever praises Yahweh lives. He or she expresses himself or herself as one dependent on the "source of life," and therefore especially alive. "I will bless the Lord at all times" (Ps. 34:1).

Insofar as the Psalms were influenced by wisdom poetry, חכמה ("wisdom") was primarily understood as "fear of Yahweh" (Ps. 111:10), a constructive, even dominant force for life. "Give me understanding that I may live" is the petition in Ps. 119:144. The question, "What man is there who desires life, and covets many days, that he may enjoy good?" (Ps. 34:12), is answered in the next verse in terms of the wisdom tradition. One is to keep his tongue from evil and keep far away from the influence of those who do evil. He is to do good, and strive for שלום (shalom). In the same way that the commands of Israel's God mean life and point the way to life (Deut. 30:15ff.), so too חכמה ("wisdom") leads to life in fellowship with Yahweh. The decisive human attitude is attentive listening and careful acceptance of what God says.

It could be seen more and more clearly that life for the men and women of Israel was Yahweh's gift, and life in the presence of Israel's God was the highest good. Only by keeping this in mind can we understand the confession, "Thy steadfast love is better than life" (Ps. 63:3). Here the "steadfast love" of Yahweh and "life" go their separate ways, and it becomes clear that life as such is *not* the highest good. That which determines, supports, and encompasses this life, that is, Yahweh's gracious, saving חסד (ḥesed, "steadfast love"), is alone the focus of attention. For anyone for whom חיים ("life") was the most valuable or even the only power, Ps. 63:3 represents a "revaluation of all values." But in Israel this "revaluation" has already taken place in that the כבוד (*kabod*, "glory") of life has its origin and basis in Yahweh's gift of his presence, of his protection and deliverance. If life encounters trouble and death, then the sign that is characteristic of that life shines in even greater certainty, "Your steadfast love is better than life." For there is something better than this mortal life—Yahweh's חסד ("steadfast love").

Like the statements about life, the concepts of death are also distinctive. It is important to remember that language and metaphor in the Psalms of the Old Testament are not to be divorced from their connection with the surrounding cultures. But it must also be emphasized that Israel was unable to see either life or death in any other way than in relationship to Yahweh. Psalm 18:4 speaks of the "cords of death" and the "torrents of perdition." These are metaphors derived from the widespread concept in the ancient Near East of chaotic, primeval waters, which swallow up all life in the primeval destruction of the *tohu wabohu* ("formlessness and void") that existed before creation (Gen. 1:2). This is one of the many metaphorical perspectives which speak of the power of death and the other forces that are hostile to life. Life passes in sickness and sorrow, and the one who is sick thinks of himself as forgotten "like one who is dead" (Ps. 31:12).

The comparison has deeper dimensions as well. If the body is burning with fever and anxiety, the sufferer can say, "Thou dost lay me in the dust of death" (Ps. 22:15); "the terrors of death have fallen upon me" (Ps. 55:4). We see here a manner of thinking and concepts that are oriented to areas which find their clearest expression in Ps. 88:3. One's "life draws near to Sheol," the realm of the dead, in which those who have passed from this life are ghosts with no real being. This was the general concept in the ancient Near East. But in Israel the world of the dead (שאול, Sheol) is judged as the place that is far from Yahweh, the God of Israel. "In death there is no remembrance of thee; in Sheol who can give thee praise?" (Ps. 6:5). Just as for Old Testament faith, praise is the characteristic mode of life, so too the silencing of praise is characteristic of the realm of death (Ps. 6:5; 30:9; 88:10-11; 115:17; Isa. 38:18-19). "With death the individual's participation in the cult was extinguished: the dead stood outwith the orbit of the worship of Jahweh, and were therefore also debarred from glorifying his deeds" (von Rad, 1962, p. 369).

The sanctuary is the sign of the presence of the "source of life," and Sheol is the God-forsaken abyss, the sphere of nonlife, of death. But this sphere of death is by no means to be localized in some static view of the world. Even if this sphere lies in the primordial depths, it still strikes out aggressively to interfere with the world of life. Its chaotic darkness is not only manifest in the places where pit and grave are dug. מות (*mot*, "death") is a hostile, many-faceted force. Wherever the diminution of life manifests itself as weakness, sickness, imprisonment, hostile threats, danger before the law, or anxiety, there the sphere of death has broken into the human realm. The epitome of terror, however, is more than anything else the fact that the ties that bind one's life to Yahweh are torn asunder. If death cuts a person off definitively from God, the conditon of "relative death" leads to the unknowable path of suffering that results from being forsaken by God (Ps. 22:1). The reality of death begins when Yahweh is silent, when a person whom Yahweh has forsaken cries out from the depths (Ps. 130:1). The modern interpretation of death sees it as beginning at the moment when physical life ceases, but the Old Testament contains an incomparably more complex and therefore more profound concept, based solely on one's relationship to Yahweh. Life and death are not unrelated things that can take on a mythological span of meaning only in the context of fateful constellations, occurrences in nature, magical powers, or the cycle of vegetation as it dies and revives. Since Yahweh's actions in history determine the nature of life in Israel, it is significant for the dead that they stand outside the deeds performed in history by Israel's God (Ps. 88:10). Yahweh does not perform "wonders" for the dead; they are cut off from his "saving help" (Ps. 80:11). And yet, although this definition is clear and absolute, the final word has not been spoken. If it is true that those who pray in the Psalms, when they acknowledge that "Thy steadfast love is better than life" (Ps. 63:3), can regard "Yahweh's steadfast love" and "life" as two separate entities, then this confession proclaims the triumph of the חסד ("steadfast love") of Israel's God, from whom even death itself cannot hide. Even though the dead and those who are near to death sink into a realm that is far from God, Ps. 139:8 shows that Yahweh's authority by no means ends at the borders of Sheol (cf. also Amos 9:2). At this point great caution is called for. We must observe quite precisely what meaning "salvation from the dead" has in the Psalms.

The starting point for a discussion of the theme "deliverance from death" should be the "totalistic way of thinking" that has just been described. It holds that anyone who even to the slightest degree has entered into the realm of Sheol is totally within its power (see Ch. Barth, 1947, pp. 93ff.). In Ps. 30:3 the psalmist speaks to Yahweh in gratitude, "Thou hast brought up my soul from Sheol, restored me (my נפש, nephesh) to life from among those gone down to the Pit!" (for the verbs that express deliverance, see Ch. Barth, 1947, pp. 124ff.). This text makes it clear that here deliverance from death involves an event that took place during the lifetime of the individual. He has been rescued by Yahweh from the sphere of Sheol. The realm of death is represented by the "pit" which has been dug for the corpse. In our way of thinking, we would conclude that the one speaking in Ps. 30:3 has not really died. But he *did* really die! For the reality of death struck deep into his life, in the concrete diminution of life that he experienced. Thus "deliverance from death" is rescue from the power of anything that interferes with one's life in an unwholesome and destructive way. Yahweh is the deliverer. The verbs of saving that are used in the Psalms stand in the context of those deeds in history by which Yahweh has declared his people acquitted. It would therefore be false if the phenomenon "deliverance from death" were studied only in the concepts that can be found elsewhere in the ancient Near East. When Yahweh intervenes, his grace and mercy are manifest, and they are acknowledged with gratitude, "O thou who liftest me up from the gates of Sheol" (Ps. 9:13). Here the "gates of Sheol" are the entrance to Sheol, which has made an incursion deep into the realm of life. Often the words "pit" or "grave" are used as synonyms for Sheol (Ps. 16:10; 88:6; etc.). The grave is also the opening of the depths of Sheol into the world of life, symbol of the realm of death that is present even in the midst of life.

The event of deliverance from death is mentioned especially in the "thanksgiving songs of the individual." In Ps. 56:12-13 the one praying expresses the intention to fulfill his or her vow to offer thanks, introducing in this way the confession, "For thou hast delivered my soul from death . . . that I may walk before God in the light of life." The existence that has been liberated from the power of destruction enters into the "light of life," into the "land of the living.'' This life is characterized by one's conduct in the presence of Yahweh. Psalm 118:17 cries out, ''I shall not die, but I shall live, and recount the deeds of the Lord.'' The context in Psalm 118 shows clearly that ''not die'' means being saved from an unwholesome death by Yahweh's intervention.

It is worthwhile to consider how in the history of exegesis the motif ''deliverance from death'' has been understood. In the interpretation of the Psalms at the Reformation it can be seen that Calvin recognized and explained with astonishing clarity the ''sensus genuinus'' of the texts. In the Christian exegetical tradition ''deliverance from death'' had usually been understood in the light of the New Testament as ''resurrection from the dead (in agreement with Acts 2:26ff.). Luther followed this tradition in his exegesis of the Psalter, but Calvin was bold enough to hold to a ''this-worldly'' understanding. In his Psalms commentary on Ps. 56:13, he wrote that the psalmist ''confesses clearly that he owes his life to the Lord alone, life that he would have lost, if he had not been preserved in miraculous manner'' (CR 59:553). On the exegesis of the theme ''deliverance from death'' in the Psalms at the time of the Reformation, see Kraus, 1972c, pp. 258-277.

Among the specific testimonies to ''deliverance from death'' as found, for example, in the thanksgiving songs of the individual, there are some basic statements that concern Yahweh's saving actions. Thus Ps. 68:20 stresses that Yahweh is the Lord over the ways that lead to death. Therefore everything in the sphere of death that contributes to the power that Sheol has over humans and to the diminution of life is under Yahweh's sovereign power. No forces of fate are at work here, no powers that could be influenced by their victim. But Yahweh pays particular attention when any who belong to him seem to be about to fall under the power of death. ''Precious in the sight of the Lord is the death of his saints'' (Ps. 116:15). Nothing that happens here is a matter of indifference. Anything that happens to God's servants has highest value. The people of Israel became more and more aware that Yahweh alone is the one who is at work in all that is dark. Thus, according to Ps. 118:18 it is not death that holds the sufferer in his power. No, it is Yahweh who had chastened him sorely, but he has not given him over to death. Statements of this sort make us aware of what has already been hinted at: Yahweh is revealed as the Lord over death. Again and again the statements tend to move beyond the limits imposed by the finality of death, and what is provisional is brought into the light of Yahweh's complete and unlimited power. But in the Old Testament the provisional aspect still dominates. Yahweh's saving actions take place in the midst of a life that is surrounded by death and faces the constant threat of being swept away into the depths. Therefore the songs of thanksgiving that testify to ''deliverance from death'' are placed in the mouth of all those who have experienced God's saving intervention and the rescue of their life from the power of sudden, unwholesome death. These realistic contexts cannot and must not be modified or swept aside in favor of ''New Testament perspectives.'' On the contrary, it must be said that the demonstration of the reality of deliverance from death in this world, as the Psalms bear testimony to it, keeps the New Testament message of the resurrection of the dead from becoming mythologized, precisely because it is found in the context of the great deeds and the miracles performed in history by the God of Israel. In this connection, the fact that Jesus of Nazareth as the servant of God used the language of the Psalms is of extreme importance (cf. chap. 7).

In Israel the aggressive power of Sheol was depicted with an unprecedented challenge to the imagination. People knew with increasing clarity how thoroughly life is surrounded by and permeated by the destructive powers of death. It is thus easy to see why Israel could adopt from the surrounding cultures the great lament over the perishable nature of all the created world. Sober reflections of this sort belong to the didactic poetry of the wisdom tradition. They proclaim the great problems of life (see chap. 6, §F). At the same time it must again be pointed out that in the Old Testament the transitoriness and limitation of human life did not bring forth an indefinite, elegiac lament. Human existence stands under the light of Yahweh's presence. A lifetime is as nothing as God's sight, it is like "a mere breath" (Ps. 39:5). Transitoriness and insignificance become truly serious when seen in reference to God. The belief that life resembles a dream does not imply a self-destructive melancholy and resignation, even though a person may think it does when one sees one's life in the light of the reality of one's God, who brings the "reality" of the human condition into question. Time is overthrown. "A thousand years in thy sight are but as yesterday when it is past" (Ps. 90:4). What is yesterday? The breath of a memory patched together from shreds. The number of our years is 70 or even 80, but "their span is but toil and trouble." The time is gone as if flown away (Ps. 90:10). Why? Because human life in its real nature is subject to God's anger, to his "No!" (Ps. 90:7, 9). Only those whom he "satisfies" with his grace and whom he makes glad (Ps. 90:14-15) are able to live amid the passage of days. Therefore, it is appropriate to pray, "So teach us to number our days that we may get a heart of wisdom" (Ps. 90:12). Everyone should learn that the days of one's life are numbered; all should know the "measure" of their days, their "end" (Ps. 39:4). Only so can life be lived in the truth of God, anticipating the goodness of God and awaiting from God alone the challenges of each day's work (Ps. 90:17).

F. The Great Problems of Life

It is a popular practice to bring general human questions to the Old Testament and to seek for answers in direct dependence on the texts. Usually there is no attempt to make a basic revision of the questions as such. For example, the great problem of human existence, "How can God permit the frightful suffering of the innocent and the unjust plundering of their goods?" is used as the key to unlock the interpretation of the book of Job and of Psalm 73. But undertakings of this sort are inappropriate. What is needed is a formulation of the great problems of life in the way in which they are encountered in the Psalter, appropriate to the framing of a "theology of the Psalms." That means, for example, that in reference to Psalms 49 and 73 we should not raise the problem of a general theodicy, but should ask the question that forms the appropriate starting point for understanding the troubles of the psalmist: "Why must the servant of God suffer?" Why do those who walk in purity in the presence of their God experience nothing but trouble, while the ungodly pass their days in respectability and untroubled well-being? Is the death of his saints really precious in the sight of the Lord? (Ps. 116:15). Is it true that God's steadfast love is better than life (Ps. 63:3) when there is no trace of this steadfast love to be found and life is threatened and disrupted by the evil deeds of arrogant foes?

It will be useful in the following discussion to follow precisely the line of argument in such a well-known text as Psalm 73, to trace the statements of this Psalm, and to interpret its basic features. Only in this way can we learn how individuals in Israel formulated the great problems of life and in the depths of torment sought to deal with them. In this reframing of the question and in the light of these tasks we must at all costs avoid combining heterogeneous textual elements and then explaining them.

Some brief observations on the form and setting of Psalm 73 must be made. (1) The usual explanation of the form and category of the psalm highlights its nature as "didactic wisdom poetry." This reference to didactic tendencies in Psalm 73 is not subject to dispute. (2) The elements of narration and confession have gained increasing recognition, especially by M. Buber (1952, pp. 39f.). But attention has also been drawn to the expressions of thanks and of trust (cf. Würthwein, 1950, pp. 532-549). All this has made it clear that Psalm 73 took the forms and structures of the song of petition and individual thanksgiving and incorporated them into the reflective method of the wisdom tradition. Or, conversely, the prayer song of an individual with its declarations of thanks, of trust, and of confession came to incorporate didactic elements from wisdom literature. (3) The situation of the one praying is that of a person who has been smitten with severe sorrows (Ps. 73:14, 26). Undergoing bodily suffering, the one who is sore tried has to see the untroubled prosperity of those who long since have turned away from God, and feels this as a bitter burden that brings into question his or her life with God, tested by suffering (vv. 2-9). Why must those who live with God and in the presence of God suffer bitterly, while the many who long since have rejected God, do not know him, and live without him—or even in opposition to him—enjoy all earthly happiness and the favor of their fellowmen? The psalm recounts these troubles, and reflects on this problem. The one who is hard beset and is in despair sought refuge in God; he or she went to the place where God is present (v. 28), to the sanctuary (v. 17). There the questions and troubles that had tormented him or her were overcome. The sufferer gained a new assurance that could triumph over all sorrow and all problems. (4) But who is the person who has suffered through all this? Can we assume that the account is based on the actual life experience of an individual? Recent scholarship has answered this question. It is characteristic of the didactic poems in the wisdom tradition that they are marked by autobiographical stylization (cf. Prov. 24:30-34; Sir. 51:13-22; 33:16-18). Von Rad (1972, p. 38) commented as follows: "Here we definitely have, rather, a traditional stylistic form in which the teacher could, from time to time, clothe his instruction, and which also allowed of being extended into larger units. Our modern interest in the biographies of the biblical authors should not, therefore, be misled, for here we are scarcely dealing with genuine experiences; at any rate they appear in a highly conventionalized form." Denying that these are "actual experiences," however, should not lead us to relegate the "stylized poem" to the realm of unreal abstractions. On the contrary, we should reflect on how human destiny and human suffering of unheard-of difficulty can be concentrated in the form of autobiographical stylization. That which individuals experienced and suffered is elevated to the level of what is typical and universally valid. Psalm 73 is to be understood on the basis of all these assumptions.

The Psalm begins with a confession (v. 1), with the praise of the goodness of Israel's God. Thus, the setting is not the depths of temptation and trouble, but the heights to which praise of Yahweh's mighty works elevates those who have been in despair. Praise and thanksgiving are more powerful than the remembrance of all the terror that one has experienced. The real theme of the psalm is not the suffering, toiling individual, but the gracious God who rescues those who trust him. But we must ask what role is played by human uprightness, the "clean heart." If that question is addressed to the entire psalm in the desire to learn what an upright, clean heart is, the following explanations suggest themselves. That heart is clean that does not let itself ultimately be deceived and overwhelmed by impressive thoughts and speech of those intent on power or success, that does not let itself be drawn under in the wake of the demonstration of a "successful life-style" that is distant from God and marked by scorn, hubris, and violence. The "clean heart" does not betray the generations of the children by God, the "cloud of witnesses" who have experienced the goodness and help given by Israel's God (v. 15). The clean heart struggles through all inward and outward contradictions to reach the place where God is present, waits for his message, and submits to his council and guidance (v. 23-24). "Blessed are the pure in heart, for they shall see God" (Matt. 5:8). It is still true that the psalm does not praise the uprightness of the "clean heart," but the richness of Yahweh's acts of kindness. The confession proclaimed in v. 1 expresses the reality of salvation that has been confirmed and exalted by the experience of life and that is valid for all time. Even amid all the confusion of life, its validity tested through all the suffering and therefore affirmed anew for future generations, the truth of the statement stands unshaken, "Truly God is good to the upright, to those who are pure in heart."

Under the sign of the confession of the always-effective goodness of Israel's God, v. 2 begins the account of the severe threats that brought the believer's trust in God into question. Thus from the outset any tendency to be dramatic disappears. The psalm does not portray an ascent from the bottomless depths, an ascent that would begin in the abyss where there is no hope. The account is enclosed in the full assurance of salvation. Therefore, the negative beginning of v. 2, "But as for me . . . ," is noteworthy. Incomprehensibly, although Yahweh has provided nothing but goodness and kindness (v. 1), the feet of the psalmist had almost stumbled. He was about to miss the way. He was in danger of going astray and missing the complete kindness of his God. It must be made clear that Psalm 73 does not present a theoretical discussion of "divine retribution," of the search for a "theodicy," or of the riddle of the "moral order of the universe." Here an individual, in whose fate numerous human ills combine, recounts how he was in danger of wandering from the fullness of the goodness of his God, and why this came about. Here too at the outset of the account that begins in v. 2, any dramatic components are excluded. The account related, "My feet had almost stumbled . . . ." "Almost!" This anticipates the outcome. De facto it did not happen. God's servant was in the greatest danger, but God did not permit him to fall.

Verses 3-12 speak of the origin of the powerful threat to life with God. These verses portray the powers whose words and actions constitute so dangerous an attack on the believer's existence with Yahweh. What are these people called, and how are their actions described? They are "arrogant" and "wicked." They enjoy health and happiness; suffering and pain are unknown to them. They push forward with arrogance and violence. Their heart, the center of their well fed and refined existence, is a fountain of evil thoughts and malicious plans, of vulgar language and words that distort the truth. They open their mouths as if they were speaking down from heaven. They are successful. The masses run after them and swallow everything they say. Their power grows and their happiness increases. Their whole way of life and action is marked by a self-confidence that denies that God is present or knows what is going on: "Who is God anyway? There is no such thing as a 'higher knowledge' or an 'ultimate insight' into our circumstances or our actions. We are in charge!'' It is important not to regard these descriptions in this psalm as expressions of the resentment felt by a pious soul who removes himself as far as possible from the ''evil world'' and pillories it with a caricature. The one speaking here is not a pious or ''pure'' individual (in the sense of a complete rejection of the godless and filthy) who watches this nauseating rabble pass before his righteous eyes. No, the one speaking is not the type to flee from the world, not the pious person disgusted with the activity of the godless. The speaker is the suffering servant of God, the child of God who is hard beset and in despair (v. 15), who in the midst of the environment portrayed in vv. 3-12 is tempted and tried to the utmost. They all press in upon him—those shining examples of successful men and women who by power and cunning, arrogance and violence have mastered human existence and have ''the good things of life.'' Not only does their tongue strut ''through the earth,'' but ''they set their mouths against the heavens'' (vv. 8-9). In all that they say and think, the true, living God is worth nothing more to them than the contemptuous question, ''How can God know? Is there knowledge in the Most High?'' (v. 11). In their life-style, they accept those who are powerful and happy as representing the real world. They take them as examples to follow, as models for the masses. Living means talking big, eating and drinking, tasting life to the full, worshiping power as the secret of eternal happiness (v. 12).

The decisive factor in all this is that what is portrayed here represents not the thought and behavior of the ''world'' that stands in opposition to or surrounds the Israelite קהל (''congregation''), but represents instead a way of life for Israelites, for members of God's people in the time of the Old Testament and early Judaism. Thus the godlessness among God's people is the issue. That is the great threat. The men and women depicted in vv. 3-12 have created a new model for the community of God. From now on only one question is important—How do I increase my power, how do I gain happiness? Everything depends on what I have to do to succeed. ''God'' is merely a word. There is no longer any need to deal with God. Human beings on earth must serve as substitutes for his might and glory. And since no one can count on his goodness any longer, the only thing to strive for is ''eternal happiness'' on earth (v. 12).

But God's servants suffer. Day after day and night after night they are ''chastened'' (v. 14). Life with God is marked by weakness, suffering, and brokenness. This is the path that God travels with his children (v. 15). And the great question arises, Is suffering, nothing but suffering, the answer which God gives to those who seek him with a pure heart? Is trouble, nothing but trouble, the portion which God gives to those who do not plunge into the stream of power, happiness, and success? How intolerable that perspective is! How terrible are the consequences of such a contrast! Verse 13 draws the despairing conclusion, ''All in vain!'' Yes, such a life with God is completely meaningless. Suffering instead of happiness, impotence instead of might, failure instead of success.

It would be easy to say, ''I will speak like those people!'' (v. 15). Can there be any other result except a turning away from this God who lets his children perish in suffering, without power, never knowing success? Isn't it time to join the multitude of those who know how to master life? This dangerous temptation is countered by the realization, ''If I had said, 'I will speak thus,' I would have been untrue to the generation of thy children'' (v. 15). The signs of Yahweh's saving faithfulness are inextinguishable among his people. It would have been an act of unfaithfulness to the ''children of God'' to adopt those principles of life that are far from God and alien to him, a repudiation of the great deeds which God had performed for those among his people who were suffering. And that was a line which it was impossible to cross.

"But when I thought how to understand this, it seemed to me a wearisome task" (v. 16). This confession speaks of resignation and despair, but above all of the impossibility of finding a solution to the great problems of life. God's servant stands before a wall too high for any leap of thought, or any formula from wisdom theology. Who could possibly answer the hard questions: Why is the whole of life filled with unresolvable paradoxes? Why do those who turn away from God find happiness and success, while the "children of God" are destined to wither and waste away in sorrow and pain? It is in keeping with the depth of Old Testament wisdom, especially that of the book of Job, that statements of hopeless despair are not covered up but are candidly expressed.

In v.17 the account looks back to the turning point that leads to new knowledge and new certainty, "Until I went into the sanctuary of God; then I perceived [there] their end." The מִקְדְּשֵׁי־אֵל (*miqdešey 'el*) are not, as Martin Buber and others have thought, "God's holy secrets," arcane wisdom; they are the "precincts of the sanctuary" (cf. Ps. 68:35; Ezek.21:2 [MT 21:7]; 28:18). The psalmist had entered the temple precincts in order to seek a solution to the problems that were oppressing him. To whom did he turn? Whether we think concretely of a priest or a teacher of wisdom, in any case he sought the "face of Yahweh." The pronouncement that he longed to hear, or the knowledge that could be imparted to him were to be received as coming from God himself. This is clear from the way the statements are framed. The expectation expressed in v. 17b is interesting: "I wanted to know what would be the end of them [the godless]" (author's translation). Why this interest in the fate of others, specifically of their end? In order to answer this question correctly we must explain the Hebrew expression אַחֲרִית (*'aharit*). The term, especially in the wisdom literature of the Old Testament, means the outcome, the end of a (complicated) process, therefore a solution, the final meaning of all that has occurred before. The question is asked, what gives ultimate and true meaning and value to life? Thereby, the unveiled ultima becomes the setting for the prima, the final revelation of life becomes the fulfillment of its foretokens. If this is granted, it is important to note the relationship of the question to the imparting of knowledge. The one in despair asks about the אַחֲרִית (*'aharit*), that is, the outcome and end of the godless that will make everything clear. Instead, what Yahweh is presently doing is made known; that is, it is revealed to one who prays that God is already at work. The end has already begun.

How is God at work? The answer is found in vv. 18-20. It is already certain, because the ground, the basis on which the proponents of power, happiness, and success have built their lives, is cracked and shifting. They are going to fall as if they were on a smooth and slippery surface. They stumble, and everything they are and have crumbles into rubble (v. 18). The existence that promised imposing, permanent security and that boasted of effectiveness vanishes. It is gone suddenly, "like a dream" (v. 20). It had no reality because it was not based on God. You awake and they are gone. You stand up and shake off the troublesome dream. The point of this disclosure can be summed up by saying that the life that denies God, however much it may expand and flourish, has no abiding quality, no future. "The axe is laid to the root of the trees" (Matt. 3:10). All the power, happiness, and success that had been won or gained by turning away from God have no reality when seen in terms of its already-vanishing basis, the foundation that is crumbling beneath it. The only life that has reality is that which is lived in fellowship with Yahweh, the God of Israel. The human apocalypse that wisdom theology has borne witness to in vv. 18-20 has its roots in prophecy—the proclamation of judgment. The world that has pressed its claim to be a splendid "final reality" is swept away like a formless dream. This does not involve a calculable or in some way attainable theory of retribution that might become the secret religious possession of all those whose lives had fallen short, or a formula for the use of the vengeful pious. Rather, it is a disclosure that causes fear and horror. Anyone who fails to recognize the prophetic depths of what is revealed in the sanctuary will of necessity misunderstand one of the decisive statements of the psalm. Even though it is wisdom theology that expresses the turn of events, the events which Psalm 73 presents in typical form correspond to a disclosure of judgment based on prophetic insight raised to universal validity.

The continuation of the account expresses clearly that what is disclosed is not some deus ex machina that sweeps away all the problems, and it is not some pious assurance that can be called on when needed. Once more the psalm portrays the situation of doubt, bitterness, and confusion that cannot be penetrated by human understanding (vv. 21-22). The one who is praying does not think that he has been granted knowledge that would permit him to comprehend how God governs the world or to grasp how God's justice works. He sees himself once more a prey to the hopeless torment of that which he cannot comprehend. He is "stupid and ignorant . . . like a beast" (v. 22).

This is followed by magnificent statements of trust and confession (vv. 23-28). Luther translated the first words of v. 23, "Dennoch bleibe ich stets bei dir . . ." ("nevertheless I remain constantly with thee . . ."). But this well-known and highly valued translation, which was often used as the basis for the unwavering "nevertheless of faith," does not represent the syntax of the Hebrew text. The verbless clause does not express an unwavering faith, a dynamic event, an act of triumph, but a state, "Yet I am continually with thee." In the face of the perishing and vanishing nature of all the power held by those who reject God, this verse speaks of that which is abiding, reliable, firm. The psalmist knows that he (she) has found refuge with Yahweh, in the faithfulness of the community which God has established and which he preserves. Verse 23 gives expression not to a "nevertheless" of faith nor to a defiant piety, but to a quite surprising assurance that nothing can destroy the covenant or disrupt the believer's communion with God. Thus we are not justified in finding here a dramatic breakthrough to totally new insight. The trust that is expressed in this confession knows that it is based on the faithfulness and reliability of God.

If we ask how the psalmist came to the point where he was able to declare, "nevertheless I am continually with thee," the next line immediately gives the answer: "Thou dost hold my right hand" (v. 23b). This points to a royal (might we even say, messianic?) procedure. The formula, "God grasps one by the hand," when the king ascends the throne and is inducted into the royal office, denotes the conferring of privilege and charisma on the king (Isa. 45:1; 42:1). When the suffering servant of God makes this formulation his or her own, it is possible to speak of his or her participating in royal, messianic privileges, but not of a "democratization of the statements of the royal ideology." As the context makes clear, this participation is to be understood as a confirmation of one's portion. This event in which "thou dost hold my right hand" is apparently an empirical, palpable experience that gives rise to a sense of assurance. In his servant's deepest sorrow, Yahweh has renewed and confirmed his covenant and his presence. From then on the servant knows that God leads and protects him or her. "Thou dost guide me with thy counsel" (v. 24). Surely the words of Isa. 55:8-9 are true also of this "counsel": "For my thoughts are not your thoughts, neither are your ways my ways, says the Lord. For as the heavens are higher than the earth, so are my ways higher than your ways and my thoughts than your thoughts."

The goal of this miraculous leading is given in v. 24b, "Thou wilt receive me to glory." In the Old Testament the verb לקח (laqaḥ) expresses a process in which one is removed, caught up (Gen. 5:24; 2 Kings 2:1ff.; Ps. 49:15). Thus Psalm 73 boldly expresses the highest assurance, that out of sorrow and suffering God's servant will be caught up into "glory," into the splendor of the realm of God. This is the אחרית ('aḥarit) of the sorrowing servant of God! But how is this expression of assurance to be understood? Does it indicate a life after death? Is it possible here to speak of an "assurance of the resurrection"? Von Rad (1962, 406) held that to introduce into the Psalms the alternative of before and after death is to import a foreign element that does not represent the true nature of the Old Testament statements. It is not, however, some unprecedented innovation if, in a world familiar with the mythology of dying and rising deities such as were to be found in Canaan, the theme of "resurrection" is introduced. All that is correct, and yet it must be emphasized that what the Old Testament says about "life" and "death" stands out as a foreign body in the world of the ancient Near East. In Ps. 73:24 the emphasis is not on a "resurrection event," but on the confession that not even death can separate a person from Yahweh. Using the code of mythological language, which can dare to adopt the concept of "being caught up," the indestructibility of fellowship with God is reaffirmed even in the face of death. The psalmist testifies to *this* miracle. And nothing should detract from it. Even when passing through that "sphere of death" that separates one from Yahweh, fellowship with God is preserved unbroken. We should not read Ps. 73:24b in the light of negations of resurrection, but instead we should ask whether the expressions of assurance found in the Old Testament do not provide an essential key to interpretation that should be placed alongside the New Testament message of the resurrection from the dead.

Assurance and trust are given further expression in vv. 25-26 in the question, "Whom have I in heaven?" This rhetorical question is a confession that for the psalmist there is in the world of powers beyond this world, in heaven, no helper in time of trouble, neither among the stars nor among the "elohim" beings (cf. Job 5:1). Even on earth there is nothing that the psalmist would place alongside Yahweh. This eliminates all expectations of happiness and assurances of שלום (shalom). God's servant has been freed to say a decisive no to all the clamoring and imposing forces of happiness and success. This is not a no pronounced in renunciation and bitterness by some pious soul turning from the world, but it is the no of a free human being sure of being led by God. The no is based on trust. Even though flesh and heart may fail, "God is the strength of my heart and my portion for ever" (v. 26). That "strength" (צור, "rock") is the psalmist's abiding, indestructible foundation (on חלק [ḥeleq, "portion"] cf. chap. 6, §D).

In vv. 27-28 the whole situation is summed up and, following the practice of the wisdom tradition, the doctrine is formulated. "For lo, those who are far from thee shall perish; thou dost put an end to those who are false to thee. But for me it is good to be near God; I have made the Lord God my refuge, that I may tell of all thy works.'' It must be said again, however, that this doctrine is not a rule of thumb, not a dogma of vengeance that could solve all the questions of life and suffering. The teaching formulated here has been elevated to the status of universal validity, but the ''I'' of the psalmist remains a testimony to Yahweh's saving faithfulness. Nothing can be divorced from the existence of men and women in the presence of God or elevated into a realm of abstract retribution. At the center of this psalm there is a prophetic disclosure. The decisive seriousness of what has become obvious is reaffirmed in v. 27 as an exhortation and as a warning. There is only one thing that has unforeseeable, frightening consequences—to turn from God, to abandon God. The terrors of the judgment lie behind each word of v. 27. But this is also the striking foil to abiding fellowship with God, which emerges clearly out of the dark contrasting picture of rejection of God. Fellowship with God based on his covenant is what is permanent; it alone is real.

Looking back on the path followed by this interpretation, it is clear that it was necessary to examine in detail the statements of the psalm and to follow its ''line of argument.'' The prayers of Israel do not confront the great problems of life with formulas or general truths. All suffering and all experiences are a story lived out with Yahweh, which is to be recounted and to which testimony is to be given. This aspect must be recognized as determinative for our understanding of all the individual prayer songs and individual songs of thanksgiving. This has been stressed again and again in this chapter. The individual in the presence of God is in the Old Testament the individual in Israel, completely caught up in the mystery and wonder of a unique history and of the encounters of the chosen people with their God.

G. The History of Israel and the Significance of David

The relationship of the Psalms to the history of Israel demands particular attention, especially in reference to the discussion in chapter 7 of ''The Psalms in the New Testament.'' In reference to the Psalms, Karl Barth (*CD* 4/3:55) rightly raised the question, ''Where did [the Psalter's] authors really derive all that they have given us in these poems by way of confession of their praise, their gratitude, their comfort, their confidence, yet also their penitence, their distress in deepest need, their hope and defiance? How do they know what they obviously think they know concerning God and themselves, God and the created heaven and earth, God's relationship to them and theirs to Him?'' Barth answered these questions by referring to the origin of the Psalms in the history of Israel and stressed particularly the so-called historical psalms, 68; 77; 78; 105; 106; 107; and 136, in which this relationship is expressed with especial clarity.

In this connection it is also necessary to take into account the Psalm headings, which point to the history of Israel, and specifically to the history of David. Even though a ''theology of the Psalms'' that is oriented to form criticism can leave aside the Psalm titles, since they were for the most part added later, it is still not possible to avoid recognizing that all these Psalms demand to be read and understood in direct relationship to Israel's history. The headings show the primary context that provides the background against which each of the Psalms is to be explained. Westermann (1967, p. 18) says in this connection, ''The history of Israel accompanies the Psalms. Throughout a thousand years the cries to God in lament and praise remain bound up with the history of God's people." "The Psalms are the clearest evidence that in Israel calling out to God was never divorced from the reality of what occurred in the realm of history and politics." Anyone who listens carefully will be able to perceive political and historical contours even in such a Psalm as Psalm 73, which at first seems far removed from history.

Finally, the name *David* must be mentioned once more, since this name stands inscribed over the greatest number of the Psalms. It is possible to ignore this, as consistent historical-critical scholarship does, and to a large extent leave the notices of origin and the historical headings untranslated. Or, following the preferences of that line of interpretation which is oriented to royal ideology, see in "David" a reference to the royal nature of the psalms involved. Both these approaches, however, fail to deal with the simple and unavoidable fact that "David" is a reference to the poet and singer and provides the origin and the goal in terms of which the Psalms must ultimately be understood, and in terms of which they have actually been understood in the New Testament, as well as in the history of Judaism and the church. It must be recognized that the heading לדוד ("of" or "for David") was intended as an indication of such an understanding. Indeed, how can we understand the reception of the Davidic psalms in the New Testament, uninfluenced by any modern reflection, if we have not at least made the attempt to grasp the hermeneutical direction of those who provided the headings at a relatively late time in the psalm tradition? Certainly a decisive factor was the desire to connect the Psalms with history, as far as that was possible. And since David was early regarded as poet and singer (Amos 6:5), the majority of the songs of praise and prayer were ascribed to him as the royal prototype of psalm hymnody. But it is possible to take a further bold step and say with Karl Barth (*CD* 4/3:55): "What we have here is not just wise or pious poetry, but this one in whom so much promise is fulfilled and so much fulfillment becomes new promise, this one whose history is as it were the history of Israel *in nuce*. His knowledge is the basis of the knowledge extended throughout the Psalter. The echo of his voice is heard in it. And as the Psalms live by his voice, or more generally by the voice of the history which moves to him and proceeds from him, even when they have the character of what are called nature-psalms they are not timeless lyrics, but epics which follow and reflect the acts of Yahweh and the experiences of Israel in their totality." Thus the hermeneutical clues given for interpreting the Psalms by those who provided the headings say that it was primarily David's voice that was to be heard in the Psalter. And this one voice, which makes audible the cantus firmus of all the Psalms, is the voice of the promised king of Israel, the Messiah.

176

7. The Psalms
in the New Testament

In the New Testament the word ψάλμος (''psalm'') is found seven times and the verb ψάλλειν (*psallein*, ''to sing praise'') four times. These specific verbal references to the Psalms will be explored in the following discussion. In addition, this chapter will examine the quotations of Psalms in the New Testament. It should be noted that some of them are identified and some are not. The clearest identification is in Acts 13:33, ''in the second psalm.'' Quotations in Luke 20:42 and Acts 1:20 are introduced by the words ''the book of Psalms,'' and the quotation in Luke 24:44, by ''in the psalms.'' All other quotations—as will be shown, there are a great many—are not identified specifically, but with greater or lesser certainty they can be identified as quotations and arranged in groups. It is appropriate to begin by examining the New Testament quotations of such psalms as were of particular importance for the kerygma of the early church. These are Psalms 2; 22; 69; 110; and 118. Then, in a concluding section, we will examine other psalm texts that are explicitly quoted.

In the whole inquiry there is a primary exegetical task, the goal of which is to identify and explain the biblical-theological contexts in which quotations were used. It would hardly be in the interest of such a procedure to present the processes of understanding which are involved in the quotations behind the texts, but the intention that is contained in the texts themselves must be explicated. What are the steps that are to be followed? (1) The context of each psalm quotation is to be investigated to determine the intention of its kerygma. This includes a precise determination of the place of the quotation in this specific context. (2) From the New Testament context we should identify the purpose for which the psalm has been quoted. Then we must identify the kerygmatic scope of meaning which the Old Testament text has helped to advance. (3) We should also reflect on the character which the New Testament context has given to the quotation in its relationship to the way the text was understood in the Old Testament. This will lead us to investigate whether the early Christian kerygma has discovered in this new use made of the text anything of relevance for our understanding of the witness borne by the Old Testament itself.

Thus this chapter presents a contribution to the study of biblical theology, a contribution distinctive in the questions it raises and the goals it sets. The usual procedure in the Old Testament studies is to interpret Psalms in the context of the ancient Near East, the Old Testament tradition history, and the history of Israel. In the investigation of the quotation of the Psalms in the New Testament, that procedure will be incorporated into a process that seeks an understanding of the whole Bible and that is concerned with furthering theological knowledge.

A. New Testament References to the Psalms

While in Judaism the Torah is at the center of worship and life, in the early church the prophetic writings and the Psalms took on especial importance. The Septuagint, the Greek translation of the Old Testament, served as the primary source for quotations. To be sure, at the time of the formation of the New Testament, the Septuagint had not yet won canonical status for all its books, but it was adopted by the early Christians in the full extent of its language and its phraseology. This is especially true of the Psalms.

In Luke 20:42 and Acts 1:20 the Psalter is called βίβλος ψαλμῶν (the book of Psalms''). Luke 24:44 identifies a psalm quotation as found ἐν τοῖς ψαλμοῖς (in the psalms''). In Acts 13:33 Ps. 2:7 is quoted with the identification ἐν τῷ ψαλμῷ τῷ δευτέρῳ (''in the second psalm''). Other readings of this text identify it as being the ''first'' psalm (cf. the Nestle-Aland Greek Testament) and thus point to a specific stage in the transmission of the Psalms at which the second psalm was the first, that is to say, a stage later than which the present Psalm 1 was placed at the beginning of the Psalter as a sort of prolog. It is interesting that the Lukan writings precisely identify the psalm quotations in the passages involved. Questions of content will be dealt with later.

The term ψαλμός (''psalm'') is also found in 1 Cor. 14:26. This passage says that when the congregation gathers, each person should contribute his or her charism or otherwise share in the proceedings. These include ''a hymn (ψαλμός), a lesson, a revelation, a tongue, or an interpretation.'' What does this reference to the psalms mean? What psalms or types of psalms are meant? Did the worship of the early church begin with an (Old Testament) psalm? Did the assembly begin with a hymn or with a prayer song? Should we assume any sort of planned order of worship? Were these really Old Testament Psalms that were sung and prayed? It is clear that for the period to which 1 Cor. 14:26 refers there were three types of psalm poetry which were inspired by the psalms of the Old Testament and influenced by its language: (1) the Jewish psalmody which is accessible in the remarkable example of the *Hodayoth* (''Thanksgiving Psalms'') of Qumran; (2) the Jewish-Christian psalmody which is seen in Luke 1:46-55, 68-79; 2:29-35; (3) the Christian psalmody which permeates the book of Revelation (Rev. 5:9-10; 11:17-18; 12:10-12; 19:6-8). In 1 Cor. 14:26 it is not clear whether Old Testament Psalms are involved. If not, it should be asked which of the two latter types was meant. The criterion of what it is appropriate to use in worship is the οἰκοδομή (*oikodomē*)—the ''edification'' of the church.

Ephesians 5:19-20 and Col. 3:16 also refer to psalms that were sung by the early Christians or used in their prayers. The worshipers are exhorted to ''be filled with the Spirit, addressing one another in psalms and hymns and spiritual songs, singing and making melody to the Lord with all your heart.'' Colossians 3:16 speaks of singing ''psalms and hymns and spiritual songs with thankfulness.'' However the word is to be understood in these two texts, it is significant that the message of the Psalms plays a decisive role. The believing community is to incorporate "psalms and hymns and spiritual songs," in their nature as paranesis and paraklesis, into its kerygmatic function. Therefore even though psalms are directed to God in petition, adoration, thanks, and song, they are also intended to speak to those hearers who are at the same time singing and praying. It can be shown that in the New Testament the kerygma of the Psalms is of great significance.

If in reference to Eph. 5:19-20 and Col. 3:16 we press the question of what psalms or types of psalms are involved, then, at least as far as Ephesians is concerned, Eph. 2:19 points to Old Testament Psalms. It says there, "So then you are no longer strangers and sojourners, but you are fellow citizens with the saints and members of the household of God." This statement points to the a priori of the existence of Christians. "There had long since been a house of God, a people of God; God had long since been revealed in his will and his promises; revelation had long since been given . . ." (Iwand, 1977, p. 21). The Gentiles have been made a part of something already existing. Anyone who reverses this relationship distorts God's plan of salvation, which is the basis of the New Testament. The Gentiles enter into the world of Abraham and David, where the Psalms had been sung and prayed. They are privileged to receive the harvest of that which grew and ripened through the trials and suffering of God's Old Testament people. This basic understanding of the matter would still hold, even if the psalms of the early church were not word for word those of the Old Testament, that is, if "new songs" were raised, which still had the basis and origin of their language and their intention to be "new" in the Psalms of the Old Testament.

New psalms were written and sung in the early Christian communities. Psalms, hymns, and songs, were, like prophecy, the work of the Spirit of God. They are ᾠδαὶ πνευματικαί ("spiritual songs," Eph. 5:19; Col. 3:16). When we examine the early Christian psalms, those transmitted in the book of Revelation, for example, it is unmistakable that large numbers of expressions, distinctive phraseology, and motifs have been borrowed from the Old Testament Psalms. The Psalter is the ground from which the language of the spirit-inspired hymns and prayer songs of early Christianity sprang. The influence of the Septuagint on this process of borrowing was especially great. The "new song" that is raised in the New Testament (Rev. 5:9-10; 14:3) has its prototype in the Psalms of the Old Testament (Ps. 33:3; 40:3; 96:1; 98:1; 149:1), even though for the early Christian hymn the eschatological turning point provided the decisive stimulus for what was new.

Let us return to the aspect of the songs and prayers of the early church expressed in their nature as paraklesis and paranesis. This aspect is especially noticeable in Col. 3:16. Lohmeyer (1964, p. 150) wrote, "For the whole early church psalms and songs are not the aimless expression of an emotion-filled faith, but they are a God-given gift with the sole purpose of 'edifying,' or, as it says here, 'to teach and admonish.' No member of the community is able to contribute such words out of his own knowledge. Everything valid heard in the community is the work of the 'spirit,' and this language of the spirit differs from human prose by being in poetic form as well. 'Psalms and hymns and spiritual songs' are therefore the way the Spirit speaks. Therefore, human teaching and human sayings are never found in them (the contrast to the opinions of the Colossians is quite clear and explains the threefold use of nouns), but only the 'Word of Christ.' " This gives us a quite clear indication of the authority which speaks through, and is at work in, the Psalms. In the Psalms we do not hear human voices raised to express noble thoughts. It is God himself who speaks in his Spirit to human hearts, to exhort and comfort, to instruct and assist. This aspect must constantly be kept in mind.

B. Psalms of Special Significance

It is clear that in early Christianity several Old Testament psalms were extremely important. They were quoted again and again and cited as "star witnesses" in the proclamation that the promises of God had been fulfilled. These are Psalms 2; 22; 69; 110; 118. It seems appropriate to begin with Psalms 2 and 110, two "royal psalms," because these two songs stand at the center of the messianic message of the New Testament and are used as witnesses to the messiahship of Jesus of Nazareth.

Psalm 2 is quoted often in the New Testament, especially in the Synoptic Gospels in connection with the baptism of Jesus and his transfiguration (Matt. 3:17; 17:5; Mark 9:7; Luke 3:22; 9:35); 2 Peter 1:17 also cites it in reference to the transfiguration. Psalm 2 is also quoted in Acts (4:25f.; 13:33), in the letter to the Hebrews (1:5; 5:5; 7:28), and in Revelation (2:26f.; 6:15; 11:15, 18; 17:18; 19:19). Two themes are stressed in these quotations in the New Testament: divine sonship (based on Ps. 2:7) and the rebellion and defeat of the hostile nations (Ps. 2:1-2, 8-9). Since particular attention has been paid to the witness to divine sonship, and the motif of the nations derives its significance in connection with the often-quoted saying in Ps. 2:7, it is appropriate to begin with that saying.

In the Septuagint the Hebrew text is translated by the words υἱός μου εἶ σύ, ἐγὼ σήμερον γεγέννηκά σε ("You are my son, today I have begotten you," Ps. 2:7). It should be borne in mind that what God says, transmitted by a prophet, had its Sitz-im-Leben in the royal ritual of the enthronement (or annual festival) of the king of Jerusalem, and that the testimony given "today" is to be understood as an act of adoption, and thus as a legal act. The ruler was installed by Yahweh as his "son," that is, as the representative of divine power and majesty. Thus the adoption took on the meaning of a choosing of the king. The chosen מָשִׁיחַ (messiah, "anointed," Ps. 2:2) is placed at Yahweh's side as the one nearest to him, as the "heir" of the realm of divine glory (Ps. 2:8-9). Here we must raise the question of whether E. Schweizer (1970, p. 356) was right when he said, "In Old Testament terminology 'son' was purely a statement of function and described the authority of the one who reigned on behalf of God over his people. A contemporary of Jesus who was instructed in the Old Testament would be more concerned about a person's action or a thing's function than about its nature. He would not be interested in the question of whether a person was God's Son 'in and of himself'; in fact, he would not have been able to understand such a question." To begin with, we may agree with Schweizer that in the tradition of the Old Testament and of Judaism there was no interest in divine sonship "in and of itself." The whole "Son of God mythology" with its involvement in the physical, in which one could speak of a *deus incarnatus*, as was the case with the Egyptian pharaohs, was foreign to Israel and was probably regarded as uncanny. It is however, another question whether the distinction between "function" and "being" which Schweizer has introduced provides an evaluative category that is appropriate to Old Testament thought. If the ruler who is addressed in Ps. 2:7 is not "in and of himself" the son of God, he is still declared to be the son of God through the legal authority of adoption, and by that event in which he is chosen as Yahweh's "representative" he is transported into the realm of the presence of God. What happens here cannot be subsumed under the distinctions that apply to "being" and "function." In any case, the king as "son of God" participates in the mystery and wonder of God's presence in the midst of his people. He is a witness to this present moment in the personality that has been transformed and renewed through the act of anointing and installation. The king is thus not only the bearer of a function, he is *per-sona* (one through whom a voice speaks). It is Yahweh's will to speak through and with the human being who has been at God's side. The context makes it clear that this "son of God" is not merely the bearer of a function. He is *heir* (Ps. 2:8-9). The categories of family law are drawn on in order to plumb the mysterious depths of the relationship between God and the king. The distinction between "being" and "function" is to be absorbed by this concept of a concrete relationship. In any case it is clear why the transcendent statements in Psalm 2 aroused an interest in this "messianic promise" in the early church.

First it should be asked how the indication of time in σήμερον ("today," Ps. 2:7) was understood in the early Christian kerygma, that is, in terms of what event the elevation to divine sonship in the Old Testament passage was understood in the New Testament. Four possibilities can be discerned in the text. (1) The "today" is the event of the baptism of Jesus. (2) In the miracle of the transfiguration Jesus was declared to be the "Son of God." (3) Jesus became the "Son of God" by his resurrection from the dead. (4) The ascension into God's heavenly world elevated the one who was humbled to be God's Son. These possibilities will be explored in detail.

At the baptism of Jesus a voice was heard "from heaven" saying, "This is my beloved Son, with whom I am well pleased" (Matt. 3:17; the second person pronoun is found in Mark. 1:11 and Luke 3:22). To begin with, the explanation offered above for σήμερον ("today") must be corrected since, although in the act of baptism by John, Jesus was declared by the "voice from heaven" to be the "Son of God," or at least so designated, the time designation has been omitted—as we shall see, for good reason. The declaration of the king as son of God in Ps. 2:7 has been connected in Matt. 3:17 in striking manner with three other texts and themes of Old Testament promises. It is necessary to pay close attention here, because Ps. 2:7, by being brought together with these texts and themes takes on a specific interpretation which casts light on the Old Testament understanding of Yahweh's statement. Yahweh is "well pleased" with his son. Isaiah 42:1 (LXX) refers to ὁ ἐκλεκτός (my "chosen"). He is the one chosen by God. This nuance, which was already implicit in Ps. 2:7 and is to be explained by 2 Sam. 7:14 and Ps. 89:26-27, is made explicit in Matt. 3:17 by being brought together with Isa. 42:1. A second important component is also introduced from Isa. 42:1. It is by the Spirit of God that Jesus is the "Son of God." The context in Luke 4 shows even more clearly by the quotation of Isa. 61:1-2 that the one who is anointed by God's spirit is the משיח (*messiah*, Luke 4:17-19). As the "Son of God," the Messiah Jesus is the one anointed by the Spirit. A pneumatic Christology is introduced. In the biblical understanding the πνεῦμα (*pneuma*, "Spirit") is a charismatic proof of the presence of God. As the one baptized by the Spirit, Jesus is in person the presence of God. What could initially be derived from Ps. 2:7 finds here its confirmation and its concrete fulfillment. Still a third aspect can be observed in the juxtaposition of formulas in Matt. 3:17. When Jesus is called ἀγαπητός ("beloved") this alludes to Gen. 22:2, 16 (cf. also Rom. 8:32). It might be asked whether through this one word (corresponding to Rom. 8:32) the *signa crucis* ("sign of the cross") of "the path of sacrifice" which Abraham walked with Isaac is brought into play. In any case, Matt. 3:17 brings together statements on the themes "choice," "Spirit," and "presence of God" and thus provides approaches to the interpretation of Ps. 2:7. The terms מְשִׁיחַ (*messiah*, "anointed") and בְּנִי ("my son") in Ps. 2:2, 7 are seen in a new light in their Christological relationships.

Matthew 3:17 raises the much discussed question of whether the voice that spoke at the baptism of Jesus, together with the event of baptism by the Spirit and the bestowal of power, provided justification for an adoptionist Christology. The question takes on sharper form when attention is directed to the aspect of adoption in Ps. 2:7. But we must reemphasize the observation made above, that in Matt. 3:17 the word σήμερον ("today") is lacking. Thus the baptism of Jesus is not a terminus a quo for his divine sonship and his receiving the Spirit. Even in the nativity accounts it is made clear that from the outset the Spirit of God determines the being and the life of the coming one (Matt. 1:18, 20, 23; 2:15). Seen in this light the baptism merely marks a specific moment of a concrete proclamation of the bestowal of power, in which the Spirit of God is united with Jesus. The voice from heaven and the nature of the event as proclamation are decisive here. From the event described we can learn that "the Spirit of God comes from above, and is God's creative power, and thus the baptism is the moment in which God chooses the man Jesus as the instrument through which he will work" (Schniewind, 1964, on Matt. 3:17). Thus this does not imply any discontinuity in the path that Jesus followed (such as that when his disciples were called to follow him, or such as the conversion of Paul). "It is the history of a unique life, in which God's presence and God's spirit appear among mankind. God's Spirit is thus not an "idea," not a reified thought beyond that which occurs here among us on earth, but it is a reality which appears in human history, in the history of the one who came from God and who reigns in exaltation, but who was a man, God's hidden king, God's obedient, suffering servant" (Schniewind, 1964, on Matt. 3:17).

It will not be possible to examine in detail the problems involved in the pericope of Jesus' transfiguration. It is enough to point out that Matt. 17:5 repeats verbatim the saying uttered at the baptism (Matt. 3:17). Note also the corresponding relationship of Luke 3:22 and 9:35. The shining forth of the light of the glory of God places the pericope in a close relationship with the accounts of the resurrection. Just as Matt. 3:13-17 bears testimony to the presence of God through the descent of the πνεῦμα ("Spirit"), so Matt. 17:1-8 testifies to God's presence through the appearance of the divine δόξα ("glory"). In both cases it is the "voice from heaven" that speaks the decisive saying. When the pericope of the transfiguration is compared with the narrative of Jesus' baptism the conclusion drawn in connection with Matt. 3:13-17 receives confirmation, namely, an adoptionistic understanding is not possible. Both pericopes agree that they are testifying to a mysterious designation of Jesus as the Son of God and not to an event which initiates his sonship. Second Peter 1:17 refers to Matt. 17:5. The apostle declares that he has been an eyewitness to the glorious majesty of Christ in the event of transfiguration. The apostolic privilege of being an eyewitness is elsewhere based on having seen the risen Christ, but in 2 Peter 1:17 it is connected with the transfiguration.

Psalm 2:7 is quoted in Acts 13:33 in reference to the resurrection of Jesus Christ. The quotation involves the entire divine saying, following the wording of the Septuagint. Thus the temporal designation σήμερον ("today") comes into play. The "today" is a reference to the miracle of Easter. Jesus became the "Son of God" through his resurrection. This Christological statement corresponds to the passage Rom. 1:3-4, which Käsemann (1980, ad rem) terms "a liturgical fragment from pre-Pauline times." Christ was enthroned as Son of God by the resurrection from the dead. "The Spirit of holiness was the power which accomplished this" (p. 11). The use of the word *designated* casts light on the event of exaltation and enthronement. It is highly doubtful that it is justifiable to speak of an "adoptionist christology of primitive Christianity," as Käsemann does (p. 12). If Rom. 1:3-4 really does contain a "fragment," then the question arises of the context in which this fragment may originally have been found. In Paul's letter to the Romans, in any case, no adoptionistic nuance can be of any importance. Romans 8:3 speaks of Christ as the "Son of God" in reference to his preexistence.

Finally, Ps. 2:7 is quoted in New Testament texts that deal with the exaltation of Christ into God's heavenly world (Heb. 1:5; 5:5; 7:28). Jesus Christ has been exalted to the "right hand of God," far above all angels. Thus he has become "Son of God," and 2 Sam. 7:14 is fulfilled, ''I will be his father, and he shall be my son.'' In this incomparable position the exalted Christ differs from all the angelic powers which played an important role in those Gnostic speculations to which the above-mentioned passages in Hebrews expressed opposition. If we examine each of the contexts in which the statements about the exaltation of the Son of God to heaven occur, two interesting observations can be made. First, Heb. 1:8-9 adds to the quotation of Ps. 2:7 a passage from a royal psalm, Ps. 45:7-8. This expresses clearly that Christ, as the exalted Son of God, is ὁ θεός. Thus אלהים in Ps. 45:7 is understood as a reference to the deity of the ruler (cf. *Comm.* on Ps. 45:7-8). This context emphasizes that as "Son of God" he is truly God. His kingdom is ultimately identical with the kingdom of God. Second, Heb. 5:5-6 combines quotations from Ps. 2:7 and Ps. 110:4. Christ does not take upon himself the honor of being God's high priest (v. 4). He is installed in office by the conferral of power in Ps. 2:7, and this means that he has been appointed a priest forever after the order of Melchizedek (Heb. 5:6). In Heb. 7:28 the two psalm passages are brought together once again, this time in the abbreviated form υἱός—εἰς τὸν αἰῶνα ("Son . . . for ever"). It is in agreement with the still-to-be-discussed Christology of Psalm 110 when the letter to the Hebrews, beginning with 4:14, deals in detail with the priestly kingship of Christ.

In addition to the Christological interpretation of Ps. 2:7, the early church drew attention to the relevance of two other themes in Psalm 2 for the decisive divine statement: (1) threats against "God's anointed" by the hostile nations, and (2) the triumph over these nations and their rulers by the son of God, who had been installed as heir and emperor. The first of these themes is developed in Ps. 2:1-2 and is cited in Acts 4:25-26. When the apostles Peter and John were released after their interrogation and went back to their supporters, they reported about being brought to trial before the elders and chief priests. The community responded with praise and adoration of God. In this context they referred to Ps. 2:1-2, as translated in the Septuagint. In v. 24 they praised the creator and Lord of heaven and earth, and in vv. 25f., with the quotation from Psalm 2, they praised the Lord of the nations. Still, the situation described in Ps. 2:1-2 of a worldwide revolution of the "kings of the earth" and the "rulers" is not applied directly to the legal accusations that Peter and John had faced, but to the judicial procedure against "thy holy servant Jesus, whom thou didst anoint" (v. 27). Herod, Pilate, and the Gentiles are named. It is remarkable how immediately the application is drawn to the trial of Jesus. In this context, and in illustration of this scene, Ps. 2:1-2 is quoted. That means that it is against Jesus as the Christ that the powers of the Gentile world rose in rebellion, and now have been crushed. In vain they dared to seek to dethrone "God's anointed." But if this is a repetition of the threat of a worldwide revolt against God and his anointed, then the community can, in the light of the Christ event—and thus in the assurance that the enemy has already been defeated—pray that God will hear and rescue them out of their present perils. What they are experiencing are in reality nothing but rearguard actions. For in the trial of Jesus the fate of the nations and their rulers has already been decided. Psalm 2 has here been fulfilled as a whole. Psalm 2:1-4 is seen in the light of the eschatological enthronement of Jesus the Christ. With the crucifixion, opposition and accusations have resulted in an event that was in accord with the will of God, and which attained its goal in the exaltation of Christ and the defeat of the hostile forces. Jesus is the "servant of God" (Isa. 52:13ff.), who astonished the nations and closed the mouths of kings (Isa. 52:15). "God was with him" (Acts 10:38). He raised him from the dead (Acts 3:26) and glorified him (Acts 3:13). Every uprising of the nations has been brought to an end in this eschatological event—an event foreshadowed in the Old Testament. The promise made implicitly in Ps. 2:1-2 is recognized as a promise in its explicitly manifested fulfillment and is proclaimed as having attained its goal. The promise of God given to David and his dynasty, with all the events involved in its accomplishment, has been fulfilled in Jesus the Messiah. From now on the hostile powers that confront the Christian community can accomplish nothing that is not the will of God. This will was accomplished in the crucifixion (by "kings and rulers"). It is also carried out by those new opponents who are attacking. Their uprising will therefore never achieve its purpose.

We should keep in mind that the quotation of Ps. 2:1-2 was made a part of a prayer of the community. On v. 27 Conzelmann (1972, p. 43) commented, "Here we find not the style of prayer but that of exegesis." It would perhaps be better to say that, as quoted in the prayer, Psalm 2 was interpreted concretely in reference to the trial of Jesus. In the early church exegesis took place in prayer. Questions of style have no relevance here. What is involved is an event in which prophetic proclamations are understood in the presence of God. This shows that Psalm 2, in keeping with a conclusion drawn above, was understood as a message, or more precisely, as a promise in the context of the Davidic history (Acts 4:25), in the context of the promises given to David, to which the Messiah's community could appeal in a situation of concrete peril.

In reference to specific questions in Acts 4:25-31 it may be noted (1) that in contrast to the Lukan passion narrative, Pilate is the one to whom blame is attached. Emphasis is placed on the guilt he incurred toward God and his Messiah. To be sure, in Luke 23:6ff. the cooperation of Herod, who represents the βασιλεῖς (v. 26) and Pilate, the representative of the ἄρχοντες (v. 27), is noted. (2) It can be shown that the designation of Jesus as παῖς θεοῦ (v. 27) is based on Isa. 52:13ff. or on Isaiah 53, but has nothing to do with Ps. 2:7, because there Yahweh's anointed is called υἱὸς θεοῦ (LXX).

The defeat of the nations foretold in Ps. 2:9 comes to fulfillment in the quotation in Rev. 12:5 and 19:15. The apocalyptic vision of the birth of the "child" in Rev. 12:5 leads up to the commission of the Son to "rule all the nations with a rod of iron." Here we find expressed the authority of Christ as judge, his sovereignty over all the nations. The Messiah is the Lord of the nations. What Psalm 2 foretold, the Apocalypse sees as fulfilled in the eschaton. So too in Rev. 19:15. Christ as the "Logos" (v. 13) appears as the judge of the nations. A sharp sword goes forth from his mouth (Isa. 11:4). He defeats the hostile nations and rules them with a rod of iron. It should be clear that Ps. 2:9 was quoted for the purpose of showing that the work of the Messiah as judge was foretold in prophecy.

One of the most serious errors of early periods of scholarship was that, in pursuit of general ideology, they drew contrasts between the "God of love" in the New Testament and the "God of hatred" in the Old Testament. In his commentary on the Psalms, H. Schmidt (1934) wrote of Psalm 2, "How different the picture of the king who shatters the nations with a rod of iron is from the picture of the one who was crucified!" This sort of contrast is a well-known cliche that suggests metaphors, but does not produce any relevant comparisons or connections in terms of biblical theology. In the context of Psalm 2 the concept of shattering vessels of clay signifies the judicial authority of the "son of God" as the heir of the world and of the nations, making use of a familiar metaphor from the ancient Near East. It must immediately be asked whether the New Testament has anything to say about the judicial authority of Christ Jesus over the nations. We have only to mention Matt. 28:18 (with the allusion to Dan. 7:14). But two passages, Rev. 12:5 and 19:15, deserve special attention. More explicit reference is made to Ps. 2:9, in order to testify to the judicial authority of Jesus the Messiah, the authority of the one who was crucified. What H. Schmidt advanced were dichotomies extrapolated from a history of piety foreign to the Bible and lacking any theological meaning or content.

While there can hardly be any doubt that the New Testament texts in which Psalm 2 is quoted contain Christological and kerygmatic emphases of the early church, when we consider the New Testament passages in which Psalm 110 is quoted we encounter quite complicated problems. There is no mistaking the fact that Psalm 110 played an extraordinary role in the early church. In v. 1 there are a number of questions which have been answered variously by biblical scholars. In addition to v. 1, v. 4 is also cited, especially in the letter to the Hebrews. Emphasis was placed on the fact that Jesus Christ had been made a high priest after the order of Melchizedek (Heb. 5:6, 10; 6:20; 7:3, 11, 15, 17, 21, 24, 28). The sovereign authority of the exalted one is proven by the quotation of Ps. 110:4. The promise has been fulfilled. In Heb. 5:5-6 the quotation that deals with Melchizedek is combined with Ps. 2:7. Heb. 7:3 takes up older Melchizedek traditions found in Gen. 14:20. In all this it is clear that what Psalm 110 says about the priest-king is used in Hebrews to bear testimony to the honor of the heavenly high priest who has been taken up into the world of God. Thus it must be noted that Ps. 110:1 plays as great a role in Hebrews as Ps. 110:4 does. Christ as the "heir" (Ps. 2:8) has sat down "at the right hand of God" on high (Heb. 1:3). In Heb. 1:13 the wording of Ps. 110:1 is cited with a clear contrast to gnostic speculations about angels. The command in the psalm to sit on the throne is addressed only to the exalted Christ. Thus when we combine Ps. 110:1 and Ps. 110:4 we have a concept of a high priest who sits at the right hand of God in heaven (Heb. 8:1) and waits for all his foes to be defeated (Heb. 10:12-13). When it is said in Heb. 12:2 that the exalted one has sat down at God's right hand on the throne of

God, this not only reaffirms what has already been applied in Heb. 1:8-9 with the quotation from the royal psalm Ps. 45:7-8, but it also quotes an Old Testament expression from the Chronicler's history (1 Chron. 28:5; 29:23; 2 Chron. 9:8).

But the specific problems raised by the New Testament references to Ps. 110:1 are hardly touched on by the observations made in Hebrews. In the Synoptic Gospels that verse is transmitted in three different contexts: (1) in the pericope "David's son—David's Lord" (Mark 12:35-37; Matt. 22:41-46; Luke 20:41-44); (2) in the passion narrative (Mark 14:62; Matt. 26:64); and (3) in the long ending of Mark (16:19).

The pericope "David's son—David's Lord" contains the quotation, "The Lord said to my Lord, Sit at my right hand, till I put thy enemies under thy feet." Luke follows the exact wording of the Septuagint. Mark and Matthew have ὑποκάτω ("under") instead of the ὑποπόδιον ("footstool") of the Septuagint. The stimulus to reflection and the remarkable discussion in the pericope must have been provided by the introduction to the psalm in the Septuagint. In the Hebrew text יהוה ("Yahweh") speaks to the king, who is called אדני (adonai, "lord"). The Septuagint, which renders אדני (adonai) as κύριος (kyrios, "lord") translates εἶπεν ὁ κύριος τῷ κυρίῳ μου ("the Lord said to my lord"). The problem is expressed in an argument that probably is pre-Markan. Schniewind (1949), in commenting on Mark 12:36, asks if it is possible to ascribe these words to Jesus himself. He answers in the affirmative and bases his position not only on the "total message and work of Jesus," but also on a Jewish tradition which is supposed to have interpreted Psalm 110 messianically. This tradition was alleged to have been consciously suppressed and only later revived. But it is scarcely possible to answer Schniewind's question in the affirmative. Closer to the mark is E. Schweizer (1970, pp. 254-255) when he begins with the following suggestion: "Perhaps the quotation in vs. 36 began to be applied to Jesus in the Greek-speaking church. The Aramaic-speaking church addressed Jesus as *marana*, 'our Lord' (1 Cor. 16:22). It is unlikely that the Hebrew word in Psalm 110:1 *adoni*, 'my lord,' would have been applied to Jesus, since it connoted a position of higher honor. This word is used in the customary way in Psalm 110:5 where it refers to God, and this is how it was interpreted in Jesus' time. On the other hand, there was only one word for 'lord' (*kurios*) in the Greek-speaking church. This word is used in Psalm 110:1 (LXX) and was frequently applied to Jesus." It must be added that no messianic interpretation of Psalm 110 in Jewish circles can be documented. In the Qumran texts the psalm was not quoted. The controversy-question which is raised in the pericope is the following: Is Jesus, as the Messiah, David's son or David's Lord? How could such a controversy have arisen? It has been surmised that Jesus' Davidic descent was either not known or not widely accepted. But no attention is paid to that issue in this passage. The problem that occupies the center of attention is that of reconciling descent from David with the dignity of κύριος. At the conclusion the main question remained open. If the one addressed is called κύριος (and receives thereby a title of honor borne by God himself), how is it possible that he is also at the same time David's son? It is at once obvious that such a problem does not exist in the Hebrew original of the psalm and cannot be derived from it. Thus the question remains of how the dilemma in Mark 12:37 can be overcome. There are two possibilities: (1) In a mysterious simultaneity the Messiah can be the son of David and also the *Kyrios*, who stands completely beside God. Schniewind says (1949): "It corresponds to the expectation that hoped for both the earthly Messiah and the son of man who was to come from heaven

186

. . .; but the unity of the two expectations, that a real person, born of the seed of David, and a person who comes from heaven are one and the same, is found in the person of Jesus. The mystery, however, remains unresolved.'' This explanation could be held, even if the words of the pericope could not be traced back to Jesus himself. (2) What appears to be a dilemma in Mark 12:36 could be resolved in two stages. By reference to Rom. 1:3-4 and Acts 2:25-28 it could then be explained that "in his lifetime, Jesus is the Messiah, i.e. the son of David. He was then exalted to be David's lord, i.e. to be Son of God (Rom. 1:3f.). Two periods in his work must therefore be distinguished, corresponding to the two stages of his being'' (Conzelmann, 1969, pp. 74-75). One could point to the summons "sit" which began an action in a temporal sequence. This can be nothing more than an attempt to find an interpretation. It is difficult to find any access to the background and the motifs of this remarkable train of thought.

Jesus' messianic self-witness has been transmitted in Mark 14:61-62. To the high priest's question whether he was "the Christ, the son of the Blessed," Jesus answered, according to the kerygmatic tradition of the early church, with a clear "I am" (but compare Matt. 26:64). This was at once surpassed by the affirmation, "You will see the Son of man seated at the right hand of Power, and coming with the clouds of heaven'' (Mark 14:62). Matthew adds the words ἀπ' ἄρτι, "hereafter." This logion combines words from Ps. 110:1 and Dan. 7:13. Jesus is the (apocalyptic) Son of man and ruler of the world, who comes from heaven. He will be seated at the "right hand of God." The meaning is that the exalted one, who is enthroned with God, will come. As far as the sitting at the "right hand of God" is concerned, the manner in which the passion narrative speaks of the exaltation of Christ is astonishing. This kerygma can only be compared with the way in which the Gospel of John proclaims that the one who was crucified is the one who is exalted. Moreover, exaltation and parousia are brought together. The exalted one is the coming one. Can it really be said that what we have here is "the result of a long preoccupation with the Bible" (E. Schweizer, 1970, p. 327)? Should we not rather reflect on how intimately the Old Testament connects the royal "sitting at God's right hand" and the designation as Son of man (Ps. 80:17)? Matthew says that "hereafter" the exalted and returning Son of man will be seen, to whom "all authority in heaven and on earth has been given" (Matt. 28:18). He will return as the judge (Matt. 25:31). Psalm 110:1 became an important element indeed in the message of the early church about the exaltation of Christ.

The New Testament saw the resurrection of Jesus Christ from the dead as the fulfillment of Ps. 110:1. The "sitting at the right hand of God" was understood as the goal of the "ascension" and as the place where he would exercise his lordship in the time between his exaltation and his parousia. In Mark 16:19, part of the later supplement to the Gospel of Mark, the "ascension" is mentioned. What is related there alludes to the Elijah narrative (2 Kings 2:11) and to Ps. 110:1. The force of the statement is that Jesus sits on God's throne as Lord and ruler. Jesus' resurrection from the dead was first mentioned in Acts 2:34-36. Then, after the comment that David did not ascend into heaven, Ps. 110:1 is quoted as a testimony to the miracle of Jesus' exaltation. By his resurrection and ascension (exaltation), Jesus of Nazareth became "both Lord and Christ" (Acts 2:36). It is clear that the exaltation theology preserved in the tradition of the book of Acts appeals for its authority to Ps. 110:1. David was not the one who carried out the striking command to sit at God's right hand and to reign there. It was fulfilled only by the one who was crucified and who rose again—fulfilled in the event of eschatological exaltation. The power of God, which Christians affirm, accomplished the resurrection of Jesus Christ from the dead and his exaltation at God's right hand, above all cosmic powers (Eph. 1:20).

The quoting of Ps. 110:1 in 1 Cor. 15:25 has particular significance. Elements of apocalyptic tradition constitute the framework in which a process of the end-time is disclosed in a reference to Ps. 110:1. Here too we see that there can be a progressive development of the psalm text. At the end, Christ will turn the kingdom over to his Father. Until then he will reign "until he has put all his enemies under his feet" (1 Cor. 15:25). In the kingdom of Christ as the "transitional kingdom," the Messiah's enemies are defeated. It is God himself who crushes the hostile powers at the feet of Christ. The lordship of the exalted Christ is thus not something to be enjoyed in a static superiority to the world, but it is movement in history, it is God's struggle and God's victory. Above all, it should be emphasized that "The last enemy to be destroyed is death" (1 Cor. 15:26). This statement carries us deep into the Psalms, in which death is seen as a hostile power and its defeat is hoped for.

According to the Old Testament's understanding of itself, the supreme significance of Psalm 110 lies in the lofty statements it contains about the chosen king. Consequently we can say that in the New Testament two of these statements of exaltation were regarded as promises that had been fulfilled. (1) God himself exalts the king and places him at his own right hand. He appoints him as coruler and confers that power on him; he overcomes all the king's enemies. (2) God's king is declared a priest (after the order of Melchizedek).

The quotation of Psalms 2 and 110 in the New Testament brings us to the central issue of the Christological titles of honor, which has long constituted a problem for New Testament scholarship. Here we can only cite the relevant literature. E. Schweizer, 1962; W. Kramer, 1966; F. Hahn, 1969; O. Cullmann, 1963. Attention may also be called to works dealing with New Testament theology, where further literature is cited. It cannot be the task of this book to enter into a thorough discussion with the works listed above. This limitation defines and clarifies the goal of the present chapter.

From the category of prayer songs of the individual, which address Yahweh in the midst of great peril, the New Testament refers especially to Psalms 22 and 69. The background for this use, especially in reference to Psalm 22, is significant. The words "My God, my God, why hast thou forsaken me?" (Ps. 22:1) are, according to Mark 15:34 and Matt. 27:46, the last which Jesus spoke on the cross. In addition, this is the only place in the New Testament in which a statement from the Psalms is cited in Hebrew. To be sure, the text has been transmitted differently in the various manuscripts, but it is clear that Jesus was not using the Aramaic language here but was taking this anguished prayer from the Hebrew Old Testament. This indicates that the Holy Scripture, the Old Testament, was known through the readings in the synagogue in the original language. It should be added that the Psalms of the Old Testament, as can be seen above all in Mark 15:34 and Matt. 27:46, were the prayer book of Jesus. We can certainly assume that the early church would scarcely have placed so unusual a quotation as Ps. 22:1 in the mouth of the one who was crucified. This cry belongs to the unforgettable remembrances of what had occurred.

Psalm 22:1 gives voice to the terrifying lament of one who has been forsaken by God. Those who regard the cry as an expression of triumph or as primarily an expression of trust (''my God . . .'') misunderstand the clear intention of this prayer which Jesus has made his own. Something unfathomable is reported. The one crucified identifies himself with those in Israel who were sinking into the depths, far from God and forsaken by him. Unless we are mistaken, the New Testament contains a twofold reaction to this event. The letter to the Hebrews speaks of immeasurable burden which Jesus had taken upon himself, that is, his being forsaken by God and his cry are signs of ultimate and extreme participation in the suffering which separates God from his children. In every respect Jesus has been ''tempted as we are'' (Heb. 4:15). ''In the days of his flesh, Jesus offered up prayers and supplications, with loud cries and tears, to him who was able to save him from death'' (Heb. 5:7). John 8:29, however, seems to intend to weaken the incomprehensible cry from the cross, when Christ speaks the words, ''And he who sent me is with me; he has not left me alone, for I always do what is pleasing to him.''

How are we to understand Jesus' solidarity and identification with the sufferings and extreme temptations of those who prayed in Israel? Two answers may be proposed here. (1) If the prayer language of Israel expresses the collective troubles, the sufferings of those forsaken by God, which far transcend the specific destiny of an individual, then, according to the testimony of the early church, it is Jesus alone who fulfills this claim. He not only identifies himself with all the suffering that finds expression in the Psalms uttered in the presence of God, but also he alone is the servant of God, in whose life and death are fulfilled all the sufferings of all those who cry out in prayer. He alone is able to take upon himself the indescribable totality of what it means to be forsaken by God and to be far from his presence. This he can do because of his mission as ''Son of God'' (Matt. 26:63-64). He alone is able to speak the language of prayer in Israel as the one who in comprehensive authority is the personification of Israel. (2) Jesus not only takes all suffering on himself, but he bears it vicariously as he gives help and rescues (Matt. 8:17). In him God himself knows what it means to be forsaken by God and in trouble, and in him God gives help (Isa. 35:4). This is the way in which the Old Testament proclaims eschatological deliverance and aid (Isa. 35:53). This is the vanishing point that provides the perspective for all the promises that we find referred to in the passion narrative. What Luther stressed again and again is still valid: it is not for himself that Jesus acts and suffers, but ''for us'' (cf. Matt. 1:21, 23).

Thus in a double sense the New Testament gives us a new situation. From now on anyone who prays the Psalms is not only entering into the prayer language of Israel but also is taking up the prayer that was fulfilled in Jesus Christ, including the cry of dereliction and despair. The one praying prays ἐν Χριστῷ (''in Christ''), that is, in the realm of language and reality that have been shaped by the suffering of Jesus on the cross. All those who in the future take the Psalms as their prayers will also perceive in them the message of the one who was crucified, who took all suffering on himself and bore it.

In New Testament scholarship much has been written about the so-called ''prophetic proof-texts,'' particularly those dealing with the cross and the resurrection, which the early church made a part of its traditions. The intention and the undertaking themselves are not in question. The concept ''proof'' is, however, questionable, if this word is used in isolation from the concrete situation. When the New Testament quotes or cites Old Testament texts we cannot assume a process of proof that is entirely obvious, that attempts with mathematical precision to demonstrate the congruence of prophecy and fulfillment. What is involved is the attempt in debates with the Jews to demonstrate that Jesus of Nazareth lived, suffered, and rose from the dead according to the Old Testament promises, prayers, and experiences of trouble and deliverance, and that he brought them to completion and fulfillment. It is a kerygmatic proof, the primary goal of which is to make it known that in Jesus, the Son of God, Israel's sonship had become reality (Matt. 2:15). The major error of many scholarly explanations is that they overlook how alive and present the language of the Old Testament was and how directly the early church could find analogies to texts dealing with Israel whenever the kerygma of Jesus was being given form and handed on. When it is said in this connection that "the scriptures were fulfilled" (Mark 14:49; 15:28; Matt. 26:54, 56; etc.) the reference to the "documentation" is far from giving us the right to turn the living process of referring to a text into a pedantic establishment of proof, completely separated from the situation of debate with the Jewish community.

The facts that on the cross Jesus cried out in the words of Ps. 22:1 and that this prayer, the cry of dereliction from the Psalms, points back to the original setting were perceived after the fact. It is possible, especially in reference to Psalm 22, that this early remembrance is closely related to other quotations and allusions to Psalm 22, and may even have called them forth. Even the Johannine tradition felt the influence of the reference to Psalm 22. The Fourth Gospel was not able in the context of its Christology to incorporate Ps. 22:1 into the passion story, but it at least included one word from Ps. 22:15, διψῶ ("I thirst," John 19:28).

Three individual motifs from Psalm 22 were incorporated into the passion narrative: (1) the deriding of the one suffering, as those passing by shook their heads (Ps. 22:7, found in Mark 15:29; Matt. 27:39; Luke 23:35; cf. also Ps. 109:25); (2) the scornful challenge hurled at the one whom God had forsaken, "He trusts in God; let God deliver him now, if he desires him" (Ps. 22 :8, found in Matt. 27:43); (3) the dividing of his clothes and the casting of lots (P s. 22:18, found in Mark 15:24; Matt. 27:35; Luke 23:34; John 19:24).

All these quotations and allusions were designed to make it clear that Jesus took on himself in detail the suffering that befell individuals in Israel in the Old Testament. More specifically we must say that according to the biblical testimony of the early church Jesus did not suffer an "individual destiny" that can be understood in terms of his personal biography, and that should be reproduced with appropriate nuances. He took on himself what was experienced in Israel as painful and was lamented in the presence of God. Ultimate suffering—and that can be seen in its depths only in relationship to the God of Israel—was revealed in the suffering of Jesus on the cross.

The Letter to the Hebrews used the quotation of Ps. 22:22 to show specifically that the suffering which Jesus underwent in his death (Heb. 9:2-3) was suffering for his people (Heb. 2:12, 17). From the quotation "I will proclaim thy name to my brethren" the conclusion is drawn that Jesus Christ was not ashamed to call those addressed here his "brothers," and thus to bind himself intimately to them. The Hebrew word לאחי ("to my brothers") in synonymous parallelism with קהל ("congregation") can be interpreted as referring to one's fellow members of the community of Israel who are being addressed while the one praying this psalm presents his thank offering. Thus also Heb. 2:12, using the Septuagint translation (τοῖς ἀδελφοῖς μου, "to my brothers") and interpreting Ps. 22:22 as referring to Jesus as the one speaking, became the basis for the brotherhood of those who share in the deliverance (σωτηρία, *soteria*, v. 10) and sanctification (ἁγιάζων, v.11). It should be noted that Jesus established this brotherhood, and that no one is authorized on his own to call Jesus "brother."

Finally, brief reference may be made to allusions to various verses in Psalm 22. Romans 5:5 has the clause ἐλπὶς οὐ καταισχύνει ("hope does not disappoint"), which can be traced back to Ps. 22:5. And when 2 Tim. 4:17 reports that the author of this letter was "rescued from the lion's mouth," the wording of Ps. 22:21 can be recognized. Revelation 19:5 reflects the wording of Ps. 22:23, and Rev. 11:15 that of Ps. 22:29. In reference to the latter passage it should be noted that Ps. 2:2 is also reflected there and that the phrase ἡ βασιλεία . . . τοῦ κυρίου ("the kingdom of [our] Lord") was taken from the Septuagint.

In the New Testament, especially in the passion narrative, the prayer song Psalm 69 plays a significant role, similar to that of Psalm 22. Psalm 69:21 is quoted in Mark 15:36; Matt. 27:34, 48; Luke 23:36; John 19:29. The commentaries are almost unanimous in declaring that this is a proof-text, and that the New Testament reports have undergone legendary expansion in view of Ps. 69:21. But can this interpretation really be supported? Is it not possible that an actual occurrence was later illustrated by reference to the Old Testament psalm? How else can it be explained that Psalm 69 has so much significance in the accounts of the passion? We must begin with the wording of the Hebrew text. Its translation reads, "They gave me poison for food, and for my thirst they gave me vinegar to drink" (Ps. 69:21). It is obvious that the suffering of the one offering this prayer was painfully intensified by the drink that was given him. "Poison" and "vinegar" did not lessen or dull the pain but intensified it. The synonymous parallelism of the verse makes this clear. This is also the case in its use in the New Testament. According to Luke the vinegar was given to Jesus in connection with the ridicule heaped on him (Luke 23:36). Matthew 27:34 shows that Jesus refused the drink, but later in his agony he had to accept it (Matt. 27:48). All the Gospels report that Jesus died after drinking the potion. The easiest conclusion to be drawn is that we are dealing here with the memory of an actual event. Jesus' foes wanted to increase his dying agony painfully and cruelly by means of this drink. The tradition then pointed to Ps. 69:21 and thereby ascribed to that psalm the great significance which it received in the New Testament. Anyone who really knows the Old Testament psalms which were sung in suffering and the pain of death may rightly ask why the scene in Ps. 69:21 was inserted into the account during the transmission of the passion story in the early church instead of one of the many other incidents which are mentioned in the portrayals of danger and suffering in the Psalter. What adequate grounds does the modern exegete have for constructing relationships which could be more easily explained by events and by the citation of Scripture? Do scholars really want to begin with the assumption that the only thing known about the end of Jesus' life is that he was crucified, and that all other features of the tradition are to be regarded exclusively as legends formed on the basis of the desire to find proof-texts? Anyone who in this way carries the confession in 1 Cor. 15:3 ad absurdum transforms tradition history into fabrication history.

In John 15:25, Ps. 69:5 is quoted. Just before this the inconceivable hatred directed against Jesus, the messenger of God, is mentioned (v. 23-24). The context indicates that sin is "hatred directed against God" (Bultmann, 1971, p. 551).

To this it must be added that this hatred falls on the Christ of God (cf. also John 7:7; 15:18, 23-24). The writer of the Fourth Gospel finds the assertion that hatred brings guilt confirmed in the baselessness of the hatred, as attested by the quotation of Ps. 69:4, "those who hate me without cause" (cf. also Ps. 35:19). There is therefore no basis or cause that could be cited for this hatred. The frightening reality is that this is innocent suffering. It is especially stressed that this is written in "their [i.e., the Jews'] law." Innocent suffering therefore is nothing new, but a mystery at the heart of Israel's world. It enables us to understand the passion, but it also brings to light the profound enigma of sin.

The way Ps. 69:9 is used in the New Testament is significant. The Old Testament passage reads, "For zeal for thy house has consumed me, and the insults of those who insult thee have fallen on me." This is addressed to Yahweh. It refers to *his* house and to those who insult *him*. At the cleansing of the temple the first half of Ps. 69:9 is quoted, "His disciples remembered that it was written, 'Zeal for thy house will consume me' " (John 2:17). This verse says, in a manner typical of the Gospel of John, that only later did it dawn on Jesus' disciples that the cleansing of the temple was the fulfillment of a passage in the Psalms. Bultmann (1971, p. 124) wrote, "Yet the meaning can scarcely be that Jesus' action was an expression of his uncommon zeal . . . . Rather, the Evangelist . . . is looking forward to what is to come—or alternately at the whole of Jesus' ministry—and he means that Jesus' zeal will lead him to his death." Thus the verb *consume* should be stressed. Jesus dies because of that which he has begun to accomplish. This interpretation corresponds to the basic meaning of the quotation of Psalm 69 in the New Testament. In addition, the other possible interpretations would be in conflict with John 4:21, 24. The second half of v. 9 in Psalm 69 is taken up in Rom. 15:3 and Heb. 11:26. Romans 15:3 emphasizes that Jesus was not acting on his own behalf in what he said and what he suffered. Instead, "The reproaches of those who reproached thee fell on me." That is to say, ridicule and contempt that were intended for God fell on his Christ. He suffered in the place of God. In Psalm 69 a motif out of the prayer songs of the people has been applied to the individual. Israel does not suffer for its own guilt, but for the sake of Yahweh (cf. Ps. 44:18-19; 74:18-19; 79:12). This motif is taken up in the New Testament. For Heb. 11:26 the ὀνειδισμὸς τοῦ Χριστοῦ ("abuse suffered for the Christ") is a fixed expression. Moses, according to the Christological exegesis, "considered abuse suffered for the Christ greater wealth than the treasures of Egypt."

While the New Testament texts thus far discussed in connection with Psalm 69 are seen in relation to the passion, other points of view of this psalm are dealt with in Rom. 11:9-10; Rev. 16:1; 3:5; 13:8; 17:8; 20:12, 15; 21:27. Romans 11:9-10, in reference to Ps. 69:22-23, but also in reference to Isa. 29:10 and Deut. 21:3, speaks of a "hardening." Ps. 69:24 is quoted with a small but significant modification in Rev. 16:1. The Old Testament passage is translated "Pour out thy indignation upon them, and let thy burning anger overtake them." It is characteristic that this "wish for revenge," which is often criticized and regarded with disfavor, but which has been cited as characteristic of the Old Testament mentality, not only was taken up in the New Testament, but the fulfillment of this longing by God, the judge of the nations is announced in Rev. 16:1. God commands his heavenly servants to pour out the vials of his wrath upon the earth. The "book of life," which is mentioned in the Old Testament in Ps. 69:28; Exod. 32:32; and Dan. 12:1, is referred to in Rev. 3:5; 13:8; 17:8; 20:12, 15; 21:27. Being blotted out of this book is mentioned only in Rev. 3:5, but Rev. 13:8; 17:8; and 20:15 speak of "everyone whose name has not been written before the foundation of the world in the book of life of the Lamb that is slain," and Rev. 21:27 speaks of those "who are written in the Lamb's book of life." All these last-named references to Psalm 69 are of only secondary significance.

The special attention accorded Psalm 118 in the New Testament can primarily be explained by the fact that this psalm had great significance in Judaism. The petition הושיעה נא ("hosanna," "save us," Ps. 118:25) was a cultic formula used in the Feast of Tabernacles. Moreover, Psalms 113–118, known as the "Hallel," were a fixed part of the Jewish cycle of autumn feasts and of Passover (cf. Matt. 26:30; Mark 14:26). Finally, it should be mentioned that in Judaism Ps. 18:22-23 was interpreted as referring to Abraham, David, and the Messiah. A messianic interpretation of the psalm was in the air. We should start, then, with Ps. 118:25-26 and point out the connection with Matt. 23:39; Luke 13:35; 19:38; Matt. 21:9, 15; Mark 11:9-10; and John 12:13. The shout of ὡσάννα ("hosanna") was taken up in the pericope of Jesus' entry into Jerusalem. The phraseology εὐλογημένος ὁ ἐρχόμενος ἐν ὀνόματι κυρίου ("blessed is he who comes in the name of the Lord") takes on in this context a messianic meaning, a total change from the meaning of the Old Testament wording, which refers to the entrance of the cultic community. To the words just cited, Mark adds the interpretative sentence, "Blessed is the kingdom of our father David that is coming!" (Mark 11:10). Matthew prefaces these words with the statement, "Hosanna to the Son of David!" Here "Son of David" means the Messiah, and therefore suggests the fulfillment of 2 Sam. 7:12-16 (cf. 2 Sam. 14:4). The Gospel of John adds ὁ βασιλεὺς τοῦ Ἰσραηλ ("the King of Israel," John 12:13, in anticipation of John 18:37). None of these messianic interpretations is surprising when we are aware of the history of the messianic interpretation of Psalm 118 in Judaism. The only thing that is surprising is that now Jesus of Nazareth, whom the people held to be a "prophet," was being proclaimed as Messiah (cf. Matt. 21:11). It is clear that here the kerygma of the early church found expression. Any doubt is removed by the quotation of Ps. 118:26 in Matt. 23:39; Luke 13:35; and Luke 19:38. Jesus says, "You will not see me again, until you say, 'Blessed is he who comes in the name of the Lord' " (Matt. 23:39). The "coming" of Jesus is set forth in Matt. 3:11; 11:3; 21:9 (and the synoptic parallels). Still, the saying in Matt. 23:39 obviously had a particular significance, which is revealed in Matt. 26:64, "Hereafter you will see the Son of man seated at the right hand of Power, and coming on the clouds of heaven." Only when the Messiah (as the Son of man) comes from heaven will he really be the "coming one" whom Daniel foretold (Dan. 7:13). Only then—and this is the meaning of this saying—will Ps. 118:26 be fulfilled.

Psalm 118:22-23 speaks of the miracle that Yahweh has performed. "The stone which the builders rejected has become the head of the corner." It could also be translated, "principal stone." The Old Testament wording is clear. A stone which the masons had regarded with contempt and thrown aside came to be included in the building as the keystone, which supports one of the corners of the house or even the portal (cf. Dalman, 1928, p. 66). To drop the metaphor, someone who had been rejected comes to high honor. In the Synoptics, Ps. 118:22-23 is connected with the parable of the evil husbandmen (Matt. 21:42; Luke 20:17). The rejection and exaltation of Jesus becomes clear. If the people of God are regarded as the temple which God builds, as is often the case in the biblical tradition, this saying means that the Messiah who was rejected and killed by his own people, carries and supports the whole house of God.

In Acts 4:11-12; Ps. 118:22-23 is understood in the exclusive sense, "he alone," because the statement is added, "And there is salvation in no one else, for there is no other name under heaven given among men by which we must be saved." Moreover, the situation of decision contained in the rejection and raising to honor of the "stone" can be singled out for attention. This is done in 1 Peter 2:7, where Ps. 118:22-23 is connected with the quotation of Isa. 28:16, in reference to faith. Then v. 8 continues, "A stone that will make men stumble, a rock that will make them fall." The Old Testament saying about the stone over which men stumble and fall suddenly appears in this passage (cf. Ps. 91:12; Isa. 8:14). The warning in Luke 20:18 is even more sharply formulated, "Every one who falls on that stone will be broken to pieces; but when it falls on any one it will crush him."

Less central in significance are other quotations of Psalm 118, for example, the word-for-word repetition of Ps. 118:6 in Heb. 13:6. Anyone who trusts the God who has promised, "I will not fail you or forsake you" (Josh. 1:5), can affirm the undaunted confession of the psalmist. He also knows—and here the quotation goes beyond the context—that he is safe from the hostility of the powerful. The declaration of the psalmist in Ps. 118:18 that the Lord has chastened him sorely but has not given him over to death is taken up by Paul in a series of statements that show the powerful influence of Psalm 119, for example, 2 Cor. 6:9, "as dying and behold we live; as punished and yet not killed . . . ." The chastening refers to the path between life and death, the road on which God constantly comes to the rescue, in reminder of the humiliation and exaltation of Christ, and also bears testimony to the deep humility of the apostle and his total reliance on the God who saves.

It should also be noted that the joy that breaks forth into shouting in Ps. 118:24 has become a part of the worship offered to Yahweh the King in Rev. 19:7.

C. Other Psalm Texts Cited or Quoted

Anyone who explores the nuances of the ways in which Old Testament Psalms are used in the New Testament will be amazed at the ways in which Israel's songs of prayer and praise were alive and present in the early church. Characteristic phraseology from the widest variety of psalms suddenly appears; sometimes only a few words are found, but they are unmistakable allusions to the Psalter. Beyond this there are, in addition to the psalms of special significance that have already been discussed, clear citations which we must now consider. Looking at the whole New Testament, we see that the Psalms, whether in quotations or in the use of isolated phraseology, are found most frequently in the book of Revelation, in the letters of Paul, in the Synoptic Gospels, and in the Acts of the Apostles. It seems appropriate to modify the method of presentation followed thus far and to trace one by one the quotations of the Psalms in the books of the New Testament, beginning with the Synoptic Gospels.

First, however, it is important to note in a general way the New Testament psalms drew on the traditional material of the language of prayer, adoration, and praise of the Old Testament. It can be said that, for example, in the hymns of Luke 1 and in those of the book of Revelation what we find is anything but a pedantic dependence. The spontaneous and direct use of turns of phrase, idioms, and concepts from the Psalms of Israel can only mean that those Psalms were so present a reality for the authors that they could pick up this or that phrase from different texts and disparate contexts and bring them together in a new context.

What follows cannot claim to be a comprehensive treatment, but it will describe the way in which in Luke 1 and in Revelation concepts and phrases were borrowed from the Psalms of the Old Testament, and how specific characteristics of the forms of praise in Israel determined the style of the New Testament hymns. Luke 1:49, 68 makes use of a theme from Ps. 111:9, and an echo of Ps. 103:17 is heard in Luke 1:50. Luke 1:51 made use of what Ps. 89:10 said about the "mighty arm" of Israel's God. The motif that the rich come to naught and the hungry are satisfied with good things (Ps. 34:10; 107:9) finds application in Luke 1:53. It is also significant that the statement "He has remembered his steadfast love and faithfulness to the house of Israel" (Ps. 98:3) was used in Luke 1:54. Doxological phraseology such as "Blessed be the Lord, the God of Israel, from everlasting to everlasting!" (Ps. 41:13; 72:18-19; 89:52; 106:48) becomes a part of the praise of God in the "Benedictus" (Luke 1:68). The messianic aspects of Psalm 132 became important, for instance, Ps. 132:17 in Luke 1:69. Traditional metaphors in which Yahweh is called, for example, "horn of my salvation" (Ps. 18:2) are found in Luke 1:69, and confessions of God's saving and redemptive action, such as those in Ps. 106:10 are found in Luke 1:71. Luke 1:72 emphasizes that Yahweh "is mindful of his covenant" (Ps. 105:8; 106:45).

The situation is similar in the book of Revelation. Special notice should be taken of the adoption of the Old Testament shout of praise, "Hallelujah!" (Ps. 104:35) in Rev. 19:1, 3, 6. Moreover, the message of the arrival of God's eschatological kingship, as it is found in Ps. 47:8 and in the psalms of Yahweh's kingship, takes on tremendous importance in its apocalyptic aspect: Rev. 4:2, 9; 5:1, 7, 13; 6:16; 7:10, 17; 19:4; 21:5. The Hebrew expression יהוה מלך ("Yahweh reigns, Ps. 93:1; 97:1; 99:1) is rendered in Rev. 19:6 as ἐβασίλευσεν κύριος ὁ θεός ("the Lord God reigns"). In the eschaton God's kingship will finally be established. Thus it is by no means the case that Israel's Psalms were speaking an exaggerated language that had no relation to reality. That which in the Old Testament, in the light of final things was only promise had now been fulfilled. The proclamation of fulfillment enables the Old Testament hymns that were qualified promises to take part in the reality that has now been revealed. As was the case in Luke 1, so too in Revelation the doxologies and doxological formulations of the Psalter find wide usage.

Attention has already been called to the modification that took place in the process of borrowing. What follows is a partial listing and cataloging of Old Testament quotations in the New Testament with attention to the interpretation of their contents, beginning with the Synoptic Gospels. Since Matthew frequently quotes the Psalms, the older of the material in this Gospel will be followed, but where references to the psalm are identifiable in Mark or in Luke they will also be mentioned.

In the pericope of the "wise men from the East" (Matt. 2:1-18) the fulfillment of a prophecy found in Ps. 72:10, 15 and Isa. 60:6 is described. In these two verses of Psalm 72, part of a royal psalm, it is said that "kings of Tarshish and of the isles" bring him presents, and bring "gold of Sheba" to Jerusalem to honor "Yahweh's anointed." Three things are significant in Matt. 2:11, where this honoring is portrayed: (1) the structure of the passage with the use of the Old Testament materials; (2) the enhancing of the statements about the "wise men" by the use of Psalm 72 and its words about "kings" that come from afar, which had effects on the tradition of the church; and (3) the messianic understanding of the entire pericope—it is God's Messiah who is being adored. The importance of the correlation of prophecy and fulfillment in the Gospel of Matthew can be assumed to be well known. Nevertheless, the specific manner in which this correlation is carried out deserves consideration in each instance.

In the account of the temptation (Matt. 4:1-11; Luke 4:1-13) the use of the Old Testament is quite different. Psalm 91:11-12 is quoted by the tempter (Matt. 4:6; Luke 4:10-11). He suggests that Jesus express his confidence in God's protection, ignoring the concrete situation. The passage shows that "the Scripture" is not something from the realm of tabu that speaks for itself and has undisputed validity "in and of itself." Clearly one's basic relationship to this "Scripture" is what is decisive. The Scripture can be misused. There can be a tendency at work that serves to tempt, that is, to separate one from God. Thus concrete, living obedience can be disrupted and disturbed by the quoting of Scripture. Certainty can be turned into security, into blindness and presumption. Thus the manner in which Scripture is put to use is of supreme importance. Matthew 4:6 and Luke 4:10-11 are impressive evidence that the "Scripture" is not a collection of holy words that by virtue of some imminent sanctity are valid and effective. In particular, the correlation of prophecy and fulfillment leads to a basic relationship to "Scripture" that is determined by the coming of the Messiah and characterized by an authoritative example.

In three places the Beatitudes in Matthew show the influence of the Psalms. Matthew 5:4, "Blessed are those who mourn, for they shall be comforted," reminds the hearer of Ps. 126:5-6, "May those who sow in tears reap with shouts of joy!" and also of Isa. 61:2. The transition from the troubles lamented in the prayer song to the deliverance proclaimed in the song of thanks, a transition indeed frequent in the Psalms, marks the structure of the Beatitudes. In Matt. 5:5 the promise, "Those who wait for the Lord shall possess the land" (Ps. 37:9), is taken up, and thereby a one-sided expectation becomes a part of the Beatitudes. All the Psalms proclaim that God finally fulfills the hopes of those who are poor, oppressed, or dispossessed from their land and gives them justice. It will not be possible to eliminate the eschatological perspective in Matt. 5:5; the renewed earth will be a place of justice (1 Peter 3:12).

Finally, the Beatitude in Matt. 5:8 draws on the phraseology of the psalms that speak of a "pure heart" (Ps. 24:4; 51:10; 73:1). The recasting of the concept is interesting. According to Ps. 24:4 those who have a "pure heart" will be permitted to enter the sanctuary (Ps. 24:4), while in Matt. 5:8 the eschatological vision of God will be the fulfillment of the promise. Thus the New Testament makes explicit in eschatological terms the old cultic formula "to see the face of God," which in the Psalms means to enter into the sanctuary, the place where Yahweh is present.

Matthew 5:35 borrows from the Psalms two particular designations of Jerusalem, "city of the great King" (Ps. 48:2) and God's "footstool" (Ps. 99:5).

The rejection of the פעלי־און ("evildoers") in Ps. 6:8 is in Matt. 7:23 and Luke 13:27 applied to those who say, "Lord, Lord": "Depart from me, you evildoers."

In the development of the parable of the mustard seed Ps. 104:12 is used in Matt. 13:32; Mark 4:32; and Luke 13:19 in order to illustrate the size of the tree that grew out of the smallest beginnings. But these are only peripheral citations.

A much deeper level of meaning is reached by the reference to Ps. 78:2 in Matt. 13:35. There in v. 34 reference is made to the fact that Jesus spoke in parables. The Gospel writer saw this as fulfilling Ps. 78:2, "I will open my mouth in a parable (מָשָׁל = παραβολή); I will utter dark sayings (חִידוֹת = κεκρυμμένα) from of old." Jesus enters into the role of the unknown, unnamed speaker of the Old Testament Psalms. He is the one who speaks the cryptic מָשָׁל (*mašal*, "parable").

It is well known that in the New Testament the idea of being judged according to one's works plays a significant role. Wherever this is said (in the Synoptics, in Matt. 16:27) we can see a reference to Ps. 62:12 (cf. also Rom. 2:6; 2 Tim. 4:14; Rev. 2:23; 20:12; 22:12). It is significant that according to Ps. 62:12 the just judgment of God is understood as a demonstration of his חֶסֶד (*ḥesed*, "loving kindness"). This is because the one who in the Old Testament is hard beset and offers prayer recognizes in the judgment on his foes a sign that Yahweh is coming to his rescue. In the New Testament this thought recedes into the background.

When according to Matt. 21:16 the children cry out "Hosanna to the Son of David!" Jesus interprets this in terms of Ps. 8:2, "Have you never read, 'Out of the mouth of babes and sucklings thou hast brought perfect praise'?" The praise which the children offer is thus an integral part of the course of events and does not represent something strange or surprising. To be sure, Ps. 8:2 is quoted according to the Septuagint, which understood it in a sense different from that of the Hebrew text. According to the Old Testament text the voices of the babes and infants form a "bulwark" against the foes of God.

In addition to the special quotations from Psalms 22 and 69 a number of individual motifs from these psalms were incorporated into the passion narrative of the Synoptic Gospels. That Judas, one of those who was eating with Jesus, betrayed him (Mark 14:18) is reported with echoes of Ps. 41:9. "Even my bosom friend in whom I trusted, who ate of my bread, has lifted his heel against me." In John 13:18 the scriptural reference is even more detailed. "It is that the scripture may be fulfilled, 'He who ate my bread has lifted his heel against me.'" Associations that lay close at hand found application here. The same is the case of the "acquaintances . . . who stood at a distance" (Luke 23:49; cf. Ps. 38:11; 88:8).

In Pss. 42:5, 11; 43:5 the one who is praying says that the despairing soul is cast down, and this is taken up in the first person expression of the sorrowing one who said in Gethsemane, "My soul is very sorrowful" (Matt. 26:38), but he added ἕως θανάτου ("unto death"). The sufferings of death crush the sorrowing soul. For Luke and also for John the cry that God has forsaken Jesus, recorded in Matthew and Mark (cf. Ps. 22:1), does not seem to have been acceptable, with its terror and in the thoroughness of its questioning of the messianic office of the one crucified. Other "final words" became incorporated into the tradition. In Luke 23:46 Jesus prays as he dies, "Into thy hands I commit my spirit" (Ps. 31:5). In the context of the Gospel of Luke, the anthropological meaning which רוּחַ/πνεῦμα ("spirit") had in the Old Testament was clearly transcended. That is to say, it does not signify that the one dying commends his life's breath, his life, into God's hands (Eccles. 12:7). As Messiah, Jesus is the bearer of the divine πνεῦμα (Luke 4:18). He surrenders to his God the spirit with which he had been anointed (Luke 4:18, 21). To be sure, ἐξέπνευσεν ("expired") is a well-known euphemism for "to die" and is employed here in an anthropological sense, but we still may well ask whether, especially in light of the kerygmatic correction of the quotation from Ps. 22:1 in Matthew and Mark, a decided Christological motivation did not lead to the use of Ps. 31:5 in Luke.

197

The Psalms in the New Testament

Only on a few occasions in the Gospel of John are allusions or quotations from the Psalms found. John 10:11, in the context of the pericope of the Good Shepherd, contains an echo of Ps. 23:1, "The Lord is my shepherd, I shall not want." In John 10:10, Jesus, the Good Shepherd says, "I came that they may have life, and have it abundantly (περισσόν)." Yahweh's work comes here to its completion and to its goal.

The quotation of Ps. 82:6 in John 10:34 is unique. Psalm 82, permeated with strongly mythologically colored statements, portrays Yahweh holding court in the midst of the assembly of the gods. Those who are mighty on earth, whose representatives tower into the heavenly world, are brought to judgment. Verse 6 says, "I say, 'You are gods, sons of the Most High, all of you.' " But this view is shown to be false, because these powers will all "die like men" (v. 7). In John 10:34 we must begin with the statement made by the Johannine Christ, "I and the Father are one" (John 10:30). The Jews who heard this statement wanted to stone Jesus because of the blasphemy expressed in his declaration (v. 33). But Jesus referred to Ps. 82:6 with the words, "Is it not written in your law, 'I said, you are Gods'?" He gives his hearers to think that on the basis of an Old Testament statement of this nature his claim, "I and the Father are one," is justified. It is obvious that especially in Judaism an Old Testament declaration of divinity such as that in Ps. 82:6 would be startling, but in this context it would simply be regarded as erroneous. It appears that the Johannine text takes notice of this. In our eyes this is a weak argument, but for Jesus' Jewish contemporaries it would at least attract notice.

Old Testament psalms are quoted with relative frequency in the book of Acts. The reference to βίβλος ψαλμῶν (the book of Psalms, Luke 20:42; Acts 1:20) and to ψαλμοί (psalms, Luke 24:44), so prominent in the Lukan writings, comes into focus when the fate of Judas and the succession to his apostolic office are reported (Acts 1:20). The narrator sees the events foreshadowed in Ps. 109:8, "May his days be few; may another seize his goods" ("office" in Acts 1:20). Both the early death and the succession to office are read out of the psalm, which in the Old Testament deals with the godless. It is clear that scribal traditions were at work here.

The quotation of Ps. 16:8-11 in Acts 2:25-29 and 13:35 raises special problems. For the meaning of the Old Testament text see what was said above on the theme "Deliverance from Death" (cf. chap. 6, §E). Resurrection from the dead is not involved. But the statements in the Hebrew text were understood differently in Acts 2:25-28. Since the starting point is the resurrection of the one who was crucified (v. 24), Ps. 16:8-11 was taken as a statement which David made about Jesus as the Messiah. Clearly a passage that announces a resurrection cannot refer to David. David is dead, and his grave can be seen in Jerusalem. Therefore David, as a prophet who knew the promise made in 2 Sam. 7:12-13, spoke prophetically of the resurrection of Jesus Christ (note also the allusion to Ps. 132:11). It is clear that the meaning of the psalm has been transformed. Acts 2:25-29 contributed in a major way to the fact that church tradition read Old Testament psalms, which were really dealing with "deliverance from death," in the light of the resurrection and interpreted them accordingly. We should keep in mind the transcending intention that moves beyond the earthly realm of this life in those psalms in the Old Testament in which life in the presence of Yahweh produced a very complex concept of life, and in which death, away from God's presence, in

Sheol, produced an equally complex concept of death. If we do, the shift in meaning with its tendency to announce the fulfillment of the original meaning, becomes more easily understood. Nevertheless, it is not legitimate to displace the kerygma that is proper to the Old Testament with a proclamation that it has been fulfilled, especially since the disputes with Judaism are long past and the method of arguing from "the Scripture" which was then possible is no longer relevant today.

Only a passing reference is possible here to the hymnodic designation of God as אל־הכבוד ("God of glory," Ps. 29:3) which recurs in Acts 7:2 in the translation θεὸς τῆς δόξης ("God of glory"). This passage, together with many others, testifies that the Father of Jesus Christ is the God of Israel. As the Old Testament people of God praised and honored him, so too he is honored in the Christian community.

A verse from a royal psalm, Ps. 89:20, is quoted in a messianic sense in Acts 13:22: "I have found David, my servant; with my holy oil I have anointed him." To this quotation is added the exclamation, "Of this man's posterity God has brought to Israel a Savior, Jesus, as he promised" (Acts 13:23). The New Testament emphasizes again and again that Jesus, who has fulfilled the promise given to David and his posterity, is God's gift for Israel.

The themes that are so frequent in the Psalms, "judgment on the nations" and "salvation for the nations," appear in the kerygma of the Acts of the Apostles: the theme of judgment in Acts 17:31 (cf. Ps. 9:8; 96:13; 98:9); the theme of salvation in Acts 28:28 (cf. Ps. 67:2; 98:3).

In addition, the relationship between God and people in the Psalms is interpreted in terms of the relationship of the Kyrios to his congregation. Psalm 74:2, "Remember thy congregation, which thou has gotten of old . . .," recurs in the form of an exhortation in Paul's speech to the elders of the church in Ephesus (Acts 20:28). It is emphasized that he "obtained" the church "with the blood of his own Son," that is to say, he chose it and made it his own.

The letters of Paul make use of the psalms of the Old Testament in numerous passages. Especially in Romans we find quotations or phraseology from Israel's language of praise and prayer. The message of the justification of the sinner receives especial support through the use of psalm texts. In Rom. 1:16-17 Paul alludes to Ps. 98:2, "for in it the righteousness of God is revealed." Psalm 98 provides clear support for the universal significance of this eschatological event. The verb ἀποκαλύπτειν ("reveal") is the translation of the Hebrew גלה (*galah*) of Ps. 98:2. If Rom. 1:16-17 is interpreted in light of Psalm 98, δικαιοσύνη ("righteousness") is the proclamation of the eschatological accomplishment of God's justice that brings salvation and renews the creation. It involves all peoples. The God of justice comes to judge the earth (Ps. 98:9). This judgment, however, is now carried out through the gospel, "for salvation to every one who has faith, to the Jew first and also to the Greek." In Psalm 98 צדקה ("righteousness") and ישועה ("salvation") are already synonymous. But the elements of judgment must not be eliminated or absorbed. Paul speaks of the "wrath of God" which is revealed "against all ungodliness and wickedness of men" (Rom. 1:18-32). Humans are thus revealed as idolaters. Romans 1:23 alludes to Ps. 106:20, where it says, "They exchanged the glory of God for the image of an ox that eats grass."

Romans 3:4 declares that God is true, "though every man be false." The last part of the sentence is a quotation of Ps. 116:11. And then the conclusion is given in the form of a quotation, ''That thou mayest be justified in thy words, and prevail when thou art judged,'' a statement taken from Ps. 51:4, where it follows the doxology of judgment and the process of *Deum iustificare* (justifying God). But the ''justification of God,'' which in Ps. 51:4 is related to a specific, concrete instance is, in Rom. 3:4, placed in a universal and eschatological dimension. ''God is no longer declared to be righteous in his temporal judgment. He triumphs over his earthly opponents in the last judgment and shows himself to be justified in the words of his revelation. What Paul gathers from the psalm quotation is that world history ends with God's victory over his foes and with the manifestation of his justice over his creatures'' (Käsemann, 1980, p. 81). Who are these foes? They are the ''godless,'' who are revealed to be all mankind, without exception. In this aspect Paul's theology differs in an essential way from the situation in the Psalter. The contrast of the righteous and the godless is abolished by a new point of view. Descriptions of the רשעים (''wicked''), which in the Old Testament serve to portray the foes of the צדיק (''righteous''), now have a part to play in the unmasking of the godlessness of all human beings. Romans 3:10-18 quotes Ps. 5:9; 14:1ff; 140:3, and Rom. 3:18 quotes Ps. 36:1. The picture of the רשע (''wicked'') given in the Psalms includes everyone, ''Jews and Greeks'' (Rom. 3:9). Thus the announcement of the *iustificatio impii* (justification of the ungodly), as voiced in Ps. 143:2 (see the *Comm.*), can be taken up by Paul in Rom. 3:20 and Gal. 2:16: ''Enter not into judgment with thy servant; for no man living is righteous before thee.'' Nothing but the ascription of God's righteousness in response to faith, without any human achievement, that is, the justification of the ungodly, can bring about the transformation (Rom. 4:5-6). In Rom. 4:7-8, Paul quotes Ps. 32:1-2 to speak of the happiness of being forgiven and not having sins reckoned against us (Rom. 4:7-8). In this way the message that produces faith is one that permeates the whole world.

In order to illustrate this universal, cosmic character of the preaching of the gospel, Paul refers in Rom. 10:18 to Ps. 19:4. The psalm announces that ''the heavens are telling'' the glory of the Creator, which resounds throughout the whole world. The same thing applies to the proclamation of the Word of God that was said in Ps. 19:4 of the *creation narrative*: ''Their voice goes out through all the earth, and their words to the end of the world.'' But do we have here merely an ''illustration''? In keeping with the intention of the Old Testament psalm must we not recognize the eschatological relationship of the message of the created world to the gospel (cf. the *Comm.* on Psalm 19; von Rad, 1972, p. 162)? Nevertheless, the fulfillment of the eschatological goal will be that all peoples praise God. For example, Paul saw the praise of the peoples, mentioned in Ps. 18:49 and 117:1 as a promise now fulfilled (Rom. 15:9, 11).

In Romans 11 Paul speaks about the situation of Israel, the people of God. If the question ''Has God rejected his people?'' can be answered with an unequivocal ''By no means!'' and is immediately reinforced with the assertion ''God has not rejected his people,'' then the message of Ps. 94:14 goes forth anew: ''For the Lord will not forsake his people; he will not abandon his heritage.'' This promise is unalterable. It is not the covenant with Israel that is proclaimed. Now the Christian community bears the designation ''the Israel of God'' (Gal. 6:16). Wishes for peace, such as those expressed in the Psalms for Israel (Ps. 125:5; 128:6) are transferred to the new people of God. Just as the Israel of the old covenant had to take upon itself suffering and death for the sake of its election (Ps. 44:22), so now, and to a special degree, the Christian community is plunged into the eschatological θλίψις ("tribulation"). "For thy sake we are being killed all the day long; we are regarded as sheep to be slaughtered" (Rom. 8:36). The foregoing discussion shows how strong and profound are the connections between the apostle Paul's message of justification and the Psalms of the Old Testament.

In the epistles to the Corinthians, the quotations of the Psalms can also easily be recognized. In the context of showing that the wisdom of this world is foolishness before God, Ps. 94:11 is cited in 1 Cor. 3:20, "The Lord knows that the thoughts of the wise are futile." In 1 Cor. 10:20 Paul shows, by reference to Ps. 106:37, that every offering that the pagans bring is offered to demons and not to God.

The quotation of Ps. 24:1 in 1 Cor. 10:26 is interesting. The unlimited freedom expressed in the formula πάντα ἔξεστιν ("all things are lawful," 1 Cor. 10:23) is based on the fact that "the earth is the Lord's, and everything in it." This also serves, however, as the basis for responsibility before God and our neighbor, because the earth is "the Lord's." The mystery of creation contains within it the dialectic of freedom and responsibility.

"All things" (πάντα) have been placed beneath the feet of Christ (1 Cor. 15:27; Eph. 1:22). He is the Lord of the world. Psalm 8:6 is brought together with Ps. 110:1 and quoted in a messianic sense, in connection with the "kingdom of Christ." In the discussion of Heb. 2:6ff. we will return to this method of interpreting Ps. 8:6.

In referring to the "Spirit of faith" which has been received, the apostle voices his confession in the words of Ps. 116:10, "I believed, and so I spoke" (2 Cor. 4:13). The statement is completely taken out of the context of Psalm 116, but it attracted attention to itself especially because the verb הֶאֱמִין ("I kept faith") occurs and because as a consequence of the certainty of faith the Psalms of the Old Testament speak out in ringing declarations. As a proof-text for the fullness of the gifts of God, Ps. 112:9 is cited in 2 Cor. 9:9, "He scatters abroad, he gives to the poor; his righteousness endures for ever."

In the letter to the Ephesians, the quotation of Ps. 68:18 in Eph. 4:8-10 is notable. In v. 7 the apostle spoke of the grace that is imparted "according to the measure of Christ's gift." The gifts are distributed by the one who "ascended on high." The two elements, "ascension to the heights" and "distribution of gifts" were the occasion for the citing of Ps. 68:18. Since the motif of enthronement is so clear in the Old Testament Psalms (see *Comm.*) the application of this text to Christ signifies the proclamation of the lordship of the exalted one throughout the world. He has ascended in order "that he might fill all things" (v. 10). The gifts which he distributes in his community have cosmic and universal meaning and effect. That which the church receives is given to the whole of creation.

In the discussion above of the use made of Psalms 2 and 110 it was shown that in the Letter to the Hebrews the Psalms of the Old Testament play a special role in the demonstration that Jesus is the Messiah and the Son of God. In the polemic against (Gnostic) speculations about angels, according to which Jesus Christ was apparently incorporated into the ranks of angelic beings, texts from the Psalms were used to show that Jesus as the Christ was exalted above all imaginable powers and forces. In order to make clear what the Bible means by "angel," in distinction to the Son of God, reference is made in Heb. 1:7 to Ps. 104:4. Angels are messengers and servants, while the nature of Christ is not comparable to anything else. In Heb. 1:10 the term ὁ θεός ("God") from Ps. 47:6 is applied to him, and following that, in Heb. 1:10-12 even a statement about God the creator

(Ps. 102:25-27) is used in reference to the one who has been exalted. The quotation of Ps. 8:2ff. in Heb. 2:6ff. is to be understood similarly. Once again the debate with the teachings concerning angels plays a decisive role. In Ps. 8:5 it says, "Thou hast made him a little less than the heavenly beings [RSV 'God']." In the LXX and Heb. 2:7 the term is rendered ἀγγέλους ("angels"). That means that Jesus has been subordinated to the angels! This subordination is explained in two ways in the context. First, in the present aeon the majesty and lordship of Christ cannot be seen. And second, Jesus has been "crowned with glory and honor" (cf. Ps. 8:5), so that "he might taste death for every one." Thus the declaration of exaltation "thou hast put all things under his feet," can be understood only *sub contrario crucis* (in contrast to the cross). It related to the "world to come" (οἰκουμένην τὴν μέλλουσαν, v. 5), and is therefore to be understood strictly in eschatological terms. In the Christology of the Letter to the Hebrews, therefore, the statements from Psalm 8 concerning subordination and exaltation are interpreted messianically and applied to the work of Jesus or to his eschatological exaltation. It is rather strange that Ps. 8:5, a verse that in its Old Testament meaning serves as a basis for the majesty and sovereign lordship of mankind ("a little less than the heavenly beings") should be taken as a statement of subordination. This is to be explained in terms of the polemic against the teachings concerning angels. In this transformed aspect a basis is established by the statement that the one humbled by the suffering of death is crowned with glory and honor, because he tasted death for every one. In the whole use of the quotation the decisive factor is that Psalm 8 is taken out of an anthropological setting into a Christological one. Behind this lies the conviction that only the Son of God can be that υἱὸς ἀνθρώπου, under whose feet all things are placed in subjection (cf. also 1 Cor. 15:27).

In other passages in Hebrews statements and exhortations to the Christian community are provided with support from the Psalms. In the warning against hardness of heart and falling away from God, Ps. 95:9-11 is cited in Heb. 3:7-11,15; 4:3-5.

To underline the fact that it is impossible to remove sins by the sacrifice of animals, Ps. 40:6-8 is quoted in Heb. 10:5-10. In agreement with Ps. 40:8, it is affirmed that true sacrifice is doing the will of God (Heb. 10:7, 9).

Finally, the exhortation always to offer to God the "sacrifice of praise" as "the fruit of the lips" (Isa. 57:19) is supported in Heb. 13:5 by allusion to Ps. 50:14, 23.

In 1 Peter references to the Psalms help clarify the kerygma. In 1 Peter 1:17 the formula "invoke God as Father" is taken from the royal psalm 89:26-27 and applied to the Christian invocation of God. 1 Peter 2:3 alludes to Ps. 34:8, in speaking of "tasting" the goodness and kindness of the Lord. There is also an allusion to Ps. 39:12 in the statement about being "aliens and exiles" in 1 Peter 2:11. Rules for life from the wisdom tradition, such as those found in Ps. 34:12-14 are taken up in 1 Peter 3:10-12. The question of what constitutes a blessed life is answered in terms of the wisdom traditions. The Old Testament exhortation, "Cast your burden on the Lord, and he will sustain you" (Ps. 55:22), is found in 1 Peter 5:7.

In 2 Peter 3:8 the quotation of Ps. 90:4 serves to demonstrate that the lamented and ridiculed "delay of the parousia" does not discredit the promise of a new world. "For a thousand years in thy sight are but as yesterday when it is past, or as a watch in the night" (Ps. 90:4). This transformation of all concepts of time is brought into play in the struggle. That which seems to last endlessly in the eyes of men is only a brief span of time for God. A thousand years are for him no more than a day (2 Peter 3:8). If we ignore the specific numbers we might well ask, following the intention of 2 Peter 3:8, to what extent the eschatological event of salvation has permeated and transformed the human understanding of time.

It has already been shown that the early Christian psalms in the book of Revelation grew out of the traditional language of the Hebrew Psalter. It only remains to point out the way in which the Old Testament Psalms were used in other contexts in the apocalyptic message. In Rev. 1:5 Christ is termed "the firstborn of the dead" and "the ruler of kings on earth." It is easy to see that Ps. 89:27 is reflected in these decisive designations of the "anointed of Yahweh."

In the letter to the church in Thyatira the formula "who triest the minds and hearts" (Rev. 2:23) has been borrowed in order to testify to God's knowledge that reaches even into the depths of the heart, and which forms the basis on which he judges (Ps. 7:9). Old Testament traditions that were involved in the institution of divine judgment in the courts of the sanctuary have been applied here to the lordship of the Kyrios over the church.

Psalm 86:9 looks forward to the worship and adoration which the nations will offer to God in the end time. This expectation is also found in Rev. 3:9 and 15:4. In the first passage "peoples" refers to those who say that they are Jews, but in fact are not. In other words, these are "Jews" who have liberated themselves from the world of Israel and therefore are no longer counted as "true Jews" (John 1:47), but are included among the ἔθνη (*ethnē*, "Gentiles" or "nations"). They are still not excluded from the expectation of the worship to be offered in the end-time.

In Rev. 7:17 the eschatological peace in the realm of God's eternity is illustrated by a metaphor that refers to Ps. 23:2, "For the Lamb in the midst of the throne will be their shepherd, and he will guide them to springs of living water."

On the other side of the picture, the wrath of God which will be poured out over the hostile nations of the world is characterized by Old Testament metaphors and traditions. The "cup of wrath" (Ps. 75:8) appears in Rev. 14:10. The apocalyptic terrors of God's judgment are portrayed in Rev. 16:4, 6 in terms of the events of the exodus (the plagues that fell on Pharaoh) in Ps. 78:44 and Ps. 79:3. And again we find in the book of Revelation the formula of the judgment doxology "The Lord is just in all his ways, and kind in all his doings" (Ps. 145:17; cf. Rev. 15:3; 16:5). References to Ps. 19:9 are found in Rev. 16:7 and 19:2, and to Ps. 119:137 in Rev. 16:5, 7 and 19:2.

But as has already been shown, it is not only the judgment of God that is proclaimed in the use of texts from the Psalms but also the marvelous demonstrations of his grace and power to deliver in the end-time. The redeemed servants of God will finally see the face of God in a fulfillment that goes beyond all promises (Rev. 22:4, in the quotations from Ps. 17:15 and 42:2). To encounter the living God, to "behold his face" was, for those who made the Psalms of Israel their prayer, the epitome of the joy of worship and the fulfillment of all expectations. In the eschaton, in God's eternal world it will be fulfilled: "They shall see his face" (Rev. 22:4) ὄψονται τὸ πρόσωπον αὐτοῦ.

Abbreviations

ANET	*Ancient Near Eastern Texts*, ed. J. Pritchard
AOT	*Altorientalische Texte zum Alten Testament*
ATANT	Abhandlungen zur Theologie des Alten und Neuen Testaments
BHT	Beiträge zur historischen Theologie
BJRL	*Bulletin of the John Rylands Library*
BK	Biblischer Kommentar
BtA	Biblisch-theologische Aufsätze
BWANT	Beiträge zur Wissenschaft vom Alten und Neuen Testament
BZ	*Biblische Zeitschrift*
BZAW	Beihefte zur *ZAW*
CD	Karl Barth, *Church Dogmatics*
CR	Corpus Reformatorum
ET	English translation
EvTh	*Evangelische Theologie*
FRLANT	Forschungen zur Religion und Literatur des Alten und Neuen Testaments
FS	Festschrift
HK	Handkommentar zum Alten Testament
HNT	Handbuch zum Neuen Testament
JB	Jerusalem Bible
JBL	*Journal of Biblical Literature*
JNES	*Journal of Near Eastern Studies*
KEK	Kritisch-exegetischer Kommentar über das Neue Testament
KJV	King James Version
MT	Masoretic Text
NTD	Das Neue Testament Deutsch
OLZ	*Orientalistische Literaturzeitung*
OTS	*Oudtestamentische Studien*
RGG	*Religion in Geschichte und Gegenwart*, 3d ed.
RSV	Revised Standard Version
SBM	Stuttgarter biblische Monographien
SBS	Stuttgarter Bibelstudien

Abbreviations

THAT	*Theologisches Handwörterbuch zum Alten Testament*, 2 vols., edited by E. Jenni and C. Westermann, 1971, 1976
ThLZ	*Theologische Literaturzeitung*
ThR NF	*Theologische Rundschau*, Neue Folge
ThZ	*Theologische Zeitschrift*
TThZ	*Trier Theologische Zeitschrift*
VT	*Vetus Testamentum*
WA	Weimar edition of Luther's works
WMANT	Wissenschaftliche Monographien zum Alten und Neuen Testament
ZAW	*Zeitschrift für die alttestamentliche Wissenschaft*
ZDPV	*Zeitschrift des deutschen Palästina-Vereins*
ZEE	*Zeitschrift für evangelische Ethik*
ZNW	*Zeitschrift für die neutestamentliche Wissenschaft*
ZThK	*Zeitschrift für Theologie und Kirche*

References

Albertz, M.
  1947   *Die Botschaft des Neuen Testaments* I. 1. 2 vols. Zurich: Evangelischer Verlag,
           1947–1957.

Albright, W. F.
  1950   "Baal-Zephon." In A. Bertholet FS, edited by W. Baumgartner et al., pp. 1-14.
           Tübingen: Mohr.
  1955   "Palestinian Inscriptions." In *Ancient Near Eastern Texts Relating to the Old
           Testament*, edited by J. Pritchard, pp. 320-322. 2d ed. Princeton: Princeton Uni-
           versity Press.

Alt, A.
  1953a   "Gedanken über das Königtum Jahwehs." In *Kleine Schriften zur Geschichte
           des Volkes Israel*, vol. 1, pp. 345-357. Munich: Beck.
  1953b   "Die Ursprünge des israelitischen Rechts." In *Kleine Schriften* 1:278-332.
  1959a   "Das Grossreich Davids." In *Kleine Schriften zur Geschichte des Volkes Isra-
           el*, vol. 2, pp. 66-75. Munich: Beck.
  1959b   "Das Königtum in den Reichen Israel und Juda." In *Kleine Schriften*
           2:116-134.

Althaus, P.
  1966   *Die christliche Wahrheit*. 7th ed.

Amirtham, S.
  1968   "To Be Near and Far Away from Yahweh." *Bangalore Theological Forum* 2.

Anderson, G. W.
  1965   "Enemies and Evildoers in the Book of Psalms." *BJRL* 48: 16-29.

Bächli, O.
  1962   *Israel und die Völker*. ATANT 41. Zurich: Zwingli.
  1966   "Die Erwählung der Geringen im Alten Testament." *ThZ* 22: 385-395.

Barth, Christoph
  1947   *Die Errettung vom Tode in den individuellen Klage- und Dankliedern des Alten
           Testaments*. Zollikon: Evangelischer Verlag.
  1961   *Einführung in die Psalmen*, Biblische Studien 32. Neukirchen-Vluyn:
           Neukirchener. ET: *Introduction to the Psalms*. Translated by R. A. Wilson.
           New York: Scribner, 1966.

References

Barth, K.
1933   *The Epistle to the Romans.* Translated by E. C. Hoskyns. London: Oxford University Press. Reprinted 1968.
1936–1969   *Church Dogmatics.* Translated by G. Bromiley and T. Torrance. Edinburgh: T. and T. Clark.
1962   *Einführung in die evangelische Theologie.* Zurich: EVZ Verlag. ET: T. and T. Clark.
1965   *Das Vaterunser.*

Bauer, H.
1933   "Die Gottheiten von Ras Schamra." *ZAW* 51:81-100.

Begrich, J.
1934   "Das priesterliche Heilsorakel." *ZAW* 52 (1934): 81-92. Reprinted in *Gesammelte Studien* (Munich: Kaiser, 1964), pp. 217-231.
1938   *Studien zu Deuterojesaja.* BWANT 77. Reprinted in Theologische Bücherei 20 (Munich: Kaiser, 1963).
1964   "Mabbul." In *Gesammelte Studien*, pp. 39-54.

Bentzen, A.
1948   *Messias, Moses redivivus, Menschensohn.* Zurich: Zwingli.

Berghe, P. von der.
1962   "*Ani* et *anaw* dans les psaumes." In *Le Psautier*, edited by R. DeLanghe. Louvain.

Bernhardt, K. H.
1961   *Das Problem der altorientalischen Königsideologie im Alten Testament.* Leiden: Brill.

Beyerlin, W.
1970   *Die Rettung der Bedrängten in den Feindpsalmen der einzelnen auf institutionelle Zusammenhänge.* FRLANT 99. Göttingen: Vandenhoeck & Ruprecht.

Birkeland, H.
1933a   *Ani und Anaw in den Psalmen.* Oslo: Dybwad.
1933b   *Die Feinde des Individuums in der israelitischen Psalmenliteratur.* Oslo: Grøndahl.
1955   *The Evildoers in the Book of Psalms.* Oslo: Dybwad.

Bonhoeffer, D.
1959   *Creation and Fall.* Translated by J. Fletcher. New York: Macmillan.

Bright, J.
1956   *The Kingdom of God.* Nashville: Abingdon.

Brunner, H.
1961   "Die religiöse Wertung der Armut im alten Ägypten." *Saeculum* 31.

Buber, M.
1932   *Das Kommende.*
1952   *Right and Wrong: An Interpretation of Some Psalms.* London: SCM.
1963   "Der Jude und sein Judentum." In *Gesammelte Aufsätze und Reden.*
1966   "Offener Brief an G. Kittel." In *Versuche des Verstehens.* Edited by R. R. Geis and H.-J. Kraus. Munich: Kaiser.
1967   *Kingship of God.* Translated by R. Smith. London: SCM.

Bultmann, R.
1971   *The Gospel of John.* Translated by G. R. Beasley-Murray. Philadelphia: Westminster.

Calov, A.
  1676   *Biblia Novi Testamenti illustrata* I.

Causse, A.
  1922   *Les "pauvres" d'Israel.*
  1937   *Du groupe ethnique à la communauté religieuse.*

Conzelmann, H.
  1969   *Outline of the Theology of the New Testament.* Translated by J. Bowden. New York: Harper and Row.
  1972   *Die Apostelgeschichte.* 2d ed. HNT 7. Tübingen: Mohr.

Crim, K.
  1962   *The Royal Psalms.* Richmond: John Knox.

Cross, F. M.
  1973   *Canaanite Myth and Hebrew Epic.* Cambridge, Mass.: Harvard University Press.

Crüsemann, F.
  1969   *Studien zur Formgeschichte von Hymnus und Danklied in Israel.* WMANT 32. Neukirchen-Vluyn: Neukirchener.

Cullmann, O.
  1963   *The Christology of the New Testament.* Translated by S. Guthrie and C. Hall. Rev. ed. Philadelphia: Westminster.

Dalman, G.
  1928   *Arbeit und Sitte in Palästina.*

Delakat, L.
  1967   *Asylie und Schutzorakel am Zionheiligtum.* Gütersloh: Bertelsmann.

Della Vida, G. L.
  1944   *"El 'Elyon* in Genesis 14:18-20." *JBL* 63: 1-9.

Dibelius, M.
  1906   *Die Lade Jahwes.* Leiden: Brill.

Driver, G. R.
  1928   "The Original Form of the Name 'Yahweh.' " *ZAW* 46: 7-25.

Dürr, L.
  1929   *Psalm 110 im Lichte der neueren altorientalischen Forschung.*

Dussaud, R.
  1941   *Les origines cananéenes du sacrifice Israélite.* 2d ed.

Eichholz, G.
  1972   *Die Theologie des Paulus im Umriss,* Neukirchen-Vluyn: Neukirchener.

Eichhorn, D.
  1972   *Gott als Fels, Burg und Zuflucht.* Berne: Lang.

Eichrodt, W.
  1961   *Theology of the Old Testament.* Translated by J. A. Baker. Philadelphia: Westminster.

Eisenbeis, W.
  1969   *Die Wurzel slm im Alten Testament.* BZAW 113. Berlin: de Gruyter.

Eissfeldt, O.
  1932   "Baal Zaphon, Zeus Kasios und der Durchzug der Israeliten durchs Meer." *Beiträge zur Religionsgeschichte des Altertums* I.

References

1950   "Jahwe Zebaoth." In *Miscellanea Academica Berolinensia* 2/2. Reprinted in *Kleine Schriften*, vol. 3, pp. 103-123. Tübingen: Mohr.

1951   "El im ugaritischen Pantheon." *Bericht über die Verhandlungen der Sächsischen Akademie der Wissenschaften, Philologisch-historische Klasse* 98/4.

1962   "Jahwe als König." *Kleine Schriften*, vol. 1, pp. 172-193. Tübingen: Mohr.

1966a   "El und Jahwe." *Kleine Schriften*, vol. 3, pp. 386-397.

1966b   "Silo und Jerusalem." *Kleine Schriften*, vol. 3, pp. 417-425.

Eliade, M.

1959   *The Sacred and the Profane*. New York: Harcourt, Brace.

Erman, A.

1934   *Die Religion der Ägypter*. Berlin.

Fahlgren, K. H.

1932   *Sedaka nahestehende und entgegengesetzte Begriffe im Alten Testament*.

Falkenstein, A., and Soden, W. von.

1953   *Sumerische und akkadische Hymnen und Gebete*. Zurich: Artemis Verlag.

Fohrer, G.

1969   "Zion-Jerusalem im Alten Testament." In *Studien zur alttestamentlichen Theologie und Geschichte*, pp. 195-241. BZAW 115. Berlin: de Gruyter.

Frankfort, H.

1948   *Kingship and the Gods*. Chicago: University of Chicago Press.

Gadd, C. J.

1948   *Ideas of Divine Rule in the Ancient East*. London: Oxford University Press.

Galling, K.

1977   *Biblisches Reallexikon*. 2d ed. Tübingen: Mohr.

Gese, H.

1969   *Die Religionen Altsyriens*. Religionen der Menschheit 10/2. Stuttgart: Kohlhammer.

1974   "Natus ex Virgine." In *Vom Sinai zum Zion*. Munich: Kaiser.

Goodman, Philip

1973   *The Sukkot and Simḥat Torah Anthology*. Philadelphia: Jewish Publication Society.

Gray, G. B.

1925   *Sacrifice in the Old Testament*. Oxford: Clarendon.

Gray, R.

1953   "The God *Yw* in the Religion of Canaan." *JNES* 12: 278-283.

Gressmann, H.

1910   *Alorientalische Texte zum Alten Testament*. Berlin: de Gruyter.

1929   *Der Messias*. Göttingen: Vandenhoeck & Ruprecht.

Grether, O.

1934   *Name und Wort Gottes im Alten Testament*. BZAW 64. Giessen: Töpelmann.

Gross, H.

1956   "Lässt sich in den Psalmen ein 'Thronbesteigungsfest Gottes' nachweisen?" *TThZ* 65.

1967   "Theologische Eigenart der Psalmen und ihre Bedeutung für die Offenbarung des Alten Testaments." *Bibel und Leben* 8.

Gunkel, H.
1921 *Das Märchen im Alten Testament*. Religionsgeschichtliche Volksbücher II/23-26. Tübingen: Mohr.
1922 *Genesis*. HK I/1. 5th ed. Göttingen: Vandenhoeck & Ruprecht.

Gunkel, H., and Begrich, J.
1933 *Einleitung in die Psalmen*. Göttingen: Vandenhoeck & Ruprecht.

Hahn, F.
1969 *The Titles of Jesus in Christology*. Translated by H. Knight and G. Ogg. New York: World.

Hanhart, R.
1967 *Die Heiligen des Höchsten*. VTSuppl. 16. Göttingen: Vandenhoeck & Ruprecht.

Hayes, J. H.
1963 "The Tradition of Zion's Inviolability." *JBL* 82: 419-426.

Hegel, G. W. F.
1937 *Vorlesungen über die Asthetik*, vol. 12. Edited by H. Glockner.

Hempel, J.
1956 "Altes Testament und Religionsgeschichte." *ThLZ* 81: 259-279.

Herder, J. G.
1780–1781 *Briefe, das Studium der Theologie Betreffend*.

Herrmann, S.
1966 "Der Alttestamentlich Gottesname." *EvTh* 26: 281-293.

Holma, H.
1915 "Nabel der Erde." *OLZ* 18.

Hooke, S. H.
1958 *Myth, Ritual and Kingship*. Oxford: Clarendon.

Horst, F.
1929 "Die Doxologien im Amosbuch." *ZAW* 47:45-54. Reprinted in *Gottes Recht* (Munich: Kaiser, 1961), pp. 155-166.
1947–1948 "Segen und Segenshandlungen in der Bibel." *EvTh* 7: 23-37. Reprinted in *Gottes Recht*, pp. 188-202.

Iwand, H. J.
1977 *Predigt-Meditationen* I. 4th ed.

Jasper, F. N.
1967 "Early Israelite Traditions and the Psalter." *VT* 17: 50-59.

Jenni, E., and Westermann, C.
1971, 1976 *Theologisches Handwörterbuch zum Alten Testament*. 2 vols. Munich: Kaiser.

Jeremias Jorg
1970 *Kultprophetie und Gerichtsverkündigung in der späten Königszeit*. WMANT 35. Neukirchen-Vluyn: Neukirchener.
1971 "Lade und Zion." In *Probleme biblischer Theologie* (von Rad FS), pp. 183-198, Munich: Kaiser.
1977 *Theophanie: Die Geschichte einer Gattung*. WMANT 10. 2d ed. Neukirchen-Vluyn: Neukirchener.

Käsemann, E.
1980 *Commentary on Romans*. Translated by G. Bromiley. Grand Rapids: Eerdmans.

211

References

Keck, L. E.
  1966 "The Poor among the Saints in Jewish Christianity and Qumran." *ZNW* 57: 54-78.

Keel, O.
  1969 *Feinde und Gottesleugner: Studien zum Image der Widersacher in den Individualpsalmen*. SBM 7.

Kees, H.
  1941 *Der Götterglaube in alten Ägypten*. Berlin: Akademie Verlag.

Keller, C. A., and Wehmeier, G.
  1971 "Der Segen im Alten Testament." THAT.

Kerenyi, K.
  1940 *Die antike Religion*.
  1955 *Umgang mit dem Göttlichen*. Göttingen: Vandenhoeck & Ruprecht.

Kinyongo, J.
  1970 *Origine et signification du nom divin Yahvé*.

Knierim, R.
  1971 "Offenbarung im Alten Testament." In *Probleme biblischer Theologie* (von Rad FS), pp. 223f.

Koch, K.
  1953 "*Sdq* im Alten Testament." Dissertation, Heidelberg.
  1955 "Gibt es ein Vergeltungsdogma im Alten Testament?" *ZThK* 52: 1-42.
  1961 "Wesen und Ursprung der 'Gemeinschaftstreue' im Israel der Konigzeit." *ZEE* 5: 72-90.

Köhler, L.
  1953 *Lexicon in Veteris Testamenti Libros*. Leiden: Brill.
  1956 *Hebrew Man*. Translated by P. Ackroyd. Nashville: Abingdon.
  1957 *Old Testament Theology*. Translated by A. S. Todd, Philadelphia: Westminster.

Kramer, W.
  1966 *Christ, Lord, Son of God*. Translated by B. Hardy. London: SCM.

Kraus, H. J.
  1951a "Freude an Gottes Gesetz." *EvTh* 8.
  1951b *Die Königsherrschaft Gottes im Alten Testament*. BHT 13. Tübingen: Mohr.
  1959 "Archäologische und topographische Probleme Jerusalems im Lichte der Psalmenexegese." *ZDPV* 75: 125-140.
  1966 *Worship in Israel*. Translated by G. Buswell. Richmond: John Knox.
  1968 *Klagelieder*. BK 20. 3d ed. Neukirchen-Vluyn: Neukirchener.
  1970 *Die biblische Theologie*, Neukirchen-Vluyn: Neukirchener.
  1972a "Gottesdienst im alten und im neuen Bund." *Biblisch-theologische Aufsätze*, pp. 195-234. Neukirchen-Vluyn: Neukirchener.
  1972b "Das Heilige Volk." *BtA*, pp. 37-49.
  1972c "Von Leben und Tod in den Psalmen." *BtA*, pp. 258-277.
  1972d "Der lebendige Gott." *BtA*, pp. 1-36.
  1972e "Zum Thema 'Exodus.'" *BtA*, pp. 102-119.
  1972f "Zum Gesetzesverständnis der nachprophetischen Zeit." *BtA*, pp. 179-194.
  1975 *Reich Gottes: Reich der Freiheit*, Neukirchen-Vluyn: Neukirchener.
  1978 *Logos und Sophia*. Theologische Studien 123. Zurich: Theologischer Verlag.

Kuschke, A.
  1939 "Arm und Reich im Alten Testament." *ZAW* 57: 31-57.

Kutsch, E.
1955 "Das Herbstfest in Israel." Dissertation, Mainz.
1963 *Salbung als Rechtsakt im Alten Testament und im alten Orient*. Berlin: Töpelmann.

Labuschagne, C. J.
1966 *The Incomparability of Yahweh in the Old Testament*. Leiden: Brill.

Lack, R.
1962 "Les origines de *'Elyôn*: Le Très-Haut dans in la tradition cultuelle d'Israël."

Liaño, J. M.
1966 "Los pobres en el A. T." *Estudios Biblicos* 25.

Lidzbarski, M.
1898 *Handbuch der nordsemitischen Epigraphik*. Weimar.
1915 *Ephemeris für semitische Epigraphik*, vol. 3. Giessen.

Lipinski, E.
1965 *La royauté de Yahwé dans la poésie et le culte de l'Ancien Israel*. Brussels.

Lisowsky, C.
1958 *Konkordanz zum Hebräischen Alten Testament*. Stuttgart: Privileg Würt. Bibelanstalt.

Lohmeyer, E.
1964 *Der Brief an die . . . Kolosser*. KEK. Göttingen: Vandenhoeck & Ruprecht.

Luther, Martin
1960 "Preface to the Psalter." In *Luther's Works*, vol. 35, pp. 253-257. Philadelphia: Fortress.

Lutz, H. M.
1968 *Jahwe, Jerusalem and die Völker*. WMANT 27. Neukirchen-Vluyn: Neukirchener.

Maag, V.
1950 "Jahwäs Heerscharen." FS L. Köhler, pp. 27-52. Berne: Büchlov.
1960 *Malkut JHWH*. VTSuppl 7. Leiden: Brill.

Maier, J.
1965 *Das altisraelitische Ladeheiligtum*. Berlin: Töpelmann.

Martin-Achard, R.
1965 "Yahwe et les 'Anawim." ThZ 21: 349-357.

Mayer, R.
1958 "Der Gottesname Jahwe im Lichte der neuesten Forschung." *BZ* 2: 26-53.

Metzger, M.
1970 "Himmlische und irdische Wohnstatt Jahwes." *Ugarit-Forschungen* 2, pp. 139-158.

Michalson, C.
1957 "The Real Presence of the Hidden God." In *Faith and Ethics*. Edited by Paul Ramsey. New York: Harper.

Michel, D.
1956 "Studien zu den sogenannten Thronbesteigungspsalmen." *VT* 6:40-68.
1968 "AMAT: Untersuchung über 'Wahrheit' im Hebräischen." *Archiv für Begriffsgeschichte* 12.

References

Miskotte, K. H.
1976 *Biblisches ABC*. Neukirchen-Vluyn: Neukirchener.

Mowinckel, S.
1921 *Psalmen Studien* 1. Oslo.
1922 *Psalmen Studien* 2.
1923a *Psalmen Studien* 3.
1923b *Psalmen Studien* 4.
1924a *Psalmen Studien* 5.
1924b *Psalmen Studien* 6.
1952 *Zum israelitischen Neujahr und zur Deutung der Thronbesteigungspsalmen*. Oslo: Dybwad.
1953 *Religion und Kultus*.
1965a "Gottesdienst." In *RGG*, 3d ed., vol. 2, pp. 1751-1755.
1965b "Kultus." In *RGG*, 3d ed., vol. 4, pp. 120-126.
1965c "Mythos und Mythologie." In *RGG*, vol. 4, pp. 1274-1278.
1962 *The Psalms in Israel's Worship*. 2 vols. New York: Abingdon.

Munch, P. A.
1936 "Einige Bemerkungen zu den *anijjim* and den *resaᵉim* in den Psalmen." *Le Monde Oriental* 30.

Noth, M.
1957a "Die Gesetze im Pentateuch." In *Gesammelte Studien*, vol. 1. Munich: Kaiser.
1957b "Die mit des Gesetzes Werken umgehen, sind under dem Fluch." In *Gesammelte Studien*, vol. 1, pp. 155-171.
1957c "Gott, König, Volk im Alten Testament." In *Gesammelte Studien*, vol. 1, pp. 188-229.
1957d "Die Heiligen des Höchsten." In *Gesammelte Studien*, vol. 1, pp. 274-290.
1957e "Jerusalem und die israelitische Tradition." In *Gesammelte Studien*, vol. 1, pp. 172-187.
1968 *Könige* I. BK 9/1. Neukirchen-Vluyn: Neukirchener.
1969 "Das Amt des 'Richters Israel.' " In *Gesammelte Studien*, vol. 2, pp. 71-85.

Oesterley, W. O. E.
1937 *Sacrifices in Ancient Israel*. London: Hodder and Stoughton.

Östborn, G.
1945 *TORA in the Old Testament: A Semantic Study*.

Otto, E.
1950 "Der Vorwurf an Gott." *Vorträge der orientalischen Tagung im Marburg, Fachgruppe Ägyptologie*.

Otto, W. F.
1955 *Die Gestalt und das Sein*.

Pannenberg, W., and Rendtorff, editors
1968 *Revelation as History*. New York: Macmillan.

Patro, S. S.
1976 "Royal Psalms in Modern Scholarship." Dissertation, Kiel.

Pedersen, J.
1926 *Israel*. 2 vols. London: Oxford University Press.

Perlitt, L.
1969 *Bundestheologie im Alten Testament*. WMANT 36. Neukirchen-Vluyn: Neukirchener.

Ploeg, J. van der
1950   "Les pauvres d'Israel et leur piētē." *OTS* 7.

Porteus, N. W.
1961   "Jerusalem-Zion: The Growth of a Symbol." *Verbannung und Heimkehr* (FS W. Rudolph), pp. 235-252. Edited by A. Kuschke. Tübingen: Mohr.

Pritchard, J. B., ed.
1969   *Ancient Near Eastern Texts: Relating to the Old Testament.* 3rd ed. Princeton: Princeton University Press.

Rad, G. von
1940–1941   "Erwägungen zu den Königpsalmen." *ZAW* 58: 216-222.
1962   *Old Testament Theology*, vol. 1. Translated by D. M. G. Stalker. New York: Harper and Row.
1965   *Old Testament Theology*, vol. 2.
1969   *Der Heilige Krieg im alten Israel.* 5th ed. Göttingen: Vandenhoeck & Ruprecht.
1971a   "Die levitische Predigt in den Büchern Chronik." *Gesammelte Studien*, vol. 1, pp. 248-161. Munich: Kaiser.
1971b   "Das judäische Königsritual." *Gesammelte Studien*, vol. 1, pp. 205-213.
1971c   " 'Gerechtigkeit' und 'Leben' in der Kultsprache der Psalmen." *Gesammelte Studien*, vol. 1, pp. 225-247.
1971d   "Das formgeschichtliche Problem des Hexateuchs." *Gesammelte Studien*, vol. 1, pp. 9-86. ET: *The Problem of the Hexateuch and Other Studies*, translated by E. Dicken (New York: McGraw Hill, 1966).
1972   *Wisdom in Israel.* Nashville: Abingdon.
1973a   "Das Werk Jahwes." *Gesammelte Studien*, vol. 2, pp. 236-244. Munich: Kaiser.
1973b   "Christliche Weisheit?" *Gesammelte Studien*, vol. 2, pp. 267-271.
1973c   *Predigt-Meditationen*, Göttingen: Vandenhoeck & Ruprecht.
1980   *God at Work in Israel.* Nashville: Abingdon.

Rahlfs, A.
1892   '*Ānī und 'Ānāw in den Psalmen*.

Rendtorff, R.
1967   *Studien zur Geschichte des Opfers im alten Israel.* WMANT 24. Göttingen: Vandenhoeck & Ruprecht.
1968   "The Concept of Revelation in Ancient Israel." In Pannenberg and Rendtorff, editors, *Revelation as History*, pp. 23-54. New York: Macmillan.

Rohland, E.
1956   "Die Beduetung der Erwählungstradition Israels für die Eschatologie der alttestamentlichen Propheten." Dissertation, Heidelberg.

Ross, J. P.
1967   "Jahweh Seba'ot in Samuel and Psalms." *VT* 17: 76-92.

Rost, L.
1926   *Die Überlieferung von der Thronnachfolge Davids.* BWANT 3/6. Stuttgart: Kohlhammer.
1965   *Das kleine Credo und andere Studien zum Alten Testament.* Heidelberg: Quelle and Meyer.
1971   "Erwägungen zum Begriff *šalōm*." *Schalom* (FS A. Jepsen). Edited by K.-H. Bernhardt. Stuttgart: Calwer.

Rowley, H. H.
1950   "The Meaning of Sacrifice in the Old Testament." *BJRL* (1950), pp. 74-110.

References

Ruppert, L.
   1973   *Das leidende Gerechte*. Würzburg: Echter Verlag.

Savignac, J. de
   1953   "Note sur le sens du terme sáphôn dans quelques passages de la Bible." *VT* 3: 95-96.

Schatz, W.
   1972   *Genesis 14: Eine Untersuchung*. Berne: Lang.

Schmid, Hans Heinrich
   1971   *Šālōm: "Frieden" im Alten Orient und im Alten Testament*. SBS 51.
   1973   "Schöpfung, Gerechtigkeit und Heil," *ZThK* 70:1-19.

Schmid, R.
   1964   *Das Bundesopfer in Israel*. Munich: Koesel.

Schmidt, Hans
   1927   *Die Thronfahrt Jahwes*.
   1928   *Das Gebet des Angeklagten im Alten Testament*. ZAW, Beiheft 49.
   1933   *Der Heilige Fels in Jerusalem*. Tübingen: Mohr.
   1934   *Die Psalmen*. HAT.
   1955   "Jahwe und die Kulttraditionen von Jerusalem." *ZAW* 67: 168-197.
   1966   *Israel, Zion und die Völker*.

Schmidt, Werner H.
   1962   "Wo hat die Aussage Jahwe 'der Heilige' ihren Ursprung?" *ZAW* 74: 62-66.
   1963   "מִשְׁכָּן als Ausdruck Jerusalemer Kultursprache." *ZAW* 75: 91-93.
   1966   *Königtum Gottes in Ugarit und Israel*. 2d ed. Berlin: Töpelmann.
   1970   *Das erste Gebot*. TheolEx 165.
   1971   "Kritik am Königtum." In *Probleme biblischer Theologie* (von Rad FS), pp. 440-461. Munich: Kaiser.
   1975   *Alttestamentlicher Glaube in seiner Geschichte*. 2d ed. Neukirchen-Vluyn: Neukirchener.

Schniewind, J.
   1949   *Das Evangelium nach Markus*. NTD. Göttingen: Vandenhoeck & Ruprecht.
   1964   *Das Evangelium nach Matthaeus*. NTD.

Schreiner, Josef
   1963   *Sion-Jerusalem*. Munich: Koesel.

Schwarzwäller, K.
   1963   "Die Feinde des Individuums in den Psalmen." Dissertation, Hamburg.

Schweizer, E.
   1962   *Lordship and Discipleship*. London: SCM.
   1970   *The Good News according to Mark*. Translated by D. Madvig. Richmond: John Knox.
   1975   *The Good News according to Matthew*. Translated by D. Green. Atlanta: John Knox.
   1984   *The Good News according to Luke*. Translated by D. Green. Atlanta: John Knox.

Seeligmann, I. L.
   1963   "Menschliches Heldentum und göttliche Hilfe." *ThZ* 19: 385-411.

Sethe, K.
   1929   *Amun und die acht Urgötter von Hermopolis*. Abhandlungen der Preussischen Akademie der Wissenschaften, Phil.-hist. Klasse.

Seybold, K.
1973 *Das Gebet des Kranken im Alten Testament*. BWANT. Stuttgart: Kohlhammer.

Smend, R.
1963 *Die Bundesformel*. TheolSt 68.

Stamm, J. J.
1940 *Erlösen und Vergeben im Alten Testament*. Bern: Francke.
1946 *Das Leiden des Unschuldigen in Babylon und Israel*. Zurich: Zwingli Verlag.
1955 "Ein Vierteljahrhundert Psalmenforschung." *ThR* NF 23: 1-68.

Stamm, J. J., and Bietenhard, H.
1959 *Der Weltfriede im Lichte der Bibel*. Zurich: Zwingli Verlag.

Steck, O. H.
1972 *Friedensvorstellungen im alten Jerusalem*. Zurich: Theologischer Verlag.

Stoebe, H. J.
1971 "ḥeṣed." In THAT, 1:607ff.
1973 *Das erste Buch Samuelis*. Gütersloh: Mohn.

Stolz, Fritz
1970 *Strukturen und Figuren im Kult von Jerusalem*. BZAW 118.

Tillich, Paul
1951–1963 *Systematic Theology*. 3 volumes. Chicago: University of Chicago Press.

Volz, P.
1912 *Das Neujahrsfest Jahwes*. Tübingen: Mohr.

Wambacq, B. N.
1947 *L'épithète divine Jahvé Sébaoth*. Paris and Bruges: Desclée de Brouwer.

Wanke, G.
1966 *Die Zionstheologie der Korachiten in ihrem traditionsgeschichtlichen Zusammenhang*. BZAW 97. Berlin: Töpelmann.

Wehmeier, G.
1970 *Der Segen im Alten Testament*. Basel: Reinhardt.

Weiser, Artur
1962 *The Psalms*. Translated by H. Hartwell. Philadelphia: Westminster.

Wellhausen, J.
1965 "Israelitisch-jüdische Religion." In *Grundrisse zum Alten Testament*, edited by R. Smend. Munich: Kaiser.

Wendel, A.
1927 *Das Opfer in der altisraelitischen Religion*. Leipzig: Pfeiffer.

Westermann, Claus
1964 "Das Verhältnis des Jahweglaubens zu den ausserisraelitischen Religionen. In *Forschung am Alten Testament*. Munich: Kaiser.
1967 *Die Geschichtsbezogenheit menschlicher Rede von Gott in Alten Testament*. Weltgespräch 1.
1969 *Der Frieden im Alten Testament*. Studien zur Frieden-forschung, vol. 1.
1984 *Genesis 1–11*. Translated by John J. Scullion. Minneapolis: Augsburg.

Whitelock, L. T.
1968 "The *rib*-Pattern and the Concept of Judgment in the Book of Psalms." Dissertation, Boston.

References

Widengren, G.
1955   *Sakrales Königtum im Alten Testament und im Judentum*. Stuttgart: Kohlhammer.

Wildberger, H.
1972   *Jesaia 1-12*. BK 10. Neukirchen-Vluyn: Neukirchener.

Wolff, H. W.
1974   *Anthropology of the Old Testament*. Translated by Margaret Kohl. Philadelphia: Fortress.
1977   *Joel and Amos*. Hermeneia. Philadelphia: Fortress.
1979   *Die Stunde des Amos*. 4th ed. Munich: Kaiser.

Würthwein, E.
1947   "Amos 5,21-27." *ThLZ* 72: 143-159.
1950   "Erwägungen zu Psalm 73." In FS A. Bertholet, pp. 532-549. Tübingen: Mohr.
1970   *Wort und Existenz: Studien zum Alten Testament*. Göttingen: Vandenhoeck & Ruprecht.

Zimmerli, W.
1971   *Man and His Hope in the Old Testament*. Translator not listed. London: SCM.
1978   *Old Testament Theology in Outline*. Translated by D. Green. Atlanta. John Knox.
1979   *Ezekiel*. Translated by R. E. Clements. 2 volumes. Hermeneia. Philadelphia: Fortress.

Zimmern, H.
1926   *Das babylonische Neujahrsfest*.
1928   *Zum babylonischen Neujahrsfest*. 2 volumes. Leipzig [1906; 1918].

Index of
Selected Hebrew Words

Index of Biblical References

Genesis
1:1—2:4a	92
1:2	165
1:26ff.	149
2	80
2:7	146
3	157
5:24	174
8:21	157
14:18-22	25, 28, 115
14:19	29
14:20	185
17:1	25
21:33	25
22:2	182
22:16	182
30:3	113
32:13-21	94
36:31	87
39:9	156
43:11	94
50:23	113

Exodus
3:14	17
12:11ff.	106
12:26f.	92
15:18	26
19:6	26
20:7	21
20:24	20
23:10ff.	85
25:9	26
25:40	26
26:30	26
32:32	192
34:18ff.	85

Leviticus
23:4ff.	85

Numbers
12:3	123
16:55	160
18:20	160
18:21	160
22:22	48
23:21	26
24:16	25
24:17	114
28	85
29	85

Deuteronomy
4:21	160
6:7	92
7:9	55
7:12	55
10:9	160
10:14	47
16:1-17	85
16:18	131
17:8-13	131
21:3	192
21:19	131
22:15	131
25:7	131
26:16ff.	58
26:19	24
27:1ff.	57
28:1	24
30:10ff.	57, 162
30:15ff.	164
31:11	34
31:19	92, 139, 140
32:35	67
33:5	26

Joshua
1:5	196
7:19	156

8:20	114
13:12	87
13:14	160
13:21	87
13:23	160
14:4	160
15:13	160
17:5	160
24:26	55

Judges
4:2	87
6:11ff.	48
8:23	52
9:8	87
20:23ff.	98
21:2ff.	98

Ruth
4:1	131

1 Samuel
1:3	74
3:1ff.	74
3:3	74
3:9f.	74
4:3ff.	19, 74
4:4	18, 26, 74, 88, 89
4:5	74
4:11	75
4:21	74
6:5	75
6:7f.	75
6:12f.	75
6:13	75
6:14f.	75
6:21	75
7:5ff.	98
7:6	98

221

Index of Biblical References

Index of Biblical References

Index of Biblical References

Index of Names and Subjects

Index of Names and Subjects